Assembling Export Markets

RGS-IBG Book Series

For further information about the series and a full list of published and forthcoming titles, please visit www.rgsbookseries.com

Published

Forthcoming

Assembling Export Markets

The Making and Unmaking of Global Food Connections in West Africa

Stefan Ouma

WILEY Blackwell

This edition first published 2015
© 2015 John Wiley & Sons, Ltd

Registered Office
John Wiley & Sons, Ltd, The Atrium, Southern Gate, Chichester, West Sussex, PO19 8SQ, UK

Editorial Offices
350 Main Street, Malden, MA 02148-5020, USA
9600 Garsington Road, Oxford, OX4 2DQ, UK
The Atrium, Southern Gate, Chichester, West Sussex, PO19 8SQ, UK

For details of our global editorial offices, for customer services, and for information about how
to apply for permission to reuse the copyright material in this book please see our website at
www.wiley.com/wiley-blackwell.

Library of Congress Cataloging-in-Publication Data applied for.

C: 9781118632611
P: 9781118632581

A catalogue record for this book is available from the British Library.

Cover image: Front cover image © Stefan Ouma

Set in 9.5/11.5pt Plantin by SPi Publisher Services, Pondicherry, India
Printed and bound in Malaysia by Vivar Printing Sdn Bhd

1   2015

Contents

Series Editors' Preface

The RGS-IBG Book Series only publishes work of the highest international standing. Its emphasis is on distinctive new developments in human and physical geography, although it is also open to contributions from cognate disciplines whose interests overlap with those of geographers. The Series places strong emphasis on theoretically-informed and empirically-strong texts. Reflecting the vibrant and diverse theoretical and empirical agendas that characterize the contemporary discipline, contributions are expected to inform, challenge and stimulate the reader. Overall, the RGS-IBG Book Series seeks to promote scholarly publications that leave an intellectual mark and change the way readers think about particular issues, methods or theories.

For details on how to submit a proposal please visit:
www.rgsbookseries.com

Neil Coe
National University of Singapore

Tim Allott
University of Manchester, UK

RGS-IBG Book Series Editors

Preface

Research projects not only write histories, they also have one. Before I began the project leading to this book, I had just had finished a project on the impact of the private food safety standard GLOBALG.A.P. on the governance of horticultural value chains in Kenya. In the course of that project, I became increasingly dissatisfied with the conceptual and methodological tools global commodity/value analysis provided to unpack the "world market integration" of firms and farms in the Global South. What about the actual *practice* of global commodity/value chains? What about the inner workings of firms and farms? What about the larger dynamics of agrifood capitalism and its underlying patterns of commodification, valorization, accumulation, and dispossession? And most importantly, could we just substitute "chains" for "markets" at a time when the practice of development was all about "markets"? Being concerned by these questions, I wanted to get a more grounded understanding of global market connections: how are they actually forged *in situ*? How do managers, workers, or farmers enact these connections and reiterate them within everyday organizational practices? What happens "backstage"? Surprisingly, there was hardly any literature on such questions in the wider field of agrifood studies. Although I could have continued to pursue these questions in regard to the case of the Kenyan fresh produce industry, I decided against joining the herd of researchers that have besieged managers, workers, farmers, and policy-makers from the 1990s onward in a country whose horticulture subsector is often called an economic success story.

Instead, Ghana's emerging fresh fruits industry attracted my attention in late 2007. Even though the country's pineapple subsector was experiencing serious structural challenges around that time, Ghana was framed as a candidate for a "horticultural take-off" in donor circles and policy papers alike. Such a narrative tied well into the political representations of Ghana as an "emerging economy." But what lurked beneath those phrases? What exactly happened on the ground? Fortunately, a group of managers, farmers, and market-makers in Ghana enabled me to tackle these questions. Without their trust, help, engagement, knowledge, and agency, this book would not exist. I therefore thank them. Although I am indebted to these people in the very first place, I am also guilty of what many researchers do: I have co-produced knowledge with participants of my research, I have flown back to a university in the Global North, I have reworked and repackaged it, and finally I have published it, surely with only a limited benefit to the people I actually worked with.

Despite the critical take on markets I develop in this book, it must be read as an acknowledgment of the daily struggles the participants of my research were involved in – managers, farmers, workers, and other market-makers. Personally, I believe that representatives of the companies I worked with had the very best intentions and had a keen interest in contributing to development and poverty reduction in the areas they were operating. Thus, this book is not a critique of the people or the organizations that so readily facilitated my research, but rather a critique of those perspectives on markets that take them for granted and render them natural, normal, stable, egalitarian, nonpolitical, and purely social spaces. *Nevertheless, geographical associations made related to the case study companies may have been altered to ensure anonymity.*

Obviously, I could not have completed this project without the help of many other people inside and outside of Ghana. I would thus first and foremost like to thank Peter Lindner and Marc Boeckler of the Department of Human Geography at Frankfurt University for their intellectual, moral, and financial support throughout this project, which they also helped to transform into a German Research Council (DFG)-funded project ("The Global Agricultural Market and its Fuzzy Margins: Forms and Consequences of the Integration of Smallholder Farmers into Transnational Commodity Chains – The Example of Ghana"). Although saddled with many other obligations, both repeatedly traveled with me to Ghana and showed a keen interest in "the field." Peter gave me every freedom I needed throughout a cordial and collegial relationship over the past six years. I would also like to thank Stefano Ponte of Copenhagen Business School for co-examining the dissertation that led to this book. Furthermore, I am hugely indebted to Kojo S. Amanor at the University of Ghana's Kwame Nkrumah Institute of African Studies in Legon, whose sharp comments made me rethink several parts of the book and gave it a more critical edge here and there. Iddrisu Azindow of the same institution kindly shared his in-depth knowledge on northern Ghana with me and helped with validating several Dagbani terms used in the book. Of course, both may still disagree with some parts of this book. I am also hugely indebted to Apiatus, Iddrisu, Daniel, and Alex for their invaluable field assistance as well as Elizabeth Arthur for her sound interview transcriptions and Twi-English translations. My Frankfurt colleagues Katharina Abdo, Veit Bachmann, Iris Dzudzek, Julia Verne, and Alexander Vorbrugg provided further critical comments that also helped improve the book manuscript. Special kudos go to Hanna Strass, David Adjei, Martin, Nanja Nagorny, Phillipe, and Maik. I would also like to thank Elke Alban, Ömer Alpaslan, Ian Copestake, Olivier Graefe, Niels Fold, Detlef Müller-Mahn, Martin Müller, Matthew Hannah, Lindsay Whitfield, and Dorothy Hauzar, who in one way or another contributed to this project. Finally, I would like to thank Neil Coe, Jacqueline Scott, and Allison Kostka of Wiley, and three anonymous reviewers for having confidence in the project, as well as Eva for having confidence in me.

Frankfurt, November 2013

The following chapters contain ideas that have been published previously. Permission to publish this material is gratefully acknowleged.

Chapter 3: Ouma, S., Boeckler, M., & Lindner, P. (2013). Extending the Margins of Marketization: Frontier Regions and the Making of Agro-export Markets in northern Ghana. *Geoforum* 48, 225–235.

Chapter 8: Ouma, S. (2012). Creating and Maintaining Global Connections: Agro-business and the Precarious Making of Fresh-cut Markets. *Journal of Development Studies* 48 (3), 322–334.

Technical Remarks

Anonymization: In this book, all names of individuals, organizations, and many geographical locations have been anonymized or altered to ensure anomymity and/or confidentiality. In some cases, sources such as reports that could identify my case studies are withheld, and the wording of the information derived from these sources has been slightly changed to ensure anonymity.

Monetary values, currencies, measurements: All monetary values used with regard to the case studies are approximations. The exact figures are witheld to ensure confidentiality. In some instances, the currency is withheld to ensure confidentiality and is simply designated as "xx" or "xy." All Ghana cedi values used in this book correspond to New Ghana cedis (GHS). As of December 31, 2008, 1 GHS = USD 0.77 = € 0.54. As of December 31, 2010, 1 GHS = USD 0.66 = € 0.50. 1 GHS = 100 pesewas. 1 acre = 0.405 hectares.

Language: Twi and Dagbani terms for certain English expressions are provided in brackets and vice versa.

List of Figures

List of Tables

Abbreviations

ADP	Agricultural Diversification Programme
AEF	African Enterprise Foundation
AgSSIP	Agricultural Sector Services Investment Programme
ASIP	Agricultural Sector Investment Programme
CSR	Corporate Social Responsibility
€	Euro
EC	*économie des conventions*
EDAIF	Export Development Agriculture Investment Fund
EMQAP	Export Marketing and Quality Assurance Programme
EPZ	Export Processing Zone
EU	European Union
FA	Field Assistant
FDI	Foreign Direct Investments
g	grams
GCC	Global Commodity Chains
GEPC	Ghana Export Promotion Council
GFZB	Ghana Free Zone Board
GHS	Ghana cedis
GTZ/GIZ	Gesellschaft für Technische Zusammenarbeit/Gesellschaft für Internationale Zusammenarbeit
GVC	Global Value Chains
HEII	Horticulture Export Industries Initiative
IMF	International Monetary Fund
IPM	Integrated Pest Management
JIT	Just-in-time
kg	kilograms
MCA	Millennium Challenge Account
MOAP	Market-oriented Agriculture Programme
MOFA	Ministry of Food and Agriculture

mt	Metric tons
NDC	National Democratic Congress
NES	New Economic Sociology
NGO	Non-governmental Organization
NIE	New Institutional Economics
NPP	New Patriotic Party
NTE	Non-traditional Exports
OFL	Organic Fruit Limited
QMS	Quality Management System
R&D	Research and Development
SCM	Supply Chain Management
SSEM	Social Studies of Economization and Marketization
SPEG	Sea Freight Pineapple Exporters' Association of Ghana
SSST	Social Studies of Science and Technology
STA	Sociotechnical *agencement*
TF	Ton:go Fruits
TIPCEE	Trade and Investment Programme for a Competitive Export Economy
UNDP	United Nations Development Programme
USP	Unique Selling Point
USAID	United States Agency for International Development
USD	US dollars

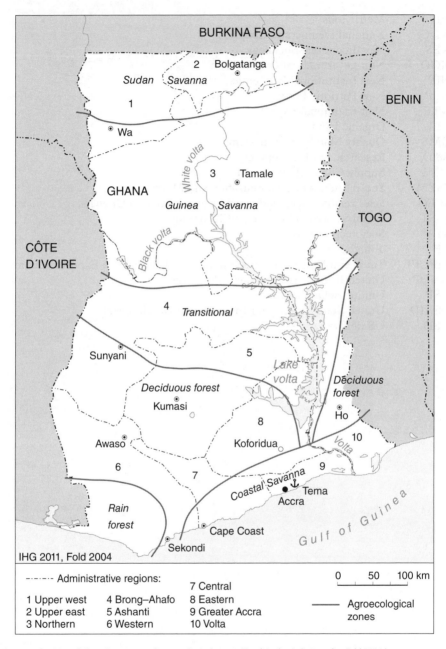

Figure 0.1 Map of Ghana's regions and agroecological zones. (From Author's design after Fold 2004.)

Chapter One
Introduction: Struggling with "World Market Integration"

It has become a familiar scene in Densu Valley, Aborobe district, southern Ghana: Trucks piled with fresh pineapples struggle through the rough rural terrain, making their way to the nearby processing facility of a multinational agribusiness company. Upon arrival, the fruits are sliced and packed, and flown "fresh from farm" and "just-in-time" to retailers in Europe, where an affluent and quality-conscious urban clientele would buy the little 200 g packages of pineapple chunks, making the farmers distant participants in the convenience food revolution.

For some time now, Densu Valley has been one of the new sites of the global agrifood economy. In the past, many farmers in the valley – until the 1950s a major cocoa-growing area, when all the plants were destroyed by disease – had mainly been involved in food crop production or had left to seek their fortunes in Ghana's sprawling cities, but it was in the late 1980s that a much more lucrative window of business opportunity opened. With European consumers hungry for fresh pineapples, some farmers and pioneer exporters ventured into pineapple production, which subsequently took off on a broad scale from the early 1990s onwards. However, "the market" was frequently deceitful, shaped by mistrust and uncertainty, with both exporters and farmers often being cheated by one another or by buyers in distant Europe, in a trade that was mainly organized around volatile spot-market relations. With the arrival of the exporter–processor Ton:go Fruits[1] (TF) in the late 1990s, times seemed to change for a few chosen ones. Through its operations, some farmers were integrated into more tightly regulated, dynamic, and demanding supply chains via more solid contractual arrangements. Under close supervision of the company's

Assembling Export Markets: The Making and Unmaking of Global Food Connections in West Africa, First Edition. Stefan Ouma.
© 2015 John Wiley & Sons, Ltd. Published 2015 by John Wiley & Sons, Ltd.

agronomists and through its financial support, the farmers were introduced to the world of European retailers, with its demands for food safety, quality, freshness, supply chain management. Many farmers fared well with the just-in-time model. Their new riches materialized through the opening of shops and the construction of houses in the area, symbolizing the relative fortunes that a new class of "big-time farmers" (as they are known locally) had acquired through the blessings of international trade.

Depending on one's theoretical inclination, the integration of Densu Valley farmers into agrobusiness supply chains may be seen through very different prisms. In their seminal work *Living under Contract*, Little and Watts (1994) conceived of the "world market integration" of farmers in the Global South through specific contractual relations with (often large) agribusiness companies as an industrial appropriation of selected rural activities, expressive of a new global regime of capital accumulation based on "global fresh" and the penetration of new agrarian frontiers (see also Friedmann 1993). In the same book, Watts (1994) reflected extensively and with impressive historical detail upon the social implications of contract farming in the rural South,[2] arguing that through such a mode of market integration "[n]ominally independent growers retain the illusion of autonomy but have become in practice what Lenin called propertied proletarians, workers cultivating company crops on private allotments" (ibid.: 64). Watts' argument can be placed in a lineage with other political economy texts that have critically discussed how agribusiness operates and takes control over production in the Global South, and what role smallholder farmers (or "peasants") play in a globalized agrifood economy (Feder 1976; Bernstein 2010).

Agrarian political economy's critical stance towards "world market integration" and global capitalism more generally can be contrasted to the position of neoclassical economics and the policy descriptions derived from it. From the viewpoint of the World Bank economists who in the 1980s and 1990s urged the Ghanaian government to liberalize markets, attract foreign direct investments (FDI), and embrace export promotion strategies, the case of TF and its farmers might have been considered as nothing less than a success story. From the 1980s onward, the World Bank singled out the promotion of non-traditional exports (NTEs) as a new panacea for development, as prices for traditional commodities such as cocoa, coffee, and sugar were declining. As part of a new paradigm advocating "private-sector development with an emphasis on export-led growth, monetary and fiscal reform, and government deregulation in agricultural production and marketing" (Little & Dolan 2000: 63), countries like Ghana were promised a rosy future, given their comparative advantage with regard to land, labor, climate and proximity to European markets. As the World Bank (1993: 40) noted back then, "[a]ccelerated growth is predicated on a rapid integration of the Ghanaian economy into world markets, and Ghana has a comparative advantage in horticulture and (potentially) fruit and vegetable processing industries."

Indeed, TF invested in Ghana owing to the country's comparative advantages and a range of tax incentives the structurally adjusted Ghanaian state provided to foreign investors under a free zone model promoted by the World Bank – which some may consider ostensible proof that export promotion policies can attract precious FDI. The case also seems to provide striking evidence that the diversification of Ghana's economy, which since colonial times had relied upon the export of cocoa, minerals, and timber, is feasible. TF moved beyond the mere export of crude fruits by adding local value through processing, generating employment and transferring skills and knowledge to workers and suppliers alike. In this regard, the company also seems to have helped evade the trap of crude (low-value) exports, the yoke under which most export-oriented economies across sub-Saharan Africa had found themselves since colonial times.

Despite their different theoretical inclination and treatment of the consequences of "world market integration", the agrarian political economy and neoclassical take on markets do share a striking commonality. Implicitly, they both render the global market an "organismic totality" (Gibson-Graham 2006 [1996]: 98). Through scholarly abstraction, an essential, absolute economic entity with a self-evident quality is created.[3] In these narratives, "the market" to varying degrees either features as a grand destructive or grand empowering force (and thus either as an object of critique or glorification), but it is rarely made an object of discussion in itself. While many critical political economy approaches often treat markets, and capitalism more gener-ally, as abstract machines whose "dominance is guaranteed by a logic of profitability, a telos of expansion, an imperative of accumulation, a structure of ownership and control, or some other quality of feature [...]" (Gibson-Graham 2006 [1996]: 15), neoclassical economics in its various disguises does so by naturalizing and dehistori-cizing them (see also Barnes 2005). By abstracting markets, these readings often unintentionally join tracks by black-boxing how markets (and "capital" more generally) come into being *practically*. Far from natural, smooth, or straightforward, this is often a contested, interrupted, and precarious process.

Many hundred miles north of Densu Valley, we encounter another frontier of the global agrifood economy. Since the late 1990s, a company, hereafter referred to as Organic Fruits Ltd. (OFL), has tried to create a market for organic mangoes in northern Ghana, a region where farmers had neither grown trees for export, nor trees under contract before. Where subsistence farming based on a slash and burn system is still the dominant mode of production, where rural land is largely held as a communal property, and daily life is deeply entangled with customary and religious values and forms of authority, market-making becomes a complex project. Ghana's north has always been marked by high incidences of poverty and food insecurity, having fared less well during Ghana's economic recovery that took shape in the 1980s. Having been structurally "underdeveloped" since colonial times, it has largely served as a labor reservoir for the cocoa, mining and urban economies in the country's south. A Ghanaian geographer attuned to critical political economy once described it as "a marginal, peripheral and 'distant' rural space in the context of capital accumulation" (Songsore 1989; cited in Kasanga 1995: 221). Choosing a different wording, even more liberal economists subscribe to such a diagnosis, arguing that the "high incidence of poverty in northern Ghana is [...] attributed to exclusion from trade" (Al-Hassan & Diao 2007: 5).

In both discourses on the developmental condition of northern Ghana, categories such as "marginal," "peripheral," "distant," and "excluded" are usually based on the idea that the market has a boundary, which, according to Mitchell (2007: 246–247), "is thought to separate the market from the large areas of material activity and resources that seem to exist beyond its limit. For countries outside the West, the idea of a boundary provides a common way not just to think about these places but to diagnose their problems and design appropriate remedies." Such remedies have become increasingly popular and manifest themselves in ambitious programs for "market integration" and "value chain development." For some time now, international development players and many African governments' ministries for agriculture, industry, and trade have embraced a market-oriented development agenda that no longer ties smoothly into the free-markets approach of the Washington Consensus era, as it wants to actively design and shape markets through reengineering economic relations and practices.

Global value chains and "inclusive markets" are now heralded as harbingers of growth if well designed, having the power to bring "development" to places "disconnected" from the global space of flows (McMichael 2013; Neilson 2014). Ghana has become a prominent laboratory for these new tools of economic engineering, which often aim at modernizing and professionalizing farming practices as a by-product. Although many of these efforts have targeted regions in Ghana's south in the past, more recently "excluded" populations in Ghana's north have been chosen for "market integration." But these populations are not naturally "outside" the market. Market integration programs need this "outside" as a "supplementary constitutive other" (Boeckler 2005: 53) to "help to extend the rules of the market into these other spaces" (Mitchell 2007: 247). These "other spaces," perceived to lie "outside" an already-existing market, enter orthodox economic knowledge and imaginations as "absent objects" (Mbembe 2001: 241) always set in relation to the full presence of "the market" or associated categories such as "capitalism," "modernity," and "development." Such differences not only inscribe qualitative, spatial, and temporal differences between places and people, and thereby justify interventions, but they also convey the idea that "the market" exists independently as a kind of transcendental being to which one could become closely connected. Indeed, extending the blessings of the market has been the goal of OFL's investment. The company undertook the ambitious effort of contracting almost 1,300 farmers in what so far has been one of the largest private investments in the agricultural sector in northern Ghana. The farmers are prefinanced through a contract arrangement, under which OFL provides inputs and services to farmers on a credit basis, while farmers provide the land and labor for the production of mangoes, which are finally marketed both locally and overseas by the company.

This book is about the two frontier regions introduced earlier. Taking the evolution of the aforesaid two agrobusiness–outgrower complexes as vantage points, its objective is to advance broader arguments about market-oriented transformations in Ghana"s agricultural sector and the rural South more generally. It is a story about firm managers and farmers who struggle to become part of, position themselves in, and make a living from global agrifood markets, which have been undergoing profound changes since the 1990s: a surging demand for fresh fruits and vegetables in the Global North; the rise of retailers, standards, and certification schemes; the time–space compression of supply chains through the power of logistics; and the consolidation of a neoliberal trade and development architecture have all altered the geography of the global agrifood economy (McMichael & Friedmann 2007). One of the most striking markers of market restructuring in North–South trade has been the rising importance of high-value horticultural exports, such as the pineapples and mangoes. But the issue goes far beyond fruits; products and assortments such as baby vegetable mixes or flower bouquets, barely known to consumers in the North just a decade ago, have become "destination goods" (Dolan & Humphrey 2004) and a core of large retailers' strategies to effectively enroll consumers by ensuring "permanent global summer time" (Blythman; cited in Dicken 2011: 271). Their demand has led to an expansion of global supply chains into new frontiers such as Densu Valley and northern Ghana, where labor and nature can be turned into resources. In addition, large agribusiness enterprises, often of foreign origin and in alliance with other market-makers such as governments or international development organizations, have been cooperating with local farmers through diverse institutional arrangements, integrating different people, modes of production, and nature(s) in distinctively new ways into global market architectures.

This book will show that there is neither something natural, nor something evolutionary or inevitable, about global market connections. Markets do not simply fall out of thin air if the environment is "enabled," as development organizations frequently claim, nor do they befall and subjugate local actors as inexorable global forces that are driven by some transhistorical law of capital accumulation, as more structuralist critiques of economic globalization or agrarian political economy usually imagine (Busch & Juska 1997). Today's global fresh produce markets, like all markets, do not reside outside the ongoing practices of market subjects, which are themselves effects of *particular* conditions that need to be *worked* upon. Humans not only have to become particular types of subjects in the very first place, but they also have to solve a range of sociotechnical puzzles in order to access, maintain, and/or expand markets. With regard to contemporary global agrifood chains, this comprises the transformation of nature into market goods, the setting of quality standards, the implementation of different production technologies, the calculation of prices, the organization of logistics, and the coordination of transactions in often uncertain environments, to name just a few. TF had to overcome such very *concrete* (but by no means "natural") "problems" of market-making, but how did all this work out? How did the company create and extend the connections sustaining its markets? What organizational forms, resources, technologies, strategies, and practices were central to this? How were these connections maintained across space and time amid competitive and regulatory dynamics, and what impact did this have on local farmers and the wider regional economy?

Such sociotechnical puzzles of market-making seem to be even more complex in the case of the organic mango outgrower scheme in northern Ghana. Although OFL had to solve similar market-making problems as TF, the complexity of constructing markets for organic mangoes revolves around one peculiar "problem": how to integrate farmers into the organic agrifood market who had never been exposed to its workings before? In each case, it will become clear that the global agrifood markets scrutinized did not simply extend into new territory, but came into being as effects of a process during which labor, nature, and the worth of goods were as much worked upon as they were contested. We often forget the contested nature of the commodity form and the manifold associations that may enable and disable it, for markets are not only mechanisms of connection and disconnection, but also of "forgetting" (Tsing 2008: 27). Global agrifood markets are no exception. When consumers finally buy the neatly packaged fruits from Ghana, vegetables from Kenya or cut flowers from Ethiopia, the reconfigurations, struggles and controversies that shaped their production are no longer visible.

It is against this backdrop that this book seeks to unmake how agri-export markets are assembled as sociotechnical arrangements, but it also seeks to unmake how these are unmade through moments of crisis, disruption and resistance. It thereby critically challenges the fetishization and (ahistorical) normalization of markets in their various disguises in the realm of agrarian development. This is an important political exercise as the contemporary governmental desire to link farmers to global agrifood markets often falls short of acknowledging the risks, disappointments, exclusions, and displacements that come with the integration into global agrifood chains, whose rules of the game are made in particular places. In order to do so, we have to unpack the ontologies and epistemologies that underlie the dominant concepts being used to render intelligible the workings of the global economy.

Rethinking Global Connections

To be fair, the study of the dynamic reconfiguration of the global agrifood economy has advanced since Watts' political economy account of the new spatial fixes reshaping global agrarian capitalism. He later clearly distanced himself from more structuralist approaches to the global agrifood economy (Goodman & Watts 1997). More fine-grained approaches such as global commodity or global value chain analysis have emerged over the last two decades with the aim of unpacking the complexities of global trade relations. Rooted in world-systems analysis and the dependency tradition, global commodity chain (GCC) analyses have contributed to our understanding of how households, capital, commodities, firms, institutions, and places are functionally integrated in spatially dispersed production and distribution networks within an increasingly complex global division of labor (Gereffi 1994). The GCC approach has helped us in theorizing and researching the global network economy in different ways, before later morphing into the global value chain (GVC) framework (see Gereffi et al. 2001), which departed in both conceptual and empirical terms from the meso-level foci of the GCC approach (Bair 2005). Both frameworks have been widely applied to North–South agrifood relations, often with a focus on African farms and firms (see, e.g., Dolan & Humphrey 2004; Gibbon & Ponte 2005; Ouma 2010). Despite the crucial insights that the "chain literature" has provided into the inner workings of the global agrifood economy, it has often focused on a rather narrow set of theoretical and empirical issues: the organization and governance of agrifood chains, questions of economic upgrading, and the re-regulation of chains by private standards (which are increasingly being proliferated in the global economy). Although these, alongside labor struggles (Selywn 2011), dynamics of "social upgrading" (Barrientos et al. 2011), and the environmental and livelihood impacts of global agrifood chains (Neilson & Pritchard 2009) remain important issues to be critically interrogated, the existing chain literature often tells us little about how global economic connections come into being, how they are assembled practically by different actors, and what such chains look like "from below" or even "from within." And while we should ask ourselves why and how managers, farmers or workers become part of global markets, there is an urgent need to overcome the "inclusionary bias" (Bair & Werner 2011a: 989) of the chain literature and likewise ask why markets break down, people lose faith in them or are actively being expelled from them.

The underlying problem here, however, is not only one of empirical focus. Although chain approaches differ in important ways from neoclassical or structuralist views on trade, they partly display a similar kind of ostensive sociology (Latour1986), privileging entities such as "global markets," "GCCs," or "GVCs" over the multiple relations, materially entangled practices, and diverse bodies of knowledge that make them up. This point has been repeatedly made by the global production networks (GPN) school, which extensively draws on relational and poststructuralist takes on economic processes in economic sociology and geography (Dicken et al. 2001; Henderson et al. 2002; Hess 2004). Indeed, many scholars working in the chain tradition predominantly advance an absolute, essentialized and overcoordinated understanding of global supply chains without considering the often precarious and contested nature of these connections across geographical, material, social, and institutional differences, and the practical work that sustains them. In particular, the now dominant variant of the approach that borrows from *New Institutional Economics* (NIE) (Williamson 1979) frequently treats markets as preconfigured and essential coordination mechanisms among other "non-market" governance forms such as hierarchies or networks (Gereffi et al. 2005) rather than as something that is socially constructed in the first place. A primordial notion of markets indeed has deeper ontological and epistemological roots in the social sciences more generally. In their quest for conceptual order and purity, economists, sociologists and geographers have often mobilized a final vocabulary such as "the market," "the firm," "the commodity," "value," "capital," or "price," which serve as stable and unquestioned artifacts of explanation that exist *a priori*. Providing the researcher with a sense of security that she can mirror her object of analysis (Rorty 1979; Barnes 2001), these orders and the final vocabulary that sustains them are often blind to the messy actualities of economic practice, the myriad of connections that finally make up seemingly stable "economic" entities, and the very (im)possibilities that shape this process.

But there is another reason why this literature has largely left untouched certain processes that are nevertheless central to the making of global agrifood economy: much of the GCC and GVC literature has embraced a rather top-down notion of order, which is considered to be produced by particular forms of governance, executed by powerful actors such as "lead firms" (e.g., large retailers, branded marketers and agribusiness companies) (Coe et al. 2008). Although we should not downplay the "rule-governed structure" (Friedmann 1993: 30–31) of the global agrifood economy, including its underlying dynamics of supranational and state regulation, corporate power, and human and environmental exploitation, the popular top-down notion of order employed in GCC/GVC studies (and, indeed, much of agrarian political economy literature more generally) often produces too crude an account to capture the more fine-grained "microphysical" processes through which particular market orders are established on the ground (for exceptions, see Loconto 2010; Raj-Reichert 2013). Besides asking what GCCs and GVCs are, how they are governed, and how they impact local firms, farms, and workers, it is likewise fruitful to explore how they become *effective* in particular places within particular historical conjunctures. Such a perspective raises a range of questions usually not addressed (or at least under-researched) by scholars working in the GCC, GVC, and GPN traditions: What about the inner life of organizations and commodities? How are prices constructed in GCCs? How are ordinary fruits turned into goods of the retail market? How does the "outgrower" or "supplier," a new kind subjectivity in itself, come into being, and how is he or she being worked upon? How is the complexity of economic life coordinated across spatial, material, and social differences – differences that often do not exist *a priori*? How do economic models of global connection structure the very organization and practical realization of markets?

Finally, we should ask ourselves whether it is appropriate to fully substitute "chains" and "networks" for "markets" at a time when economy, society, and even nature are all about *markets*, and when market-led development has become a new panacea? This is a deeply political question, resting on a particular notion of critique. While ideas about the societal impact and reach of markets have remained contested throughout history (see, e.g., Polanyi 2001 [1944]; Swedberg 2005), the rise of neo-liberalism from the late 1970s onwards, and the demise of politico-economic alternatives after the fall of state socialism in various countries, have led to a new absolutization and ontologization of markets. These processes have not only deeper roots in the history of modern economic thought, but have also been reified in the language and practice of market-fetishizing politics. Such market fetishism manifests itself in the typical tropes often mobilized in a variety of different settings. In an attempt to justify political decisions and projects of economy-making, economists, planners, business people, and politicians alike often uphold notions that "the market" demands, empowers, determines, is nervous, promises, connects, clears, allocates, or even loses trust in a certain country, as we could witness for the ongoing Euro crisis. "The market" frequently acts as an unquestioned referential meta-category, as a final vocabulary in a Rortyian sense, according to which decisions are justified.

The realm of development provides one of the most striking examples. For instance, two major international development organizations note in their manual on "making markets work for the poor" (M4P) – a new paradigm of development that is currently being globalized alongside similar ones such as the value chain approach – that "there's little point being against markets *per se*. Like breathing air, they're there" ([italics in original] Sen; cited in DFID & SDC 2008: 9). More generally, in its most abstract form, as an efficient mechanism for allocating scarce resources based on the principle of supply and demand, "the market" seems to have become a concept so familiar that its mere existence and nature are taken for granted often in such power-ful ways that it is not only difficult to imagine alternatives, but also to demonstrate what ongoing constructive work actually goes into this seemingly natural and absolute economic formation. As one could witness with the global financial crisis that ensued from 2007/2008 onward, even in times of systemic market failure, the fetishization of "the market" persists.

Against this backdrop, it should become clear that despite the fact that this book is about the construction of agro-exports markets in Ghana, a broader scope of analysis and reflection is necessary. I can do nothing but agree with Çalışkan and Callon (2010: 22) when they assert that "[i]f the dynamics of economic markets are to be understood, then they must be placed within the context of broader movements that bring the economic into being." This is an important point, as it is associated with a particular understanding of critique embraced in this book. While the GCC, GVC and GPN literature, as well as economic sociology and geography accounts of markets, more generally often advance an *ipso facto* critique (Castree 2003: 291), arguing that one approach/discipline or another (especially economics) does not represent "the economic" correctly, my project is more closely aligned with Foucault's take on critique, who understands it as a "historical interrogation of the conditions of possibility of things being as they are" (Elden 2010: 800).

Grounding Commodity Chains: Geographies of Marketization

To come to terms with the expansion of global market relations through the work of a variety of market-makers (ranging from businesses and traditional authorities to NGOs and governments), I shall draw on what has been called the "social studies of economization and marketization" (SSEM)[4] (Callon 1998a; Çalışkan & Callon 2009, 2010). Taking inspiration from the social studies of science and technology and their constructionist take on "scientific facts," as well as its intellectual offspring, actor-network-theory (ANT), scholars in this field argue that economic facts like "the economy" or markets can be considered outcomes of historically variegated processes of economization. In this book, the latter refers to all the processes that constitute the "behaviors, organizations, institutions, and objects which are tentatively and often controversially qualified as "economic" by experts and lay persons" (Çalışkan & Callon 2009: 370).

Thus, I understand marketization as a particular but now dominant form of econ-omization, denoting either the creation of new market relations around new goods, or the reconfiguration of existing markets and goods according to new modalities of valuation and accumulation. The power of this approach is that it helps unsettle both (global) commodity chains and markets as unquestioned entities, providing not only a sympathetic critique of the GCC/GVC/GPN literature, but also challenging the ontologies and epistemologies of modern economics, this "sole science of the market in practice" (Fine & Milonakis 2009: 12). Although markets are at the heart of modern economics and take "center stage in capitalist processes of circulation and exchange, they have rarely been made an object of study" (Berndt & Boeckler 2009: 535; see also Frances et al. 1991; Coase 1988). What instead prevails in the "age of the market" (Lie 1997: 341) is a neoclassical trope, whose bits and pieces have become part of how many professional and lay economists make sense of economic realities:

> The theoretical picture of the market is one of impersonal exchange. [...]. At a given price (or, more precisely, given all prices), individual agents choose how much to supply and how much to demand. These supplies and demands are simply added up; when the prices are such that total supply equals total demand in each market, equilibrium prevails. There is no particular relation between a supplier and a demander; that is, a supplier is indifferent about supplying one demander or another, or vice versa. (Arrow 1998: 94)

This "theoretical picture" is based on the (often implicit) premise of secure property rights over goods, the full availability of information, the homogeneity of goods, full competition, and stable, pre-given preferences of rational individuals in the market-place. A utilitarian rationality as the exclusive mode of economic action lies at the core of such a research program, which advances an ahistorical picture of particular economic subjectivities.[5]

In contrast, the marketization perspective attunes us to the fact that particular market configurations, economic subjectivities, and goods are outcomes of specific historical struggles. It acknowledges that there are not only many ways to organize and perform "the economy" (Polanyi 2001[1944]; Gibson-Graham 2006 ([1996]), but also many ways to organize and perform markets.[6] For instance, local markets for fish, and maize markets in Ghana, work according to quite different principles than export-oriented (or extravert?) markets for crops such as pineapples. At the same time, this perspective is sensitive to the power-laden reconfiguration of particular markets in space and time. Many global agricultural markets, for instance, have been reshaped according to a capital-friendly program of marketization, where even the knowledge relevant to production and exchange has been commoditized (Guthman 2007). Such processes are embedded into a range of wider techno-economic struggles, regulatory shifts and the ongoing practices of actors such a retailers, agrobusiness firms and (new) market intermediaries such as certification bodies, who all try to extract profit from agriculture (Amanor 2009; Ouma 2010; McMichael 2013).[7]

The social studies of markets/marketization program has sparked a considerable interest among economic geographers (see, e.g., Berndt & Boeckler 2009, Boeckler & Berndt 2012; Peck 2012), but its full thrust is yet to be explored in both theoretical and empirical terms. Unfortunately, many studies committed to the social studies of markets/marketization program have so far focused on so-called advanced capitalist economies (but see Çalışkan 2010). However, by confronting this program with the concrete historical and material realities of southern and northern Ghana, I show that marketization is never a straightforward process but one marked by improvisations, controversies, recalcitrances, and crises. In order to imagine marketization as much more frictional than conventional readings, I shall draw on additional insights from earlier ANT work, the *économie des conventions* (EC) (Boltanski & Thévenot 2006 [1991]), and what I call the "anthropology of universals" (Mitchell 2002; Tsing 2005, 2008).[8] In their own ways, each of the latter approaches sensitizes us to the historical and geographical situatedness of particular practices framed as "economic," and the often-skewed ways in which marketization wrestles with or is entangled with other forms of economization. I provide a detailed discussion of the synergies, unacknowledged links, and frictions between these largely more-than-human and anti-essentialist strands of thinking about economies.

In order to underscore the analytical power of the approach developed in this book, it is briefly necessary to situate it in the non-economics social science disciplines, particularly the *New Economic Sociology* (NES), from which the sociology of markets emerged as a more recent intellectual field. Taking inspiration from the work of Polanyi (2001 [1944]), White (1981), and Granovetter (1985), among others (e.g., Weber, Marx, or Simmel), the sociology of markets has become one of the most vibrant frontiers of sociology. Even though there exist some notable internal differences, for instance, with regard to whether one conceives of markets as networks, institutions, or fields (Fligstein 2001; Fourcade 2007; Aspers & Beckert 2008), market sociologists inspired by the NES are unified by a distaste for the neoclassical conceptualization of markets as socially thin, decentralized mechanisms for the efficient allocation of goods and services, with exchange solely being structured by the laws of supply and demand. Starting from the basic premise that there is nothing law-like, natural, self-organized, or spontaneous about markets, they argue that this type of exchange already contains a great deal of social structure:

> Market actors have to find one another. Money has to exist to allow market actors to get beyond bartering non-equivalent goods. Actors have to know what the price is. Underlying all exchange is that both buyers and sellers have faith that they will not be cheated. Such faith often implies informal (i.e., personal knowledge of the buyer or seller) and formal mechanisms (i.e., law) that govern exchange. Furthermore, market actors are often organizations, implying that organizational dynamics influence market structures. For sociologists, market exchange implies a whole backdrop of social arrangements that economics does not even begin to hint at. But the sociology of markets goes further than just questioning the institutional embeddedness of an anonymous market. It is prepared to unpack the black boxes of exchange, competition, and production. Sociologists begin by realizing that market actors are involved in day-to-day social relationships with one another, relationships based on trust, friendship, power, and dependence. (Fligstein & Dauter 2007: 113)

The program of the NES-inspired sociology of markets has been highly influential. Except for mainstream economics, there is now a growing consensus in the social sciences that markets are "constructed socially with the help of actors who are interlinked in dense and extensive webs of social relations" (Berndt & Boeckler 2009: 536). On this basis, social "scientists" have delved into a wide array of phenomena that economists usually undersocialize. Economic geographers, in particular, have taken up many key insights of the NES to study the social embeddedness of economic activities from a territorial and topological perspective (Henderson et al. 2002; Hess 2004; Peck 2005; Grabher 2006), even though they have been somewhat hesitant to engage more comprehensively with its market-oriented offspring (Peck 2012). Taken as a whole, the NES-influenced research program in and beyond sociology offers a more socially grounded take on economic phenomena (firms, markets, inter-firm linkages, economic agency, etc.) than mainstream economics does. However, it also suffers from a range of shortcomings[9] that need to be addressed if the question of how marketization takes effect in the new frontier regions of global agrarian capitalism is to be answered:

1. While at least a few market sociologists have addressed the making of new markets (Fligstein 2001; Aspers 2009), they – like many economic geographers – usually disregard the specificities of market constructions and market behavior; they instead dissolve markets by embedding them into networks, institutions, and fields, which then become privileged as analytical categories. But what if "[m]arkets exist and so does rational behavior [...]" (Barber 1995: 389)? Indeed, even the most abstract markets should be understood as truly social (and thus not "disembedded") entities (Knorr-Cetina & Bruegger 2002). This calls for an approach that takes seriously the spatially variegated social construction of market arrangements and interrogates the specific conditions under which they emerge (Peck 2005). Thereby, the terms *social construction*, *arrangement*, and indeed *the social* itself, have to be put under critical scrutiny (Latour 2005). We have to move beyond the ontological divide that separates the "economic" from the "social" in much of the NES-inspired literature, with the former said to be embedded into the latter (Krippner 2001).

2. NES-inspired works in economic sociology and geography often neglect the powerful and effective role of different bodies of knowledge, including more or less formal economic models (or templates), when they interrogate the architecture of markets. Yet, for many agricultural markets in Eastern Europe, Latin America, and Africa, for instance, economic models have played a crucial part in transforming social, economic, and society–nature relations, be it through the implementation of the macro-economic models which underpinned structural adjustment programs (SAPs) in the 1980s (McMichael 1998) and the privatization of collective farms in post-socialist Russia in the 1990s (Lindner 2008), or, as we have witnessed more recently, through the global proliferation of micro-economic models such as food safety and quality standards, or supply chain management (SCM) tools. Reconstructing how certain bodies of economic knowledge are not only constitutive of the construction of markets but also become more effective than others becomes an analytical-cum-political project that requires more attention.[10]

3. Although some economic sociologists have addressed the question of how markets are made and how they work *in situ* (e.g., Abolafia 1998 on financial markets), they have usually done so from a distance. Yet, as Knorr-Cetina and Bruegger (2002) demonstrate so strikingly in their ethnographic study of trading rooms, or as Elyachar (2005) shows for the making of micro-enterprises in Cairo as part of neoliberal entrepreneurship promotion programs, specific practices are constitutive of markets and have a productive–inventive, reproductive, and reinventive–destructive function, and they must be put under ethnographic scrutiny.

4. While scholars embracing an NES-inspired research program have frequently noted that economic relationships are imbued with politics and power, both are often "rendered contingent and contextual, and, as a result, they are only haphazardly theorized" (Peck 2005: 147). If these are recognized, it is usually in a top-down fashion. The sociology of markets (and, also to a lesser extent much of economic geography) has largely not addressed the more fine-grained, "microphysical" processes and arrangements that produce market orders and subjectivities *in situ*. This represents a missed opportunity to link up questions of social theory and society-/economy-making more generally (Fourcade 2007). Some economic geographers and sociologists working on global connections provide valuable entry points in this regard (see, e.g., Hughes 2001; Loconto 2010; Ramamurthy 2011; Raj-Reichert 2013), but these are yet to be more explored in relation to a theory of market-making.

5. Different strands of the NES-inspired sociology of markets operate with an over-coordinated notion of order that is grounded in formal and informal institutions and/or shared understandings, which coordinate human actions. However, the notion of an institution as defined by network scholars and neoinstitutionalists seems to be too restricted to describe the spatially variegated arrangements of power, knowledge, rules, material devices, and technologies that make up markets (Callon 2005: 8). From this, it follows that we need to take seriously the socially transformative, redistributive, and stabilizing role material devices play in markets (Pinch & Swedberg 2008). They are central in facilitating the coordination of market activities across space and time, as Knorr-Cetina and Bruegger (2002) demonstrate for the working of financial markets. At the same time, materials not only have an exchange-facilitating role, but they themselves lie at the very heart of exchange as "transformed nature" (Hudson 2008). The "double-materiality" of markets must therefore have a firm place in any study of marketization.

6. Even though economic sociologists and geographers have reworked many of economics' assumptions and categories, they have often shown limited interest in reflecting on how these categories come into being and become effective in both shaping our worldview as researchers as well as the very practical processes of market-making.

Although this book in fact acknowledges many overlapping concerns with both the GCC/GVC/GPN and the sociology of markets literature, the program developed here aims to portray "world market integration" processes as discursive, material, and social all at once. In short, they are about (re)assembling the market social, as an extended reading of Latour (2005) would suggest. By grounding such processes in regions widely underrepresented in economic geography, economic sociology and global political economy (Murphy 2008; Carmody 2011), this book deliberately straddles the divide between economic sociology, anthropology, geography, and "development studies" at large.

Matters of Concern

Given my own ambition to rethink "world market integration", I first and foremost critically engage with the problems raised earlier by de-centering absolutist and preconfigured readings of global market connections. Instead of either embracing or assuming away "the market" as a final object, the overall goal of this book is to reconstruct how global market connections are being *constructed*, *ordered*, and *performed* in concrete places for concrete agro-commodities.

This "how" question will be addressed for the two market-making projects introduced earlier, which in their own right mark two typical frontiers of the global agrifood economy. In addition, they also epitomize the resurgence/refashioning of contract-farming arrangements across Africa, and the Global South more generally (Oya 2012). While in many African countries contract farming was practiced for traditional commodities such as cotton, oil palm, tobacco, tea, or sugar in the early post-colonial period (1960s–1970s), and was promoted by development organizations such as the World Bank or the United Agency for International Development (USAID) as a "dynamic partnership" between small farmers and private capital across the Global South since the late 1970s (Glover & Kusterer 1990; Watts 1994),[11] it has recently been refashioned in development discourse as a "win-win tool" to facilitate the market integration of smallholder farmers into highly demanding retail markets. This discourse maintains that by linking farmers to agribusiness companies through contractual arrangements, they would benefit from market access, technical expertise, and financial support provided by contracting companies, which would enjoy a stable supply of products at the right time and quality.

The rise of new commodity spaces in Ghana fits well into this discourse. Thus, my case studies by no means stand alone but must be situated into the wider experimental space of Ghana's agricultural sector, which over the past decade has experienced a series of new market-making projects for fresh fruits such as pineapples, bananas, mangoes, and citrus, and also for staples such as maize. Agribusiness companies of different sizes and origin, large Northern retailers, development organizations, certification bodies, governments, consultants, industry associations, farmers, and traditional authorities to varying degrees have been central actors in these market-making projects. At the same time, at least the fresh fruits subsector has also experienced significant restructuring due to regulatory and structural changes in global agrifood markets. While export-oriented horticulture contributes little to Ghana's overall agricultural GDP in comparison to staple crops such as maize or traditional export crops such as cocoa, my case studies do offer something to rethink the remaking of agriculture and the (Ghanaian) economy more generally.

As introduced earlier, my first case study focuses on the operations of OFL. It is a telling case because it is representative of a nucleus–outgrower model, where a large company organizes farmers as "outgrowers" under a long-term contractual arrangement, seasonally serving the organic mango market. At the same time, farmers are supported through a long-term-credit scheme and technical services that should allow for the optimal production of mangoes.

The second case study revolves around the operations of TF and was selected because it is representative of a centralized "hub-and-spoke model" of agribusiness organization, whereby a processor–exporter links up with a pool of small-, medium-, and large-scale suppliers, serving highly demanding retail markets on a just-in-time basis throughout the year with a variety of tropical fruits products. The focus here is on the market segment for fresh pineapples and the farmers supplying them. Located in Ghana's coastal savannah zone, the case study area has experienced rapid institutional, economic, environmental, and cultural transformations over the past decades.

These contextual factors differentiate this case study from the mango project, which is embedded into the distinct institutional, social, ecological, and infrastructural setting of northern Ghana. Historically, southern Ghana has been shaped by processes of commodification since the early 19th century (first through the extension of export-oriented palm oil production and later through cocoa production). Ghana's north, on the contrary, has a different history of land administration and economy-making. Consequently, the commodification of land and labor in the north has progressed far less than in Ghana's south. Indeed, many farmers in northern Ghana have never been exposed to the workings of the "world market" as tree farmers. Despite these differences, both case studies do not, however, simply stand for themselves, but in fact will serve as entry points for critically reflecting upon more general issues pertinent to the workings of the global economy. To me, they are catalysts, not cameras.

The Practical Means of Marketization

In regard to both case studies, I am specifically interested in the "practical means" (Latour 2005: 66) that co-produce markets: How is nature being turned into goods for the "world market"? What organizational forms, subjectivities, tactics/strategies, material devices, practices, and ways of knowing are being mobilized to construct and maintain such market connections? How are specific market encounters being organized, and how are these being stabilized/destabilized in the course of everyday market practice? An overall interest lies in the question of which new forms of South–North connection and disconnection are being established through assembling and performing export markets. Because I am interested in the new forms of (dis-) connection that emerge from the latter, I shall put under ethnographic scrutiny the new alignments of power, knowledge, and materially entangled practices that lie at the heart of new export market orders. In this regard, it should be noted that while the traditional themes of agrarian political economy – economic impact, social differentiation (including the dimensions of "citizenship," "ethnicity," "age," and "gender") and agrarian change are still important points of reference when dealing with processes of "world market integration" (see, e.g., Amanor 2010a; Oya 2012; Ramamurthy 2011; Selwyn 2012), I am more specifically interested in how markets, and for that matter "the social" itself, are being assembled through the ongoing practices of market agents and how they become effective (or not), rather than only focusing on what (re)distributive or stratifying effects they bring with them. Thus, this book aims to reconstruct the quotidian and interdependent making of organizations (the agribusiness–outgrower complex), markets, and the "economy" at large.

Marketization as Proliferation

Studying how the intricate geographies of global capitalism come into being, however, is not devoid of theoretical, ontological, epistemological, and methodological challenges for which we have to be sensitized. This is probably best done in Anna Tsing's *Friction*, a remarkable ethnographic study of the penetration of the Indonesian rainforest by Japanese-Korean "capital" (Tsing 2005). She reminds us that conceiving of markets or capitalism in dynamic unfolding relations rather than mere substances must defy any essentialism, and that processes of "world market integration" are usually much messier *in practice* than one might think. Speaking with Tsing, universals such as markets or commodity chains need to be engaged locally for them to become "global" in the very first place. It is through friction "that universals become practically effective," but "they can never fulfill their promises of universality. Even in transcending localities, they don't take over the world" (ibid. 8).

In order to unveil what it takes to accomplish global market connections in a heterogeneous world, I explore the very practical *problems* that lie at the heart of agrarian marketization processes. These "problems" need to be solved practically before something ostensibly abstract like a market can take its form and function. Marketization is, hereafter, conceptualized as a "proliferation" (Tsing 2005: 26) of engaged arrangements that respond to a number of problematizations that are pertinent to contemporary market-making projects in the global agrifood economy. As Foucault (1997 [1984]) reminds us, problematizations are by no means innocent, and they are often highly productive undertakings. Certain domains, objects, relations, rationalities, or practices only become problems at particular historical conjunctures, and these are usually followed by (not necessarily successful) interventions that aim at solving them in particular ways. Export-oriented marketization is no different.

Of Frontier Regions and Borderlands

Tsing's notion of engaged universals also has profound implications for my conceptualization of the term *frontier*, which hereafter does not simply denote a terrain of expansion of market modernity (Turner 1921), where unvalorized nature is appropriated by resourceful men (sic!). The term I propose here is neither synonymous with the notion of "frontier" often advanced in critical agrarian political economy (Amanor 1994: 24–26; Watts 1994: 71; Agergard et al. 2010), as it does not assume the expansion of a universal and essential form of "capitalism" into spaces which had previously been dominated by other modes of production, for instance, subsistence agriculture. Instead, I am here more inclined towards Mitchell's concept of the "frontier region" (Mitchell 2007: 247). Defying any methodological territorialism, frontier regions are discursive-cum-material "borderlands of global capitalism" (Boeckler & Berndt 2012) where struggles over new agencies, commodities, encounters, entitlements, rights, obligations, and material devices, as well as with the "inside" and the "outside" of the market are fought out.

Similarly to Tsing's notion of "engaged universals," the notion of "frontier region" allows us to capture the heterogeneous, at times messy, arrangements of global markets, and the extensive work that is needed to sustain them across geographical, material, social, and institutional difference. By being interested in the relational production of markets in two specific frontier regions, I also refute what Hart (2004: 97) calls the "impact model" of globalization – the popular perspective that renders the "local" as a mere passive object of inexorable "global" forces, thus privileging the universal (the abstract) over the particular (the concrete) in an often deterministic mode of thinking. This relationship, as will be shown, is less one of determinations, or one of "dialectics" – a notion which despite its emphasis on the mutually constitutive quality of the abstract and the concrete has too often fallen short of explaining how the abstract is assembled, stabilized, destabilized, and reassembled in practice – but one of translations, hybridizations and, to use Tsing's term (2005), "friction." Thus, I will show that global market connections require "particular conditions of existence to appear at all" (Hall 1985: 113). But they are not simply multiply articulated, as Hall and others would put it (see, e.g., Bair & Werner 2011a).[12] Instead, they emerge within the "sticky materiality of practical encounters" (Tsing 2005: 1). As such, they need "to be positively sustained by specific processes" (Hall 1985: 113), yet they can break down at any time.[13]

All in all, the two frontier regions presented here have to be conceived as heuristic sites in a larger global setting of agrarian marketization. The case studies are experimental sites that could undoubtedly have been located elsewhere – global capitalism has many frontier regions where it is being *worked* upon. Although this work is about the construction of agro-export markets in Ghana, it thus relates to wider debates on the expansion of markets and new processes of commodification in various social domains and places.

How This Book Unfolds

In order to set the scene, in the next chapter I sketch some key prisms through which we can imagine market-making processes. Drawing on a bricolage of ANT, the social studies of economization and marketization, the EC, as well as the anthropology of universals, I develop a vocabulary that helps grasp the very practical problems that lie at the heart of making global market connections. In general, cross-fertilization between these different intellectual strands represents a frictional project, but one that produces productive friction.

Chapter 3 first outlines the structural and policy context of my case studies, which are then introduced in detail. Even though both serve different markets in different structural settings, similar dynamics of market-making can be observed. While I attend to commonalities and differences between the case studies in the empirical part of the book, this prelude to the empirical sections underscores that these projects of global connection only became possible at particular historical conjunctures and in turn have influenced other projects of economy building in Ghana more generally. My rather detailed discussion of the structural and policy context also points to something larger: that we cannot think of marketization without considering the multiple technologies, forms of regulation, material devices, discourses, and calculative practices that constitute "the economy" at large.

Chapter 4 maps out the methodological approach of the book, which is inextricably linked to the theoretical conceptualization of markets embraced here. I spell out the basic traits of what I call a "critical ethnography of marketization," which allows for capturing how markets are arranged and performed as heterogeneous actor-networks. My key methodological concern is to outline an approach that is not only sensitive to *what* things are done and *why* they are done but also to *how* they are done – how the messy work of making markets plays out *in practice*. I show, however, that "following the actors" and the multiple linkages which made up markets in my case studies was inevitably bound up with various methodological challenges as it called for in-depth ethnographic research in agronomy departments, in busy packhouses, and on remote farms over an extended period of time. It also required maneuvering at the frictional interstices between agribusiness companies and their farmers. Consequently, I will discuss these challenges in detail.

Chapter 5 provides a detailed genealogy of the two case studies and how global market connections have been forged in each one. I put the investments of OFL and TF "in place" and discuss the underlying economic models. Taking into account the very different nature of frontier regions and global connections (seasonal mango production in Ghana's north versus just-in-time production in the south) in each case, I also demonstrate how micro constructions became macro, how more complexly coordinated global connections evolved, and what factors supported or hampered such processes of enlargement.

In Chapter 6, I reconstruct how global market connections were enacted *in situ* by unpacking the more microphysical, disciplinary processes that lie at the heart of "world market integration". The global connections I described in the previous two chapters could not become effective without the making of particular agencies (among farmers) that valuate simple crops as goods that have (a legitimate) exchange value, take ownership over them, perform the roles assigned to them in the market-making program, and become responsible, autonomous, and accountable "market agents."

Chapter 7 delves more deeply into issues of power and asymmetries in markets, highlighting the ambiguous character of markets as (anti-)political encounters. I explore the question of how encounters between ostensibly "powerful" companies and ostensibly "powerless" farmers were organized, without resorting to a top-down and preconfigured notion of power. Instead, I address *how* hierarchies came into being, were performed, and resisted, highlighting the mundane and technical manifestations of power in agrifood chains. First and foremost, I demonstrate that power relations are not only articulated in specific relations of definition, as the previous chapter shows, but also in specific relations of calculation and accounting.

Chapter 8 deals with the issues of crisis and change in markets. A performative and processual take on marketization needs to address both order and disorder in markets. I thus show how market arrangements in the two case studies were destabilized into different directions over the course of time. In the pineapple case, the just-in-time model slid into crisis owing to the cumulative effects of changing preferences in the world pineapple market, the global economic crisis, price pressures and increasingly fierce competition in buyer markets, and the destabilization of supply chain relations amid new dynamics of competition in the raw material market in Ghana. In the mango case, the entry point is a different one altogether. I here highlight how "nature" itself was the source of crisis as it could not simply be turned into a resource, a fact that had a significant impact on the organization and trajectory of the market-making project. In each case study, I am interested in how company managers and agronomists reengineered market arrangements in the wake of crisis.

The book's conclusion tackles the question of how we can grasp and qualify the ambivalent dynamics of connection and disconnection that come along with marketization projects in the Ghanaian policy context as well as in the age of "global capitalism" more generally – projects which strive to instantiate particular forms of market modernity.

Endnotes

1 In this book, all names of individuals, of the case study companies and related organizations, and their geographical associations have been anonymized, are withheld, or have been altered to protect sources. Development organizations and programs associated with the Ghanaian agricultural sector more generally are referred to by their original names.

2 Contract farming can be defined as "forms of vertical coordination between growers and buyers–processors that directly shape production decisions through contractually specifying market obligations (by volume, value, quality, and, at times, advanced price determination); provide specific inputs; and exercise some control at the point of production (i.e., a division of management functions between contractor and contractee" (Little & Watts 1994: 9).

3 The absolutization of markets has been a long-standing problem in economic and social theory. For an early take on this, see Barber (1977).

4 This program also goes by the name "social studies of markets" (Çalışkan 2010) and is sometimes narrowly referred to as the "performativity program" (MacKenzie et al. 2007).

5 I am aware that "economics" is a diverse field, including strands of feminist, evolutionary, institutional, Marxist, and ecological economics that break with these assumptions in many respects. Yet these are not part of the discursive core of a highly centralized discipline (see also Peck 2012).

6 Indeed, markets, including capitalist markets, have historically taken a variety of forms (see, e.g., Polanyi 1992 [1957]; Swedberg 2005; Peck 2012), which one should not subsume under one grand market narrative.

7 I am not suggesting here that the peculiarities of global horticultural markets and other types of markets with bilateral oligopolies are features of all markets. I am grateful to Kojo Amanor for pushing me to be clearer on this.

8 Note here that economic anthropology more generally provides some crucial (and welcome) insights to help make sense of markets as material, institutional, semiotic, and discursive formations, including their very making (see, e.g., Polanyi 1992 [1957]; Geertz 1978; Carrier 1997; Graeber 2001; Rankin 2004; Escobar 2005; Hann & Hart 2011).

9   In what follows, I concur with optimistic reviewers such as Fligstein & Dauter (2007) and Aspers & Beckert (2008) that different theory camps in the sociology of markets share common interests, yet often obscure these owing to the use of jargon or ignorance. There-fore, we can only but benefit from an "engaged pluralism" of approaches that allows us to conceive of markets as "boundary objects" (Barnes & Sheppard 2010). However, I will also demonstrate that there are notable ontological, epistemological, and methodological differences between the SSEM program and network, neoinstitutionalist and field approaches to markets.

10   Note that the need to study how firms, inter-firm relations and markets come into being in practice has also been repeatedly emphasized by economic geographers (Yeung 2003; Hess 2004; Jones & Murphy 2011), but there seems to be a considerable gap between theoretical and methodological ambition and actual research practices, as such calls have rarely been followed up by a more ethnographic research program (for exceptions, see Rankin 2004; Dunn 2005).

11   The earliest experiments with contract farming in Africa indeed have colonial roots. The first contract farming scheme goes back to sugar cultivation schemes in Kenya in the 1920s, back then a white-settler colony. Amanor (1999: 35) reports that in Ghana smallholder-focused contract farming was introduced for cocoa, oil palm, cotton, and tobacco sectors as well as for the production of rice and vegetables under irrigation from the 1970s onward.

12   Hall utilizes the concept of articulation in order to distance himself from deterministic and essentialist readings of Marx. "Essentialist" here denotes the "specific presumption [...] that any apparent complexity – a person, a relationship, a historical occurrence, and so forth – can be analyzed to reveal a simplicity at its core" (Resnick & Wolff 1987: 2–3; cited in Gibson-Graham 2006 [1996]: 24).

13   What is commonly referred to as the "local" then is hereafter not understood as something that is given or subordinated to the "global." It is an epistemological category, not an ontological one. It indicates the effective "sites" (Marston et al. 2005; Schatzki 2005) of market practices that are associatively enacted by multiple connections and have to be positively sustained.

Chapter Two
Querying Marketization

Somewhere in an outgrower scheme in northern Ghana …What counts here are *practical* problems, getting things done, meeting the requirements of customers, consumers, and standard setters in spatially distant but institutionally close Europe. Market-making in northern Ghana is hard work. Not convinced? Ask the outgrower manager, the one who is supposed to turn "peasants" into tree farmers. One day back in July 2008, he and I drive on a bumpy road, inspecting some mango farms in the western and eastern part of the outgrower scheme. Our trip is a test for the pickup truck, because during the rainy season between May and October the bumpy feeder roads turn into a reddish stretch of ferralitic clay on which the vehicles of Organic Fruits Limited (OFL)[1] would frequently get stuck. As the pickup sneaks through the rough terrain, the outgrower manager – a white man in his fifties from East Africa who had been hired by the OFL directors owing to his extensive experience with agro-industries and smallholder farming across East Africa – constantly talks about how difficult his job is. Expectations from the shareholders and the buyers are high, yet the work of forging global connections is tedious. It was about "First World expectations" amid "Third World production realities," as the manager remarks while reflecting upon his daily work.

We move out of the car, checking on the progress of some newly established block farms. The manager is not happy. Important things have not been fixed; the picture is similar at another farm. The farmers have not fenced their plots against stray animals, who love to feed on young mango trees, nor have they cut down the grass to prevent bush fires that so frequently strike in this region during the dry season. Instead, weeds

Assembling Export Markets: The Making and Unmaking of Global Food Connections in West Africa,
First Edition. Stefan Ouma.

compete with mango trees. The water tanks on the fringe of the farm, essential for irrigating the trees in their early years, are half-empty, and the water has probably been taken for domestic use, or cattles, instead of for the trees; pests have attacked the trees on one plot. His is a 24/7 job. It is a struggle for particular farming practices, but it is also a struggle against the material environment, including "nature" itself.

★ ★ ★

As the reader might guess from the just presented ethnographic account, the work of making markets such as the mango project is large in scale and scope. Such architecturing touches upon a diverse range of "social," "economic," and "material" issues. How to integrate farmers into global organic markets, when they had never been exposed to their workings before? How to gain access to land and render it an accessible production factor in a region where land is still held as a communal property? How also to invoke the responsibilities of the contract, the responsibilities of producer and buyer, of debtor and creditor, in order to recover the huge investment the company had made through loans granted to the farmers? These are only some of the practical problems that lie at the heart of market-making in northern Ghana; similar problems could be outlined for the frontier region in Ghana's south, where the local Smooth Cayenne pineapple variety has to be turned into a just-in-time pineapple that meets the standards of the world's most demanding retailers.

What should become clear from this account is that in order to address these very practical problems of marketization, we need an approach that places the historicity, practical construction, and spatiality of markets at center stage. In order to do so, we need to overcome an *ostensive* understanding of markets (Fourcade 2007: 1019) in favor of a *performative* one (Latour 1986).

Here, the social studies of economization and marketization (SSEM) provide an excellent entry point. While marketization usually denotes the extension of the market principle into previously state-governed domains as part of neoliberal policy shifts (see, e.g., England & Ward 2007), an SSEM perspective offers a more material and pragmatic take on the making and remaking of markets. Spurred by the seminal work of Michel Callon (1998a), a burgeoning body of literature has since emerged with the goal of studying the multiple processes through which markets of various shapes and sizes, in various places and social domains, are constructed, ordered, performed, reproduced, reordered, or fall apart. Callon rejects "contextual explanations" (Barry & Slater 2005: 107) such as the embeddedness argument so prominent in the *New Economic Sociology* (NES) and economic geography, instead arguing that one "must not imagine society as a context for different types of activities including economic activities, [but] [...] imagine the processes through which collective relations are constructed, including relations that can be called economic relations" (ibid.). The argument, rather implicitly, builds on the more general notion of performativity advanced in language philosophy and social theory, which rejects both realist accounts of reality and a transcendental treatment of categories such as "gender," "the state," or "the economy," instead turning our attention to the "set of processes [...] that work to bring into being certain kinds of realities or [...] that lead to certain kinds of socially binding consequences" (Butler 2010: 147).

From a performative vantage point, markets are not quasi-natural and *per se* absolute and stable forms of exchange but highly presuppositional sociotechnical arrangements[2] that "require a set of investments and operations to shape calculative agencies, to qualify and singularize goods, and to organize and stabilize the encounters between goods and agencies" (Callon 2005: 8). Markets cannot be reduced to a singular form or essence for there are multiple ways to organize them. Financial markets, for instance, where sellers and buyers switch roles and trade highly abstract products in real time, are very different from agricultural markets, where roles are fixed, nature has to be transformed, other technological infrastructures are at work, and the processes of product qualification are radically different.

In the remainder of this chapter, I take these insights as a starting point to map out the contours of a performative approach to the making of global agrifood connections. It is deeply informed by the SSEM, yet developed in dialogue with other sociological, geographical, and anthropological approaches to studying "the economy." First, I contextualize and spell out the key tenets of a performative approach to marketization.

I then propose to conceive of marketization as a process of proliferation that hinges on the solution of a distinct set of practical problems, and I demonstrate what specific research questions each of these practical problems produces. In this regard, it should be noted that research questions are always fictitious artifacts of scholarly practice. We need them to justify our projects, to attract money and to prove the scientificity of our own work. On paper, they give us a sense of orientation and provide a starting point for our projects, but when released into the wild, they often create frictions and may morph if we allow them to do so.

My own work is no exception. The questions formulated after discussing each practical problem of market-making were more effects of ongoing research practices than solid starting points for my research. This point warrants special emphasis. Too often, research in both the natural and social sciences is presented as a "relatively finished object" rather than as the contingent, "sequenced, step-by-step unfolding of action" (Pollner & Emerson 2008: 128–129) (see also Chapter 4). Thus, what follows is by no means a theoretical framework that had been developed in advance of my field research and was "applied" to my "object" of research. Instead, it has been the product of a circular and reflexive process that interweaved sensitizing concepts, empirical research, "data" analysis, reading, and writing. It is a "vocabulary" (Geertz 1973: 73) – though not a final or substantivist one – through which the *praxis* of global market connections can be expressed.

Studying Markets as Practical Accomplishments

A performative take on markets is clearly informed by what is often fuzzily referred to as actor-network-theory (ANT).[3] Although this approach was initially developed for the social study of science and technology (SSST) (Callon & Latour 1981; Callon 1986; Latour 1986; Law 1986, 1992), why not extend it to the study of markets? Why not advance a social study of markets and marketization? In order to capture the full thrust of such a research program, one has to understand the methodological stance that distinguishes ANT from other social sciences schools of thought.

First, ANT defies any analytical essentialism that delineates "the economic" from "the social"/"the cultural," "context" from "content," "nature" from "society," "subjects" from "objects," "the macro" from "the micro," "structure" from "agency," and "the global" from "the local" (Law 1999: 3). Instead, it highlights the composite quality of social phenomena through the continuous demarcation of these entities within a web of heterogeneous relations. In this regard, ANT is informed by both ethnomethodology and pragmatism and their sensitivity to the situativeness of social order (Garfinkel 1967; Overdevest 2011), but moves beyond a social constructivist stance by embracing a symmetrical approach to humans and nonhumans, acknowledging the socially transformative power of the latter (Callon & Latour 1981: 284). According to this reading, everybody/everything that "produce[s] differences, alter[s] the state of the world, produce[s] unexpected events, and trigger[s] changes which would not have happened without" "it" counts as an actor (Callon 2009: 24).

Second, ANT conceives of social phenomena as consisting in dynamic, unfolding relations rather than mere substances, forces, or universals. At the core of this research program is a sociology of heterogeneous associations, rather than one which thinks of the social in mere essences, abstract structures, or durable substances (Latour 2005: 43–46). The term net-*work* literally captures what is in focus here: the distributed work that is needed to forge and sustain associations between humans and nonhumans that make up ostensible entities such as "society," "the economy," or "markets."

Third, ANT rejects the attribution of agency to a single, closed actor who has the individual capacity and resources to *act* (Giddens 1979). Instead, it conceives of agency as a relational, often precarious effect of heterogeneous associations binding human and nonhuman elements together that finally act as a network – hence the term *actor-network*.

Altogether, each of these reworkings of modernist ontologies is grounded in the broader cultural turn and practice/pragmatic turns that have swept through the humanities and social sciences since the early 1990s (Crang 1997; Thrift 1997; Schatzki et al. 2001; Slater & Tonkiss 2001; Boeckler 2005). Even though calling each of these intellectual movements a turn may ascribe far too much coherence to what is in fact a diverse array of intellectual projects, some commonalities between these movements can be identified. Influenced by semiotic, poststructuralist, feminist, and postcolonial theories, "the cultural turn" has torn down the binaries, stable categories and proliferated truths that constituted the project of modernist reasoning. Instead, it recognizes the intricate relationship between knowledge, language, representation, power, and practice, as well as the situated relationality of social categories. No more grand narratives, no more "us" and "them," no more separation between "the economic" and "the social"/"culture," no more distinction between "society" and "nature," and no more final vocabulary and "ocular metaphors" (Rorty 1979: 318) that could solidify the multiple relations which make up society and naturalize the "truths" represented by them. Instead, what the cultural turn envisages is to lift the veil (Berndt & Boeckler 2007: 218), to uncover the (often hidden) presuppositional arrangements that organize the world, including "economic life."

The SSEM are sympathetic to the project of "lifting the veil," but due to their grounding in the anthropology of science and technology, they do not merely envisage a *deconstruction* of "social facts" – of the discourses and representations of economic entities such as markets (Escobar 2005) or firms (Yeung 2003) – but aim to reconstruct the "ongoing practical accomplishment" (Garfinkel 1967: 3) of these "economic quasi-entities" (Berndt & Boeckler 2011a: 1061). Treating even the hardest "scientific facts" as practical accomplishments was exactly what the anthropologists of science and technology did in the late 1970s and early 1980s, when they tried to move beyond the Mertonian sociology of science and knowledge dominant at that time. Attending to science *as work* through close observation, these scholars demonstrated that one of the central pillars of modernity – the "scientificity of science" (Latour 1983: 143) – in fact, rested on the bringing together of a variety of heterogeneous elements inside and outside the laboratory which eventually made up "scientific facts." Thus, against this ethnomethodological and pragmatic backdrop, the program of the SSEM is more closely aligned to what Schatzki et al. (2001) call the "practice turn in contemporary social theory," or what Muniesa et al. (2007: 1) more specifically deem "the pragmatic turn in the study of markets and economic activities in general."

Latour captures the thrust of a pragmatic approach toward the production of social reality quite nicely: "Dispersion, destruction, and deconstruction are not the goals to be achieved but what needs to be overcome. It's much more important to check what are the new institutions, procedures, and concepts able to collect and reconnect the social" (Latour 2005: 11). Materials are firmly a part of assembling the social, which makes it less appropriate to talk of a "social constructivist" approach (Mitchell 2002: 4–5). Accordingly, the term *constructionism* captures far better the empirical program associated with a pragmatic turn in the study of markets and "society" at large. "Construction" can be defined as "a process by which something is being built from existing material (in contrast to *creation*, which, at least in principle, starts from nothing)" (Czarniawska 2008: 5).

Constructionism then refers to the study of the messy assembling of social phenomena, and one of its central empirical concerns is to ask *how it is* that "the social" becomes durable (Knorr-Cetina 1989; Law 1999; Latour 2005) – in short, how something ostensibly stable like a market is constructed from heterogeneous associations.

Markets as Sociotechnical Agencements

Building on a critical reworking of modernist ontologies, capitalist markets can then be understood as "hybrid collectifs" (Callon & Law 1995) or sociotechnical arrangements that align humans, living organisms, technological infrastructures, specific resources, different ways of knowing, conventions, emotional qualities, standards and procedures, systems of metrology, and aspects of political regulation in such ways that commodities together with the property rights attached to them can be circulated "through the contradictory encounter of quantitative and qualitative valuations" (Berndt & Boeckler 2013: 425). From such a perspective, markets are no less social or embedded than other forms of economic exchange, as is often argued, but are indeed very social things: heterogeneous associations of various elements that produce their inside and outside as ongoing effects (Law 1999: 3).

Conceiving of markets as hybrid collectifs also allows a movement beyond the role dichotomy of modern economics, which divides market participants into producers and consumers (Pinch & Swedberg 2008: 11). Firms, consumers and their organizations, civil servants and industry bodies which draw up regulations, consultancies, patent offices, researchers, technological engineers, certification bodies, lawyers, accountants, business gurus, professional economists, and international organizations all have their share in these constructions (Berndt & Boeckler 2007). The latter two are particularly important engineers for extending the frontier regions of marketization to the Global South, as we will see in some of the later sections. As argued previously, the constitutive pillars and actor-networks of markets, including global agricultural markets, are by no means natural, but a result of historical struggles, as part of which actors strive for profit, market share, and regulatory power (McMichael & Friedmann 2007). For instance, there are still many local and far less capitalistically organized markets around the world which are made up by quite different hybrid collectifs than contemporary global agrifood markets that largely work according to the program of powerful actors such as retailers or transnational agrobusiness firms.

In order to foreground the fact that markets need to be sociotechnically arranged on the one hand but invoke a particular type of agency on the other hand, one could rethink markets as sociotechnical *agencements*[4] (STAs) (Callon 2007). Speaking to Foucault's notion of *dispositif* (Foucault 1980: 194), as well as to Deleuze's posthumous interpretation of it (Deleuze 1992), the term conveys the idea of a (spatial) array of heterogeneous elements that have been meticulously adjusted to each other. It deliberately transcends the dichotomy between human agents (those who arrange) and things that have been arranged (Callon 2007: 319–320). Refining the notion of markets as hybrid collectifs that I introduced earlier, *agencements* can be considered as "arrangements endowed with the capacity to act in different ways according to their configuration" (ibid.: 320; see also Berndt & Boeckler 2009: 543). According to this understanding, market/calculative agency is formatted via, equipped by, and distributed according to the sociotechnical arrangements producing it. Yet calculative agency is only one of the many types of agency that populate the world:

> Depending on the configurations and equipments of STAs, agencies can be deliberative, have adaptive behavior, reflexive competencies, calculative or non–calculative capacity or disinterested or selfish subjectivity, whether collective or individual. (Çalışkan & Callon 2010: 10)[5]

This take on agency has the advantage that it does not resort to any *a priori* conception of the nature of agency. It breaks with conceptions of economic agency in neoclassical economics in radical ways, but also with those popular in critical political economy and the sociology of markets. While the former has naturalized and universalized market behavior as utilitarian and calculative agency via the construct of the *homo oeconomicus*, the latter approaches have rejected this construct on the grounds of ideological or analytical misrepresentation, arguing that calculative behavior "is marginal and at best an ex post rationalization for choices grounded in other logics" (Callon & Muniesa 2005: 1230). Following Callon, however, one could argue that the *homo oeconomicus* (and thus instrumental, calculative behavior) indeed exists, but only as an emergent property of network associations. He "is not an a-historical reality; he does not describe the hidden nature of the human being. He is the result of a process of configuration" (Callon 1998a: 22).

Consequently, the fact that "an agent calculates or does not has nothing to do with her or his inherent selfishness or altruism; nor is it due to the nature of the relationships in which it is engaged (a market transaction or, by contrast, love, friendship or the family)" (Callon 1998a: 15). It is, instead, the formatting of these relationships "which will orientate the agent towards calculativeness or disinterestedness" (ibid.). Accordingly, there is no such thing as the famous "law of the market," but only format-ted relations that produce markets and market subjectivities as ongoing effects. Thus, marketization rests on a particular form of *agencement*-ization.

A second gist to a performative take on markets is that not only are *material*, *procedural*, *monetary*, and *legal* elements constitutive of markets (Callon 1998a: 22), but economic theories themselves: "Economics, in the broad sense of the term, performs shapes and formats the economy, rather than observing how it functions" (ibid.: 2). Economics, in short, has performative effects; it intervenes in the world it claims to describe; it is firmly entangled with the practical realization of markets.[6] In this vein, Callon's notion of performativity oscillates between the speech act theory of philosopher John Austin and the "performative idiom" (MacKenzie et al. 2007: 3) in the SSST, transcending the divide between formalism and substantivism that characterized anthropology's golden age (Hann & Hart 2011). The attention shifts from what economics *says* and *represents* to what it *does*.[7]

Adopting a broad notion of economics that encompasses different bodies of economic knowledge, ranging from the formal theories of "caged economists" (e.g., university-based economists) to the practice theories of what Callon calls "economists in the wild" (business gurus, marketing professionals, accountants, standard setters, other social scientists, etc.) (Callon et al. 2002: 196), we can posit that economic theories in the broadest sense (discourses, texts, theoretical statements, and models) play a constitutive role in the construction and formatting of the calculative spaces that make up many contemporary markets. The economy, one could provocatively argue with Polanyi and Granovetter in mind, "is not embedded in society" but, at least partly, "in economics" (Callon 1998a: 30). Although the performativity thesis is frequently related to the power of neoclassical economics, such an exclusive correspondence, however, risks bypassing rejuvenations in economics (value chain theories, social capital theories, behavioral economics, theories on imperfect markets, market design, etc.) (see Fine & Milonakis 2009; Boeckler & Berndt 2013). Because a performative take on markets in principle allows conceiving of economics in a broader sense, these rejuvenations can be likewise addressed from an SSEM perspective.

Both anthropologists and geographers have similarly problematized the power of economic models and their effects on "real economies" (Miller 1998; Hughes 2004).

Yet this has often happened through a "colonization of cultural life lens" (Crang 1997: 9) – just as if economics worked somewhat outside the realm of the "real" economy and its "virtual" theories were simply superimposed on human beings through the workings of ideology and power (Callon 2005; Holm 2007). Yet these models, as abstract as they may be, do not operate outside the realm of reality but at the same ontic level. They are firmly part of the world they envision. They may have effects "even if the users of the system don't believe the model, don't understand it, or even don't know that it exists. Economics is embodied in procedures and physical artifacts, not just in ideas" (MacKenzie 2009a: 13; see also Elyachar 2005: 5). In empirical terms, at the heart of an SSEM program, then, lies the "studying up" of "all the theoretical and practical, expert and lay knowledge, know-how and skills developed and mobilized" (Çalışkan & Callon 2010: 19) in the process of designing, implementing, maintaining, and reproducing market arrangements.

The performativity of economics thesis has a firm empirical grounding. Scholars working on markets for financial products (MacKenzie 2009a), carbon emissions (MacKenzie 2009b), fishery quotas (Holm 2007), and land (Mitchell 2007) have demonstrated how "the model of the world becomes the world of the model" (Thrift 2000: 694) through the discursive-cum-material workings of economics. What is striking, however, is that few studies have extended a performative approach to the study of global agrifood markets (for exceptions, see Busch 2007; Loconto 2010; Berndt & Boeckler 2011a). The empirical sections contained in this work will, however, show that contemporary agrifood markets are full of less caged practice theories.[8] Food safety and quality standards such as GLOBALG.A.P (now the largest private agricultural food safety and quality scheme in the world), environmental, social, ethical, fair trade, and corporate social responsibility (CSR) standards, or various benchmarking and accounting tools, are all templates for formatting socio-technical associations in contemporary agrifood markets (Larner & LeHeron 2004; Freidberg 2007; Ouma 2010), a point that will be explored in detail later. One could even imagine the proliferation of new supply chain management (SCM) models over the past two decades as instantiating new modes of performing global market relations, replacing the spot-market relations of earlier times (Busch 2007).

More recently, standards, SCM models and various practical derivations from the commodity/value chain approach have even become powerful templates for market-oriented development programs in the Global South, as will be unveiled in subsequent chapters. Most outstanding in this regard are the UK Department for International Development (DFID), the German Agency for Technical Cooperation (GTZ, now GIZ) and the United States Agency for International Development (USAID), which over the past few years have been chief promoters of micro-economic models for the making and remaking of markets across the Global South, with the value chain approach only being the most prominent one (Neilson 2014). As part of neoliberal governmentality programs (Larner & LeHeron 2004), these projects attempt to reorganize local–global–relations in distinctively new ways.

In sum, the notion of market STA alludes to the performative role of different bodies of economic knowledge (academic, non-academic, professional, lay, codified, practical/tacit) when new sociotechnical relations are forged in the process of marketization. Any study of market constructions must thus be sensitive to this diversity of economic knowledge. What warrants more emphasis than is usually displayed by the literature is that the performativity thesis does not principally assume a literal translation of abstract market models into concrete practices, as some critics bemoan (Miller 2002). Market models may have a transformative power within specific sociotechnical arrangements, but this is not a given. Gibbon and Ponte (2008) have, for instance, demonstrated this for the case of SCM models in the US manufacturing industry.

Against this backdrop, Callon (2007, 2009) recently introduced the notion of *performation*, a term I prefer throughout this book because it speaks more directly to Deleuze's convincing posthumous interpretation of Foucault's *dispositif* (Foucault 1980). The performation of markets is about articulating a tangle ensemble of "lines of visibility and enunciation, lines of force, lines of subjectification, lines of splitting, breakage, fracture, all of which criss-cross and mingle together, some lines reproducing or giving rise to others" (Deleuze 1992: 162). Performing the economy cannot be merely reduced to the smooth enactment of economic statements, including the anthropological program of the *homo oeconomicus*; it is instead an action, a material operation, and it is often frictional and contested (MacKenzie et al. 2007: 15). This is exactly what the more historically oriented anthropology of universals reminds us of (Elyachar 2005; Tsing 2005; 2008). It is, in particular, the historically rich work of Timothy Mitchell (2002) that shows capitalism needs to be locally engaged; that economics sometimes fails to achieve its aspirations; that establishing commodity relations is often a contested process; that nature sometimes cannot simply be turned into a resource; that marketization often clashes or is complexly intertwined with other geographically and sociotechnically situated ways of performing the economy; and that projects of economy-making often have unintended side effects that may bounce back in incalculable ways.

"Problems" of Market-Making

From the discussion of these ideas, it becomes clear that we must do away with the flawed distinction between "the economic" and "the social" that is so often perpetuated in economics, sociology and economic geography, because what is commonly defined as "economic" is, first and foremost, a very social or associational "thing" (Latour 2005). As I argued in Chapter 1, this must shift attention away from the question of what economic behavior or what "the economy" is to the historically variegated process of economization (Mitchell 2008).

Both the economy and markets represent ongoing, historical accomplishments (Garfinkel 1967), which, however, are never devoid of frictions and recalcitrances. Often, during the process of accomplishing "reality" "a lot of hurts were done along the way" (Law 1994: 15), and markets are no exception. It is usually the successful fetishization and smoothing of those hurts that grants particular markets their sheer ubiquity and stability, and unveiling what it takes to make a market *in practice* in many ways equals a micro-history of sociomaterial problematizations (Callon 1986;

Foucault 1980). According to Rabinow's rereading of Foucault, a "problematization [...] is both a kind of general historical and social situation – saturated with power relations, as are all situations" (Rabinow 2003: 19). Problematizations are imbued with the relational play of "inside" and "outside," "right" and "wrong," "true" or "false," "good" and "bad," "standard" and "non-standard," as well as a "nexus of responses to that situation. Those diverse but not entirely disparate responses [...] themselves form part of the problematization as it develops or unfolds over time" (ibid.).

As I posited in Chapter 1, certain domains, objects, relations or practices only become problems at particular historical conjunctures, and these are usually followed by interventions that aim at solving them in particular ways. The (re)making of global agrifood markets is no different. In the context of export-led marketization processes in rural areas across the Global South, specific market STAs are being proliferated, which frame problems, carry solutions, and render them economic *and* technical (Li 2007a). Such STAs establish new relations between human and nonhuman elements, responding to the urgent need[s](Foucault 1980: 194) of a power-saturated agrifood economy as new places become redefined as sites of "opportunity," "deficiency," "improvement," and "investment" by retailers, agrobusiness capital, non-governmental organizations, and governments (Freidberg 2007). They are orderly and generative at once (Legg 2011).

Contemporary marketization processes in frontier regions of the global agrifood economy must accordingly be understood as a series of problem defining and solving processes "that emerge in relation to [...] a more general situation" (Rabinow 2003: 19) – a situation of what more structuralist accounts call the "third food regime" (Burch & Lawrence 2009; McMichael & Friedmann 2007). They involve, first, the "right" qualification and objectification of things amid multiple modalities of valuation and their transformation into detachable and calculable goods; second, the formatting of calculative and evaluative agencies who respond to a "proliferated" modality of valuation in a given market; third, the framing of market encounters during which the coordination of the performances and interests of heterogeneous market agents can be organized; fourth, the stabilization of markets, which is firmly entangled with all the other three problems. Concerning the latter point, the argument developed here is that the regular functioning of agrifood markets requires ongoing stabilization and maintenance work amid uncertainties, disruptions, and recalcitrances. These may stem from a variety of sources, such as cooperative problems between two or more transacting parties, dynamics of competition, regulatory shifts, changing notions of what counts as a legitimate practice or good in markets, or from the difficulty to fully pacify nature or devices used for market construction. I will show that the stability of global agricultural markets and, indeed, capitalist markets more generally, rests on distinct processes of smoothing and depoliticization that enable heterogeneous actors and elements to stick together. While I am well aware that there are different markets for different products with different configurations, it can be argued that finding a "solution" to the four practical problems presented here is crucial for making a wide range of markets work, including export-oriented agrifood markets.

Overall, I am not so much interested in the genealogy of market *agencements*, but rather in their local *engagement* (Tsing 2005: 8). This requires unpacking the mechanisms through which farmers and nature in Ghana become effectively enrolled into specific projects of market-making.

Exchanging Goods the "Right" Way

As numerous scholars have previously pointed out, at the heart of market exchange lies the monetized circulation of things which are transferred as "commodities" from one owner to another. However, things do not circulate out of nothing, but do so because they are valued, and it is because they are valued according to specific criteria that they become commodities[9] (Dewey 1915; Çalışkan & Callon 2009: 1389).

How this valuation takes place has been a long-contested issue in economics, sociology, and anthropology (Beckert & Aspers 2011), with classical political economist Adam Smith arguing that the value of a good is a reflection of the time used for its production. Such a notion of value came under attack in the 19th century from Karl Marx, on the one hand, and neoclassical economists such as Léon Walras on the other. While neoclassical economists refuted Smith's objectivist conception of value by advancing a subjective theory of value anchored in the concepts of marginal utility and preferences, Marx had earlier criticized Smith and other liberal economists for hushing up the relational historicity of the commodity form.[10]

Marx's approach to commodities thus represents a valuable starting point. Appadurai (1986) critically extends his production-centered interest in the historical and material-relational character of commodities by showing how objects can change status within their "total trajectory from production, to exchange/distribution, to consumption" (ibid.: 13). A commodity must accordingly be understood as an achievement rather than a starting point, and objects can be moved into (but also out of) a commodity state. Each commodity has a complex "sociogeographic trajectory" (Castree 2003: 274) made up of multiple relations and multiple situations. Consequently, commodities do not possess a value *a priori* (Çalışkan & Callon 2009: 386), but may change their status in the course of their life. Such a position clearly moves beyond both the Marxian notion of labor-value – denoting that the value of a commodity is eventually derived from the labor mobilized to create it – as well as the subjective value theory of neoclassical economics which roots it in the utility calculations of individuals (see Zafirovski 2000).

The notion of the social life of things helps us dissect the making of markets if we likewise ask how this life is grounded – how it is unfolding within *concrete* arrangements. In today's global agrifood economy, three interrelated processes underpin the complex sociogeographic trajectory of "market things": qualification/objectification, detachment/calculation, and singularization. Although I discuss these processes in the context of global agrifood markets later, unraveling them further extends beyond the scope of this book. Doing so, however, allows for a more nuanced engagement with the ongoing proliferation of market STAs that nurture contemporary global capitalism.

Qualified Objectifications

Over the past decade, the rise of private food safety and quality standards has been one of the most outstanding trends in the global agrifood economy, changing the rules of the game for participant firms and farms. The proliferation of these standards is rooted in the restructuring of consumer markets, competitive dynamics in the retail sector, and the regulatory devolution of quality assurance from public authorities to retailers and certification bodies in North America and the European Union (EU). Responding to various food scares that swept through these markets in the 1990s, and increasing concerns of both consumers and public regulators about the origin of food, large retailers have reorganized their supply chains around notions of traceability, food safety, and quality assurance (Guthman 2007; Ouma 2010). Moreover, these standards have become more than mere private governance devices enforcing the safety of food. Indeed, food safety is now widely treated as a noncompetitive factor in the marketplace, with retailers increasingly trying to compete less over sanitary and phytosanitary issues than by embedding "extra quality" into product and process standards through claims of sustainability, well-being, fair trade, and morality (Ponte & Gibbon 2005; Freidberg 2007).

What this brief account of the global proliferation of agrifood standards shows is that for something to become a commodity, it needs to be qualified and rendered a tradable object in the first place (Thomas 1991: 32; Çalışkan & Callon 2010: 5). Processes of commodification, however, do not occur in a vacuum but according to specific collective modes of qualification. Various strands of thinking in economic sociology argue that processes of qualification are always ambiguous, marked by uncertainties because there are many potential ways to qualify a good, a large number of agents with conflicting ideas and interests are involved in transactions, and buyers can never be sure about the true state of a good or the intentions of a seller (Beckert 2009; see also Akerlof 1970). Accordingly, market agents invest in stable forms such as rules or standards (Thévenot 1984: 11), which help to channel uncertainty by coordinating the practices of producers or workers, for instance, by prescribing exactly how nature should be transformed into a product. In order to tease out how we could think about the qualification of both objects and subjects in detail, it is worth confronting the SSEM program with insights from both the *économie des conventions* (EC) and the anthropology of universals.

Now gaining increasing recognition among economic sociologists as an exciting approach to economic affairs, the EC evolved as an interdisciplinary project in France in the 1980s, comprising economists, sociologists, statisticians, and historians (Jagd 2007). Even though there are different strands of the EC school, the common ontological stance is probably best captured by Boltanski & Thévenot (2006 [1991]),[11] who argue that human interaction, for example, market exchange, requires coordination. Coordination rests on establishing equivalence between different people or objects *in actu*, involving a form of judgment according to some higher principle of generality. Yet the practice of establishing equivalence, and therefore the qualification of a person or an object according to a specific principle, is generally exposed to different forms of generality (or worth), which brings about a situational uncertainty among actors: "The same persons have, on the same day and in the same social space, to use different devices for assessment, including the reference to different types of worth, when they shift from one situation to another" (Boltanski & Thévenot 1999: 369). Nevertheless, for interaction to be coordinated, a situational equivalence between different forms of worth finally needs to be established.

From such an ontological viewpoint firms, markets or other sites of the social can be thought of as being populated by a plurality of what Boltanski and Thévenot (2006 [1991]) called "orders of worth." Thévenot (2001a) later preferred to deem these somewhat more openly as "conventions" or "pragmatic regimes" (Thévenot 2001b): "Conventions channel uncertainty on the basis of a common form of evaluation that qualifies objects for coordination" (Eymard-Duvernay et al. 2003: 9). They inform the qualification of persons and goods (including services), drawing on broader narratives on what counts as a legitimate practice and what counts as a legitimate "good" in a specific exchange situation.

The term *good* has a twofold meaning in this regard. More generally, it denotes an object which can satisfy needs, is good, and sought after (Callon et al. 2002: 197). But the term also indicates that every process of qualification not only involves an objectification, but also judgments and justifications of people who have a "critical capacity" to do so (Boltanski & Thévenot 1999). The crucial question from such a perspective is how something is made "good" for exchange and what frame of qual-ification/justification (or "order of worth") is invoked to define a "right" or "just" good when it enters a public space of engagement such as a market, where critique holds sway (Thévenot 2001a: 57). Eventually, every market good has to make that transition from a "familiar" to a public space – from a realm of idiosyncrasy to one where a broader generality over a good prevails (Thévenot 2001a: 68). In this regard, it is appropriate to distinguish a "product" from a "good," where the former is a process, a series of transformations, whereas the latter represents a qualitative state (Callon et al. 2002: 197) – a moral state.

In the broader field of agrifood studies, several sociologists, political economists and geographers have enthusiastically embraced a conventionalist perspective (Wilkinson 1997; Murdoch et al. 2000), at times extending it to the study of global food connections (Freidberg 2004; Ponte & Gibbon 2005). Often devoid of a prag-matic empirical stance, these studies have nevertheless shown that over the past decade, global agrifood markets have become populated by different conventions of qualifying goods, making up a diverse and reflexive "economy of qualities" (Callon et al. 2002). As I will show in Chapter 6, such conventions are by no means devoid of power relations, as the forms of expertise being mobilized in North–South market encounters privileges certain actors over others. But despite the fact that certain modes of qualification may gain dominance during the coordination of economic affairs, one always has to be sensitive to the *frictions*, and the new possibilities of action, that occur when these "universals" are "practically engaged" (Tsing 2005: 8).

By "repragmatizing" economic sociology (Diaz-Bohne 2008: 3), the EC is firmly interested in the situational production and coordination of social order. In doing so, it shares considerable interests with the SSEM: It likewise defies any essentialism and moves beyond economic/non-economic, micro/macro, subject/object, structure/agency, or collective/individual binaries. It also does not resort to the methodological individualism of neoclassical or transaction cost economics (Wilkinson 1997: 328), but conceives of agency as being informed by collective principles which are articulated inter-situationally in different ways (Murdoch et al. 2000: 113; Eymard-Duvernay et al. 2003: 7). Furthermore, the scholars working in the EC tradition are likewise suspicious of the notions of "institutions," "discourse," or "habitus" that are so central to the sociology of markets and (economic) sociology more generally. These often serve as all-encompassing categories for describing a presumably stable and coherent coordination of practices. Conventions, instead, have a polyvalent character. They express the versatile principles of evaluation/justification *in use* rather than a self-standing body of abstract rules or institutions that exist independently from actual practices (Stark 2009: 15). What EC scholars equally bemoan is that much of the literature influenced by the NES misses "the specificity of market coordination" (Jagd 2004: 16). In this vein, similarly to the SSEM, the EC does not embrace a mere social constructivist approach to social phenomena, but always considers economic processes to be *technical* and *organizational* processes (ibid.: 12).

In this book, I use the friction produced by rubbing the SSEM program against the anthropology of universals and the EC constructively in order to imagine markets as sites of multifarious accountability, where the quality of goods is continuously being tested and evaluated (Eymard-Duvernay et al. 2003: 12). In this regard, I adopt a more fluid and contingent perspective that partly draws on, partly reworks, conventionalist takes on the economy. The kind of "pragmatics of valuation" (Çalışkan & Callon 2009; see also Appadurai 1986; Thomas 1991) I have in mind here grants more agency to technical devices such as quality management systems, metrological systems, texts and other material infrastructures which help *perform* qualifications. These more or less immutable devices serve as practical means of association: they help to organize which elements are taken into account ("entangled") during qualification processes and which are not.

Furthermore, we should not *a priori* limit the list of potential qualifications[12] by resorting to rigid classifications such as "orders of worth"[13] or "pragmatic regimes," but propose a more contingent approach which "attends to the conditions of complexity and mobility in the relations between things, people and their context" (Çalışkan & Callon 2009: 384). In this line of thinking, there is no pre-established worth of things. The status of a good must instead be conceived as an effect of STAs that are often destabilized during the "market as a process" (Callon 1998a: 28). Of course, some heterogeneous relations may be bundled together so that "complexity disappears and we are left with simplified categories" (Murdoch et al. 2000: 114) which resemble conventions and grant some sort of durability to qualifications, but only *in association* with various other devices that "encode and stabilise particular socio-technological capacities and sustain patterns of connection" (Whatmore & Thorne 1997: 292). Yet, while some quality associations may become more or less durable over time due to the stabilizing effect of consolidated or punctualized "bundles of relations" (Law 1992), they are not devoid of situational controversies, material recalcitrances or uncertainties arising from the proliferation of new quality associations which challenge old ones.

Often these uncertainties stem from the re-regulation of markets – for example, because a practice such as using a certain pesticide is no longer considered to be legitimate – or from new dynamics of competition which fuel the proliferation of new notions of quality when certain market participants attempt to create differentiated market positions for themselves (see Chapters 5 and 8). We can observe both of these processes in contemporary agrifood markets, which have become increasingly reflexive, differentiated, and competitive. Moments of stability and uncertainty with regard to which goods are considered to be legitimate go hand in hand in these markets and, indeed, in capitalist economies more generally (Beckert 2009). In order to capture the dynamic, multi-associational and inter-situational character of quali-fication processes, it seems to be more appropriate to talk of multiple "modes of ordering" (Law 1994) or "modalities of valuation" (Çalışkan & Callon 2009: 386; Stark 2009: 7), the term used hereafter, rather than resorting to more or less stable, definite, and ideal-type "orders of worth." We would be blind to the complex spa-tiotemporal trajectory of commodities and the politics underpinning it if we limited their state to a small and preconfigured number of quality conventions, even if we conceived of them as being in dynamic interplay in practice.

Finally, a pragmatics of valuation perspective is more closely aligned to the critical project of a "history of the present" (Foucault 1991: 76). While the pragmatic strand of the EC acknowledges that people actively participate in the process of valuation and need to be qualified and competent to do so, it is less interested in the historical dynamics of such processes. A pragmatics of valuation embraces a micro-history of the market-present. Humans are not born as qualified market agents but have been historically "configured and formatted as subjects who are technically and mentally equipped to enact" specific valuations (Çalışkan & Callon 2009: 389), a point that will be further explored later.

Detachment/Calculation

As various economic anthropologists have shown, for goods to become objects of market exchange they need to be disentangled from the web of network relations which shaped their production and qualification (Thomas 1991). They need to be placed in a context in which they can have exchange value, "detached from the seller's world and attached to that of the buyer" (Callon & Muniesa 2005: 1232). Detachment denotes a process through which goods become stable, tradable things with objective (non-ambiguous) traits that can (a) have exclusive property rights and (b) a price attached to them (ibid.: 1233).

In a more classical Marxian register and within anthropology, such a process has been called *alienation* (Castree 2003: 279; Thomas 1991: 14–15), a term one could reject on the grounds that it conflates "being quits" with "being aliens" (Callon & Muniesa 2005: 1032). Participants in a transaction may depart once the transfer of ownership has been concluded, but they may know each other or be otherwise related (Granovetter 1985). They may not be "alien" to each other. Thus it is more appropriate to talk of detachment. Callon grasps this process through the notion of "framing," which he borrows from Goffman (1974). The act of framing demarcates those network relations (qualifications) that are taken into account during a monetary transaction from those which are ignored (Callon 1998b), and it is through such acts that the destructive socioecological or exploitative labor relations into which a commodity's production might have been embedded are black-boxed (Berndt & Boeckler 2011a: 1060).

Framings, however, are never complete and their content is constantly threatened by *overflowing* (Callon 1998b)[14], a term which describes the intrusion of those elements/ relations that were meant to be excluded from a transaction and which may cause the proliferation of new controversies and conflicts.[15] Nevertheless, the act of framing may temporarily "pacify" the unruly character of a good so that a worth and a price can be attached to a discrete and disentangled object (Çalışkan & Callon 2010: 5–8).

Such "framings of worth" – the term preferred hereafter as it corresponds more closely to a pragmatics of valuation perspective – are informed by particular modalities of valuation. These are frequently inscribed in "valuation technologies" (Fourcade 2011: 45) such as process management standards, including GLOBALG.A.P or the British Retail Consortium (BRC) standards (see Chapter 6), two of the most widely applied quality assurance schemes in global agrifood markets (Ouma 2010). These technologies help enact the unambiguous qualification and objectification of a good prior to a transaction, facilitate its framing for exchange and also help provide long-term governance solutions to the pacification and coordination of markets "at a distance" (Miller & Rose 1990; Larner & LeHeron 2004; Gibbon/Ponte 2008). This process of pacification enables both an act of quantitative calculation and qualitative judgment, which allow for the attachment of a worth to a good, and which form an integral part of the sociomaterial life of a commodity. As interdependent acts of "qualculation" (Callon & Law 2005),[16] they are both effects and constitutive of market STAs. On the one hand, they depend on the capacity of market agents to perform judgments about the legitimate character of a good/commodity; on the other hand, they depend on the capacity of market agents to perform monetary calculations of a good/commodity, with both processes eventually resulting in the formation of a price.

Singularizations

For the sociomaterial life of a commodity to be complete, it not only has to be detached from its original context of production and owner but also reattached to its buyer; that is, it has to enter the world of the buyer and be accepted as a legitimate, useful, and/or signifying good. A good not only has to become a "thing" for commodity exchange to happen, but "it has to be a thing whose properties have been adjusted to the buyer's world, if necessary by transforming that world" (Callon & Muniesa 2005: 1233). While standardization is a prerequisite in order to make goods comparable and, indeed, has been one of the defining traits of Fordist production, they need to be "singularized" at the same time (Callon et al. 2002; Aspers 2009).

It is particularly in those markets where the value of a product has become detached from the fulfillment of purely functional needs (Beckert 2009) that producers increasingly try to attach consumers to their products by investing in marketing technologies. We can witness such processes of singularization in many contemporary (post-Fordist) markets, and foremost in markets for cultural industry products, where a huge number of potentially substitutable goods exist. Even though many agricultural commodities continue to be singularized in rather simple ways, the proliferation of various food safety and quality standards, CSR models, and credence goods show that singularization plays an increasingly important role in the global agrifood economy, where both retailers and producers have tried to carve out protected niches or spaces for extra profit by singularizing goods amid competitive pressures (White 1981; Freidberg 2007; Guthman 2007; McMichael & Friedmann 2007) (see Chapter 5).

★ ★ ★

Considering the fact that qualification/objectification, detachment/calculation and singularization are constituent elements of the process of marketization, the questions to be answered to varying degrees across all empirical sections of this book are how these processes are arranged *dynamically* in the two frontier regions, and what investments in forms and technical devices support, transform, and manipulate the qualculation of goods.

Knowing *and* Doing Markets

Markets are sites populated by different evaluative and calculative agencies, which may cooperate, compete, conflict with, or disconnect from each other (Callon & Muniesa 2005: 1237). Yet, as highlighted previously, these agencies do not exist *a priori* or follow some transhistorical market law, but can be considered as effects of particular sociotechnical arrangements.

These sociotechnical arrangements, of which procedural rules and standards as well as various technical devices are part, format the agency of market agents in such ways that a product can be qualified, objectified, calculated and detached according to a specific modality of valuation (Çalışkan & Callon 2009: 386). Governing market-making is all about normalizing agencies in their relations to certain bodies of knowledge, devices, and procedures (Miller & Rose 1990; Dunn 2005; Gibbon & Ponte 2008). For instance, in contemporary retail agrifood chains, specific forms of record-keeping, rituals of accountability and audit technologies contribute to the normalization of agencies among managers, farmers and workers by molding local behaviors according to the expectations of consumers, retailers, and standard-setting bodies so that products can circulate globally from one place to another without friction, as I will show in more detail in Chapter 6. Markets, indeed, have disciplinary effects, as Callon (1998a: 56) notes in a rare reference to Foucault, but the "disciplining of the market" is by no means "mechanical, irreversible or irrevocable" (ibid.: 26). Along the frontier regions of the "new global agricultural market" across the rural South, the formatting of specific market agencies is meant to guarantee the frictionless circulation of goods and capital at new spatial scales. Companies investing in these places, market-makers such as development organizations or service providers, and governments all participate in framing these market agencies among managers, workers, or farmers, who actively contribute to (or resist) their own qualification as "accountable" market agents. But how are such new agencies framed *in practice*? How effective are such processes? And how can we conceive of them in conceptual terms?

Answering these questions necessitates coming to terms with two underexplored issues in the SSEM. The first one is the relationship between knowledge and practice. Even though much of the work in the SSEM acknowledges the fact that markets are practical accomplishments partially sustained by different bodies of economic knowledge, the conceptual link between knowledge and practice often remains opaque. However, making this link is central to understanding how markets are realized as ongoing accomplishments. The second issue is related to the question of how to avoid relativism and depoliticization. Solving this problem must take critical political economy's concern with material distribution ("who owns what"; "who gets what"; see Bernstein 2010) and power produced through and in markets seriously, while inverting it at the same time.

From Market Knowledge to Knowing Markets

The performativity program seems to be all about the practical effectiveness of different bodies of economic knowledge. But how can the relationship between market knowledge and market practices be conceptualized within an SSEM program when the issue of knowledge in social theory is usually discussed in unison with a subject who is (or at least is made) knowledgeable? The SSEM, one could argue, seem to radically de-center a stable subject by embracing the notion of *agencement*, which builds on a symmetry between subjects and objects and the notion of distributed agency (Hutchins 2001).

So, does such a perspective risk losing touch with real-life, flesh-and-blood managers, farmers, workers, and other market-makers? Not necessarily. Contrary to what critics often assume (see, e.g., Miller 2002), neither ANT nor the SSEM would deny "that human beings usually have to do with bodies" and "have an inner life" (Law 1992: 384). Both schools simply emphasize that agency and knowledge can never be located in bodies alone and are effects of sociotechnical *agencements* (Latour 2005: 213; Callon 2009: 24; Çalışkan & Callon 2010: 21). This must shift our attention from *knowledge* as an abstract and self-standing body to *knowing* in practice (Nicolini et al. 2003: 19). "Knowing markets" can thus be understood as the capacity to effectively align human and nonhuman elements in such ways that a good can be qualified and objectified to a given modality of valuation, calculated, and detached. From an ANT/SSEM perspective, markets gain their stability through the sedimentation of "knowing" in associational routines and through its anchorage in material devices (such as contracts or quality management handbooks) "that retain traces of interactions with the environment, as well as the kind of evaluations in use" (Eymard-Duvernay et al. 2003: 21–22). This eventually makes knowing a network property.

This notwithstanding, I suggest that the substantive, corporeal, and emotional elements of market *agencements* must derive more empirical attention than they currently get in the SSEM. Taking such elements into account prompts us not to forget about the flesh-and-blood, embodied yet formatted manager, farmer, or worker. Such a perspective also helps advance a differentiated engagement with the performativity of economics thesis. A too linear understanding of performativity may risk sliding "into the rigidity of synchronicity," that is "both the supposition that certain relations have intrinsic effects, and the hegemonic belief that we have specified the character of ordering so comprehensively that contingency has been vanquished" (Law 1994: 22).

Contrary to what a more narrow Foucauldian (Hughes 2001; Escobar 2005) or Bourdieusian (Bourdieu 2005) argument would suggest, as I shall show in more detail in Chapter 6, *agencements* never come along with fully stable agencies, or complete subjects or "durable and transportable dispositions" (Bourdieu 1977: 169, translated). This is not only due to the fact that they may be marked by *situational* frictions and emotional/bodily recalcitrances, but also because the materials and devices that are part of formatting processes "are themselves plastic, open, reconfigurable and, moreover, constantly reconfigured" (Callon 1998a: 26). Economic agents such as managers, workers, or farmers can never be understood as mere passive "subjects" that are externally managed through a variety of relations, rules, devices, organizational forms, and forms of expertise (Li 2007a). Although the reproduction of market practices relies on the principle of iterability (Boeckler 2005: 71), it may be shaped by competing modalities of valuation. This is particularly true of global supply chains. The links making them up usually interconnect a variety of sites and are often only "intelligible enough" (Tsing 2008: 41).

In other words, it is not only the front-stage arrangements of global market connections that matter, but also the backstage activities (Goffman 1974) and subtle materialities that structure the game. As mentioned before, this is why we should not stick to a rigid interpretation of the performativity thesis but instead be sensitive to the messiness and polyvalence of economic practice. As I will show throughout the empirical sections, the "everyday realities" of global connection "are notoriously stubborn" (Berndt & Boeckler 2011a: 1059), and often they have to incorporate different forms of knowledge and practices (frequently deemed "non-capitalist") to maintain their legitimacy and effectiveness (Mitchell 2002: 271).

Power in/through Markets

Markets are not the egalitarian spaces that most economists usually imagine, a claim that sociologists, geographers, and anthropologists of various *couleurs* would support. But where does "power" enter the SSEM program? This brings us back to the processes of qualification, objectification, and calculation. The capacity of agencies to effectively qualify, objectify, and calculate a good is by no means distributed evenly across time and space and is heavily influenced by their cognitive and material equipments. Markets seem to thrive on these asymmetries. Because agencies must be conceived as being unevenly equipped, this position opens up another perspective on the production of asymmetries and power relations in markets, as powerful agents are those who manage to impose "the rules of the game, that is to say, the rules used to calculate decisions, by imposing the tools in which these rules are incorporated" (Callon 1998a: 46), thereby allowing "certain calculating agencies to decide on the location and distribution of surpluses" (ibid.).

From this, it follows that market STAs "create differentiated agents and positions in the market" (Çalışkan & Callon 2010: 9). Thus, the framing of goods is fundamentally entangled with the distribution of qualculative and definitional power, which are effects of the market arrangements at work (Callon & Muniesa 2005: 1239). These are underpinned by specific and often unevenly distributed reservoirs of knowing, resources, and material equipments that not only shape the creation, enhancement, distribution, and capture of value (Henderson et al. 2002) but also its qualculation. Each of these acts is power-laden. The politics of value are in many contexts not only a "politics of knowledge" (Appadurai 1986: 6), but also a politics of equipment. How particular power relations with the capacity to produce asymmetries come into existence and structure markets is then a pivotal concern from a pragmatics of valuation perspective and will be a recurring theme throughout this book.

Conceiving of markets as asymmetrical spaces brings to the fore what constitutes power in markets, which agents can be considered to be powerful, and how surplus value is produced and distributed: the person who is able "to make the rules that others must follow" (Busch 2007: 254), who knows how to manipulate them and who manages to impose his or her calculative apparatus on other agencies can then be understood to be a powerful agent. However, agents cannot do this without the help of a whole bundle of relations and auxiliary objects. Delving a little bit deeper into the annals of ANT helps to sharpen this argument. As various authors have shown, certain agents – for instance, empires, states, retailers, or transnational agrobusiness corporations – must not *a priori* be imagined as big leviathans (Callon & Latour 1981; see also Law 1986; Whatmore & Thorne 1997). Their ostensibly all-encompassing power depends on a myriad of relations and devices. It is often exercised through "apparently humble and mundane mechanisms" which allow for "action at a distance" (Miller & Rose 1990: 8). From such a viewpoint, power can be considered to be diffused and inscribed into the relations that make up sociotechnical arrangements such as global markets. It is then those actors who manage to incorporate others into markets (or commodity chains) according to specific rules, smooth out conflicts during this "drawing together" and achieve certain outcomes that can be considered "powerful" (Busch & Juska 1997; Hess 2008).[17]

Against the backdrop that a performative take on markets is, indeed, sensitive to power relations in markets, a criticism often leveled against the SSEM and indeed ANT's application to economic affairs more generally must be put under critical scrutiny. Critics often lament that ANT "lacks an appreciation of the structural preconditions and power relations that inevitably shape production networks" (Henderson et al. 2002: 441; see also Peck 2005; Sunley 2008). Consequently, ANT applied to markets is accused of being blind to issues of power, inequalities, surplus extraction, and exploitation, providing only a descriptive and a-political analysis of markets rather than addressing the big "why-questions" or providing an explanatory account of market dynamics (Fine 2003). Even worse, some argue, is the fact that in the SSEM "capitalism" is virtually absent as a category of analysis, as are related subcategories such as "capital," "accumulation," "crisis," "class," and "ideology" (Fine 2003: 481; Barry & Slater 2005).

In a similarly scathing critique, anthropologist Daniel Miller finds that "Callon's work amounts to a defence of the economists' model of a framed and abstracted market against empirical evidence that contemporary exchange rarely if ever works according to the laws of the market" (Miller 2002: 218). The gist of his argument is that Callon's take on markets lacks flesh and life, and mistakes values and ideology for calculation. Callon is rendered a "quintessential economist" who reduces all values into which market exchange is embedded to price calculation, with disrespect for the various social entanglements of market exchange (ibid.: 231). From such a stance, a performative approach to markets would be as de-politicizing, de-socializing, and naturalizing as the one taken by economists.

Unfortunately, this represents only a superficial reading of Callon's argument that neglects what economics does in favor of a critique of what it says and represents (Holm 2007; Mitchell 2007: 247). A "Millerian" critique simply misses the point that "[t]heories here do not merely legitimate existing power relations but actually constitute new sectors of reality and make new fields of existence practicable" (Miller & Rose 1990: 8). A careful reading of the SSEM (and ANT) not only helps to denaturalize, de-ontologize, and de-absolutize markets, but also allows for a more detailed study of how asymmetries and power relations[18] are produced *in* and *through* markets, and what needs to be done to change them. At the core of such a critical project lies the reconstruction of how "relations of domination" (Callon 2005: 16) in markets come about and what sociotechnical arrangements maintain them.

My own approach here is that we have to take both markets and capitalism (as well as their social and material effects) seriously – not as abstract behemoths, but as "engaged universals" and "practical projects" achieved in a heterogeneous world (Tsing 2005: 8).

★ ★ ★

Processes of marketization are always about the proliferation of novel market agencies formatted to produce, qualify, calculate, and detach goods according to a given modality of valuation which in turn relies on concrete sociotechnical arrangements that are built on a set of material, textual, and other investments. Therefore, a central concern of the empirical chapters to follow will be to show how the (re)configuration of both market agencies and the supportive sociotechnical arrangements works in the two Ghanaian frontier regions. How are the heterogeneous elements that make up market STAs drawn together? Particularly detailed attention will be given to the question of what economic models, ways of knowing, and sociotechnical relations make up and sustain particular market STAs (Chapters 5), what agency effects they bring with them among company staff and farmers (Chapters 6 and 7) and what frictions and controversies occur during the ongoing assembling of global connections (all empirical chapters).

Such an empirical program is not blind to questions of power, as I will show in Chapter 7. However, rather than attributing power as a stock *a priori* to a particular "lead firm" that drives the supply chain – as much of the global commodity chain (GCC)/global value chain (GVC) literature does – or to agribusiness capital which "appropriates" local farmers (or workers) (Feder 1976; Watts 1994), the position embraced here shifts attention to the "practical means [...] through which inertia, durability, asymmetry, extension, domination is produced" (Latour 2005: 85)[19] as part of new market arrangements. These may in turn create differentiated positions for market participants such as retailers, agribusiness companies, workers, or farmers. If there cannot be market agencies without work, this must equally apply to leviathans, hierarchies, and "capital" itself.

Formatting Market Encounters

As argued earlier, markets can be conceived of as collective devices for the qualification and calculation of goods. These processes are only possible if goods can be qualified and calculated by "qualculative" agencies "whose encounters are organized and stabilized to a greater degree" (Callon & Muniesa 2005: 1245) to reduce the uncertainties of exchange. But how does this happen? Excluding distributed uncertainty from its theoretical frame, neoclassical economics locates the stabilization of market encounters in an "abstract space in which aggregate demands and supplies encounter and cross one another" (ibid: 1239). The NES-inspired literature, on the contrary, solves the problem of stabilizing exchange encounters by invoking notions such as networks, institutions, culture, or shared heuristics. The SSEM takes a different approach and draws attention to the multiple ways through which market encounters between goods and agents are framed. In some way, this resonates well with some economists' calls to return to the study of concrete markets (Coase 1988) and the project of economic anthropologists who have gone into the field and studied "markets in flesh," such as peasant markets (Geertz 1978) or trading floors (Abolafia 1998).

However, the formatting of market encounters must not be solely understood as a localized system of social relationships (Geertz), or as a "cultural formation" (Abolafia), but must instead be conceived of as a formative setting involving technical and organizational devices (instruction lists, procedures, scopic systems such as computer screens, metrological systems such as weighing bridges, material settings such as warehouses, price algorithms, negotiations, etc.) as well as embodied competences (Knorr-Cetina & Bruegger 2002; Çalışkan 2007b; Berndt & Boeckler 2011a). The formative setting (or qualculative space) of markets is not restricted to the actual moment of a transaction, as new economic sociologists usually posit in accordance with Max Weber (Weber 1978; cited in Beckert 2009: 248), but comprises "the conception, production and circulation of goods" (Çalışkan & Callon 2010: 10). Although my own work privileges a focus on the realm of production, it makes no sense to separate it from the realm of exchange or consumption, as, for instance, Marx (2008 [1867]) does when he argues that commodities only attain their "value form" during the act of exchange. Encounters between market agents during the stage of production – for example, when farmers are trained in the latest standard in agrifood markets by experts – cannot be treated as isolated from the broader process of circulation. Encounters during the realm of production are firmly part of market orders. They are situated in "local settings [...] configured in terms of an orientation toward distanciated interaction" (Knorr-Cetina & Bruegger 2002: 911) with buyers and consumers elsewhere. Market encounters must be carved out of heterogeneous networks in distinctive ways ("performation") so that a situation can be qualified as a market situation, grounding the processes of objectification, qualification, calculation, and detachment in the situated performances of market agents made "accountable" for these situations (Garfinkel 1967: 1; Eymard-Duvernay et al. 2003: 12; Latour 2005: 53). *Performation* (arranging market situations) and *performance* (the skilled activity of enacting market situations) go hand in hand (Berndt & Boeckler 2007).

Market encounters are the empirical prisms through which we can approach the performation and performance of concrete markets. As I will show throughout my empirical sections, in the context of global markets these are also always "worldly encounters" (Tsing 2005: 4), as a variety of actors transact across political, material, institutional, and sociocultural differences.

Out of the many factors shaping market encounters, the algorithmic procedures of pricing play a central role: no market without price! Price has been *the* central category of neoclassical economics, but that prices are central to markets would equally be confirmed from a sociological or SSEM perspective. However, rather than searching "for a primal or final cause largely outside the context of society – in nature (physical scarcity), technology (production costs or labor), psychology (marginal utility or satiation), etc. – as done by (neo) classical economics" (Zafirovski 2000: 298), or simply embedding prices socially or culturally, as economic sociology or anthropology usually does (see Geertz 1978; Beckert 2011), we should conceive of prices as the concrete outcome of manifold sociotechnical relations. At the same time, a price may serve as a "prosthetic form" (Çalışkan 2007b: 257), a strategic "market device" which is used by a market agent to achieve his or her objectives or to incorporate others into transactions (ibid.: 248).[20]

* * *

Against the backdrop that power asymmetries are usually inscribed in relations of qualculation, the procedures of value[21] determination and pricing open up an analytical space to study the unequal allocation of returns (Callon & Muniesa 2005: 1242) and therefore become important empirical prisms in the study of frontier regions. As I have shown earlier, market agencies are by no means equipped equally in terms of qualculative capacity, and it is during market encounters that asymmetries may be invoked and become effective. Indeed, work on outgrower schemes elsewhere has shown that the technicalities of encounters between farmers and exporters are crucial in shaping who gets what during specific market encounters and that these encounters are never devoid of controversies, conflicts and power struggles (Glover & Kusterer 1990; Watts 1994; Singh 2002; Vellema 2002). An SSEM perspective sheds new light on such issues. Hence, one of my key concerns is to reconstruct crucial market encounters in the two outgrower–exporter complexes in Ghana in order to provide a more situated and sequential picture of marketization processes in frontier regions of the global agrifood economy. How are such encounters organized? How (un)equal are they? How are prices being constructed? What sociotechnical arrangements structure these processes? What controversies arise during such encounters? Although the problem of organizing market encounters runs through all the empirical chapters, it will be put under particular scrutiny in Chapter 7.

Asking questions about how different market encounters are organized brings me to another related question that is central to the production and reproduction of markets more generally: how are they stabilized and maintained across time and space, and is stability really all we should write about?

The Order(ing) of Markets

If markets are indeed sites of encounters between qualculative agencies and qualified goods, organized, and stabilized to a greater degree (Callon & Muniesa 2005: 1245), then one question has only been addressed tentatively so far: How is the practical problem of stabilization being solved? How, to put it in more mundane economic terms, are these encounters *coordinated*? Answering these questions requires pulling some so far rather loosely arranged strings together: Indeed, approaching one of the main puzzles of social theory more generally, the question can be asked: How is social order being produced and reproduced (Schatzki 2001)? Implicitly or explicitly, theories of markets have always been theories of social order (Slater & Tonkiss 2001; Fourcade 2007). But if we have to rethink the relationship between "the economic" and the "the social" in order to rethink markets, we likewise have to rethink the "social order of markets" itself (Beckert 2009).

In neoclassical economics, "order is grounded in each agent acting rationally to maximize his or her own preferences within the constraints of a competitive economy" (Gould 1991: 92–93). Order is not a problem but rather the aggregated result of self-seeking individuals who make means–ends calculations in the marketplace that finally result in a price equilibrium. However, as soon as we "depart from the idealized assumptions of neoclassical theory," the "problem of order returns" (Beckert 2009: 249).

For the sociological literature that imagines markets as networks, institutions or fields, the problem of market order is of central interest and has been addressed through different prisms. Contrary to what neoclassical economists claim, new economic sociologists argue that market agents cannot be sure about the quality of a product, nor do they have complete information about other transacting parties. Furthermore, in many markets, participants do have *repeated* encounters, establishing more or less permanent relationships that differ from the idealized spot markets of neoclassical economics (Arrow 1998). Markets are also not free from culture, politics, structural power, hierarchies (for instance, between a large firm and its suppliers), or mutual observation among competitors, which often develop collective structures to manage competition and standardize products or occupational categories (White

1981; Fligstein 2001). These are all arguments frequently made by those influenced by the NES, who solve the problem of market order by invoking the idea of institutions or different varieties of embeddedness (Hess 2004; Fligstein & Dauter 2007). Despite internal differences in the broader field of the NES-inspired sociology of markets, as well as within cognate disciplines such as economic geography, the commonality between these approaches is that market participants (with the help of the state of other auxiliary institutions such as industry associations, standard-setting bodies, etc.) develop stable structures of interaction in order to overcome uncertainties related to value ("how to be sure about the right quality of a product?"), cooperation ("how to be sure that somebody's behavior is predictable/trustworthy?"), and competition ("how to manage competition in 'healthy' ways?") (see Beckert 2009). Through such means, coordinated economic activity is possible, "despite the heterogeneous motives and interests of the participating actors" (ibid.: 6).

While these ideas have been largely stuck in a territorial ("region," "industry," "national economy"), topographical imaginary (Amin 2002), GCC, GVC, and global production network (GPN) analyses have taken the problem of social order to a global, topological level. Framed through the concept of "governance," this camp has been interested in how the geographically dispersed but functionally integrated activities of different actors are governed across time and space, often by making reference to agricultural markets (Henderson et al. 2002; Gereffi et al. 2005; Ponte & Gibbon 2005; Hess 2008).

Earlier versions of the GCC approach were mainly interested in how the allocation of labor and value is governed by powerful lead firms such as retailers, and therefore operated with a distinctive concept of governance as "driving power" (Gereffi 1994). Commodity chains were conceived to be distinctly different from free spot-market relationships due to their functionally integrated and power-laden character.[22] With the reformulation of this approach into the GVC framework (Gereffi et al. 2001), however, this focus shifted to the question of how different economic activities in a value chain are *coordinated* (Bair 2005; Gibbon et al. 2008).

From such a perspective, the key questions related to the governance of GVCs asked are (1) what is to be produced, covering product design and detailed specifications; (2) how it is to be produced, covering the production process, including technology, quality systems, and labor and environmental standards; and (3) logistics, covering how much is to be produced, when it is to be produced, and how it is transported (Dolan & Humphrey 2004: 492). In this now dominant version of the approach, the problem of governing chains is related in particular to the question of through which institutional mechanisms coordination does work. However, rather than drawing on the NES literature, the leading authors adopt a transaction cost framework on which different ideal-type modes of coordination are modeled in opposition to an essential spot-market mode of coordination (Gereffi et al. 2001).

According to this "information-theoretic functionalism" (Law 1994: 101), governance structures are treated as self-emergent coordination mechanisms that result from the actor-configuration of particular chains and the nature of the product (or asset) being transacted.[23] Besides its functionalist reasoning, such a view of governance is problematic for a number of reasons. First, the focus on coordination shifts

attention away from the earlier concerns of GCC research about the unevenly distributed power to *drive* particular value chains (see Gibbon et al. 2008).

Second, it tells us little about why the information to be codified and transmitted
actually exists and what asymmetrically structured fields shape the production,
proliferation, and effectiveness of knowledge (see Ouma 2010).

Third, owing to its black boxing of intra-organizational agency, be it in firms or on
farms, the actual practices of value chain participants deserve no further attention
(Coe et al. 2008). Upstream actors such as exporters or farmers supplying mighty
buyers are rendered as passive objects of governance, lacking any more substantiated
form of agency.

Fourth, owing to its anchoring in the *New Institutional Economics* (NIE) (Williamson
1979), this take on chain governance reifies the metacategory of the market even
though it develops a more complex understanding of the coordination of economic
transactions. As in the NIE-inspired governance literature more generally, markets
are taken as starting points not end points of analysis. It is implied that "markets
occur naturally or spontaneously, in the sense that actors do not deliberately plan or
construct them in advance of actual transactions" (Campbell & Lindberg 1991: 348–349,
cited in Krippner 2001: 786). The actual existence of "natural" markets "precedes the
development of hierarchies [or other intermediate forms of coordination] insofar as
actors will begin to organize their activity through hierarchies [or other forms of
coordination] only when extenuating circumstances arise which cause the market to
break down" (ibid.). Thus, the arranged, relational material and performative nature
of markets deserves no attention – it virtually remains a black box.

Starting from a performative perspective, we not only have to adopt a critical stance
toward the treatment of markets in neoclassical economics, the NES-inspired sociology of markets, and the GCC/GVC camps, but also toward their conceptualization of
coordination/order.[24] Against the backdrop that markets can be conceived as effects
of heterogeneous arrangements, we can neither render absent the question of order,
nor can we treat coordination (and thus order) as all-encompassing and assume its
effectiveness *a priori*; we can also not simply anchor it in social networks, institutions,
or trust, nor can we or think of order – as tempting it may be – in static terms.

As I have argued so far, in the contemporary global agrifood economy heterogeneous actors, nature, modalities of valuation, technical devices, procedures, texts, and so
on, have to be brought together in order to allow a stable and legitimate qualification,
objectification, and exchange of goods. Although I have shown what kinds of associations of different elements are necessary for organizing market encounters, so far
I have only tentatively demonstrated what makes these associations durable across
time and space – how the various human and nonhuman elements that make up
markets come together and hold despite their heterogeneity. How do nature, workers,
farmers, managers, buyers, ways of knowing, organizational forms, technical devices,
and so on, act as one network over distance and through many seasons? Or how, to
put it into the words of the EC, is coordination being achieved despite the fact that
market encounters are usually populated by different modalities of valuation that may
compete, be at frictional interplay, or clash? Different vocabularies exist to render
intelligible this "drawing together" in practical terms.

As touched upon before, ANT scholars introduced the notion of "punctualization" to describe the appearance of unity, the acting of a network "as a single block" (ibid.: 385; see also Callon 1991: 153). The concept may also be extended to study the stabilization of market STAs. Punctualization usually allows for the simplification of the complex relations making up markets into a pattern of routines and "resources" (sociotechnical devices, organizational forms, etc.) that ensures the enactment and reproduction of those networks through time and space, although punctualization is "always precarious" as it may face resistance, "and may degenerate into a failing network" (Law 1992: 385). Nevertheless, some patterns and network relations may become more or less irreversible and thereby become normalized (Callon 1991: 152). Punctualization and, therefore, coordination/order, are always processes or relational effects of heterogeneous networks, which recursively generate and reproduce themselves as structures. But what may tentatively be interpreted as a social structure must be treated as a verb, not as a noun (Law 1992: 386). Hence, from an ANT perspective, there is no such thing as social order but only multiple modes of *ordering* (Law 1994) that structure actor-networks such as markets, including those for agrifood products (Whatmore & Thorne 1997). These orderings are never fully complete, nor are they devoid of imponderabilities, frictions, and controversies, for instance, when it comes to the qualification of goods. The coming into being of markets may be hampered by the recalcitrance of both human and nonhuman elements, as I will show in detail in Chapter 6. Sometimes, small players have more power than we think (Coe et al. 2008).

Moreover, punctualization can only happen through a process of *translation* that reduces complexity within networks, ends polyvalence (e.g., with respect to what counts as "quality"), pacifies controversies (e.g., with respect to what is a "just" price), and unifies heterogeneous human and nonhuman elements so that they can act as a network/market. Such a process of translation is transformative, producing a "shared space, equivalence and commensurability" (Callon 1991: 145) so that one thing (e.g., a product or an actor) can stand for another (e.g., money or a network) (see also Callon 1986). The more it becomes "impossible to go back to a point where [...] [a] translation was only one amongst others" and the more one translation "shapes and determines subsequent translations" (Callon 1991: 150), the more durable an actor-network becomes. Although many social spaces, including markets, are permeated by more or less durable translations that effectively structure the possibilities of association and reassociation, translations nevertheless represent contingent and situated processes. Every translation faces "critical moments" (Boltanski & Thévenot 1999: 359) from time to time. As will be shown in more detail in the book's empirical sections, in economic terms *translation* is often the hidden precondition for *situated* coordination.

As a body of theory that is concerned *par excellence* with the question of how human activities are coordinated, the EC takes issue with the somewhat abstract and contingent notion of translation. The common argument goes that Callonistics cannot explain into which direction certain translations (and punctualizations) go or *why* they become stable or capture the potential tensions between multiple conventions of qualifying things and people (Thévenot 2001b: 408; Jagd 2004: 13). EC scholars anchor the internal heterogeneity of organizations or markets not in the unruly character of different elements enrolled in a network with unspecified linkages, but in the frictional multiplicity of predefined conventions/orders of worth that inform economic practices and make coordination cumbersome (Boltanski & Thévenot 1999).

For instance, in a firm, a pure and short-term market orientation resting solely on "price" may clash with an order of worth resting on long-term planning and the technical sophistication of products (see Thévenot 2001a). In a similar way, during exchange, a pure price orientation may be at frictional interplay with orders of worth that valuate personal relationships, sustainability, or community benefits – something we can currently observe in the markets for fair trade or ecologically certified goods (see Ponte & Gibbon 2005; Jaffee 2007). Similarly suspicious of static notions of order as ANT scholars, practice-attuned conventionalists assume that coordination can only be achieved if pragmatic compromises are made between different orders of worth in a firm or a market. If held to be legitimate, such compromises must refer to a higher common principle (Boltanski & Thévenot 2006 [1991]: 140).

While I sympathize with ANT/SSEM as well as with EC understandings of "coordination" – and the latter indeed reminds us to pay close attention to "translation regimes" (Callon 1991: 147) that give global connections some durability – I test both notions in Chapter 7. In doing so, I will to some extent move beyond both notions to foreground more explicitly the power-laden and crises-prone nature of market encounters and the political questions associated with market-making more generally.

* * *

I have provided this detailed account of how we can conceive of market coordination because it not only equips us with a better practical understanding of how markets as *heterogeneous* STAs are stabilized across space and time, but it also helps us understand how and why they may be destabilized or even fall apart in the wake of both internal and external disruptions. With regard to my case studies, I am particularly interested in the questions of how both human and nonhuman elements are brought together in such ways that a stable qualification and exchange of goods is possible and how the coordination of heterogeneity plays out at the organizational interfaces between agribusiness companies, farmers, and associated market-makers, such as development organizations and service providers, Northern buyers, and the state. The latter should certainly not be forgotten when we talk about marketization and market-making (Fligstein 2001; Peck 2012).

I am, moreover, interested in the question of what distributed and materially entangled practices allow for the (re)production market STAs in the two agribusiness–outgrower complexes. The quest for stabilization and ordering stretches through all chapters. However, as I will show in Chapter 8 on "market crises" in more detail, market STAs do not result in a state of equilibrium, but are constantly threatened by dynamics that are so central to "capitalism." Because stability and uncertainty are two sides of the same coin under capitalist conditions (Beckert 2009), any engagement with markets that would only be concerned with the reproduction of stability would not be a pragmatic study of markets.

It is here that we have to advance the frontiers of the SSEM program, which, surprisingly, has privileged order and stability over crisis, breakdown, and change (Butler 2010, Overdevest 2011). As I will show in Chapter 8, the SSEM can learn a great deal from the NES and the GCC/GVC/GPN literature on how dynamics of competition or the proliferation of new products may lead to the breakup of established relationships and the forging of new ones or how modalities of valuation in markets may change, clash, or compete. We can also learn a great deal from works in political ecology that sensitize us to the fact that nature or material infrastructures may defy being fully incorporated into the calculative apparatuses of capitalism, something which may have seriously disruptive consequences for particular projects of economization. Thus, capitalist markets, as both material and social projects, constantly oscillate between cooperation, competition, conflict, crisis, and change.

It is against this backdrop that I shall explore in more detail in each empirical chapter how the case study companies tried to stabilize their market arrangements in often volatile and unpredictable environments. Although market arrangements more generally are threatened by ongoing destabilizations, it is in frontier regions in particular where their durability is continuously put to the test and has to be worked upon.

Conclusion

In this chapter, I mapped out the key tenets of a performative approach to the making of markets that takes inspiration from the SSEM, the EC, and the anthropology of universals. In this regard, it should be noted that we should not narrow down the study of marketization to the thesis of performativity. What is at stake here is a pragmatic approach that, in the tradition of an "engaged pluralism" (Barnes & Sheppard 2010), is open to other relational and practice approaches in sociology, geography, and anthropology, but is nevertheless distinguished by a set of key propositions. Market-making requires the drawing together of a wide range of human and nonhuman elements in specific ways so that goods can be qualified, objectified, calculated, and legitimately detached; qualculative agencies can be assembled; exchange encounters can be organized; and some form of stability can be granted.

The SSEM provide some tangible entry points to study such processes through the notion of market STA, being at the same time open to accounting for the messiness, dynamics, and contingencies of quotidian market-making that warrant a study from *below* rather than from *above*. Rubbing ANT/the SSEM against the EC, as well as the anthropology of universals, produces productive friction. An assemblage of these intellectual traditions reminds us that (1) goods have no value *per se* but acquire worth during often contested and frictional processes of valuation; (2) humans are formatted as market agents endowed with the capacity to evaluate and calculate goods, but the distribution of such truly political endowments depends on the configuration of sociotechnical arrangements; (3) we have to attend to the situative arrangements of the market as *a process* rather than resorting to substantive categories (institutions, power, embeddedness, commodity/value chains, capitalism, discourse, etc.) when it comes to unpacking the ordering of markets; (4) market-making aims at enrolling nature, agencies, and material infrastructures into new circuits of circulation, whose stability rests on processes of translation and punctualization that align humans and nonhumans in specific ways and directions; (5) such connections, like all proliferations of the social, are quite precarious because they continuously face trials of strengths and critical moments, and sometimes friction turns into fire (or crisis).

These prisms will help make sense of how the frontier regions of marketization were being expanded and reconfigured in northern and southern Ghana. In this regard, it should be emphasized that even though the SSEM program so far has mainly focused on the "inside" of markets, there is nothing to prevent it from incorporating the broader context that shapes the proliferation of specific STAs. As Muellerleile (2013: 1631) points out in reference to the contextually rich work of Polanyi, the "challenge is to construct a methodology that takes seriously both the assemblage of market entities emanating outward – and – the broader context, whether geographical, historical, or institutional that lays the groundwork for the market system to begin with."

While I have already outlined the key questions that will be addressed in the empirical sections, one set of questions can only be answered at the end of the book: What new kinds of connectivity can be found in the frontier regions of the new global agricultural market and how can we qualify them? How can we embed these connections into broader processes of economization and society-making (Fourcade 2007)? If one paid attention to connections only, one would lose sight of the disconnections, disarticulations, and displacements of global network capitalism. As Berndt & Boeckler (2011a: 566) note so aptly, "[m]arketization is about establishing and severing linkages, it is about incorporating and expelling places, people and things." My conclusion will engage with this ambiguous character of contemporary processes of agrarian marketization in frontier regions across the Global South.

Endnotes

1   In this book, all names of individuals, of the case study companies and related organizations, and their geographical associations have been anonymized, are withheld, or have been altered to protect sources. Development organizations and programs associated with the Ghanaian agricultural sector more generally are referred to by their original names.

2   Throughout the book, I use the terms *sociotechnical* and *sociomaterial* interchangeably.

3   On the skewed history of the term, see Latour (1999). ANT is, in fact, less a "theory" but more a method for studying society and technology in the making. It should be added that Callon (still) prefers the term "sociology of translation" over ANT (Callon 2009: 23).

4   The French term *agencement,* rooted in the work of Deleuze and Guattari, is often incompletely translated as *assemblage* in English (Phillips 2006; Legg 2011). Assemblage, now *en vogue* in geography and cognate disciplines (Anderson et al. 2012), has a somewhat passive connotation, thereby losing the semantic power of the term *agencement.* The latter refers to something that is well arranged (*les agencements* = fixtures, fitting; *bien agencé* = being well equipped) and that allows for agency (*agence*) at the same time (MacKenzie 2009a: 20–21). However, *agencement* should not be confused with Foucault's notion of apparatus (*dispositif*), which is more static. According to Rabinow (2003: 55–56), assemblages or *agencements* are an "experimental matrix […] not the kind of thing that is intended to endure", while apparatuses are "stabilized and set to work in multiple domains".

5   It should be noted that what Polanyi (2001[1944]) referred to as reciprocity or redistribution or what the anthropologist Marcel Mauss called gift exchange can be included in this conceptualization of agency (Thomas 1991; Graeber 2001).

6   This insight takes up what other poststructuralists and SSST scholars have noted before: that "theories [...] in part [...] create the reality they seek to interpret" (Barnes 1992; cited in Crang 1997: 12).

7   Judith Butler's "bodily"/performative rereading of Foucault is only marginally referenced in the SSEM literature.

8   As indicated earlier, the performative power of economics must not be limited to formal (neoclassical) economic theories. Processes of economization, that is, the processes of qualifying what counts as "economic", must be understood in broad terms ("economics at large", Callon 2007: 335).

9   A thing turns into a commodity when it becomes a precisely defined object of economic value (Appadurai 1986: 3). It is anything (including services) intended for monetary exchange (ibid.: 9). This is to be distinguished from objects that are meant for barter or gift exchange, as economic anthropologists and historians such as Mauss, Malinowski and Polanyi have shown.

10 For Marx an object's value was simply a representation of the "labor-time socially necessary for its reproduction" (Marx 2008 [1867]: 53). For him, value was not simply rooted in the things *per se*, or in the amount of time an individual spent on producing an object, as Smith and other liberal economists would argue, but was a materialization of specific social and technological conditions under which the exchange of things becomes dominant over the use of things. It is during exchange, when things produced for exchange acquire a commodity form, which provides the basis for exploitation and surplus extraction. The extraction of surplus value is practically possible because laborers, alienated from the fruits of their work and embedded into unequal relations of production stabilized by an institutional and ideological superstructure, receive far less for their products than is actually realized by capitalists in the marketplace. According to Marx, under capitalism these unequal social relations are hidden in the abstracted nature of the commodity ("commodity fetishism"), which obscures the fact that exchange is actually a social relation between human beings and not between "things" (Marx 2008 [1867]: 86). It is this commodity fetishism and the systemic features of capitalism that allow for its reproduction.

11 Note that one can make the distinction between a strategic and a more pragmatic approach to conventions mainly associated with the work of Boltanksi and Thévenot (Ponte & Gibbon 2005: 24). In this work, I will only engage with the latter approach.

12 On an early engagement with the problematic quest for classification within the EC, see Callon (1991: 158).

13 A true pragmatics of valuation would need to overcome the Eurocentrism engrained in Boltanski's and Thévenot's orders of worth, which were derived from rereadings of European moral and political philosophy.

14 Callon (1998b), referring to Goffman (1974), notes that what happens inside the frame is never fully detached from the outside world.

15 As I will show in Chapter 6, this could be negative social or environmental externalities or simply other forms of agency that might be at frictional interplay with a purely calculative agency. Thus, framings always have to face a "reality test" (Boltanski & Thévenot 2006 [1991: 40]) or a "trial of strengths" (Latour 2005: 53).

16 The act of framing should not just be limited to situations of calculative exchange, but can be likewise applied to other situations in the long life of a good/commodity. It always relates to a specific context of entanglement or disentanglement of a good, and, as we will see, can be extended to include agencies and encounters.

17 If extended to objects, an ANT notion of power is quite Foucauldian (Foucault 1982: 794; Latour 1986: 279; Schatzki 2005).

18   From the very beginning, ANT has been a method to study power.

19   Foucault (1982) makes a similar argument.

20   Çalışkan's notion of the price as a "prosthesis" derived from his work on pricing in global cotton markets, is, in fact, far more encompassing than used here (Çalışkan 2007b).

21   According to Beckert and Aspers (2011: 27), "[m]arket price is not the same as economic value. The market price is the outcome of different assessments of the economic value of a product in the market process". At the same time, prices can be considered effects of wider heterogeneous associations, or what they call the social structure of markets.

22   For instance, Humphrey and Schmitz (2002: 7) restricted the concept of governance to "non-market coordination" of economic relationships.

23   Adopting at least implicitly the "governmental gaze" of a lead firm (such as a retailer), Gereffi et al. (2005) identify five types of governance (market, modular, relational, captive, hierarchy), which depend on the complexity of information and knowledge involved in a transaction, the ability to codify and transmit this information between different chain actors, and the capabilities of suppliers to fulfil the requirements of the transaction. Depending on the interplay of these factors, a "higher force" will rationally decide whether supply chains/supply chain segments are coordinated through markets, different intermediate forms, and/or hierarchies.

24   Note here that certain variants of the GPN approach embrace a similar notion of order (and power) as I do here (see, e.g., Dicken et al. 2001; Hess 2008).

Chapter Three
Remaking "the Economy": Taking Ghanaian Horticulture to Global Markets

I am in an air-conditioned office in the headquarters of a US development organization in upper residential Accra. In front of me sits Jim, a Canadian probably in his late
forties, a high-ranking officer at the Trade and Investment Programme for a
Competitive Export Economy funded by the United States Agency for International
Development (USAID).[1] Often simply called TIPCEE, the program has tried to
connect Ghanaian horticulture to global markets since 2004. On the shelf behind my
interviewee, I spot a copy of Michael Porter's *Competitive Advantage of Nations*. Jim
himself has, indeed, a "strong business background," as he tells me, having worked for
a large retailer before he ventured into development. This was exactly why he was
hired – because he knew how the private sector works. Jim is emblematic of the
rapprochement between business and development that has been going on since the
beginning of the new millennium. As an economist in the "wild,"[2] his task was to
develop strategies that would facilitate the integration of Ghanaian agribusiness and
farmers – the latter are still the backbone of Ghana's agricultural sector[3] – into
"modern supply chains." As we can read from Jim's words, such an outward-oriented
development strategy rests on specific problematizations:

> The traditional approach to small farmer integration and supply chains was [that] farmers
> produce and then we try to develop advocacy systems that they get their best price in
> it and pricing was deemed proportional to the quality level. [....] We're working in
> systems that don't work like that anymore; that's the way that trade was organized prior
> to the 80s. Now people require varied types of supply chain integration, and contracts are

Assembling Export Markets: The Making and Unmaking of Global Food Connections in West Africa,
First Edition. Stefan Ouma.
© 2015 John Wiley & Sons, Ltd. Published 2015 by John Wiley & Sons, Ltd.

negotiated not necessarily on the basis of price; price is a resultant of a whole series of performance criteria that have to be met, in order for the system to generate the adequate added value. [...] So, what that means is that the farmers have to develop a whole new set of skills to be able to perform those basic quality assurance tasks, understanding the tasks, monitoring those control points, and making sure that they deliver on a whole series of criteria [...]. It's the quality assurance world, it's the new way of doing business [...]. (Interview, 2008)

★ ★ ★

TIPCEE has not been the only program aiming at facilitating the integration of African firms and farms into global agrifood markets. The development of horticultural industries across several African countries has received attention in development policy circles since at least the late 1980s and 1990s. With the promise of relatively higher returns on "high-value crops" such as fresh vegetables, cut flowers, and tropical fruits compared to traditional agro-commodities, rising consumer demand for these commodities in the Global North, and opportunities for local value addition through processing, several international donor organizations such as the World Bank have promoted the creation of horticultural industries as a strategy for export-led development (Little & Dolan 2000). Consequently, fresh produce industries across a number of African countries have experienced significant growth rates since the mid-1990s (see Figure 3.1).

One of these countries has been Ghana. While countries such as Egypt, Côte d'Ivoire, Morocco, Kenya, and South Africa are still far ahead of Ghana in terms of fresh produce export volumes, the country has been rendered a new market frontier in donor circles, news reports, and policy papers. Such a framing ties in well with the political representations of Ghana as an "African emerging economy" and a "top reformer" in Africa. Between 1998 and 2007, Ghana experienced new FDI in the fresh produce industry, particularly in the pineapple, mango, banana, and citrus subsectors. Such investments occurred in a context where, after the demise of the Washington Consensus, economic policies had steadily shifted from a faith in the developmental outcomes of free markets and simple export-promotion efforts to a market-oriented agenda based on "value chain promotion," "agrobusiness-farmer-linkages," and "shared growth and development" (Addo & Marshall 2000; Amanor 2009; Neilson 2014).

The two case studies I introduce in this chapter, one dealing with the making of markets for organic mangoes and the other with the making of just-in-time (JIT) markets for fresh-cut pineapples, partly relate to those larger developmental shifts. They represent salient frontier projects in different regions of Ghana that only became possible at particular historical conjunctures of economy building; at the same time they have given a new impetus to the project of reframing the horticulture subsector as a vibrant part of the Ghanaian economy, a field of investment, and an object of development more generally. They tell us what *agencements* instantiate the "seamless flow of products" in pipe-like markets, as Jim put it, and what it means to be a laboring subject in the "quality assurance world."

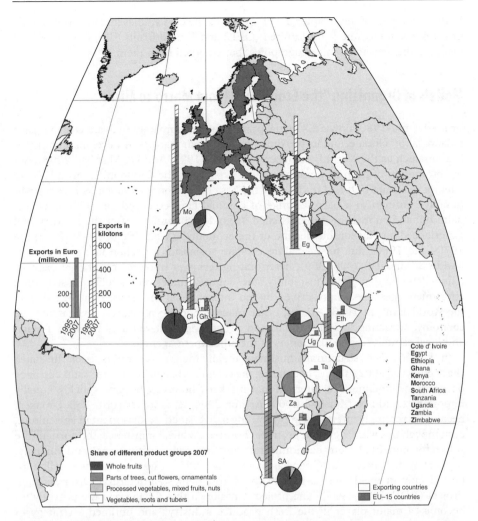

Figure 3.1   Trends in and composition of horticulture exports from selected African countries to EU-15 countries. (From Eurostat/Comext 2008; Ouma et al. 2013; Reprinted with permission of Elsevier.)

In the first section of this chapter, I introduce the industry and policy context of my case studies. In spite of the fact that the origins of my case studies date back to the end of the 1990s and thus before the rise of a market-oriented development agenda in Ghana, other market-making projects and the remaking of agriculture into an outward-oriented, globally competitive part of the Ghanaian economy bring to the fore the same questions and processes as my own case studies do, and indeed can be studied with the same tools. The reader will re-encounter some of the market-making projects described in the next section in later parts of this work, as they intersect in often crucial, sometimes awkward, ways with the evolution of the two case studies.

In the remainder of this chapter, I will introduce the case studies in detail, putting the investments of Organic Fruit Limited (OFL) and Ton:go Fruits (TF) in context and mapping the new economic geographies that emerged from them.

Models of Organizing "the Economy": From Macro to Micro

From the mid-1980s onward, Ghana, praised for its comparative advantages in regard to land, labor, climate, and its proximity to European markets by development organizations such as the World Bank (see World Bank 1993; Addo & Marshall 2000), put the promotion of fresh fruit and vegetable exports on the development agenda in an attempt to attract FDI and to diversify the base of its economy, which had been traditionally confined to a narrow range of colonial agro-commodities such as cocoa, palm oil, and rubber, or minerals such as gold and bauxite. After the country had experienced an "inexorable decline of the economy" (World Bank 1993: IX) in the 1970s and 1980s due to the failure of state socialism, a decline in cocoa exports (Addo & Marshall 2000: 359), deteriorating terms of trade for traditional exports, rising debts and political instability, the country underwent neoliberal structural adjustment measures as prescribed by the International Monetary Fund (IMF) and the World Bank in 1983. Among other macroeconomic measures, diversifying the economy, attracting foreign capital, and promoting joint-ventures between foreign and local capital were central tenets of the adjustment agenda.

In the early days, structural adjustment mainly focused on "rolling back the state" (Peck & Tickell 2002), that is, liberalizing the economy, balancing budgets, and currency devaluation. Openness to international markets, however, became quickly equally important (Addo & Marshall 2000; Arthur 2006; Amanor 2010b). Policy-makers became increasingly interested in promoting a diversified export-oriented agriculture, even though this was a slow and protracted process. While, for instance, the horticulture subsector benefited from economic reforms and some institutional and financial support by donors and the Ghanaian state in the 1980s, it was more strategically supported only in the 1990s as part of the World Bank's Agricultural Diversification Project (ADP, 1991–1999). The project envisioned that Ghana had the potential to become "a major player in the fresh produce industry" and outlined a strategy to "create a modern, competitive, professional industry capable of anticipating and responding to the demands of the market" (Dixie & Sergeant 1998: 6).

In the late 1990s, the horticultural subsector recorded considerable growth.[4] The export of pineapples, mangoes, and other produce received a significant boost. However, the former experienced a huge setback due to a demand shift in the global pineapple market from 2005 onward that led to a marginalization of smallholder farmers and a corporate consolidation within the subsector (Amanor 2012; Fold & Gough 2008; see also Chapter 8). Pineapples had already been cultivated at a larger scale since the 1970s, and the first commercial pineapple exports – organized by local businessmen who reinvested their profits from trade into agriculture – took off in 1984. This happened, however, with little government support (Whitfield 2010). Only from the mid-1990s onward did several donors promote the export of pineapples and other fresh fruits more emphatically (Voisard & Jaeger 2003; Danielou & Ravry 2005). The pineapple industry attracted some notable FDI owing to macroeconomic liberalization and the designation of export processing zones (EPZs)/free zones as part of the ADP and the Agricultural Sector Investment Programme (ASIP, 1993–1999). Alongside being granted duty-free import of goods, free zone enterprises were exempted from tax payments for a period of ten years. ADP and ASIP were followed by the World Bank–funded Agricultural Services Subsector Investment Programme (AgSSIP, 2000–2006), which aimed at reforming agricultural technology generation, institutional strengthening, the restructuring of the Ministry of Food and Agriculture (MOFA), and the development of farmer-based organizations.

Despite the obvious growth of the horticulture subsector between the mid-1990s and early 2000s, export-oriented interventions in agriculture did not tie into comprehensive sectoral policy. For instance, it was only in 2004 that a USD 9.0 million horticulture component was added to AgSSIP, after a report had identified key constraints to sectoral development and outlined a comprehensive investment program. This component was called Horticulture Export Industries Initiative (HEII), and related to newly established donor initiatives such as TIPCEE (2004–2009), or the Market Oriented Agriculture Programme (MOAP, 2004–2013) funded by the GTZ (now GIZ).

These initiatives conducted a number of experiments in order to enhance the "efficiency" and "competitiveness" of farms and firms in subsectors for both food and export crops (including pineapples and mangoes), targeting high potential areas in the coastal savanna region, the Afram Basin (Eastern Region), and northern Ghana. Different components such as institutional capacity building, business-service development initiatives, support to farmer-based organizations, the provision of high-quality seedlings to mango and pineapple farmers, the implementation of food safety and quality assurance schemes such as GLOBALG.A.P., and infrastructural upgrading were key ingredients in these experiments. Contract farming was heralded as a crucial means of providing smallholders with access to credit, extension services, technological knowledge, and global markets.

Some of these interventions, such as the promotion of farmer-based organizations, the implementation of quality assurance schemes, and the enhancement of value chains, were further pursued under more recent programs such as the Millennium Challenge Account (MCA) (2007–2012), the African Development Bank–funded Export Marketing and Quality Awareness Project (EMQAP, 2007–2012), the USD $105 million Northern Rural Growth Program (NRGP, 2007–2015) supported by the International Fund for Agricultural Development and the African Development Bank or the USAID-funded Agricultural Development and Value Chain Enhancement Programme (2011–2015). All these programs unfolded in an environment where the Ghanaian government, both the one led by the New Patriotic Party (NPP) (2001–2009) (Arthur 2006) as well as that run by National Democratic Congress (NDC) (2009–present), increasingly embraced the promotion of an agricultural sector that is private sector-driven, market-oriented, diversified, and globally competitive.

Although not all activities associated with the aforementioned initiatives were tightly coordinated or achieved their ambitious goals, they differed from earlier initiatives in terms of the practical tools and underlying economic models mobilized. Earlier interventions were based on macroeconomic recipes of fixing the economy (exchange rate liberalization, tariff reduction, "getting the prices right") and guided by a belief that this would unleash the curative power of market forces, followed by poverty reduction strategies that were meant to address the needs of different categories of farmers as a kind of acknowledgment of the failure of the Washington Consensus agenda (Amanor 2010b). Although such concerns still endure in Ghana's agricultural policies, more recent interventions in agriculture have embraced meso- and micro-economic concepts such as "agrobusiness-farmer linkages" or "value chains" as a means to support sectoral development.

While projects for integrating Ghanaian farmers into the "world market" for agri-cultural commodities are nothing new *per se* (see Amanor 1999), recent frontier projects differ from their predecessors in that farmers are now seen as "subjects of improvement" within market assemblages of different scales (regional, national, global), not simply as primary producers or cheap labor force. In other words, in the age of market-oriented development, farmers are not addressed as "producers" that may respond to the opportunities provided by liberalized market environments but as "subjects" capable of knowing the economy through particular calculative practices (Larner & LeHeron 2004: 219). The program of market-oriented development is not performed by a single state or corporate entity but by multi-stakeholder networks that involve government agencies, international development organizations, NGOs, and private companies, with the former three helping to establish the redefined conditions for private accumulation in the global agrifood economy (Amanor 2009).

Among donors to countries such as Ghana, creating an enabling market environ-ment has been perceived as the necessary precondition for a horticulture-based "take-off." Elaborate programs, strategy papers, and donor reports mobilize the idea that it is possible to reengineer the agricultural sector of an entire country and to transform its subsectors, including horticulture, into diversified, "well-organized," and globally competitive units (see Figure 3.2). These are programmatic inscriptions of the belief that global market connections promise huge opportunities for Ghanaian entrepre-neurs, farmers, workers, and rural communities, a belief that is put to the test in the chapters that follow.

The shift to a "market access via value chain integration strategy" for agricultural and agribusiness development is also exemplified by the new Food and Agricultural Sector Development Policy (FASDEP II) of MOFA, drafted in 2007, and its opera-tional equivalent, the Medium Term Agriculture Sector Investment Plan (2011–2015)[5] (MOFA 2010). Both represent a break with past policies. While previous policies and strategies of the ministry, as in many other African countries, aimed at reducing poverty by promoting *production* (technology transfer, promotion of extension services, productivity enhancement), there has been a shift to promoting *markets* and *market integration* to achieve ("pro-poor" or at least "shared") growth, and the format-ting of novel goods, market agencies, and encounters among a variety of actors has been central to the programs outlined earlier. The cases of TF and OFL tie in well with the market-led development discourse,[6] even though these projects had started before its rise. At the time my project started, they were widely considered as showcases

Figure 3.2   "Ready for take-off": brochure published by TIPCEE 2008. (Author's photo.)

for the kind of developmental model envisioned by those that wanted to "modernize" farming and foster agribusiness-farmer linkages – as so-called "offtakers" (Fynn 2011: 5) that can lead farmers to the "world market."

A Tale of Two Frontiers

Although since the late 1990s several new frontier regions have evolved in Ghana for both traditional and nontraditional exports that deserve to be studied, this book focuses on two specific ones. The new sites of the agrifood economy are experimental spaces in which agribusiness companies, farmers, retailers, and auxiliary market-makers such as NGOs, bilateral and multilateral development agencies, service providers, traditional authorities, and state actors are involved with reworking or advancing the frontier regions of agrarian marketization. This diagnosis should not, however, suggest that the case study regions lay fully "outside" the workings of (global) capitalism or the (world) market before – this would come close to an unacceptable "economic othering" built on "a dubious anthropology of the 'primitive' or 'before' of modernity" (Gidwani 2004: 531). Instead, it takes seriously the historical, spatial, material, and relational specificity of economic orders established via the integration into contemporary fresh produce markets (McMichael & Friedmann 2007). Indeed, the western, central, and southern parts of Ghana had been integrated into global markets for colonial commodities such cocoa, palm oil, timber, or rubber for decades, and several authors have shown how the extraversion of these regions has bred new subjectivities, challenged prevailing regimes of property, and produced new social orders in farming communities (Hill 1963; Amanor 1999, 2010a; Fold 2008). Likewise, in the past some farmers in Ghana's north produced cashew and cotton for the domestic market, the latter under contract arrangements (Poulton 1998).[7] However, the "quality assurance world," dominated by powerful retailers and shaped by distinct entry barriers (especially for smallholders) created by market demands for quality, flexibility, and scale, brings with it with novel framings of goods, agencies, and economic encounters. It engenders specific pathways, modalities, and technologies of marketization.

Markets for Development: Organic Mangoes in Northern Ghana

Whereas Ghana's horticulture subsector is most prominently associated with the export of whole pineapples, for some time now mango exports have been on the rise, increasing from 62 mt to 1,098 mt between 2001 and 2008, with the overall production standing at 70,000 mt in 2008 (MOFA 2010: 8). Although this still appears to be low in comparative terms – Côte d' Ivoire and Brazil (one of the leading exporters) exported 11,250 mt and 95,322 mt of mangoes, respectively, to the European Union (EU) in 2008 (NRI 2010: Ep3) – large-scale mango cultivation for export and local agro-processing, nevertheless, represents a new market frontier in Ghana, where novel dynamics play out. At stake here are processes and principles and not scale.

Since the late 1980s, market analyses and consultants had recommended mango production as a promising field for Ghanaian agriculture, and created an atmosphere that stimulated new production initiatives. Between 2000 and 2008, more than 7,000 acres of new mango orchards were established (GEPC 2008b), and in 2010, the Ghanaian government launched a new initiative aimed at planting about 20,000 acres of mango trees in the Northern, Upper East, Upper West and Brong-Ahafo Regions, as well as in the northern part of the Volta Region. Much of the new faith in mango production for export can be attributed to the pioneering of OFL and its outgrowers. When its director decided to start an organic mango project in northern Ghana in the late 1990s, it was a bold step, as one manager remembered during one of my first encounters with the project: "There was no mango being grown in the north. I mean we were the first company to come and do it as a business and outside of that you will hear people say we are crazy to do it up here in the north" (Interview, 2008).

Apart from not having any history of commercial mango farming, the region was off the radar of most large foreign and domestic investors. The lack of infrastructure, the complexly layered land tenure system, and farmers' inexperience with export agriculture all seemed to have deterred investors despite the common perception that northern Ghana, particularly the Northern Region, is blessed with an abundance of "idle" and arable farm land.

On top of that, attempts to develop commercial farming in the north had had a checkered history. Both the colonial state (through the *Gonja Development Company* founded in 1951, which tried to enroll farmers into groundnut production) as well as the post-colonial state (under both civil and military administrations) tried to push investments in commercial food production in northern Ghana. This included state-led investments into rice (in the 1960s and 1970s), cotton (from the mid-1960s onward),[8] and tomatoes (from the 1960s onward) (Amanor 2010b; Khor 2006). In the 1980s, the state was rolled back as part of structural adjustment programs (SAPs), and the promotion of commercial agriculture in the north was left to NGOs, which promoted crops such as cashew nuts. All these projects had either failed or not led to a "take-off" that would benefit local farmers on a broad scale.[9] Large-scale investments in rice farming, pushed under the military government between 1972 and 1979, had had a particularly troubled history, leading to the burning of rice farms and the damage of machinery when villagers rebelled against the appropriation of land and new patterns of accumulation fueled by urban-based capitalist farmers (Goody 1980; Konings 1984). The schisms produced in the era of large-scale rice farming are said to have had considerable consequences for the conditions for agrarian marketization and capital accumulation in the north, as Blench (1996: 12) notes: "The long-term consequence has been to deter (sic!) potential large-scale capitalist investors [...]."

Given the troubled history of large-scale investments in Ghana's north, it may now be clearer why OFL's investment was considered "crazy" by some observers, as the aforementioned manager put it. However, seen from a different angle, it actually could be considered a true case of entrepreneurial wit, at least if we assume that the "source of entrepreneurship lies in differences in information about opportunities" (Shane 2000: 449). Frontier regions of marketization are, in fact, explorative zones in which entrepreneurs recognize opportunities for commodification and surplus extraction that had either not existed before or which others are unaware of or find too risky to explore. As Tsing (2005: 30) notes so adequately, "[r]esources are made by resourcefulness [...]." The case of OFL strikingly echoes such insights.

First, the director of OFL and his associates realized that the organic mango market was growing rapidly at the end of the 1990s.

Second, they perceived that northern Ghana has the right climatic and soil conditions for the production of organic mangoes. Although Ghana's south offered two harvesting seasons for mangoes (May to July; October to November), the north had two locational advantages. On the one hand, the extended dry season between November and April would mean fewer pest and disease attacks, which was crucial given that organic farming cannot resort to conventional chemical solutions. On the other hand, the mango harvests in the north fell in a season when other major exporters into the EU such as Brazil, Peru, and South Africa would not have fruits. OFL would thus have its mangoes just ready when there was a huge gap in any EU importer's schedules. Given these factors, the director and his associates saw considerable space for arbitrage:

> There are no mangoes in Europe in my time, so I do have the upper hand. I don't know for how long because I compete with the Côte d'Ivoire, Mali, Burkina Faso. And I'm organic. It is a little bit different also, it's organic and with organic you have for the next, I think, six years, you'll always have the edge, but it will come to a stage where you'll have to start fighting for markets, but for now we are still fine, we have no problems. So organic gives me the upper hand and I'm in the right season. Because when the mangoes are very, very scarce, I can come in, for instance, with my mangoes beginning March, let's say March, April, May, those three months, I'll be the richest man in two years. I promise you, because the prices they'll be giving will be huge because there are no mangoes. South Africa ends beginning March, and then there's nobody, so March, April...actually March people always ask me "Do you have mangoes? Do you have mangoes?" – there is nothing in the market at that moment. (Interview with senior manager OFL, 2008)

Third, the director had extended business connections in Europe through another of his companies in Ghana, which was crucial for establishing a future market.

Fourth, he had spent a considerable time in northern Ghana in the past and had a "desire to see the development of the north," as another OFL manager put it (Interview, 2008). He had been involved in development projects in the north in the late 1970s, and ARAMIS, OFL's mother company, evolved from this engagement. Today, ARAMIS is a major player in Ghanaian agriculture, and has good connections to the state apparatus. Thus, the director of OFL and his associates knew their "ways left and right" in Ghana, and its north in particular, as another manager at ARAMIS stated confidently (Interview, 2009). They had crucial knowledge about the power geometries, land access, and "cultural peculiarities" in northern Ghana.

Starting with such favorable endowments, the OFL director and his associates initially planned for a large nucleus estate (see Eaton & Shepherd 2001), to which 200 acres under outgrowers were to be added at a later stage. The farmers would cultivate the trees on their own plots, using mainly family labor. Through the mediation of a powerful chief[10] whom the director became acquainted with in the late 1970s and by intervention of the overlord of Dagbon,[11] the company managed to secure a large piece of land in proximity to the White Volta – a move that was not welcomed by all members of the host community, including the local chief. MOSP, a Belgian governmental program for private sector investment, helped the company to establish a 385 acre farm. When more and more farmers in the local communities around the nucleus farm began to show interest in mango farming, the company decided to extend the project to a larger number of smallholder farmers. ARAMIS had already gathered experience with financing farmers and contract farming in the cocoa sector, and OFL incorporated this model into the mango project. The model was based on a seemingly simple formula, as a senior manager at ARAMIS explained during an interview:

We are highly commercial! But it is commercial from two ends. We start with the farmer and then we go because once that farmer makes money, our money will also come. That makes it sustainable, if we will do a project whereby we only think about ARAMIS that means in three years time the project will collapse so our income is gone, so we work from the farmer's point of view and if the farmer is successful, our money will come [...]. (Interview, 2009)

OFL also incorporated experiences from the *Ghana Oil Palm Development Corporation* (GOPDC) project, a large-scale outgrower scheme for palm oil that was set up in 1976 with funding from the World Bank (see Amanor 1999).

Additional knowledge was brought in by hired consultants who had studied mango farming projects in Côte d' Ivoire, Burkina Faso, and Togo. They were convinced of the viability of the project, assuming that northern Ghana had similar edaphic and climatic conditions as parts of Mali and Burkina Faso, where commercial smallholder mango orchards have a long tradition. On the basis of these assumptions, an ambitious expansion plan was developed. Costs and benefits were calculated; the developmental potential of an outgrower scheme was explored.

For the expansion of the project, OFL mobilized additional financial support from a number of international development organizations. Attracted by the potential developmental impact of the project and driven by the latest fashion of private-sector-/ market-led development (Amanor 2009; McMichael 2013), these organizations aided the enlargement of the outgrower scheme by providing several loans and grants. In 2001, MOSP provided financial assistance to the first 50 pioneer outgrowers. In the same year, the Association of Organic Mango Outgrowers (AOMO) was established with the help of OFL and the Belgian NGO DIAROC. AOMO was supposed to represent the interests of the farmers, and both organizations envisioned that it could take over some of the technical services that OFL provided so far. While it may sound paradoxical that a company pushes for the political organization of its "market alteri," there was, in fact, a sound economic interest behind this, as the responsible program officer at DIAROC explained at her Brussels office: "They can't work a few thousand unorganized farmers; they need people who can speak on behalf of totality for them to be efficient as a company, so in that sense they need organized farmers if they want to be effective" (Interview, 2009).

Notwithstanding the goal of organizing farmers, AOMO virtually remained an empty shell until 2004, when DIAROC supported it with a large grant to support its organizational development. DIAROC also supported the participation of another 400 outgrowers in the project through an even larger loan allocated to OFL. DIAROC's support was embedded into its experimental program Small Producers in the Value Chain, which adopted a "market-oriented approach" to development and recognized "the important role of the private sector as a key stakeholder in market or value chains." Within this program, the value chain approach was used "as a way to analyze the position of small-scale farmers and afterwards to decide about the kind of DIAROC support, and whether to intervene starting from the farmers, or through the SME [small and medium enterprises] angle, or through the banking/MFI [microfinance institutions] sector."[12] DIAROC's support was grounded in the refashioned trickle-down assumption that mango farmers could eventually develop "from informal groups into registered commercial 'village enterprises'."[13] Given its focus on empowerment and smallholder development, DIAROC played an active role in the drafting of the contract for the supported 400 farmers, which also became a template for organizing the relationship with other (non-DIAROC supported) farmers joining the project at a later stage.

DIAROC's significant support served as leverage for attracting other donor agencies. In 2005, the United Nations Development Project (UNDP) sponsored 100 outgrowers, and in the same year the African Enterprise Foundation (AEF), a US-government development organization with a special focus on enterprise development and empowerment, supported another 240 farmers. Shortly after that, MOFA decided to support the project and helped to erect office buildings for AOMO. The World Bank also provided grant assistance by paying for new seedlings via HEII. USAID helped OFL via TIPCEE, which supported training activities on organic composting techniques, the development of so-called farmer passports,[14] and the implementation of a GIS-based farm management system.

The investments of these various stakeholders enlarged the outgrower scheme considerably. What had started as a small trial became one of the largest private investments ever in northern Ghana. Even though the target of 2,000 outgrowers has eventually never been reached owing to production problems, by 2011 the scheme had incorporated 1,295 farmers spread over 43 villages.[15] Of these farmers, almost 500 had started harvesting, with some farmers enjoying good yields and returns, while many others were disappointed by production failures (see Chapter 8). In several villages, OFL has not only invested in agriculture but also fostered community development projects as part of its corporate social responsibility (CSR) agenda.

Obviously, the case of OFL and its farmers is a fascinating one for several reasons. First, it represents a case of true "boundary work" (Mitchell 2007: 267) as the project is situated in a region where most farmers had never been exposed to export agriculture. The OFL farmers were what some would call "peasants" (Silverman 1979), even though such capitalocentric and substantivist categories require postcolonial scrutiny (Gidwani 2004; Bernstein 2010; Chakrabarty 2011). Despite the fact that some farmers had been engaged in cotton and cashew farming in the past, as well as in the petty trade of shea nuts for export, the production of tree crops through a long-term contract farming and marketing arrangement presented to many a very new market model. Tree crops such as mangoes come with very specific farming practices as well as with distinctive property and socio-natural relations (Prudham 2003), which distinguishes them from short-term crops such as pineapples.

Second, the project adopts an approach of agribusiness organization commonly practiced in many countries across the Global South: the "nucleus-estate model" (Eaton & Shepherd 2001: 50). Under this organizational model, a financing company "also owns and manages an estate plantation, which is usually close to the processing plant" (ibid.: 50). The company farm is "often fairly large in order to provide some guarantee of throughput for the plant, but on occasion it can be relatively small, primarily serving as a trial and demonstration farm" (ibid.: 50; see also Vellema 2002). Although this model has already been practiced in the past for many colonial crops – for example, for palm oil in Ghana (Amanor 1999) or tea in Kenya (Grosh 1997) – it is currently enjoying a revival in several African countries for both traditional (e.g., rubber, cotton) and nontraditional commodities (Brüntrup & Peltzer 2006; Amanor 2009; Oya 2012). This form of contractualization is said to allow small-scale farmers to participate in high-value/high-quality supply chains as it guarantees an efficient and effective control of production (see World Bank 2007). Applying this model to fruit tree farming represents a *novum* in northern Ghana, and its implementation raises important questions of economy-making.

Third, the case of OFL and its outgrowers substantiates the previously made assertion that contemporary global agrifood markets are not only made by producers and consumers but by an array of market-makers. Here, a number of different actors are brought together for the creation of new markets, linking an extended loan scheme with contract production. Across the Global South, these hybrid market-making projects, building on "public-private linkages and civil society incorporation/co-option" (Amanor 2009: 248), have become increasingly widespread as part of market-oriented agricultural development agendas (McMichael 2013). Their organizational configuration makes them a tangle of different interests and framings of worth. The engagement of the aforementioned market-makers in one of Ghana's poorest regions (see Excursus 3.1) was a direct expression of the recent proliferation of models such as "value chain promotion," "private-sector-led development," and "making markets work for the poor" in Ghana and the Global South more generally.

Excursus 3.1   Ghana's south–north divide:

In development circles, the state of poverty and "underdevelopment" in Ghana's north has often been attributed to a number of historical and structural factors (Songsore 2011). Much of the economic growth induced by the fresh produce industry over the last two decades has benefited Ghana's more prosperous south, thereby exacerbating interregional disparities. In spite of exports contributing 40% to the increase in Ghana's GDP between 1985 and 2005, this growth was largely based on increases in gold, cocoa, and horticultural products, none of which are commodities produced in the country's north (Al-Hassan & Diao 2007). Patterns of extreme poverty continue to persist in a region that has been structurally neglected since colonial times (Songsore 2011), serving as a labor reservoir for the economies in the south. Furthermore, the region was hard hit by the termination of subsidies for inputs under the SAPs in the 1980s. Although the national poverty rate declined from 51.7% in 1992 to 28.5% in 2006, with Ghana's south scoring a remarkable reduction from 48% to 20% during the same period, the country's three northern provinces (Upper East, Upper West, and Northern Region) fared less well. Although the regional poverty rate dropped from 67% to 63% between 1992 and 2006 (with a poverty line set at USD 1.08 per adult per day in 2009) (World Bank 2011: 3), high population growth even led to an increase in the absolute number of poor people (ibid.: 5). This situation is aggravated by persistent structural poverty, with many villages still not having access to piped water, electricity, agricultural services (such as banking), or tarmac roads. Getting physical access to markets is still a serious problem for many farmers in the region. Until the setting up of the MCA in 2007,[16] the north had never featured prominently in policy frameworks as an area of horticulture and agribusiness development, nor has it broadly benefited from the overall growth of the Ghanaian economy since the 1980s, which economists usually attribute to "the low representation of the region's production in international trade" (Al-Hassan & Diao 2007: 3).

Fourth, the area where OFL operates is embedded in a distinct cultural, institutional, and environmental setting: most of the farmers are Muslims and belong to the hierarchically structured Dagomba kingdom (*Dagbon*) (see Abdulai 1986); outside urban areas, land is largely considered communal property and – contrary to the south, where the commodification of land (and labor) has steadily advanced since colonial times – strongly vested in the institution of the chief (*Naa*) within a complex system of non-formalized[17] tenure rights (Kasanga & Kotey 2001; Abdulai & Ndekugr 2008); the northern semi-arid savanna climate differs from the tropical climate of the coastal savanna zone, with a single rainy season alternating with an extended dry season (Blench 1996). As we will see later, these structural factors often shape the pathways of export-driven marketization in northern Ghana in unexpected ways, making it a cumbersome struggle against other ways of performing the economy, material infrastructures, and "nature" itself.

Fresh from Farm: JIT Pineapple Markets

My second story revolves around the operations of TF, a multinational company that has been producing JIT fresh-cut products since the late 1990s in Ghana's coastal savanna zone. It delivers high-value/high-quality fruit assortments to European retail markets throughout the year, sourcing from a range of small-, medium-, and large-scale farmer-suppliers in southern Ghana. The company was founded by a Swiss entrepreneur who saw a window of opportunity in the rapidly expanding fresh-cut market in Europe. In the late 1990s, minimally processed fruit was the fastest expanding sector in the fresh produce industry with a growth of around 20% per year (Dixie & Sergeant 1998: 22). Until then, fruits had been processed in the country of consumption, incurring high labor and waste disposal charges. "Fresh from farm," ready-to-eat fruits appeared as a promising venture to the entrepreneur, and not many other companies servicing the market, including vertically integrated companies such as Dole or Del Monte (mainly sourcing from Latin America), could offer such a product around that time.

Not just the market opportunities but also locational advantages made Ghana a place to invest in. Several factors shaped the company's investment decision: prior knowledge about the local institutional setting; a rather stable political climate; favorable climatic conditions; proximity to European markets and competitive air freight rates; investor incentives granted by the Ghanaian government under the Free Zone Act (see Excursus 3.2); relative availability of cheap labor, land, and a stratum of farmers who had already had experience in export-oriented pineapple farming; and important personal connections with an established exporter, who later would also act as an intermediary to secure land for a factory and introduce the entrepreneur to local farmers. With investment capital mobilized abroad, a processing facility was set up. Old connections to one of the major retailers in the European market helped TF to create a market for sophisticated convenience products from scratch. In the difficult fresh-cut market, these connections were crucial as future buyers had to be convinced about the feasibility and competitiveness of the planned product and why they should have confidence in a newly emerging company.

Excursus 3.2   The free zone model

The global proliferation of the free zone model was part of the "counter-revolution in development economics" (Daviron & Ponte 2005: 19). This counter-revolution dismissed the earlier state-driven model of import-substitution industrialization that many Latin American, Asian, and African countries (including Ghana) embraced, instead promoting market liberalization, export diversification, and export-oriented industrialization strategies "as a means of keeping up with the shifting international trade environment" (Addo & Marshall 2000: 355).[19] Free zones were heralded as generic "enabling environments" for export-oriented industrialization across the Global South by institutions such as the World Bank since the late 1970s. The free zone model was not only considered crucial for attracting foreign investors as harbingers of capital, technology, and expertise, but for harnessing local manufacturing and value addition. In the neoliberal register, cases such as Indonesia, Malaysia, Mauritius, Mexico, and Thailand were considered economic "success stories" (see World Bank 1993; Bräutigam 2005), and structurally adjusted countries such as Ghana were advised to follow these paths.

The World Bank reckoned, in one of its EPZ-promoting reports, that "Ghana needs a much more aggressive export drive focusing especially on agriculture, agro-processed products, and light manufacturing industries" (World Bank 1993: XI), and the free zone model was meant to play a crucial role in this regard. Ghana's government was a late but nevertheless docile student. In 1995, the parliament promulgated the Free Zone Act, and the Ghana Free Zone Board (GFZB) started its operations in 1996. The act allowed the GFZB to designate special zones treated as an "uncustomed territory," which granted foreign investors such as TF a wide range of tax incentives.

A free zone enterprise is expected to export 100%, but up to 30% of the companies sales can also be sold locally. Free zone enterprises are fully exempt from direct and indirect taxes and duties on imported inputs and exported output (Cook 2000: 12). They also enjoy a corporate tax holiday for ten years, after which a profit tax of between 2% and 8% applies (the normal corporate tax rate is 25% per annum). Firms are also exempt from paying withholding taxes on dividends from free zone investments (ibid.: 12). Taxes for import duties only apply to the goods sold in the domestic market.

Furthermore, the free zone model does not create any barrier for capital as there are no restrictions to the repatriation of profits or dividends from free zone activities. The free zone status can be applied to geographically bounded areas (the classical EPZ) as well as to single-site factories (such as TF) outside the clusters usually associated with the free zone model (ibid.: 11). Unlike the Mauritius model (see Bräutigam 2005), for instance, the Ghanaian free zone model does not employ extra-territorial labor regulation, and the national labor law also applies within the zones, even though companies in consultation with the workers may opt for a place-based "union." Free zone enterprises need to allocate 1% of the wage bill to train workers. In 1999, just around the time when TF's operations took off, the free zones had attracted 65 firms, most of which produced relatively low-value-added goods. These firms relied heavily on primary commodities, such as wood, metal, and petroleum (Cook 2000: 13).

The company sent its first container of fresh-cut pineapples to Europe in the late 1990s. Until 2008, TF fared well with the JIT model, recording an impressive turnover growth year after year. Fruits would be supplied to the factory by farmers, sliced, packed, and labeled and then transported by airfreight to high-street retailers in Europe. By 2008, the company sourced raw material from many dozens of smallholders, medium-sized, and large-scale farmers in southern Ghana, some of whom had grown considerably since becoming a supplier to TF. The company processed several hundred tons of fruits a week, commanding a considerable share of Ghana's pineapple exports. It boosted the local economy both through wages and farm purchases, making it a weighty economic player in southern Ghana. What started as an enterprise with a few employees had developed into a full-fledged multidivisional company with many hundreds of workers by 2008, after the company had expanded into several other countries in order to be able to provide its customers with a more diverse range of products throughout the year. The incorporation of new locations created a cross-continental production network, in which the European headquarter served as an import, sales, and marketing branch and category manager[18], while the management of the production sites was devolved to Ghanaian staff. This extensive network complemented the company's product portfolio in important ways, helping it ensure a perennial and consistent supply of fruit assortments in which pineapples and mangoes "fresh from farm" were strategic ingredients. As sales were increasing over the years, TF also upgraded its cooling and processing facilities in Ghana.

TF has been also very proactive in the adoption of international food safety and quality standards. Besides meeting mere technical and public production standards, it became compliant with many major retailer-owned and collective private standards. As we will see in Chapter 5, it knew how to position itself in a global "economy of qualities" (Callon et al. 2002). The company also championed CSR projects, investing in social amenities and health care for workers as well as in community projects among pineapple farmers in Ghana's coastal savanna zone. Such CSR practices, similarly to those of OFL in the north, were an innovation in the Ghanaian pineapple subsector. In a market dominated by powerful transnational corporations such as Del Monte and Dole, which have been repeatedly accused of poor labor and supplier relations (ILRF 2008), such investments were markers of difference. In the words of its founder, TF was "much more than a factory, much more than a workplace. It [was] a way of life" (Interview 2008).

Seen from one perspective, the case of TF and its suppliers reads like a true success story. Even though fresh produce firms in countries such as Kenya, Zambia, and Zimbabwe (for vegetables) (Dolan & Humphrey 2004; Freidberg 2004) had developed similar JIT models, often combined with CSR activities (Blowfield & Dolan 2008), TF was both a pioneer and leapfrogger in the Ghanaian pineapple subsector and fresh produce industry more generally. This achievement becomes clearer if we consider the state of the Ghanaian pineapple subsector from a historical perspective.

In the 1980s, Côte d' Ivoire dominated pineapple imports to the EU, while Ghana carved out a niche as a primary supplier of high-quality air-freighted pineapples. Ghana entered the sea-freight pineapple market in the mid-1990s, a segment that recorded significant growth until the early 2000s. Dixie & Sergeant (1998) report that in the late 1990s there were between 50 and 70 companies exporting pineapples at any one time, and 40% of exports came from smallholder production. By the early 2000s, Ghana's share of the European fresh pineapple market had reached 10%–11% of the European market (ibid: 28; see also Fold 2008; Amanor 2012).

Notwithstanding the impressive expansion of pineapple production in Ghana's south in the 1990s, the subsector lacked more sophisticated, value-adding operations and was mainly made up of many small and often struggling domestic exporting firms with low profit margins and limited access to capital and innovational capabilities, as well as a vast number of non-organized smallholder farmers who would feed the exporters through spot markets. More consolidated contractual relations between exporters and farmers (such as those promoted by TF) did not exist, and mutual deception and moral hazards were common. Sometimes, low-quality fruits would be exported owing to poorly managed supply chains. At the time TF set up its operations, there was only one factory that processed non-export-quality produce into juice for the local market and only two companies that exported more than 2,000 mt of crude pineapples *per annum* (Dixie & Sergeant 1998: 31). Furthermore, there was hardly any intra-industry coordination or collaboration between the state, the industry, and research institutions (Whitfield 2010).

Even though TF built on the existing skills of farmers when it arrived, it took the production of fresh pineapples to a new level. Although the actor landscape of the Ghanaian fresh produce sector had changed significantly by 2011 (see Chapter 8), with new domestic and foreign players entering the game,[20] the achievements of TF seem to be remarkable from a historical perspective as it virtually put Ghana on the map of Northern retailers. These achievements were due to sufficient access to capital mobilized abroad, raw material, market information, technical know-how, and close connections to European markets in the very first place, but the free zone model contributed equally to sustaining the growth and expansion of global market connections. Being exempt from import taxes and enjoying other corporate tax benefits made a "dramatic difference" to the operations of the company (Interview senior manager, 2008).

It is against this backdrop that industry observers have frequently dubbed TF's venture as a "model for development" that has "created opportunities to access high value export markets and add value in Ghana," as a development agency report put it back in 2007. It seems to prove that it is indeed possible to evade the "commodity problem" (Daviron and Ponte 2005: 8) – that more sophisticated and vertically integrated market connections can be forged from the "periphery" if only the right conditions are created. No wonder that Jim, the director of TIPCEE, would constantly refer to the company's operations during an interview back in 2008. For him, the case of TF was a striking example of how smallholders can become part of "quality assurance world." It was a model of this "seamless flow" that directly connects the production base like a pipe to end markets.

Thus, this case reads like a realization of theories of the economists in the "wild" who advised the Ghanaian government in the 1980s and 1990s as part of the SAPs. The economists of the World Bank and other like-minded organizations predicted that accelerated growth would depend "on a rapid integration of the Ghanaian economy into world markets" (World Bank 1993: 40), including those for nontraditional exports (NTEs) such as pineapples. "Integration" was said to be facilitated by adopting the policy models of the time: getting the prices (e.g., through a conducive exchange rate regime) and institutions right (e.g., through secured property rights over land and other assets), utilizing comparative advantages in resources and labor, and enhancing investor confidence by creating an enabling environment condensed in free zones would unleash the beneficial forces of the market (Addo & Marshall 2000: 356).

Seen from another perspective, the case of TF, when put in the larger context of the boom–bust cycles of the Ghanaian pineapple subsector, provides a telling example of the volatility and disciplinary powers shaping contemporary retail agrifood chains. Entering these means entering specific market *agencements*. There is nothing natural about their existence. Becoming part of these markets is all about ontological recon-figurations (Çalışkan & Callon 2010: 25). They are not simply there, "like air" (Sen; cited in DFID & SNC 2008: 9), but are an outcome of historical struggles for particular kinds of goods, agencies, encounters, and the productive, temporal, con-nective, and power relations that link these. In other words, when the JIT model was launched, the Smooth Cayenne pineapple grown for more than two decades by the Densu Valley farmers had to be requalified according to the modalities valuation of the retail world; new standards had to be set, implemented, and enforced; the pineapples of selected farmers needed to be framed as corporate resources, and ownership claims needed to be attached to them; nature had to be transformed, manipulated, and controlled in new ways; suppliers and workers had to be reformatted as qualcula-tive agents; logistics and air-based supply chains had to be set up, and eventually coordination had to be achieved between heterogeneous actors in order to allow the stable and legitimate exchange of JIT fruits.

From such a perspective, it may also be emphasized that not all farmers in Densu Valley could join the JIT world. Since 2005, Densu Valley farmers have been increas-ingly marginalized owing to a preference change in the European pineapple market from the popular Smooth Cayenne variety to the MD2 variety – an industrial crop designed by the agrobusiness giant Del Monte for the plains of Costa Rica. Many farmers and smaller exporters simply could not cope with the technical and monetary requirements the cultivation of the "designer pineapple" brought with it (see Chapter 8). By 2010, Ghana's share of the EU pineapple market had plummeted to 3% (Loeillet & Paqui 2010), giving way to imports from Costa Rica that were driven by Del Monte and other large pineapple exporters. The result has been a shattered industry that consolidated around a few large-scale exporters cultivating MD2 pineapples in a new frontier west of Densu Valley (see Chapter 8). Although a few lucky farmers contin-ued to serve the high-value (but by no means stable) JIT chains of TF, most other smallholders either dropped out of business or struggled under increasingly precarious market conditions.

Thus situated in the larger context of the competitive and regulatory dynamics of the global agrifood economy, the case of TF and the pineapple farmers of Densu Valley seems to prove agrarian political economy scholars such as Amanor (2009: 261) right, who argues that contemporary retail-driven agrifood markets are shaped by "the two processes of exclusion and inclusion – which are necessary outcomes of the creation of market governance, standardization, grades and quality controls" and which "may lead to increasing social differentiation, expansion of a small class of wealthy but still vulnerable farmers." While we should be careful about the capitalo-centrism that is sometimes ingrained in statements of this kind, the case nevertheless prompts us to ask critical questions about the differentiation of the world of farming in the Global South into those connected (at whatsoever price) and those discon-nected and expelled from global markets (Berndt & Boeckler 2011b). This process of differentiation, whose outcomes organizations such as the World Bank (2007), many other donors in Ghana (remember Jim's words from the beginning) and many scholars

(Collier & Dercon 2014) nowadays normalize as the new rural heterogeneity of a global market present, cannot be captured by established notions of class and rural social stratification (Bernstein 2010), but must be understood as a complex border-land of new positionalities and subjectivities.

All these contextual features make the TF–outgrower complex an interesting case study. First, the company and its suppliers deliver to highly demanding upmarket retailers, which differentiates it from the first case study, where a company sells seasonal produce to importers in Europe, who would then distribute it to supermarkets. Thus, it stands for one of the most technologically advanced frontier regions of the global agrifood economy, shaped by the regulatory and highly competitive dynamics of JIT retail markets (Gibbon & Ponte 2005). Second, the case study represents a centralized "hub-and-spoke-model" of agribusiness organization. This is a vertically coordinated model in which a company purchases a "crop from farmers and processes or packages and markets the product" (Eaton & Shepherd 2001: 47). Increasingly, the hub-and spoke model has been promoted in development policy circles as a means for building up processing industries (Shepherd 2007).

The contextual factors outlined earlier contribute in their own skewed and unfore-seen ways to the performance of markets in the studied cases, yet they also relate to more general and sometimes overlapping aspirations and dynamics.

Sites of Attention

For both case studies, I take the two agribusiness companies as starting points. They are treated as focal sites from where the processes of market proliferation and the "integration" of farmers into new market arrangements are studied, an approach that is embraced for both pragmatic and conceptual reasons. On the one hand, it is virtu-ally impossible to study the companies and their farmers in symmetrical detail, on the other hand the companies serve as translators and crucial co-producers of market arrangements and thus are given a prominent role as organizational sites for studying processes of export-oriented marketization in the two frontier regions. Nevertheless, in both case studies, the contracted farmers within their wider social and environ-mental setting play an important role.

In the case of OFL, the research presented here took off from its headquarters in northern Ghana. The outgrower scheme stretches across a vast area, cutting across more than 40 villages, which makes it rather difficult to cover it for a study, and so for the project a pragmatic compromise had to be found. Therefore, a small number of farmer groups and individual farmers in different zones of the outgrower scheme were selected for a more detailed study. Most of the farmers in the study area make a living from livestock, groundnuts, maize, cowpeas, rice, fishing, and shea nuts trade. But this project also involved (sometimes unexpected) encounters with NGO officials in New York and Brussels, a manager of the company at an organic fair in Germany, the managing director of the mother company in Kumasi, Ghana-based development experts, and local chiefs. The latter encounters were particularly important because the chiefs, as "traditional" authorities, played a crucial role in the market-making project by allocating land for mango production and granting political support to the project.

In the case of TF, I focus on a group of 23 to 25 small- to medium-sized pineapple farmers (the number fluctuated over the course of time) because pineapple products account for most of the turnover of the company (see Excursus 3.3).

This precludes the large-scale farmer–exporters TF was sourcing from at the time of study. These farmers live and produce in Densu Valley, an area in the Aborobe District of Ghana's Eastern Province. Decades ago, the valley was one of the prime cocoa frontiers, but those days are long gone, and local farmers shifted to pineapple production in

---

Excursus 3.3   Are TF suppliers smallholder farmers?

In general, the notion of "smallholder" has the connotation of limited land availability. However, it is usually assumed that "many other aspects of smallness are critical to characterizing resource-poor small farmers in the developing world, such as limited capital (including animals), fragmented holdings, and limited access to inputs" (Chamberlin 2007: 3). Characterizing the non-exporter suppliers of TF as "smallholder farmers" is by no means unproblematic. The question of what actually makes up a smallholder farmer is a contested one and, furthermore, itself represents a problematization. Definitions differ from country to country as well as from crop to crop (see Ouma 2010).

The suppliers of TF were not simply smallholder farmers at the time of research, even though the company frequently rendered them thus. They already represented a selected and formatted stratum of the pineapple growers in Densu Valley. One could deem them "rural petty capitalists" (Hill 1963), and some of them had managed to farm considerable portions of land over the course of time. The majority of the non-exporter Smooth Cayenne pineapple suppliers of TF cultivated between 10 and 50 acres in 2008, with two of them cultivating more than 100 acres. Each of them had additional land at his disposal. This is considerable, given that average farm sizes for most pineapple farms in the valley were below 5 acres.[21] The TF suppliers employed waged laborers on a permanent basis (rather than using household labor) in addition to several casual workers for labor peaks (field preparation, harvesting, and weeding). Many of them had extensive experience in the pineapple businesses before joining the JIT world and had at least some basic formal education, with two farmers having been trained beyond secondary school level. A few of them cultivated other cash or food crops or developed non-farm side business.

This sharply contrasts with the profile of mango farmers in northern Ghana, who usually cultivated a few acres of land, largely produced for subsistence needs, were mostly illiterate (>95%), and mainly used family labor for mango and food crop production, even though the latter was also done through customary forms of group work (kpariba).

Most of TF's suppliers acquired land by approaching the head (abusuapanyin) of a well-known local family and/or local chiefs. The latter, like in the north, hold the allodial title to land. In a few instances, farmers acquired land through their own matrilineage (abusua) or through inheritance. In the first two instances, the land was allocated on a lease-hold basis, often on conditions of what farmers perceived as freehold. This corresponds to the general finding that quasi-land markets and land privatization exist in many parts of southern Ghana, where commodification of land and labor has been going on since the early 20th century (Hill 1963; Amanor 2010a), particularly in areas close to larger cities. Of course, it would be worth investigating further what new spatial and social patterns of rural transformation have occurred in Densu Valley over the past decade owing to pineapple production.

the 1980s. Until 2004/2005, the valley had been the main producing area for two local pineapple varieties, Smooth Cayenne and Victoria, which were mainly cultivated by smallholder farmers. They would sell them to exporters, some of whom also had their own farms. From mid-2000 onward, a second more large-scale market frontier was carved out westward when the pineapple sector attracted new FDI, and some existing exporters shifted to a new pineapple variety (see Chapter 8).

At times, however, cross-reference is made to other pineapple farmers in the region and players in Ghanaian agriculture order to make a certain argument. In a similar vein, I include TF's relation *vis-à-vis* its large-scale suppliers, global buyers, global and local competitors, the Ghanaian state, service providers, and standard-setting bodies in order to explain the dynamic (re)configuration of the market frontier.

What may appear to be an approach erratic in focus has indeed a processual method behind it. Taking inspiration from what some have called a "multi-sited ethnography" (Marcus 1995),[22] I followed crucial sites and connections in the respective market arrangements, either physically or at least via interviews or by tracing artifacts. Altogether I spent 34 weeks in Ghana between February 2008 and September 2011 (plus brief return visits in 2012 and 2013), even though most of the field work was completed by October 2010. At times, the physical boundaries of the field would become fuzzy, as did the boundaries of the "objects" I studied. While I treat the companies and the farmers' fields as focal sites in my study, this does not mean that the other sites, people, and organizations can simply be rendered as an "external environment" to the agribusiness–outgrower complexes. This point warrants emphasis as organization theorists usually distinguish between an organization and its external environment framed as a "market," "suppliers," "competitors," "governments," "consumers," etc. (Schatzki 2005: 479). In my own empirical work, I have always worked beyond such a distinction and studied different sites of market-making in concrete organizational settings without separating these settings from their "environment." In this regard, I was inspired by Schatzki's view that

> the environment of a social formation is a net of practice-arrangement bundles (regardless of the terms that are used to denote features and slices of this net, for example, 'competing firms,' 'markets,' 'hostile states,' and 'NGOs'). An organization's relations to and interdependencies with extra-organizational formations consist of concrete connections and interactions between the bundle that composes the organization and those that compose extra-organizational phenomena. As with the internal workings of an organization, studying an organization's relations with other phenomena requires delving into the details of these connections and interactions and not averting to a theory about the relation between an organization and its 'environment'. (ibid.: 479)

Although Schatzki, due to his more philosophical inclination, eventually develops a different practice-oriented approach to organizations/markets than most scholars in the social studies of economization and marketization, this quote serves well to situate the rhizomatic empirical approach I adopted. Traces of global markets can be found in many sites: during audits; on farms disciplined by global standards; in quality handbooks; during price negotiations between a company and its outgrowers; in management meetings; on factory floors; in chief's palaces, where the allocation of farm land for export production is decided upon; or in northern NGO headquarters, where the funding for market-making projects in the South is approved. These apparently mundane and dispersed sites are part of the net of practice-arrangement bundles that make up global agrifood connections.

Conclusion

In this chapter, I outlined the structural and policy context of my case studies, which represent two salient frontier regions of marketization in Ghana. Whereas the case of TF stands for a dynamic JIT frontier where a processing facility as one node in the multinational production network of a company is linked flexibly to farmers who function as "suppliers" of a wide range of fruits, the case of OFL and its outgrowers is distinct because it is based on a long-term and loan-financed contract scheme that focuses on the cultivation of perennial tree crops that come along with specific institutional arrangements. OFL sells its fruits seasonally to distributors in Europe and not directly to retailers. Furthermore, the scope of OFL's project – the goal of integrating 2,000 outgrowers into global horticultural markets in a region that has not been exposed to export-oriented tree cultivation – is far more ambitious. Even though both case studies serve different markets with different organizational models in different structural settings, similar dynamics of market-making can be observed. In the empirical sections, I will attend to the specificities and commonalities of agrarian marketization in both cases.

What the reader should take from this chapter, moreover, is that these market-making projects only became possible at particular historical conjunctures and in turn influenced projects of economy building in Ghana more generally. In many more recent policy discourses, the pioneer projects of TF and OFL feature as success stories and models upon which a vibrant agroindustry that meets the demands of the "quality assurance world" could be built upon. For instance, early versions of the MCA in 2006 used the organizational models behind the operations of TF and OFL as templates for the "expansion of higher value agribusiness" (Karikari 2006: 3).

Though the origins of both case studies date back to the time before Ghana made a shift to the post–Washington Consensus market-oriented development agenda, the case studies intersect with this agenda either as a source of inspiration or because they link up with or are influenced by the activities of many of the programs launched after 2004. Of course, this book cannot trace the pathways and regional effects of these other market-making programs. It warrants emphasis, however, that the remaking of agriculture into a market-oriented, globally competitive domain of the Ghanaian economy under the auspices of the new "value chains for development agenda" brings to the fore the same questions and processes as my own case studies do, even though many markets for staples such as maize, yam, or cassava in Ghana continue to be far less "agencementized" than contemporary fresh produce markers serving Northern retailers.

Endnotes

1   In this book, all names of individuals, of the case study companies and related organizations, and their geographical associations have been anonymized, are withheld, or have been altered to protect sources. Development organizations and programs associated with the Ghanaian agricultural sector more generally are referred to by their original names.

2   I am aware of the problematic colonial history of the term "wild" and the Orientalism informing it, particularly with regard to the African continent. Deeply inscribed in Western modes of binary and racist thinking, the term has often been applied to regions said to be untouched by "Western man," "modernity," and "civilization". "Wild," as I use it here, is simply used in opposition to "caged."

3   According to the 2000 census, 50.6% of the labor force, or 4.2 million people, were directly engaged in agriculture. About 90% of farm holdings were less than 4 acres in size, a state that has not significantly changed (MOFA 2007: 4).

4   Exports of nontraditional agricultural crops (such as yam, shea nuts, pineapples, papayas, mangoes, cashew, fish, and sea food) more than doubled between 2000 and 2007 from USD 74.54 million to USD 197.24 million (GEPC 2008a). The total exports of fruits and vegetables rose from 9,800 to 131,422 mt between 1992 and 2007 (GEPC 2008b). In 2004, NTE contributed 23.7% of the total foreign exchange earnings from agriculture, the remaining coming from traditional products such as cocoa and timber (Afari-Sefa 2006: 3).

5   METASIP rests on six pillars: (1) Food security and emergency preparedness; (2) improved growth in incomes; (3) increased competitiveness and enhanced integration into domestic and international markets; (4) sustainable management of land and environment; (5) science and technology applied in food and agriculture development; and (6) enhanced institutional coordination.

6   The policies of the Washington Consensus mobilized a free market agenda. The new market-oriented development agenda is distinctively different in that it embraces interventions into value chains with regard to the requirements of "the market" (see Neilson 2014).

7   Many farming women in northern Ghana have also participated in "world markets" at a distance by collecting shea nuts and selling these to traders and exporters (Chalfin 2004). As a gendered crop, income from shea trade has both economic and social ramifications. The shea tree (*vitellaria paradoxa*), however, is neither cultivated, nor do tightly integrated shea value chains exist.

8   Cotton production was introduced in the 1920s to northern Ghana under British colonial rule but failed to take off. It was only in the 1960s that cotton production was promoted on a larger scale as part of Ghana's import substitution strategy, which received further political backing with the incorporation of the Ghana Cotton Development Board in 1968 (Poulton 1998).

9   Since 2007, northern Ghana has attracted several new investments (both foreign and domestic) in agrofuels, maize, cotton, and sorghum production, the latter three under contract-farming arrangements.

10   The chief was also given a share in the company.

11   In Dagbon, the practice of land allocation is firmly entangled with the customary administrative system made up of a hierarchy of chiefs (Abdulai 1986: 79). The paramount chief or overlord of Dagbon has to approve any major allocation of farm land to outsiders. The paramount chief who authorized the release of farm land to OFL, *Ya-Naa Yakubu Andani II*, was murdered in 2002. Since then, there has been a struggle around his succession that has divided Dagbon into the factions of the *Andani* and the *Abudu*. This fissure has also run through the outgrower scheme.

12 Quotes taken from program brochure (2005). DIAROC started this market-oriented program in 2003, breaking with its past, when it took a more classical approach to rural development. It started piloting contract farming/outgrower programs across a number of African countries.

13 Quote taken from project report (2003).

14 These helped to make farmers legible (Scott 1998: 2), documenting their personal details, farm details, and what kind of training they had so far received. Such passports facilitated compliance with the GLOBALG.A.P. and Organic Movement standards, which regulate food safety, occupational safety, and health, environmental, and organic practices in the agribusiness–outgrower–complex. They require extensive documentation on the qualification of persons and products alike. The Organic Movement is one of the most powerful organic certification bodies in Europe.

15 One village, interestingly the one where the OFL nucleus farm is located, dropped out as the project progressed.

16 See http://www.mcc.gov/pages/countries/overview/ghana (accessed: 23/08/2013) as well as Whitfield (2010).

17 According to Kasanga and Kotey (2001: 20), 80% to 90% of all the undeveloped land in Ghana with varying tenure and management systems falls under customary authority. It is estimated that 78% of that land is not formally recorded (Karikari 2006: 9).

18 Category management is a constitutive element of the shareholder-value-driven retail economy and is a part of retailers' profit-maximizing/risk-externalizing strategies (Gibbon & Ponte 2005). The basic idea is that retailers manage their operations on a product category basis (for example, fruits), and a large part of its management is transferred from the retailer to a "category captain" or "category manager" (Dolan & Humphrey 2004: 503).

19 It should be noted that such an open-door policy also brought "new pressures for land titling and institutional reform in the organisation of land relations" (Amanor 1999: 81) in order to entice investors with secure property rights. The agenda of the MCA can be read in this way (Grain 2010).

20 This included large-scale investments by a subsidiary of a Compagnie Frutière (owned by the transnational Dole), which moved over from troubled Côte d'Ivoire; another fresh-cut company with foreign stakes; and the investment of a European importer-exporter who tapped into new niche markets of pineapples in Europe. Moreover, new juice factories opened from 2009 onward, targeting the underserved domestic market.

21 Chamberlin (2007: 7) reports a national average land holding size of 5.47 acres, even though there are regional per capita variations. In the coastal and forest zone, most households operate on 4.9 or less acres. The median for the northern savanna zone was 4.9 acres.

22 The approach adopted here represents a rather thin version of Marcus' approach if we define multi-sited ethnography as "designed around chains, paths, threads, conjunctions, or juxtapositions of locations in which the ethnographer establishes some form of literal, physical presence, with an explicit, posited logic of association or connection among sites that in fact defines the argument of the ethnography" (Marcus 1995: 105).

Chapter Four
Critical Ethnographies of Marketization

I am sitting in my rented house in Saanga, northern Ghana, sometime back in 2008. I have just come home from the field – literally – struggling to locate some food in the village. It is 7 p.m. and already dark, yet the dry season's heat is still striking; 7 p.m. and it isn't any cooler? It must be the iron sheeted roof, a material marker of wealth in this area, but for me an ambivalent sign of progress. What a rough place! Could I stay here any longer? What must it be like to work here for nine years cultivating global connections, as one of the expatriate managers of Organic Fruits Ltd. (OFL)[1] has done? Could I do the same? I don't bother about this postcolonial moment. I am too tired to engage with the practices I observed and was told about or to note down what I may have actually missed. I can't simply inscribe the past events and turn them "into an account, which exists in its inscriptions and can be reconsulted" (Geertz 1973: 67). The *Moleskine* remains closed.

One year later, I left the house in Saanga behind and moved into the nearby house of a manager I had befriended. Food I knew, conversations in English, warm water and electricity, air conditioning, if one wished for. It was a comfortable place to stay in, but was it a place to do proper ethnography? A place to study markets in the making? A site of the subaltern?

★ ★ ★

My anxieties regarding how to go about my research in northern Ghana were part of a series of uncertainties I encountered when trying to provide a situated account of

Assembling Export Markets: The Making and Unmaking of Global Food Connections in West Africa, First Edition. Stefan Ouma.

global agrifood market connections. When one is lost, one may seek orientation by looking at how others have done it. Concerning the study of marketization processes, this is easier said than done. Although there now exists a burgeoning literature in anthropology, sociology, and geography of how to study globalizing processes (see, e.g., Marcus 1995; Burawoy 2000a; Crang & Cook 2007), it still remains rather opaque as to what a performative take on marketization may mean in methodological terms. Even though some works in the social studies of markets and finance have made such attempts (e.g., Abolafia 1998; Çalışkan 2007a), much of the literature black-boxes its methodological practices. This represents a striking commonality with antecedent "schools," actor-network-theory (ANT), and the social studies of science and technology (for exceptions, see Latour & Woolgar 1979; Law 1994).

Of course, the question remains as to whether many scholars following these intellectual traditions want to practice this "stepping out" at all (Barnes 2007: 17). One could argue that a constructionist research program is mainly about telling a very situated story from which it is difficult to generalize a clear-cut, fixed, impersonal, and standardized methodology that could easily be recommended to struggling ethnography rookies (Knorr-Cetina 1989; Law 1994: 4). However, without "stepping out," the reader may not get a feel for what it means to research organizations or markets *in the making* in *practical* terms. If one of the ambitions of this book is to treat markets, and the social more generally, as ongoing practical accomplishments, then why not subject research projects to the same ontology? Wouldn't such "practiced consistency" underscore more firmly that there are no such things as preconfigured entities (such as markets or organizations), but that actual hard work must go into their making? If this holds true for markets, this must also hold true for books.

Accordingly, this chapter shows how I assembled the material that informs this book. In this regard, I fuse a reflexive reconstruction of my own field work with more general methodological, epistemological, and political considerations.

In the remaining sections of this chapter I first introduce the tenets of what I call a "critical ethnography of marketization." I disclose how this approach was accomplished in the course of the research project. What is presented here is, however, rather an *ex-post* reconstruction, as already hinted at in Chapter 2, not an *ex ante* approach that was readily deployed. Ontological, epistemological, methodological, theoretical, ethical, and personal uncertainties and struggles were part and parcel of my research.

After discussing some of the "technical" practices through which the material informing this book has been produced, I spell out two particular challenges that I faced during the research process. These are, indeed, emblematic for the craft of ethnography and qualitative research more generally. First, the challenge of field access, whereby "the field" is not simply lying idly out there for the researcher to be discovered but is the product of hard work imbued with questions of power, politics, positionality, and legitimacy.

Second, the challenge to capture market practices inscribed in dynamic, ongoing relations. In the last section of this chapter, I address the problem of leaving "the field," writing/representation, and ethics.

Researching Markets in the Making

It is one thing to claim that we have to come to terms with how (agrifood) markets are made and extended and another to actually study such processes. So, how does one study markets in the making? How did I access the sites of "the market" *in situ*? In what follows, I outline the tenets of what I call a "critical ethnography of marketization."

First, the approach I propose here rests on the ontological, epistemological, and theoretical premises of a constructionist take on marketization, putting the formatting of goods, market agencies, and encounters as well as the stabilization of markets *in practice* at the center of empirical interest, while at the same time acknowledging that markets are always in the making, which involves processes of destabilization, crisis, and reconfiguration. This approach is "critical" in a Foucauldian sense (Foucault 1997[1984]) because it undoes capitalist markets more generally as self-evident, natural, and normal entities by defamiliarizing their sociotechnical foundations (Roy 2012: 34).

Second, a critical ethnography of marketization must not be understood in a methodologically reduced manner as mere participant observation. It is "less a practice of a specific method and more and more an orientation, a way of undertaking problematizations of the world" (Roy 2012: 34). Instead, it stands for a way of arranging sensitizing questions, sites of interest, and different methods of text generation and analysis in a recursive and reflexive manner (Davies 2008: 77; Ybema et al. 2009: 6) in order to unsettle the taken-for-granteds of global capitalism. The linchpin of such an approach is not only the researcher's relationship with the actual research process itself, but also to the "subjects" of research. What lies at the core of the ethnography of marketization being advanced here is a situated, embodied approach that conceives of "knowledge," "subjects," and "objects" as constituted by relationally, materially, and temporally embedded practices (Nicolini et al. 2003; Yeung 2003; Jazell & McFarlane 2010).

Third, as already highlighted in Chapter 2, such an empirical program does not envisage a mere deconstruction of a diversely articulated market discourse, as more representational approaches would do (Thrift & Olds 1996; Thrift 1997; Escobar 2005), but aims at the reconstruction of materially entangled market constructions.

Fourth, a critical ethnography of marketization does not render the "periphery" or the "local" a passive object subjugated by global forces (Nash 1981: 388). It traces proliferations of the social (in the sense of new associations), moving beyond the global–local dichotomies that populate much of the globalization literature:

> [W]henever anyone speaks of a "system," a "global feature," a "structure," a "society," an "empire," a "world economy," an "organization," the first ANT reflex should be to ask: "In which building? In which bureau? Through which corridor is it accessible? Which colleagues has it been read to? How has it been compiled?" [...] Inquirers, if they accept to follow this clue, will be surprised at the number of sites and the number of conduits that pop up as soon as those queries are being raised. The social landscape begins to change rather quickly. (Latour 2005: 183)

The program I am proposing here leans toward what is now known as "global ethnography" in anthropology, sociology, and geography (Gille & Riain 2002), but tries to eliminate the capitalocentric undertones of some of its strands. In this regard, it is Burawoy's sociologically grounded version of global ethnography that is particularly worth highlighting (Burawoy 1998, 2000a, 2000b) – the more so, as it has been productively used to study global commodity chains by other authors (Neilson & Pritchard 2009).

When coming from a social studies of economization and marketization (SSEM) and ANT corner, Burawoy's take on global ethnography at first appears quite attractive because he tries to move beyond the "sedentary-Trobriandan" tradition of anthropology (Boeckler 2005), striving to situate the concrete into its "extra-local," historical, and relational context ("extending out") without resorting to simple global–local dichotomies or causal determinisms (Burawoy 1998: 21). Yet, a closer reading of Burawoy's take on global ethnography suggests that his frictional bricolage of post-structuralist reflexivity, ethnography, and Marxian historical materialism is still at risk of perpetuating global–local determinisms (Hart 2004: 97). In his introduction to *Global Ethnography*, Burawoy states on one occasion that his project of "extending out" from concrete process to more general patterns does not treat the "micro as an expression of the macro," only to add that his reading of global ethnography focuses on the "extralocal determinations" of local phenomena (Burawoy 2000a: 27). Eventually, his project of global ethnography is committed to a reflexive approach "that extends *existing* theory to accommodate observed lacunae or anomalies" (ibid: 28).

The risk of sliding into global–local determinisms by embracing a close reading of Burawoy's take on global ethnography becomes even greater if we consider the thrust of his other works (see Stark & Bruszt 2001). Putting his version of global ethnography in the context of his broader (impressive) *ouevre*, one could provocatively argue that, despite the rhetoric about unwanted global–local determinations, similar to many other Marxists, Burawoy is "willing, for the sake of complexity, to play with difference so long as there is the guarantee of unity further on up the road" (Hall 1985: 92): the capitalist *telos*. Nevertheless, his take on global ethnography and the extended case method can serve as a productive contrast script. If given a different thrust, approached from an ANT-influenced perspective, the emphasis on history and "extra-local factors" in Burawoy's framework can have a sensitizing function. From such a perspective, the making of history would instead be conceived of as taking place "in many connected locales at once" (Moore 1987: 730; see also Mitchell 2000: 11). Past constructions often indeed have effects on present constructions as "structurally stable attributes" (Kleinman 1998: 286), as the literature on food regimes reminds us (Friedmann 1993; McMichael & Friedmann 2007). However, while there are times, or "fields of possibilities," as I would put it, following Foucault (1982: 789), when certain associations or effects are more likely than others, they should not be rendered so powerful and pervasive that the messiness of economic practice all but disappears.

Finally, the ethnography advanced here does not aim to mimic the accurate work of anthropologists for whom deep immersion in the field (Abolafia 1998) and "thick description" (Geertz 1973) have been the ultimate litmus tests for good ethnography.

I use the term "ethnography" not so much in an orthodox anthropological sense but as a marker for an epistemological strategy that is sensitive to the "ethnofoundations" (Burawoy 2000b: 344), or more precisely, "ethnotechnical" foundations of global agrifood markets.

So how does one trace the proliferation of a new market social? How does one study the "global agrifood economy" in concrete sites? How does one open the doors to the organizational settings in which in vivo market experiments (Çalışkan & Callon 2010: 20–21) take place? Finally, how does one make sure that the descriptions produced (in retrospect) are trustworthy?

Outside/Inside "the Market"

The main tenet of ethnographic research is often said to be the practice of deeply "immersing" oneself into the life world of practitioners (Emerson et al. 1995; Pollner & Emerson 2008: 118) in order to grasp the indexicality of actions and verbal expressions – the "actions-in-context," as Garfinkel (1967: 10) once put it. Only ethnographers who have never had encounters with poststructuralism, feminism, or postcolonial theory believe that such an immersion can fully succeed or take place "innocently" (Rose 1997; Jazeel & McFarlane 2010; Chakrabarty 2011; Werner 2012). If we adopt a relational approach to knowledge production, whereby "researchers" and "researched" alike are considered to co-generate what realist ethnographies usually deem as "data," ethnographic research needs to be understood not only as research *about* social relations, but also as one mediated *through* social relations (Crang & Cook 2007: 9; Rankin 2004: 6). But how are those relations forged? How does one deeply immerse oneself into large agribusiness companies, organizations that we usually encounter as black boxes? How can we translate Bruno Latour's programmatic postulate to "follow the actors" (Latour 2005: 63) and "study up" (ibid.: 98) into an "ethnographic strategy" (Neyland 2008: 25) when actors probably do not want to be followed in the very first place, when we are simply not in a position to do so, or when, thanks to our own desire for "structured" research, we do not let them choose their own paths? Shouldn't we likewise think about following the apparatus (Rabinow 2003; Roy 2012), or better, the *agencements*?

Couched in somewhat less abstract terms, similar questions occupied my mind when I approached the two case study companies in early 2008. I wanted them to become focal sites in my work, without even being sure whether the decision-makers would approve of this. Being aware that the project would collapse if the managers declined my request to study their operations, I dwelled in an uncomfortable state of uncertainty. The first step I took was to obtain information about the companies through the networks I had forged in advance with some local industry representatives and development practitioners, some of which had developed out of my previous research project on Kenyan horticulture (Ouma 2010). How high would the entry barriers be? As high as in most sectors of advanced capitalist economies, where "market-making is the province of corporate elites [...] [who] can let you in or keep you out and once you're in, you can still be asked to leave at any time," as Abolafia

(1998: 78–79) notes? Would the respective decision-makers be ready to allow an outsider to actually observe how "their market" is being performed on a day-to-day basis in a sector that is all about reputation?

After selecting the case studies, it dawned on me that the "corporate field" might be locked by many doors, and opening them was key to making the project a success. Consider the case of Ton:go Fruits (TF): when I knocked at the gates of the company on a hot and humid day, so typical for Ghana's tropical south, back in February 2008, the doors seemed to be left ajar. After I had fortunately managed to conduct a brief interview with a powerful senior manager of the company, he welcomed my study but thwarted my hopes for an in-depth ethnography:

> Ok, well let me just respond first of all to the confidentiality point you made: we live in a world which has in all fields become fiercely competitive and you've come from a worthy university in Germany, and we've now broken into that market and we are staggered at the response from other would-be entrepreneurs who've come in with similar products and almost to be the direct copies of what we're doing, we've been around for nearly eleven years now and yet we are suddenly faced with this competition. So, that has a bearing on what we like people to look at and so on. I don't, everything I read in your letter here and in the reference that backed it up gives me confidence that you're totally good of idea, but that doesn't mean to say that your readers are going to be totally good of idea [...] and I wouldn't, I don't particularly want to present all [the] opportunities which at the moment we're trying to use. The meetings with the farmers are pretty harmless to be honest with you, I don't see any real difficulty there [...]. We do, we are nervous about the factory, we are very nervous about the factory, outside, fine [...] but to actually look at the nuts and bolts of the internal part? [...]. I will put the lid on the inside of the factory myself, we just ask people not to do that [...]. (Interview, 2008)

Two-and-a-half years later, I again approached the company gates, which, for me in the meantime had become a powerful marker for being inside/outside. I was on my way to an early morning crisis meeting of the upper management in the same factory on which a lid had been put from the very beginning. When joining the meeting in the operations room, I was introduced as an "old friend of the company" by the manager quoted above – an affirmative statement which put my presence on new solid grounds. I felt I had arrived at the said "internal part," the "nuts and bolts" of my object of interest. What had happened in between? Answering this question necessitates a brief reflection on the factors on which my access to the field rested on and what can be learned from this.

When speaking of "the field" in the way many anthropologists have done for decades (Gupta & Ferguson 1997), one should bear in mind that it does not simply lie idly out there, just waiting to be discovered by the anthropologizing researcher, but that it is a genuinely associational project framed by the connections one is able to forge.[2] Forging connections in the case of TF and its farmers implied talking to the right people while respecting organizational hierarchies, assuring decision-makers' confidentiality and anonymity, and convincing them that I had a keen interest in even the most mundane things and routines. In this regard, I benefited from having won the consent and trust of two senior managers of the company who acted as important power brokers and did not object to my project, and therefore legitimized it in the long run. At the same time, I managed to link up with some lower management staff who became crucial key informants, brokers of knowledge without which ethnographies would not be possible (see Abolafia 1998: 80; Neyland 2008: 50). They not only facilitated my entry into their world of practices, providing multiple accounts, but also helped me forge important contacts with farmers.[3]

As time went by, I was also able to exploit networks in TF to gain access to backstage practices (see the following text), which raises certain ethical issues to be addressed in the last section of this chapter. My own positionality as a male, German-Kenyan academic probably also had a certain leverage effect during the research process because it helped me to get access to the mostly male managers in the company's agronomy department, who would sometimes sympathetically refer to my own "Africanness," a hybrid and situationally performed identity in itself. Gaining access to the agronomy department was central as it was the prime link to the farmers.

My account may quickly be interpreted as suggesting that an ethnographer has been successful when she has become a "member" and, thereby, has become part of more stable social relations that mediate and constitute "the field" at the same time. But the story of doing critical ethnographies is a more complex one. First, becoming a member (Neyland 2008: 51) is never fully complete but resembles a continuously negotiated relationship, imbued with the fine-grained workings of power, politics, controversies, conflicts, and accounts. Second, it is a double-scripted story, one that is about familiarizing oneself with others in the sense of "forging connections" while defamiliarizing the materially entangled practices these relational others are engaged with at the same time (Roy 2012). All this reminds us that research is an ongoing practical accomplishment in itself.

Similar dynamics played out in the mango case study, where I quickly forged relationships with key managers of OFL and the administrator of the Association of Organic Mango Outgrowers (AOMO), a Dagomba with extensive knowledge of the area. He arranged meetings with farmers, acted as a translator and organized many aspects of my "field access," from transportation to accommodation in a local community where I stayed for some time. Access to the farmers, mostly Dagomba who often only spoke their vernacular *Dagbani*, proved to be quite difficult owing to their scattered location, so the administrator's work was of great help.[4] Fortunately, my immersion into the "corporate field" went much further in this case, although my presence seemed to be treated with suspicion by some managers at the very beginning as they had become tired of development tourists coming to visit the project.

Yet, by and by, I was able to forge more stable social relations with the company and AOMO staff. This was also due to the fact that I became involved in working for AOMO in 2009, helping the organization's administrator with applications for funding from development organizations. Gradually, I became more and more embedded into the outgrower complex by wandering between the sphere of AOMO and OFL. Frontiers can be lonely places, and some of the higher-ranking OFL managers, some of whom were expats hailing from different countries, gradually welcomed my "being there." I became a guest of various OFL managers in the course of the research project, sharing food and social space. These "veranda conversations" gave me a very different idea of what occupied their work and private life alike, namely, the tedious making of markets in northern Ghana. The stable links to AOMO and OFL provided me with many opportunities for an extended exposure to the outgrower scheme, giving me privileged "access" to manifold verbal, practical, and written accounts.

What may appear as a linear and smooth research process to the reader, however, resembled a precarious interactional order in practice. Questions about my positionality and the legitimacy of my work lie at the core of this problem. Knowledge production must always be conceived of as situated – as being dependent on the position of the researcher in local/translocal, materially entangled, and power-laden social relations. What is often staged as an act of autonomous knowledge production by realists is *de facto* an intersectional, often asymmetrically structured cogeneration of knowledge (Rose 1997; Burawoy 1998: 14–15). Both of my case studies demonstrate what many other ethnographers of organizations have noted elsewhere: that knowledge production itself equals a relational, practical accomplishment that is not only mediated through power relations and politics, manifold processes of (non-/mis-)translation and social performances related to "class," "gender," "age," "race,"[5] and so on, but also requires a great deal of legitimacy. Both the positionality and the legitimacy of ethnographic work are constituted in inter-situationally dynamic ways, and a researcher's identity and positionality may shift during the course of research (Marcus 1995: 112; Rose 1997: 314).

During my project, the production of identity and legitimacy generated itself as an ongoing balancing act. They were truly performative and "negotiated in context" (Schwartz-Shea & Yanow 2009: 60): how do you communicate a "critical" research theme to informants? How do you justify your ongoing presence even during times of crisis[6] (see Chapter 8)? How do you respond to the demands of managers or farmers who may relate to you as an "expert" from a reputable European university who could help them to fix certain problems? Or do you explain to farmers that you are independent of the company staff they had seen you hang around with so many times? Variations of these problems kept me struggling throughout the project. Tackling them required not only situational accountability, but also the nurturing of durable social relations through the performative-cum-reiterative construction of trust (see Beckert 2005). Thus, some of the findings of this research were eventually shared with the case study companies.

In the mango case study, the perceived pressure to establish legitimacy for my research was even greater as some of my counterparts would repeatedly ask me how I could help the mango project. Eventually I got involved with AOMO and did some capacity building work with them, which put my presence on new legitimate grounds. My justification for hanging around in the outgrower scheme was thus no longer based on simply doing research but "working with AOMO," as I would frequently state during my accounts toward OFL managers and farmers alike. Such acts of situated engagement can frequently vault one into a limbo between familiarization and defamiliarization – between careful distance and local engagement (*familiarization*) and disconnecting ontologically (*defamiliarization*), a process which in itself is *always in the making*.

But the classical anthropological call to become a member begs another important question when it comes to studying hybrid market encounters: which "group" to become a member of? In the setting where I conducted my research, I often sat awkwardly on the fence, working with company staff and farmers alike. Some farmers were not sure about my role and feared talking openly about specific problems, probably because they thought I was either working with TF or OFL. On one occasion, this perception went so far that some farmers supplying TF refused to give me any further information, arguing I was more on the side of the company than on the side of the farmers. Other farmers simply tried to avoid encounters. Although some of these misunderstandings could be solved in the course of the project, I nevertheless had the constant feeling that I was "stuck in between," and that this could sooner or later thrust me into local politics, which it did several times. In retrospect, of course, the question arises whether one can be stuck in between when groups themselves are always in the making (Latour 2005: 27).

"Reconstructing" Market Practices

Before I deal with the question of how I attempted to grasp crucial practices of market-making as part of a critical ethnography of marketization, some remaining epistemological issues need to be addressed. What "claims of knowledge" (Neyland 2008: 42) can be made within the framework of the type of ethnography proposed here and how "trustworthy" (Schwartz-Shea & Yanow 2009) are they?

As already briefly outlined in Chapter 2, the basic epistemological assumption of a constructionist ethnography is first and foremost that performative, reality-accomplishing ways of knowing are embedded in relationally, temporarily, and materially entangled practices (Nicolini et al. 2003). The term "practice" includes the verbal and nonverbal aspects of action as representations and agents' "(self-) descriptions, conceptualizations and analyses are themselves socially organized practices" in a broader sense (Pollner & Emerson 2008: 122–123). The knowledge inscribed in these practices can only be explicated to some extent by informants during interviews, something that is not the case with theoretical, discursive knowledge (Giddens 1979: 40).

Therefore, the attention must shift to the "submundane practices" (Ybema et al. 2009: 3) of market agents associated within a common setting (e.g., an organization, a specific market site, an industry). This is exactly what "follow the actors" asks us to do: to allow informants[7] to unfold their own frames of reference, vocabularies, and theories by temporarily suspending (or at least trying to) one's own frames of reference as a researcher (Latour 2005: 30). This postulate applies to both the conduct of interviews and the ethnographic gaze of the researcher. "Follow the actors" by no means implies that the "search for order, rigor, and pattern is [...] abandoned" but that "it is simply relocated one step further into abstraction so that actors are allowed to unfold their own differing cosmos, no matter how counter-intuitive they appear" (ibid.: 23). Thus, regardless of the fact that some consider Latour's program (Krarup & Blok 2011) or the "Callonistics" (Fine 2003) associated with it as a recipe for a new empiricism that lacks explanatory power,[8] my own take on "follow the actors" is to understand it as a sensitizing methodological concept: frequently, the sociotechnical *agencements* through which seemingly "social facts" such as markets are enacted are much too fragile, messy, and frictional for them to be molded into preconfigured, stable categories,[9] though abstraction, with all its postcolonial pitfalls (Jazeel & McFarlane 2010; Werner 2012), must have its place in later stages of the research process.

This performative stance formed the backdrop of my empirical work, even though it was not systematically explicated as an *ex ante* position. Given the SSEM's interest in the diverse forms of knowledge, know-how, and skills produced and mobilized in the process of marketization (Çalışkan & Callon 2010: 19), a more profound engagement with epistemological and methodological aspects was needed than had been displayed in much of the work in the SSEM at the time when I started the project.

In order to transcend this problem, I drew on earlier works in both ANT as well as in organizational ethnography (Law 1992; Nicolini et al. 2003; Neyland 2008; Ybema et al. 2009). From an ANT perspective, the practically grounded knowledge involved in building a market must neither be understood as a mental substance inscribed in individuals, nor can it be imagined as a self-standing body of knowledge (an object) or an all-embracing discourse; it is instead a process inscribed in collective practices and material devices (e.g., management handbooks, contracts, etc.). Hence, I focused particularly on the distributed forms of knowledge mobilized within the making, reproduction, and remaking of market STAs in the two case studies, which manifest themselves in not only what people say but also in what they do (and use).

Technicalities?

As discussed in Chapter 2, "knowing the market" can be understood as the capacity to effectively align human and nonhuman elements so that a good can be qualified and objectified to a given modality of valuation, calculated, and detached.[10] What I did during my research was to trace how people performed these alignments during interviews or their daily work. Such reconstructions are never mere technical processes but constitute themselves particular ways of imagining and working upon the social.

In order to grasp the market performances related to my case studies, I at first utilized a range of methods for text cogeneration. I conducted in-depth interviews with senior and ordinary managers and farmers for each case study between February 2008 and October 2010. In the beginning, these interviews contained a selection of quite focused questions because I needed to develop a basic understanding of organizational processes and practices in an unfamiliar environment. In the course of my research, this approach became increasingly at odds with the praxeological stance I was increasingly developing. Accordingly, I tried to frame much more open-ended interview questions at later stages of the project. Yet, even those interviews still contained a number of key topics and issues that were to be covered during the interview. Several managers and farmers were interviewed repeatedly over the course of the project, and this enabled me to capture opinions, perceptions, justifications, attitudes, and practical accounts at various stages of the market-making projects, or to confront informants with issues that remained unclear to me after previous interviews. Even though the foci of the interviews were informed by some general perspectives and prior knowledge on the working of the global agrifood economy, they were adjusted in the course of the project in response to newly emerging themes, ad hoc ideas, or crucial events that impacted the trajectories of the two case studies. The interviews also recorded some structural characteristics of farmers.

This set of interviews was complemented by interviews with auxiliary market-makers such as development practitioners, service providers, or NGO officials, who provided important contextual information on the industry and policy context. This approach was adopted for both case studies, but slightly modified for the research in northern Ghana. For the latter, I also interviewed officials of NGOs in New York, and Brussels, who were supporting the mango project. When possible, all interviews were tape-recorded.

Various other techniques of text cogeneration were employed. For the mango case study, several focus group discussions were conducted in 2008 in order to capture a variety of accounts from different groups in different localities of the outgrower scheme. These groups were selected according to three criteria: (1) year joined; (2) "success" (in terms of perceived performance and productivity, which was established by talking to the AOMO administrator as well as by looking into production statistics); (3) land-related problems, which were assumed to be an indicator of the potential negative effects of mango cultivation and marketization. Three of the groups were revisited for interviews in August 2010. Even though the focus group discussions were not as productive as envisioned owing to language barriers and the unwillingness of many farmers to discuss critical issues in public, these, nevertheless, provided some tentative insights into different opinions, perceptions, and accounts of the mango out-growers. In some cases, individual farmers were selected from the groups in order to gain a more detailed insight into certain issues. This was complemented by interviews with individual farmers, who were perceived to be particularly good informants owing to their literacy levels (such as the chairman of AOMO).[11]

Focus group discussions were only conducted in the mango case study as it was difficult to organize pineapple farmers in the south for such meetings because many of them were hesitant to voice their opinions in public. Further, I thought focus group discussions in the mango case study would do more justice to the sheer size of the outgrower scheme and make it possible to at least capture a glimpse of the different practical realities in the scheme.

Moreover, ethnographic interviews with managers, farmers, or market-makers helped me to collect more situated perspectives formed off-side the rather staged, formal interview. These ethnographic interviews were closely entangled with my participation in the daily routines of company staff, managers, and some farmers, which I documented in a field diary. These "written accounts" (Emerson et al. 1995: 1) gave my material a more grounded and reflexive touch, helping to counterbalance some of the mistakes I made during interviews, where I sometimes did not manage to tap into the practical knowledge of my informants despite my initial goal of doing so. It further allowed me to study some of the backstage activities informants either would not reflect upon or were hesitant to talk about during formal interviews. Thus, the field notes served an important supportive and reflexive function in my project.

My ethnographically inclined take on practices of market-making also comprised the collection of artifacts such as quality handbooks, contracts, or cost calculations, which later served as important material entry points for studying market STAs in the two case studies. When selecting informants or situations for participant comprehension, I adopted a purposive and theoretical sampling strategy through which I tried to enhance my "exposure" (Schwartz-Shea & Yanow 2009: 67) to different lived experiences, practical contexts, and controversial situations as much as possible.

At a later stage of the project, I also experimented with "participants' diaries" (Neyland 2008: 121) in order to compensate for the fact that where the action is the ethnographer is not (Law 1994: 45). In the pineapple case study, this task was assigned to one of my key informants, whose identity and organizational affiliation cannot be further revealed. His/her task was to note down market-related events that had a significant impact on the daily practices in the agribusiness–outgrower complex. In the mango case study, a similar task was assigned to a staff member of AOMO. Given the fact that the mango case study revolved around the solution of a number of market-making problems that differed from those of the pineapple case study, the research assistant was instructed to note down production-, group-, organization-, land-, and community-related problems, as well as other interesting observations. Altogether, the participants each documented a period of eight weeks in 2010, but the quality of the observations differed very much in terms of detail, articulation, and focus.

These ethnographic techniques were complemented by an analysis of secondary data provided by policy papers on Ghana's horticulture subsector and fresh produce market information systems.

The methods employed here produced a very heterogeneous text material that was not always easy to analyze or integrate. Although the heterogeneous nature of the material must not be ignored, its quality is a direct result of my empirical strategy, which had been evolutionary rather than preconfigured, often responsive to the ongoing transformation of my own research "object" and my own positionality. Experimenting with different methods allowed me to illuminate different facets of the market-making projects.

Knowledge Production: Heuristics and Limitations

How did I coproduce the knowledge that informs this book, which heuristics did I use and what are the limits to the knowledge claims made hereafter?. For the reconstruction of market practices, insights from different approaches were pragmatically combined. Elements of grounded theory (Strauss & Corbin 2003), particularly the use of methodological, theoretical, and empirical memos, helped to organize spontaneous thoughts or reflexive moments into a dense narrative.

Both during the actual processes of text generation as well as during the analysis of the material, the use of "sensitizing concepts" (Bowen 2006) such as "practices," "qualification," "ordering," "*agencement*," or "framing" helped me reflect upon what I heard or saw in the field without molding anything immediately into preconfigured or closed concepts. Insights from ethnomethodology attuned me for the precariousness, situatedness, relationality, and the composite character of social orders (Garfinkel 1967; Thévenot 2001a). It also raised my awareness of the importance of accounts during social encounters, equipping me with a sense of reflexivity toward my own accounts during different field encounters.

Furthermore, in the tradition of a processual ethnography, I paid particular attention to what anthropologist Sally Moore calls "diagnostic events" (Moore 1987; see also Elyachar 2005: 94–95), a variant of a "situational analysis."[12] For Moore, speaking initially about processes of social change and changing relations of property in Tanzania, these are events that reveal "ongoing contests and conflicts and competitions and the efforts to prevent, suppress, or repress these" (Moore 1987: 730). Focusing on these events allows the researcher to identify the disruption of historical structures in social settings, which only then become evident as "social" structures in the first place. For my peculiar endeavor, I modified the concept and applied it to situations where either the formatting of goods, agencies, and encounters, and thus the work of stabilizing agrifood market STAs, became particularly evident (e.g., during audits, quality checks, training sessions for farmers, management meetings, etc.); or to situations when controversies and conflicts threatened or disrupted the stability of market STAs, interrogating their historical configuration, durability, and effectiveness.

In this regard, it should be noted that the postulate to follow the actors must rather be understood as a sensitizing warning, as it can never be fully achieved. Market practices can never be fully grasped in the context of coexistent, divergent, and at times frictional frames of reference that pop up during the worldly encounters of ethnographic practice. Even though mistranslations can be cushioned to some extent by triangulating the process of text generation with respect to time, place, person, and choice of method (Yeung 2003: 455) – something I tried to do throughout the research process – global ethnographers are nevertheless always predisposed in relational, material, and cognitive terms – they "cannot be outside the global processes they study" (Burawoy 2000a: 4).

Disclosing what these relational, material, and cognitive dispositions were, and how far one actually succeeded in allowing actors to unfold their own vocabulary and frames of reference before they are captured in more abstract terms at a later stage, significantly determines the quality of the reconstruction process. Even if a full suspension remains an illusion in the end, such a reflexive approach at least brings to the surface the knowledge struggles that underpin any kind of social research. Far too often, the problem of the struggle of different frames of reference for knowing and doing the social is fetishized by a ritualized description of a frictionless and straightforward research process. I myself, for instance, often failed to actually follow the actors in the way I had initially envisaged. For instance, at the beginning of the project, during interviews with managers or farmers, I often followed my interview questions too rigidly and, therefore failed to pick up on invitations from my informants to move more toward issues that really mattered to them during the daily performance of markets.

Furthermore, the ambitious aim of following managers and farmers was often thwarted by a range of very practical problems: some informants often had little time, others (such as some farmers) were entangled in asymmetrical relationships with the case study companies or even interpreters, while many conversations, especially those with farmers, were shaped by physical or language barriers of varying degrees. While I only had to use an interpreter for a few interviews with farmers in the pineapple case study, I had to use an interpreter for almost all interviews with farmers in Ghana's north. Other conversations or observations were simply not feasible because the action was *there* but I *was not* (Law 1994: 45). For instance, owing to teaching commitments, I never had a chance to be present during the actual harvesting of mangoes around April in the northern case study, obviously a crucial market encounter during which a range of dynamics and controversies may play out (see Chapter 7). I could thus only reconstruct these encounters via interviews or from the notes of my research assistant.

However, the problem described here goes beyond "being at the right place at the right time" and is also rooted in the fact that with regard to organizations or global supply chains, we always have to make the Goffmanian distinction between "frontstage appearances" and "backstage activities" (Ybema et al. 2009: 5) – between idiosyncratic and public spaces of economization (Thévenot 2001b). By not only making others an object of research but also one's own research practices, struggles, and anxieties via an "auto-ethnography" (Neyland 2008: 54), the hardship of following the actors, with all its (often unintended) silencing, dominating, and normalizing effects (Rose 1997; Burawoy 1998), at least becomes traceable for the reader. This hardship is by no means a merely methodological or technical matter but is also a very physical one, as the ethnographic snapshot presented at the beginning of this chapter suggests. One's own feelings, bodily experiences, and affective decisions during the laborious act of research are firmly entangled with what Geertz (1973: 67) calls "inscriptions," often impinging in significant ways upon the quality of the claims of knowledge that can be made in retrospect.

After "the Field": *Veni, Vidi, Vici*?

The great anthropologist Clifford Geertz once posed a simple question only to give an even simpler answer: "What does the ethnographer do? – he writes" (ibid.: 67). Of course, Geertz thought that ethnography was a more complex endeavor. He posed that question deliberately to reject a "veni-vidi-vici-conception of writing" (ibid.), in which the ethnographer simply observes, records, and analyzes as if these were smooth and autonomous operations. Writing ethnographies is surely a more complex issue (Clifford 1986). Theory, methodology, interpretation/analysis, and writing cannot be separated into autonomous acts. Instead, these must be conceived of as different·layers of textualization that we cannot disentangle as we move between them (Van Maanen 1988, cited in Wolfinger 2002: 86). Those layers of textualization are shaped in process and interrelate dynamically in the processes of writing and research more generally. Accordingly, the empirical accounts that follow are not the product of a linear process but of such dynamic textual interdependencies and feedback loops.

Equally important, Geertz noted long before Giddens (1983), anthropological writings are "not [a] logical reconstruction of a mere reality" (Geertz 1973: 67), but are second- and third-order interpretations; they are "fictions, in the sense that they are 'something made,' 'something fashioned'" (ibid.: 64; see also Clifford 1986: 6). One does not need to be wedded to a Geertzian version of "thick description" to acknowledge the intricacies of writing ethnographies, and one may even extend this to texts based on qualitative research more generally (Boeckler 2005). Against this backdrop, what follows in the empirical sections is a practical accomplishment, and I am firmly part of it. It is a reconstruction of constructions, albeit a modest and at times a messy one, one that never fully succeeds in following the actors.

However, there is more to the process of writing, the time often simply rendered as "after the field." After we have left it and eventually assemble our manuscripts, the relationships we forged during our research do not simply disappear. To some extent, this has always been the case, but in times of digital connections and mobile phones, such social relationships are more likely to persist or experience unexpected twists. Former research assistants may approach you for financial help; former interviewees may want to read about your research results. All this is embedded into a wider communicative field where "researcher," the "researched," as well as contextual, technological, and institutional parameters (e.g., the pressure to publish in international journals accessible via the Internet) interact in dynamic ways (Clifford 1986: 6; Crang & Cook 2007: 154). Important personal and ethical questions are attached to this. "Publishing commodity chains" (Hughes & Reimer 2005) is a delicate issue, as Cook has so vividly demonstrated in his research on Jamaica–UK fruits trade relationships (Crang & Cook 2007: 30–32). What if former interviewees see one's work on the Internet and feel themselves misrepresented? How does one avoid disclosing confidential information whose publication might harm informants or their organizations but retain a critical stance throughout research? I had been occupied with such questions from the very beginning of my research and not just when I "wrote up" my findings.

One way to counter this problem was to assure all of my interviewees anonymity, and a responsible treatment of the research material – interviewee names, places, product destinations, customers, and even competitors would be given other names. I always made clear to corporate interviewees that I was interested in the question of what their daily work was like, not in "undigging" anything or creating negative publicity. I underlined that conflicts and controversies are naturally part of business life and that I did not consider them as something unusual. I was there to observe and understand, not to judge and uncover. It somehow worked. But winning the trust and help of so many people made writing difficult as I continued to be embedded in some of the networks I had forged. Everyone reading the following sections should be aware that I could not simply "write up" things.

Writing up was a constant struggle in a field marked by four gravitational forces: First, the research relationships I had forged, and the promises, obligations, and pressures associated with them. Second, the need to write the kind of critical, "vivid, in-depth account of [...] field experiences which good ethnographies are supposed to contain" (Crang & Cook 2007: 154–155). Third, the insight that one can never get it fully "right" and that my view of things does not necessarily correspond with the view of the people I researched. Fourth, the point that I may have missed something, dominated or silenced voices from the field, or normalized what I observed in such ways that it became graspable with my own vocabulary (Burawoy 2000; Jazeel & McFarlane 2010). Thus, what follows is my own situated account enmeshed into a complex network of different (postcolonial) relationships. It is against this backdrop that I can only but agree with Elyachar (2005: 36):

> Ethnographies are analytical constructions of scholars; the people they study are not. It is part of the anthropological exercise to acknowledge how much larger is their creativity than what any particular analysis can encompass.

"Being there" does not mean "getting it right." As Jazeel & MacFarlane (2010: 111) note, "[t]he 'field' has its own politics, urgencies, necessities." Thus, the account that follows is guilty of partly decontextualizing knowledge though abstraction, and mis-translations are part of the game. I hope, however, that what I write here is a responsible account and at least follows the actors as much as the postcolonial politics of knowledge production permit.

Conclusion

In this chapter, I provided a reconstruction of my own reconstruction of market con-structions in the two frontier regions. My goal was to convey a sense of what it means in *practical* terms to research global (agrifood) markets in the making, arguing that we cannot simply black-box how we go about studying processes of marketization, given that a range of methodological, epistemological, political, ethical, and personal questions are entangled with such a project. I outlined the tenets of a critical ethnography of mar-ketization, an approach that is sensitive to the "ethnotechnical" foundations of seemingly global economic entities, even though mine is a modest ethnography that does not aim to mimic the detailed work of anthropologists and their thick descriptions, but aims to defamiliarize the market social. I also demonstrated the special character of ethnographic research, which is not just research about social relations but research embedded into social relations. Like all more durable social relations, they are shaped by dynamics, conflicts, obligations, and accounts, all of which warrant a constant reflection on the side of the researching subject with regard to the fact that the practice of ethnography always resembles a difficult and skillful navigation whose "field" is grounded by dynamic, unfolding social relations. Like the phenomena it studies, critical ethnographies of mar-ketization must themselves be considered as being "always in the making."

The critical project I outlined here does not simply end after we left "the field." In today's globalized world, we cannot simply disentangle ourselves from the networks we have forged in "the field," as writing ethnographies of marketization is often influ-enced by network effects reaching beyond the actual empirical "field." Networks in the digital age are stronger than we sometimes wish.

Endnotes

1   In this book, all names of individuals, of the case study companies and related organizations, and their geographical associations have been anonymized, are withheld or have been altered to protect sources. Development organizations and programs associated with the Ghanaian agricultural sector more generally are referred to by their original names.

2   In their comprehensive review of how "the field" has been conceived of in anthropology, Gupta and Ferguson (1997: 5) note that the term is often being used as "a clearing whose deceptive transparency obscures the complex processes that go into constructing it."

3   One even acted as a translator in a double sense. On the one hand he explained backstage market practices to me as an outsider, and on the other hand he translated interviews with farmers from the local Twi dialect into English. Even though certain power effects on the informants cannot be denied given the informant's affiliation, he appeared to be generally perceived as somebody trustworthy by the farmers because he was a member of the lower management and interacted with them on a daily basis as part of his job assignment.

4   Owing to resource and time constraints, no retranslations of these interviews were made.

5   It should be noted that many ANT scholars, for all their reflexivity, tend to neglect these factors when they write about "following the actors." As much as we would like to follow the actors, the "translations" from local to academic knowledge are still mediated by multifarious power relations (Rose 1997: 315; Jazeel & McFarlane 2010) and interpretative struggles (Giddens 1983: 14–15; Schwartz-Shea & Yanow 2009: 56).

6   See Bachmann (2011) on this problem.

7   "Informants" refers to people interrogated in formal interviews but also to those who are simply being observed or interrogated *in situ* (via so-called "ethnographic interviews").

8   In discussions about the critical potential of ANT, the question of whether it can move beyond mere description and provide explanations for certain phenomena is often posed. For many ANT scholars, the distinction between explanation and description is obsolete. A good descriptive account that shows how something becomes socially durable (or better, how controversies about the "social" are stabilized) is explanatory at the same time (Latour 2005).

9   See Law (1994: 46) on this problem.

10   "Knowing the market" is itself a matter of qualification.

11   In all, 97 semi-structured interviews were conducted: 21 with single TF suppliers; 11 with single mango outgrowers, including one chief (two others were interviewed ethnographically); 12 group focus discussions with mango outgrowers; 29 with company managers, staff, and directors; 5 with other exporters in the pineapple subsector; 16 with auxiliary market-makers such as development organizations; and 3 with representatives from farmers groups in Densu Valley, who were former *Farmapine* members (see Chapter 8). Furthermore, complementary survey data were collected on farmers in both case study regions.

12   For his study on contract farming in the Philippines, Vellema deployed a "situational analysis," for which I have great sympathy. Such analysis "implies detailed descriptions of particular instructive events. It also implies the incorporation of organizational politics and technological puzzles as a normal rather than an exceptional part of social process in contract farming communities [...]. [It] provides a close-up view of social interaction and problem solving, in order to elucidate how the social relation works out in everyday, problematic situations" (Vellema 2002: 18).

Chapter Five
The Birth of Global Agrifood Market Connections

When leaving the regional hub Tamale to the north, one enters an area where land still seems abundant. Villages made up of Dagomba compound houses often hosting several households border the tarmac road to Burkina Faso. Outside the villages, farmers work in their maize farms. Women return from collecting groundnuts, skillfully balancing the filled bowls on their heads. Others are in the "bush" collecting shea nuts, which they later sell to traders from Tamale. The nuts, and the butter derived from them, generate an important additional income for many households here and have been indeed the first global commodities to be exported from northern Ghana. Some cattle stroll in between, guarded by Fulani herdsmen, who often work as trustees for other farmers' livestock in exchange for land and crops. In low-lying alluvial lands, farmers plant rice. Most of the farmers living in this area are "peasants," cultivating a few acres of maize, cowpeas, rice, or groundnuts with family labor. Well-off farmers have some livestock. Where people have access to streams such as the White Volta, they usually back up their meager incomes with fishing. Others engage in petty trade or hunting. Seasonal food insecurity is rampant in an area with low crop productivity levels, poor infrastructure and government support, and vulnerability to flood and drought.

As already argued in Chapter 1, when observers try to make sense of such landscapes, they often do so by rendering them as "absent objects" (Mbembe 2001: 241), as spaces that have been left untouched by the blessings of "modernity," "development," "capitalism," or "the market." In 1937, a British colonial agricultural officer described

Assembling Export Markets: The Making and Unmaking of Global Food Connections in West Africa, First Edition. Stefan Ouma.
© 2015 John Wiley & Sons, Ltd. Published 2015 by John Wiley & Sons, Ltd.

northern Ghana (then known as the Northern Territories) as follows: "Farming is regarded as a custom and not as a business, with the result that in crop production and in animal husbandry the maximum is left to nature" (Lynn 1937; cited in Blench 1996: 1). Such "economic otherings" continue to persist in various disguises in popular, academic, and policy discourses. As previously argued, in addition to structural-historical factors, the failure of the post-colonial state to engineer development and the conspicuous absence of private investments are said to have contributed to the "underdevelopment" of northern Ghana (Songsore 2011).

The Organic Fruits Limited (OFL)[1] project promised prosperity, at least for a few chosen farmers. Covering large swathes of land, mango orchards have become a marker of change in several districts of northern Ghana. OFL has not only been supporting local farmers by providing interest-free loans used to finance the growing of mango trees, but has also heavily invested in social and material infrastructure. These markers of "community development" are visible in several villages. Schools have been built, irrigation systems have been installed, and food crops have been introduced in order to provide additional security to farmers who in the past would often face food shortages before the annual harvest of their crops.

Each (agrifood) market has its own temporality in that it is a variegated series of *agencements* that organize the production, exchange, circulation, and consumption of goods. This becomes strikingly evident if we move some several hundred kilometers down south to the splendid processing facilities of Ton:go Fruits (TF). Taking a walk through the modern factory equipped with cutting-edge cooling and processing technology, one is immediately struck by how deeply just-in-time (JIT) principles have permeated contemporary agriculture. It is a typical early morning. At the gate, some casual workers hope for a job. They may be lucky if orders are high and additional labor is needed in the factory. A farmer has just arrived with pineapples from his farm, waving his supplier tag, and waiting for the turnpike to be lifted. The agronomy department looks a busy place. Some agronomists are sitting over the supply and planting program for pineapples. Are the forecasts right? Do supply and demand match? How much to grow for the next season? Others are preparing for the GLOBALG.A.P. audit to come around next week. The "pre-harvesters" are out in the field, checking whether suppliers' fruits are ready to harvest. At the fruit in-take, a crucial rite of passage for every incoming fruit, another farmer offloads his truck brimful of pineapples (see Figure 5.1). Meticulously ordered in crates, they are still fresh, having been harvested only few hours ago. He must be relieved. After 14 tiresome months of production, the delivery day has arrived, and the farmer is ready to cash in on the fruits of his (and his laborers') work after his delivery day had been postponed owing to changing orders from the retailers. The pineapples are weighed, and a quality assurance officer checks whether they meet the strict quality criteria of the company. There is no time to waste; there is a pressing order. The fruits then enter a washing basin and are processed in the high-care facility, an area governed by tight hygiene regulations. In this sterile and cooled place, women under pressure to meet lead times skillfully top, tail, skin, and cut the pineapples, which are then weighed, sealed into 200 g tubs, and labeled according to the specifications of one of the dozen or so retail customers. The tubs are then cooled, packed into cardboard boxes, and transferred to

Figure 5.1   A truck being loaded with pineapples on a farm. (Author's photo.)

a cargo container, ready for dispatch just 45 minutes later. It is a unfamiliar sight to
see Ghanaian men and women wearing thick winter jackets, gloves, and bonnets to
protect themselves against the 5 °C cold environment in the dispatch area. As part of
the free zone arrangement (see Chapter 3, Excursus 3.2), an on-site customs officer
inspects and seals off the container so that no precious time is lost at airport customs
control. The container is ready to fly. In the operations room, the production manager
is relieved as the mission has almost been accomplished. It is a hard job as orders may
rise or drop as little as 24 hours in advance of the agreed delivery time. Some European
retailers are, in fact, not the most reliable customers. It's about time. In the late
afternoon, a large cooled company truck leaves the premises and heads toward the
airport in Accra. The driver rushes to catch the evening flight to a city in Europe,
maneuvering his precious yet fragile load through the thick traffic jams of the sprawling
metropolis. At the airport, the containers are packed onto the plane, which heads off
to Europe. The pineapples arrive in Europe in the early morning hours of the next
day, from where they are taken to the airport perishables-handling center. The quality
is checked again and the fruits are brought to the distribution center of a large retail
chain. It is about noon. The fruits are sorted according to the retailer's store order.
Delivery to the store is made in the early morning hours of the next day. From
7:00 a.m. onward, an affluent but time-poor urban clientele buys the fruits "fresh
from farm," probably having an "exotic" breakfast. In less than 48 hours, the pineapples (or other fruits, depending on the order) have made it from "field to fork." On
their journey, the fruits have not only crossed physical barriers but also regulatory

ones. As the company is certified to a whole range of product and processing standards of European provenance, their product is not simply "fruits" but a highly regulated and complexly framed good that has found its way from the plains of Aborobe to Northern tables. Having passed through a tightly coordinated supply chain that folds together heterogeneous human and nonhuman elements within a closely defined window of time, the good itself is a collective accomplishment that should attract our interest.

★ ★ ★

In this chapter, I show how parts of southern and northern Ghana were turned into focal sites of export-oriented marketization through the projects of some quick-witted entrepreneurs and their managers. Yet it will become evident that such projects of "world market integration" do not represent smooth transitions. Neither in the organic mango nor in the JIT pineapples project were local farmers simply "incorporated" or "encadred" (Amanor 1999: 34) into new sociomaterial relations, as if market-making was a process of "diffusion" (Latour 1986: 266). As I have already suggested in Chapter 1, universals do not simply take over the world (Tsing 2005: 8) but have to "mobilize adherents" (ibid.: 8), some of whom are quite recalcitrant. No mobilization is without friction. Everything starts small. Accordingly, in the first section of this chapter, I shall disentangle how corporate investments turned into complex market arrangements – how micro-actors grew to macro-size (Callon & Latour 1981: 277). In the subsequent section, it will become clear that the making of organic mango outgrowers and JIT suppliers required extensive ontological recon-figurations. These in turn hinged upon diverse monetary, social, technical, proce-dural, and scientific investments. In the last section, I demonstrate that assembling export market connections in both cases was not only about making outgrowers/suppliers, implementing "market hardware" and "outflanking nature," but also about linking up with buyers abroad as well as producing goods that fit into their world. As a whole, I am particularly interested in the multiple agendas driving the two marketization projects and their formative stages.

As can be seen from the foregoing ethnographic snapshots, producing JIT pineapples for European retailers is characterized by significantly different dynamics and complexities than the seasonal production of organic mangoes. Even though there is common ground between both market-making projects with regard to the qualifica-tion of goods, managers, farmers, and workers, they represent two distinct market models at different stages of development, enacted within different "worldly encounters" (Tsing 2005: 4).

Nothing Was Packaged for (High-value) Export

One day in 2009, I sat in the spacious conference room of TF with Mr. Sneijder, the founder of the company, talking to him about the development of the Ghanaian pine-apple business. How fortunate I was! He was a busy person, and it should by no means be taken for granted that he would spare some time for a "field-making" academic.

It had all started with a 15 minutes interview in early 2008 that he had willingly granted me at the beginning of my research. Over the course of time, we repeatedly met, and he would share and reflect in considerable depth upon what it means to forge global market connections from Ghana. He also facilitated my entry into various corporate meetings. Mr. Sneijder was a hands-on person, respected by many workers and farmers alike. He was the driving force behind TF, a visionary entrepreneur who was proud of the corporate model and the "culture" the company was based on. He seemed to live the corporate "culture" he was promoting, knowing many of his workers by name, stopping here and there for a joke or a word of motivation. Yet at the same time, he was commercially minded, a sound strategist, knowing how to steer a business of this size even through troubled times. Sitting in the conference room over a cup of coffee, we talked about how to set up a business like TF in Ghana and why others had failed to do so. Not immodestly, he told me that it had all started with an entrepreneurial vision, the recognition of an unexploited opportunity:

> You know, when, you know, any entrepreneur, who's made it, will tell you that the first thing you do is find a market. You have to go and get the market. When I started this business, I started with the market and I came not with an order, that's where the risk comes in, but I look a guy in the eye, he says, "yeah I'll take it." I don't ask him for a piece of paper, I don't ask him for any guarantees, that's good enough for me. Fine, you got the market, or a good percentage chance to get in the market, then what you do is, you then go to find where your suppliers are, so you start to locate and secure your suppliers. Once you have those two, you do the easy bit, which is the last bit, which is to build a factory. (Interview, 2009)

During our conversation, Mr. Sneijder outlined several important factors that allowed his investment to grow from micro to macro size. The first problem to be tackled was to find a "market." When he approached his future customer – a large Swiss retailer – back in the late 1990s, it was a high-risk undertaking like so much else in the retail sector, where many transactions are conducted without formal contracts. Thanks to his prior knowledge of the fresh-cut industry and his "relational proximity" (Murphy 2012) to his future customers, Mr. Sneijder eventually "got the market," or at least had "a good percentage chance" to get into it. The next market-making problem to be solved was locating and securing suppliers and developing a close relationship with them in order to sustain a demanding JIT model. Yet, like in the mango project, the "resources" necessary to sustain the new JIT market arrangement did not exist at the outset – they had to be secured, mobilized, and framed according to the demands of European retail markets. In this regard, we should refute popular understandings of frontiers as spaces where the availability of resources is taken for granted – where it is clear "who owns what" and things just appear as "packaged for export" (Tsing 2005: 29).

Market Enrollment, Not Integration

When Mr. Sneijder came to Ghana, nothing was packaged for export – at least not for high-value JIT exports. He met a subsector built on sandy ground. Farmers were not organized and produced the local Smooth Cayenne variety, which they sold to "cowboy exporters" (Whitfield 2010: 28), who would often not pay them or order fruits without collecting them. It was an industry largely characterized by precarious relationships, opportunism, and low levels of trust, embedded into an environment with very little legal security for any transacting party, not to speak of any collective structures to manage common problems, conflicts, and competition (Granovetter & McGuire 1998).

"The change came when we met TF," Kwame recalled (Interview, 2008). Through the mediation of a befriended local pineapple exporter, Mr. Sneijder and his freshly employed agronomists were introduced to some farmers in Densu Valley who were more than willing to join the "fresh from farm" project and demonstrated the ability to produce high-quality fruits – farmers such as Kwame. Because entrepreneurship is not just about recognizing unexploited opportunities or recombining resources and ideas in new ways (Schumpeter 1947), but also about "heterogeneous engineering" (Law 1987), the company had to find ways to mobilize adherents for its project of JIT connections. Human and nonhuman elements had to be engineered in ways that ensured access to raw material as well as the stable qualification/objectification, calculation, exchange, and circulation of goods according to the anthropological program of European retail markets. But who knew whether farmers would smoothly become part of such a project and stick with it? After all, markets are not only sites of cooperation but also sites of struggles about opportunities for surplus generation and resource control (Baker et al. 1998: 153; Fligstein & Dauter 2007: 114), and no market is complete without conflict – an observation already voiced by Max Weber in his famous phrase that the market was "a battle of man against man" (Weber 1978 [1922], cited in Swedberg & Granovetter 1992: 9).

Indeed, when TF set up its operations, competition for fresh pineapples was often fierce, market relations were "hazardous" and "capricious" (Baker et al. 1998: 148), and local farmers had many other options available. Thus, the challenge was to enroll farmers from other existing market arrangements in the pineapple subsector in order to create reliable resources.

Furthermore, the farmers had to remain with TF. Any dynamics of competition disrupting the supply base or encouraging the development of "shadow markets"[2] on which supported suppliers side-sell their produce to other exporters when market demand was high would have had serious repercussions for the company's business model. Given its market orientation, such dynamics would have been even more destructive. In a world with stiff competition among retail suppliers, where supply chains compete against supply chains (Busch 2007: 141), the JIT model demanded the availability of high-quality fruits *throughout* the year without any supply breakdowns. It required a system of permanently "greased pumps." What it did not require were confrontations between "capital" and "labor" or "suppliers," respectively – the "no go" for JIT systems (see Herod 2001).

According to the Mr Sneijder, the key to enrolling the farmers was a "simple philosophy," namely, to nurture "a culture of mutual respect and one of trust" in order to "earn loyalty and most importantly commitment to quality and quantity" (Interview, 2009) from the farmers. Achieving this required a range of associational investments that had been unprecedented in the hitherto "socially thin" pineapple subsector:

> We've done something that no one, nobody else has ever done. In order to build up loyalty, we pay our farmers well, we pay them much more than everybody else does, we have a certain relationship with them, we train them, we finance them, we help them, we're friends with them, it's a powerful relationship. (Interview, 2009)

The strong "family culture" practiced at TF was, indeed, a frequent topic in interviews with managers and had its material and performative expressions at the factory level. While at this stage I cannot delve into the underlying complexities surrounding the term in a corporate context, suffice it to say that it must not be understood as a substance but as a form-giving and materially entangled mode of ordering. The story about "family culture" was a performatively reiterated device of *interessement* (Callon 1986) that mobilized adherents; redefined roles from antagonistic to cooperative; and produced the stability under which resources for the JIT project could be secured. It begs emphasis here that stories and histories themselves can be interpreted as "ordering resources for working on and making sense of the networks of the social" (Law 1994: 71).

As part of this "cultural project," the company provided interest-free loans to pioneer farmers so that they could expand their farms. The loans would later be deducted from supplies to the factory. Through this scheme, the farmers had access to cheap capital in an environment with extraordinarily high interest rates for agricultural loans.[3] Furthermore, TF guaranteed prices above industry average, paying farmers within 14 days after delivery. It also paid some of the pioneer suppliers in foreign currency, which protected them against exchange rate fluctuations and made it even more attractive to deliver to the company. Both the loans and above-industry-average prices worked as "prostheses" (Çalışkan 2007b: 257), as strategic market devices that helped to effectively enroll the farmers. Although such a strategy could be interpreted as a subordination of farmers through credit and debt (Watts 1994: 66; Ramamurthy 2011), these investments into durable relationships were highly risky given the widespread opportunistic practices, the low enforceability of contracts, and the weak legal environment in Ghana's agricultural sector. Yet it was a risk inevitably attached to the worldly market encounters between a Swiss businessman and the farmers of Densu Valley:

> Well, I don't think there was that much confidence [...] as entrepreneurial risk, and, that's what I do, and you look at something, you take a deep breath, you listen, you make sure that you absolutely minimize the risk by understanding all the bits and pieces, don't do anything blindly, and you take a deep breath and go through it. And that's what we did and it worked. (Interview with Mr Sneijder, 2009)

Did it really work? When asked in the beginning, indeed many farmers confirmed a close attachment to TF, forwarding descriptions such as "we got a very good relationship," "they have been a lot of help to us," "it's very good and it's cordial," "for the past ten years, there is no week TF has not taken our fruits," or "I am developing from TF" to characterize their relationship with the company. Even though some farmers provided a more nuanced picture when I got to know them better, all agreed that the company had done much for pineapple farming in Ghana and that their relationship with TF was indeed "powerful." This is, of course, not to deny that several of the pioneer farmers no longer worked for TF at the time of research. There were several reasons for this, one of them being that the relationship was probably more "powerful" than some farmers wished it to be.

Thus, the crucial issue to be addressed in Chapter 7 will be the power geometries inherent in the JIT supply chain and the materially entangled practices that sustained them. After all, markets are also spaces of confrontation and power struggles (Bourdieu 2005; Çalışkan & Callon 2010), and those struggles are firmly about making others join particular networks of qualculation and so prevent their defection to alternative ones. The words of David, one of the pioneer suppliers to TF, speak for themselves:

> It's like in the beginning, remember, someone didn't come from Europe and gave money to expand my farm. Somebody came from Europe and wanted to do business with me and find me to be trusted. Have my farm, need to lure me to his side for me to supply, not to give it to any other exporter. [....]. So you have to get me for me to be supplying you. So [...] they didn't just walk to the street and find someone to give the person the monies. You came to my farm [...] seeing what I am doing before you gave me the money to invest in what I am doing [...]. (Interview, 2009)

As argued before, enrollment, or "luring another person to one's side," is equivalent to a laborious act of translation, during which the possibility of interaction and the frames of maneuver are negotiated (Callon 1986: 203). But there are different translations; some are more powerful than others, and some serve a particular purpose better than others.

* * *

So given that in the frontier regions of export-oriented marketization neither resources nor cooperating market agents can be taken for granted, how did the process of enrolling outgrowers into the organic mango project work out in Ghana's north, which, contrary to the south, had no history of export-oriented agriculture apart from the export of a few wild tree products?

When the OFL director and his associates started the mango project, they may have known their way around northern Ghana, but they did not anticipate the enormous monetary, social, institutional, procedural, scientific, and material investments that would have to go into the qualification of goods as well as the formatting of market agencies and encounters in their scheme. The Herculean task was to transform subsistence farmers into tree outgrowers in a region that had no history of commercial mango farming and lacked adequate market infrastructure. There was no way to "go to a book and say this is what I have to do," and much of this ontological reconfiguration had been "trial and error," one senior manager reckoned during our first conversation in 2008. John, another senior manager, and a "northener" with an extended experience in agro-forestry, recalled the uncertainties that surrounded the company's investment in northern Ghana in the very beginning – uncertainties that partly persisted throughout the evolution of the project:

> [...] It is a new idea altogether in the north here. It is not that there are no tree crops for export, there are tree crops for export but these tree crops are not planted. For example, the shea tree, the *dawadawa*, and then the tamarind leaves.[4] [....] They pick them from the wild and sell them but growing the tree crop for the export market is something very, very new to them. So when we started with these mango plantations, some people say "oh it will not succeed, it will not fruit" and all that [...]. (Interview, 2009)

Another manager, Claire, a Belgian with prior volunteering work experience in northern Ghana who had worked in the mango project from the very beginning, succinctly summed up the challenges the company faced throughout the project: "And also let's face it how it is, we're creating history now. We are not reading from history" (Interview, 2008). Referring to the process of mango market-making as "creating history" actually points to something larger, namely, the fact that the activity at the frontier is to work on human subjects, material objects, and "nature" itself (Tsing 2005: 30) (see Figure 5.2). Dagomba and Mamprusi "peasant farmers" had to become "outgrowers"

Figure 5.2   Outgrowers in their farms, assisted by OFL staff. (Author's photo.)

who stick to a contract and produce organic mango trees according to the demands of northern buyers; seedlings had to be nursed, planted, and turned into organic mango trees; irrigation equipment had to be installed; an extension system had to be set up; staff had to be trained and disciplined; and packing and cooling infrastructure had to be built. All this had to form a stable ensemble in which the peasant-turned-outgrower was the lynchpin.

Although contracts, like prices, may serve as prostheses to foster such stable enrollments, they are not enough to guarantee them, as Durkheim's idea of the non-contractual elements of the contract suggests (Durkheim 1977 [1893]: 251). This applies in particular to environments with little or low enforceability of contractual rights such as northern Ghana, where suing smallholders involves prohibitive transaction costs (Grosh 1997: 250). In such environments, "[i]t is not unusual for companies to suspend any faith in formal legal institutions and rely instead on painstakingly constructed relations of trust, patronage, and traditional reciprocities – a moral economy of sorts – rather than the word of the law" (Watts 1994: 66). TF's cultural project seems to support this claim, and, as we shall see, one could also apply it to the market enrollment of the mango farmers. What matters for making "capital" is to create stable relations that allow for investments, access to resources, as well as the production, qualification, and the exchange of goods, including the redistribution of (surplus) value.

However, such productive relations cannot merely be rooted in the power of the contract or a more informal moral economy of sorts but must encompass a wide range of "emotional, corporal, textual and technical elements" (Çalışkan & Callon 2010: 21). As Callon and Latour (1981: 296) put it: "In order to grow we must enroll other wills by translating what they want and by reifying this translation in such a way that none of them can desire anything else any longer." As in the pineapple case, enrolling farmers into a hitherto unknown market arrangement of sufficient durability across space and time was exactly what was at stake at the beginning of, and effectively throughout, the organic mango project. Farmers who had until then produced food crops were to be enrolled in "common 'translations' and visions" (Gouveia & Juska 2002: 375), preventing their defection to other networks. More generally we could reread the work of enrollment as the mobilization of all the devices "by which a set of interrelated roles is defined and attributed to actors who accept them" (Callon 1986: 211). This must shift our attention to the "practical means" (Latour 2005: 66) of market enrollment. As we might frame it in Latourian terms: no work, no "outgrowers"; no work, no "suppliers."

But what is the place of farmers in the whole story? Were they simply passive subalterns to be worked upon? Or did they display voice, agency, or doubt? When the OFL managers started the outgrower project, they encountered a mixture of hope, uncertainty, and mistrust among many local farmers. Although some pioneer farmers were keen on joining the project for a better future, others were hesitant for several reasons. Many farmers "were thinking that the white man would own the project and for that matter if we made a mistake and gave our land to the White man to do the project at the end he is going to benefit [and] we won't get anything until [...] we realized that we have to own the mangoes but [are] only supported with the inputs" (group interview with farmers, 2008, translated). Such was the tenor in many group discussions with farmers. In the beginning, there was much uncertainty about the "*siliminga* company" (White man's company) and its true intentions.

Other farmers were hesitant because of the failure of past development projects. Over the years, farmers in the region had been repeatedly approached by NGOs, among others, with projects for cashew and teak cultivation, but these projects had been introduced as quick-fix solutions typical of the aid economy that has thrived in northern Ghana for the past 20 years or so (see Mohan 2002). Apart from teak cultivation, none of these projects had long-lasting effects. The NGOs often left after project funding ended, leaving farmers with crops but no markets. Market-making in the past was indeed a series of failures and disappointments. Thus, trust for the market had to be manufactured in the first place – a piecemeal endeavor as the chairman of AOMO, Dauda noted: "Our people here actually have never gone actually into projects of that nature, so it needed time and patience for you to be able to push them to accept it" (Interview, 2009).[5]

Such reservations notwithstanding, many farmers quickly joined the outgrower scheme, and the project rapidly grew in size and complexity in order to reach the shareholders' target of 2,000 outgrowers by 2008. The farmers had their own reasons for joining the scheme. During focus group discussions, some of them provided a whole range of situated justifications for why they had become "mango outgrowers." Some simply mimicked their neighbors in joining the project; others were hesitant to join and changed their mind when they saw some of their colleagues cashing in on their first harvests in 2006; many dreamed of living a better future from the very beginning. In a drought-prone environment where seasonal subsistence farming prevailed, commercial mango farming appeared as an investment that extended into the future, as was disclosed during a group discussion in the village of Daseba:

> We joined the scheme because of the hardships related to subsistence farming and life in the community here. We hoped to fight poverty and at least to provide a better future to our children even if we could not benefit ourselves. Mango farming is like building a house and gives some additional security compared to the drought-prone farming of other crops in the area. Furthermore our group has heard of other farmers in the area who benefited from the project. Our expectations were high, but could not be assessed, because we ourselves have not harvested yet. (Interview, 2009, translated)

Read differently, mango farming was also perceived as a chance to escape the perils of "inherited poverty" – as a means of adopting new practices of economization that broke with the past. Yet joining the project was "not a matter of blind copying; it was a powerful claim to a chance for transformed conditions of life – a place-in-the-world" (Ferguson 2006: 19). We can neither dismiss the farmers' aspirations to become part of the world market as an effect of the workings of discourse or false consciousness, nor can we assume that they were simply "incorporated." Instead, the prospective mango farmers had their own aspirations – they *acted* and *decided*.

This notwithstanding, uncertainty loomed large on both sides, on the farmers' as much as on the company's. Frontier regions are imaginative projects as much as they are imponderable spaces (Tsing 2005: 32–33); they are ambiguous zones where material aspiration and disappointment sit closely together. The mango frontier was no different. Even though OFL managed to attract a critical mass of farmers who decided to join the project, enrolling that many farmers into a market arrangement of considerable scale, according to a senior manager, posed "a massive risk" (Interview, 2008). Not only did the director and his associates invest their own capital in farmers who had never cultivated trees on a commercial basis before, but they also borrowed money from some of the development organizations involved (see Chapter 3). For instance, OFL had to pay back DIAROC's loan with annual (below-market) interest.[6] *De facto*, the outgrowers were not bound to pay back their loans unless they produced marketable mangoes. OFL mobilized several strategies of *interessement* in order to firmly attach the farmers to the company in an uncertain market environment. Earning returns on capital invested is hard work.

First, respecting local power geometries and customary arrangements (including land tenure arrangements) was a crucial step in mobilizing support for the project. The aspiration to "make the farmers as much a part of us as we are of them" (Interview with Claire, 2008) required the OFL managers to become closely entangled with local customary practices and "domestic" arrangements (Boltanski & Thévenot 2006 [1991]). Paying respect to chiefs and "abiding by the same rules as they do" (Interview with Claire, 2008) was a central precondition for establishing legitimacy for the project. The company managers were often not only economists but also anthropologists in the "wild." In one way or another, economics has always been an anthropology (Callon 2005: 8), but the politico-economic landscape of northern Ghana made the OFL managers literally follow Geertzian footsteps. Achieving such close entanglements with farmers often required a deep immersion into local systems of reference and "customary" practices, which often led to compromises between corporate interests and local orders of authority, property, and worth.

Second, OFL, in partnership with some of the NGOs involved, invested heavily in community development projects in order to mobilize adherents for its market-making project. Most outstanding in this regard was a school-upgrading project through which village schools were supported with books, food, and the provision of housing facilities for teachers. In a project with a scope of many years, the calculation behind such a move was also to secure the huge investments for OFL over a considerable period of time. After DIAROC had strongly pushed for it in an effort to socialize the value chain (see the following text), the company also supported many farmers with the planting of intermediate-value crops such as groundnuts and a grain variety in order to help bridge the long gestation period of mangoes and to alleviate the concerns of farmers about joining the project. This arrangement represented an important food security component against the background that one frequent criticism laid at the door of export-oriented outgrower schemes in the Global South was that scarce resources were diverted to meet the needs of affluent consumers in the Global North (see Glover & Kusterer 1990: 17).[7] The arrangement also formed part and parcel of the strategy to qualify mangoes as something "worthy," as will be illustrated in Chapter 6. Of course, some of the strategies for amassing reputational capital through investing in community development had been practiced in the past in outgrower schemes in Ghana and elsewhere (Amanor 1999; Vellema 2002; Blowfield & Dolan 2008) and, indeed, have seen a rise as part of the "value chains for development" agenda (Amanor 2009). However, they appear in a new light when conceived of as a project of enrollment from a social studies of economization and marketization (SSEM) perspective.

Third, the OFL managers realized that many outgrower schemes in sub-Saharan Africa in the past failed not only because of "moral hazards" on the part of the farmers, but also because companies were frequently not transparent and were manipulative in their dealings with farmers. Thus, the ambitious strategy of the senior management was to "do everything above the table" (Interview with senior manager, 2009). This included the effort to administer the loan scheme in such ways that "the outgrowers know at any point and time and any moment [that] they can find out how much money they owe to OFL for the inputs they've taken" (ibid.) as well as the transparent setting of prices.[8] Farmers would receive detailed debit notes for every input supplied to them. Furthermore, the OFL management made sure it paid the highest prices at the time of harvest in order to attach farmers closely to the company. After the harvest, farmers would be given a breakdown of the costs so that they could see how much OFL received for the fruits sold in local and export markets and how much money was deducted for loan repayment, handling, transportation, and marketing. Trust building, after all, played a part in stabilizing relationships with farmers, even though it was only one element.

Manufacturing trust, however, was a piecemeal project, and there were several incidents that shattered the trust-building process between the farmers and the company. Firms and organizations more generally are not monoliths "characterized by preset goals which they work (…) towards" (Thrift & Olds 1996: 319). Instead, they are sites of distributed practices. The lower-management staff of the company would at times pursue their own agendas. Thus, trust had to be constructed performatively over the years, and the senior management took an active part in such constructions. In this regard, it should be noted that "trust" does not simply exist as a lubricate substance, as is often assumed in the *New Economic Sociology* (NES), economics, and economic geography more generally (see Grabher 2006); it rather has to be nurtured and practically reiterated in concrete situations "by acts that signal trustworthiness" (Beckert 2005: 5).

The manufacture of trust seemed to have paid off to a large extent until 2010, when the project slid into a crisis (see Chapter 8). When asked in 2008 and 2009, all the farmers interviewed said that their relationship with OFL was good and that the company had a reputation for being honest in its dealings. In turn, no side-selling was reported on the part of the farmers during the period between 2007 and 2010 despite reported attempts by traders from the south to buy fruits. Yet, the managers were well aware that the success of OFL's alignment strategies on a large scale could only be judged after a few years. How would the farmers frame the mangoes when the trees matured? According to mere market imperatives or according to personal attachments to the company?

In conclusion, the various practical means by which farmers were enrolled into new market arrangements prompt us to rethink Durkheim's famous notion of the "non-contractual elements of the contract" (Durkheim 1977 [1893]: 251, translated). In a region where farmers had never produced mangoes commercially and in an environment with little enforceable legal and property rights, the contract as an ideally interlocking device required a range of "associational" investments in order to produce durable enrollments. As such, neither in this case nor more generally, are contracts merely of "social origin" as Durkheim (1977[1893]: 255) once argued. This recognition must shift attention from "contracts" to the entangled devices of *interessement*, the series of processes by which company managers tried to lock farmers into the roles that had been proposed for them in the program of market-making. As Callon (1986: 211) notes so accurately, "to describe enrolment is thus to describe the group of multilateral negotiations, trials of strength and tricks that accompany the *interessements* and enable them to succeed." The corporeal and subjective elements of this enrollment, without which market sociotechnical *agencements* (STAs) cannot exist, will be described in more detail in the Chapter 6.

The Messy Economics of Outgrowing

So, how does one make sense of the incorporation of smallholder farmers into outgrower schemes? In many accounts of the economics of contract farming (see e.g., Glover & Kusterer 1990: 7; Grosh 1997; Eaton & Shepherd 2001: 46), contracting models largely appear to be the rational outcomes of economic and political considerations. These are said to commonly emerge in situations where a company needs to achieve economies of scale/scope to be competitive or to pay for additional investments but can only do so by relying on smallholders owing to limited access to land or because such a move is politically more acceptable in settings where foreign investment in land is a sensitive issue. Amanor (1999), arguing from an agrarian political economy perspective, foregrounds the more structural forces behind contracting, which he finds to be driven by the logic of capitalist accumulation. According to him, outgrower schemes "are a means of camouflaging the expropriation of land, by appearing to give farmers a role in new development projects" (ibid.: 37). They "maintain the cheapness of communal and domestic labor while absorbing the peasantry into relations of commodity production that are dependent upon industry and capital" (ibid.: 87). From such a perspective, contract farming projects use the "unpaid, family labor of smallholders which now generates exchange value" (Ramamurthy 2011: 1035; see also Watts 1994). While these are valid points, both case studies call for a more differentiated interpretation, as the configurations and models at work here cannot be described by purified accounts of "the economic."

Let me qualify this with regard to the mango project. In many of my conversations with OFL managers, different justifications for the project were mobilized, which echo some of the orders of worth Boltanski and Thévenot (1999, 2006 [1991]) are so fond of . The project was expanded for market and industrial reasons, because the shareholders needed to achieve economies of scale to justify additional investments. They strategized to enhance their market power, but managing a large-scale plantation under tree crops would have resulted in considerable sunk and organizational costs;[9] for political/domestic reasons, because acquiring huge tracts of land in Dagbon could have sparked off conflicts within the host village or within adjacent communities; and for redistributional/civic reasons, because the company's directors (and shareholders) wanted to see development and poverty reduction in the north.

Although one does not have to fully buy into the categorical universe of Boltanski and Thévenot, many interviews with OFL managers nevertheless provide a sense of the multiple aspirations and framings of worth that drove the organic mango project. Add to this the agendas of other involved market-makers such as DIAROC and the African Enterprise Foundation (AEF), with their focus on empowerment, or of local chiefs who wanted to bring "development" to their communities or enhance their standing in local political hierarchies, and you have an assemblage of heterogeneous actors and motifs.

When situated into a broader developmental context, the case of OFL and its out-growers seems to unite the "power of markets with the authority of universal ideals," reconciling "the creative forces of private entrepreneurship with the needs of the disadvantaged" (Annan 1998). Thus, the project tied well into the Post–Washington Consensus discourses on "growing inclusive markets,"[10] "making markets work for the poor" (DFID & SDC 2008), and compassionate agribusiness (World Bank 2007: 137). When it comes to agriculture and the rural poor, these discourses have often been entangled with the programmatic renaissance of contract farming as a motor for regional development (see Eaton & Shepherd 2001; Brüntrup & Peltzer 2006; World Bank 2011: 11). The organic mango project was embedded into this new discursive space where attention shifted from the "developmental state" to the "developmental market" (Amanor 2010b).

We should take these particular historical conjunctures and the new models of market-making associated with them seriously. The project, similar to the JIT fron-tier, cannot be reduced to a case of "strategic philanthropy," as Ferguson (2006: 203) and other critical voices would put it (Blowfield & Dolan 2008; Amanor 2009), but it is instead a bricolage of older models of agribusiness organization and new ideas about multistakeholderism, community development, value chain pro-motion, and empowerment, each of which comes along with distinct framings of worth. The emergence and proliferation of these ideas is expressive of the fact that universals such as "the market" cannot just take over the world but have to be locally engaged. If this peculiar economic social is to spread beyond a given locality with any hope of durability, and markets have done so quite often, then it must mobilize adherents, as I shall subsequently demonstrate. Thus, it does not impose itself naturally or compellingly. By doing so, markets are "locally reconfigured, even as they are held by a wider-reaching charisma" (Tsing 2005: 246). In our global modernity, there is *something* universal about markets, but there is *nothing* natural about them.

Market-making as Boundary Work

Market-making in outgrower schemes is all about the relational-material produc-tion of resources that can be tapped into and turned into qualified and exchangea-ble goods. How was this production of resources organized in detail? How did the frontier regions of export-oriented marketization evolve in southern and northern

Ghana? How was control over land, labor, and pineapples/mangoes assembled in risky business environments, and what impact did this have on local regimes of property and economization? Answering these questions fully lies ahead of us in this and the following chapter, but it warrants emphasis that once we go "backstage" we learn "about the skills of practitioners" (Latour 2005: 90). Furthermore, we see "the puzzling merger of human activities and non-human entities" (ibid.). It all starts off small. But enrolling farmers, "nature," and new infrastructures into circuits of capitalist circulation is never a straightforward process, but one marked by trials of strength, recalcitrances, and practical surprises. It is not simply about extending the margins of "the market"; rather, it is about the coming into being of a material-cum-discursive line that separates the "inside" from the "outside" of the market and that is constantly being worked. Such *boundary work* (Mitchell 2007) was far more complex in Ghana's north than in Densu Valley, an old cocoa-growing area where land and labor had been commodified for decades. Whereas mobilizing land for pineapple production in Densu Valley was not a fundamental problem for TF and its suppliers, it formed a complex political element in Ghana's north. Although outgrower schemes have long been discussed as indirect means of commodifying land (see Amanor 1999), a complementary view sensitizes us to the fact that marketization often wrestles with other forms of economization during frictional encounters. This makes the organic mango project a particularly interesting case to study for it helps us ground marketization in the messy socialities and materialities of economic practice. History tells us that the proliferation of the capitalist market social is not as straightforward a process as strong notions of performativity suggest (Elyachar 2005; Mitchell 2002; Polanyi 2001[1944]).

Against the background of the huge risk OFL was taking, the work of assembling global connections had to be carefully designed, taking into account monetary, social, political, material, and biophysical factors. OFL's mother company ARAMIS hired both international and local experts to achieve these goals. The company's pioneer management was made up of two foreigners with considerable local expertise and a group of "northerners" familiar with the language, environment, power geometries, and customary arrangements in Dagbon,[11] and the team was later strengthened by white (male) managers from East Africa who had considerable expertise with commercial agriculture and were accustomed to living and working in rural environments. Such combined expertise allowed OFL to maneuver through the complex cultural and institutional landscape of Dagbon (and parts of Mamprusi). Respecting local power geometries and land tenure arrangements was key to framing new resources on which claims of ownership could eventually be laid.

Substantiating this argument requires additional background information on land tenure arrangements in Dagbon. Land there is held in trust[12] by chiefs[13] (see Excursus 5.1), and in much of rural Dagbon, it is still largely considered an "inalienable wealth" (Thomas 1991: 22), "[...] protected against the rules of private property and the market" (Mitchell 2007: 246). Within a given community, every member has a right to cultivate land. Such rights can be inherited from father to son, or brother to brother,[14] and therefore represent a secure proprietary claim over land, even though

Excursus 5.1   Land tenure arrangements in Dagbon

The allodial interest over all land in Dagbon (excluding state-owned land) is vested in the institution of the paramount chief (Ya-Naa), who, however, does not have an absolute right of disposition over the land (Abdulai 1986: 78). The so-called tindemba, earth priests who are descendants of the pioneer settlers who had populated the area before the Dagomba people migrated to northern Ghana from what is today northern Nigeria between the 12th and 15th centuries, have largely lost their distributional power over land and are restricted to spiritual matters. In parts of Upper West, however, they still hold distributional power (Abdulai 1986: 75; Kasanga & Kotey 2001: 14).

In practice, much of the power over land allocation has been devolved to divisional, subdivisional, and village chiefs, whose proprietary rights in land increase inversely to their position in the political hierarchy. "Each chief, including the Ya-Naa, is directly responsible for land matters in his own unit of administration (tengbani)" (ibid.: 77). Yet, if large tracts of lands are to be allocated to "outsiders" or foreign investors, such a decision must be approved by the Ya-Naa as royalties would have to be paid for the lease of land. Under Ghanaian law, foreign investors such as OFL can hold property under lease agreements with a maximum term of 50 years, which might be renewed for another 50 years or less depending on negotiations (Kasanga 1995: 27).

In many cases, patrilinearly structured families have become a secondary distributional mechanism. This is different from the areas such as Densu Valley in Ghana's south, where a matrilinear tenure system prevails (Fold & Gough 2008; Goldstein & Udry 2008). Abdulai (1986: 87), building on research conducted in the early 1980s, argues that once land has been allocated, farmers have secure and inheritable rights over it as long as it is being cultivated and not even chiefs can contest those rights, prompting him to reject the term "usufruct rights" that is commonly used in this regard. Most of the land in the north is not formally registered. For instance, Yaro (2010: 203) reports that only 11% of the respondents to a regional survey on land matters registered their plots with the Lands Commission, the responsible government institution. Trees come with a specific bundle of rights, depending on the nature of the tree (wild or planted, tree species) (Poudyal 2011). Yaro (2010) also provides a more recent and nuanced picture of the land situation in northern Ghana and argues that land access and security have become highly unevenly distributed in the wake of mounting demographic pressures (particularly in Upper East) and subsequent commodification, though no "evidence" for this could be found in the study area. Customary arrangements have been radically transformed and monetized in urban and peri-urban areas, particularly in and around Tamale (the largest city in northern Ghana), where land markets similar to Ghana's south have developed, and land is basically sold as a commodity by chiefs and property owners. Al Haji Yakubu, a chief I interviewed in one of the mango communities, described Tamale as a "polluted place" where "they have sold everything." He made a sharp distinction between economic practices in the rural study area and Tamale, the regional capital: "Some of us feel that Tamale is no more a Dagomba land as such. I do think it is not. What is happening here is different from what is happening in Tamale, and what is happening in Tamale is different from what is happening here." (Interview, 2009)

this usually involves a great portion of negotiation (Abdulai 1986). These complex customary arrangements, which orthodox economic discourses and land-focused development programs in Ghana (such as the Millennium Challenge Account (MCA) or the World Bank–funded *Land Administration Project*; see Chapter 3) commonly render as "obstacles" to investment (DeSoto 2001; Karikari 2006; Abdulai & Ndekugr

2008; Goldstein & Udry 2008),[15] were assembled into the mango project. In the following excerpt, Charles, the outgrower manager, gives a vivid illustration of how the process of becoming an outgrower worked in practice:

> We don't really get involved with land. We will say, listen, we want to establish so many acres of mangoes. [...]. As the AOMO administrator is the officially employed representative, he would then help them to facilitate the whole discussion. And then they will identify land. They will identify individuals who should participate. And then when OFL will get that list, we will then investigate: Is that person a resident of that village? Are they a farmer? Are they in good standing to be able to make as much of a success of the farming operation as possible? We look at the land, then we get them to dig holes, profile pits we call them. We inspect the soil. Is it suitable for mango production? So then that's when [...] our scientific qualifications and experience come into it. We want to make sure that their investment and our investment are secure through making informed and good decisions on their behalf. And once those people have been identified as "yes, they should join the outgrower scheme," then they need to pay a registration fee [...]. It's paying for becoming a registered farmer with the outgrower scheme. So it's just a sense of commitment [...], and once they've paid [the] registration fee, then the loan account is open. Then we can start issuing them with their tools and water and fertilizer and seedlings and services. So the land is theirs. OFL, especially of late, we stand back completely. (Interview, 2008)

Mobilizing adherents for the mango project was indeed the first step in a series of distributed calculations and judgments through which individual farmers and land became part of a new market arrangement. For the purpose of enhancing the stability of the project, local power geometries and modes of economization were incorporated into it. Only after a willing farmer and "disentanglable" land had been identified by AOMO in consultation with the respective communities and chief did OFL move in to qualify a farmer and the land, transforming these qualifications into calculative heuristics that decided whether a farmer would become an outgrower or not. According to the AOMO administrator, the company was looking for farmers who were convinced that they "could obey" and "adjust" themselves (Interview, 2008). Would the farmers be patient enough to work continuously over an extended period of time without any returns? Could they[16] mobilize additional family labor? Would they be willing to sacrifice some income for the first three to five years as they would have to divert their attention away from food and other cash crops such as maize?

Another requirement was that the farmers live in the community in order to prevent practices of absentee farming or the capture of the project by urban-based elites, a common problem for many outgrower schemes and irrigation projects in Ghana (Kasanga 1995), sub-Saharan Africa (Yaro 2010), and beyond (Glover & Kusterer 1990; Eaton & Shepherd 2001; Vellema 2002). OFL then required successful candidates to join the project in groups of a minimum of 10 farmers, because it would not have been economical for the company to set up irrigation infrastructure or service individual plots. If farmers found secure land, were assessed as suitable, and managed to form a group, they were then asked to pay a bag of maize as a registration fee.

Table 5.1   From "peasant" to "outgrower"

Expression of interest from the farmers
A group needs to be formed and secure (releasable) land has to be found
Farmers and soils are "screened"
Contract is signed with individual group members
Initial training by OFL
Provision of inputs by OFL
Field preparation under the guidance of OFL staff
Installation of water tank/pipes
Provision of trees and organic manure
Regular field checks and instructions for maintenance and pruning by OFL
Annual harvests, selection, and sales
Repayment of loan from sales

Demanding such a "sense of commitment" was perceived to be crucial to ensure that only motivated farmers willing to "invest" participated in the project. In a region where farmers were used to "handouts" from NGOs, the registration fee represented a precious sacrifice.

Finally, a written contract had to be signed that was the framing device that transformed "peasants" into "outgrowers" (see Table 5.1). Afterward, the loan account would be opened, and the respective farmers became productive parts of the organic market arrangement. They acquired the right to receive certain inputs necessary for mango production but at the same time became "debtors" who had to repay these advances in future. They were attributed a position as the lowest link in a chain of sociotechnical relations stretching from the command centers of Northern standard-setting bodies such as the Organic Movement and GLOBALG.A.P., over to the outgrower management down to technical field assistants (FAs) who supervised the process of cultivation (see Table 5.1).

Yet this process of enrollment was not always smooth. Frequently, it involved tedious and careful work, as various artifacts such project progress reports, e-mails circulating between the outgrower department and OFL upper management, as well as minutes of AOMO-OFL progress meetings document in painstaking detail. The release of land was often preceded by lengthy negotiations with chiefs or former cultivators (or family members, in the case of Mamprusi areas) over the land in question, who sometimes refused to release the land or protested against its release and which eventually slowed down matters enough to prevent the managers from reaching the ultimate goal of gaining 2,000 outgrowers by the end of 2008:

> There are always issues over land, unless it is already owned by, that whole block is owned by the chief and he says "yes, you can use this." Or there is one person that says "I've got a hundred acres, I'll release it for half of my community to use," and it happens. Then there is no issue. But where there are existing blocks of farm land within that area, each individual will need to release their land and it can be backwards and forwards and backwards and forwards. But we facilitate, we get people together and get them to get on with it and make decisions. (Interview with outgrower manager, 2008)

Rendering land a resource that could be incorporated into new sociotechnical arrangements was by no means an uncontested process and required sensitivity. This was, however, only the first laborious framing in a sequence (see Chapter 7) that had to be worked upon in order to transform "subsistence farmers" into "mango tree outgrowers."

Overall, the enrollment of farmers into the new market arrangements did not just resemble a brokered integration (Vellema 2002: 65), nor was it simply a matter of appropriation, persuasion, enticing, or the benevolent unfolding of universal market forces. In a region where many domains of life, including property relations, had hitherto been organized along other forms of economization, the mango project represented a true case of "boundary work." If we look closer, its tedious nature becomes evident. Backstage, such boundary work "turns into a terrain of negotiations, the claiming of rights, relations of power, attempts at encroachment and exclusion. Rather than a problem of transferring assets from outside the boundary to inside, there are rearrangements of power, inequality, and poverty at stake" (Mitchell 2007: 260). Although the long-term "disarticulations" (Bair & Werner 2011a) of such rearrangements, including its impact on power geometries within communities (see Boamah 2014 on this), cannot yet be fully assessed, one issue begs particular emphasis.

On the one hand, tree cultures such as mangoes in the long run may create problems within local communities as they lock into a rather flexible system of land use and, therefore, represent *de facto* claims to land (Fortman 1985). This might eventually exclude others (e.g., local hunters, other farmers) from its use and adversely affect customary entitlements (see Fold 2008: 116–117; Amanor 2010a). During a research project conducted by anthropologist Iddrisu Azindow of the University of Ghana in 2012, it became evident that some farmers considered the planting of trees to be a means of securing land in areas where it was under pressure. I myself, however, heard of only one case where farmers saw their entitlements threatened after the local chief had allocated land to a group of mango farmers. This resulted in a few trees being cut down by the protestors, but the case was later resolved through mediation between AOMO, the respective chief, and the farmers. However, after the Ghanaian government decided in 2011 to support mango production in the north through its *Export Development and Agricultural Investment Fund* (EDAIF) and OFL gave mango cultivation a name in northern Ghana, it is likely that pressure on land will increase in the region. There is a danger that this will happen at the expense of shea trees, which generally support women by providing them with regular income.

Outflanking Nature?

Global markets are often discussed "after birth." They simply appear to work, while their formative stages and the practices that produced them often escape our analytical gaze. This not only relates to the sociality of markets but also to their infrastructures and the biogeophysical transformations they thrive on. Both logistical infrastructures and "nature" are often imagined as objects of promethean visions – objects that can easily be implemented or tamed, respectively. The material reality of global connections is stubbornly different, however. The case of OFL gives us some intriguing insights into the intricate work of turning markets into "after thought" (Cowen 2012), but the points made below could equally serve as prisms to unpack the "black box" of JIT connections in Ghana's south. Getting fruits from farm to shelf in 48 hours is a logistical nightmare.

For the outgrower scheme to fully "take off," new physical infrastructure had to be set up and tested. While this may sound rather mundane – every market-making depends on material investments – this represented an extraordinary challenge in a region with no history in commercial mango cultivation and a lack of market infrastructure (electricity, irrigation facilities, tarmac roads), located many hundred miles away from the port in Accra/Tema. In the very first place, the bio-materialities of organic mango production had to be assembled. Owing to the lack of planting material in Ghana in the beginning, OFL imported mango seedlings from neighboring Burkina Faso, which had had a much longer history of mango cultivation than northern Ghana and similar climatic and edaphic conditions. These imported seedlings were later found to be substandard, and therefore, the company invested into a nursery that had the capacity to accommodate 342,000 improved seedlings in all, irrigated with a micro drip system linked to the White Volta. Although much of the nucleus farm of OFL was planted with substandard seedlings – which later would seriously affect yields (see Chapter 8) – most of the outgrowers were given improved seedling varieties.

Furthermore, equipment such as trucks, irrigation systems, and drying facilities for mangoes had to be bought – often from abroad – and brought to northern Ghana and made to work. The managers from East Africa, used to improvising with farm equipment in rural environments, often proved their value in such situations by finding makeshift solutions to even the most complex hardware problem. Yet, equipping the outgrower scheme in material terms often entailed unforeseen investments, as probably best exemplified by the case of irrigation infrastructure. Initially, consultants calculated that the mango trees would require irrigation for only the first three years after planting. Building on contracted expertise, OFL designed a makeshift irrigation system using polythene water tanks. Every block farm was allocated a number of these tanks, and farmers had to water their farms with buckets every two days. Yet such a system was soon found to be uneconomical given the high wastage of water, high refill costs (the trucks were operated by the company), the high labor intensity, and the fact that trees needed much more water than initially calculated. Thus, for farms close to streams, a mechanized drip irrigation system was implemented that soon covered 50% of the outgrower scheme. This cost was added onto the loan roll of the farmers, who were envisaged as future owners of the irrigation scheme.

At a later stage of the project, the company also needed to set up a packhouse and develop a functioning cold chain that would ensure smooth transport of the mangoes from the hot savannas of northern Ghana to the ports in distant Europe. How to get harvested mangoes at 9 °C from the packhouse to ports in France and Belgium was a sociotechnical puzzle to be solved.

These material investments point to something larger. One of the central characteristics of modern capitalist agriculture is the structuralized imperative to outflank "nature"[17] and to control the biogeophysical dimension of production, processing, or distribution processes (see Goodman & Watts 1997; Murdoch et al. 2000; Boyd et al. 2001). Pests have to be controlled, growth patterns of crops have to be manipulated, nutrients need to be applied, temperatures have to be adjusted, and sometimes rain has to be created. For markets to become collective calculative devices, nature itself must be pacified, socialized, and rendered a calculable object, while various other auxiliary devices must be mobilized to support such a process (Gouveia & Juska 2002). Nature must become part of an "administrative ordering" (Scott 1998: 4).

Yet nature must not only be understood as mere "resources to be transformed, almost as if we were omnipotent" (Busch & Juska 1997: 691) – a position widely adopted in mainstream economics and critical political economy (see Castree 2003: 282); nor must auxiliary devices be treated as obedient tools that help transform nature without friction. Both are active but often recalcitrant elements in market arrangements and partly determine whether markets succeed or fail, as we will see in more detail Chapter 8. Neither nature nor other auxiliary devices such as seedlings, cooling infrastructure, or irrigation pumps are reliable "partners" in making markets, as the OFL managers often learned the hard way. They may defy efforts to control, leading to the disruption of market STAs.

Outflanking "nature" indeed posed a huge practical problem for OFL and its out-growers and was part of its struggle to forge global connections from northern Ghana, a fact well exemplified by a field note I took in summer 2009 after I had bumped into Claire, the packhouse manager. Frustrated about the continuous material setbacks the company experienced when trying to experiment with the processing of fruits[18] at the packhouse, and forced to order spare parts from South Africa for the broken-down system that took one week for them to arrive in Ghana, she complained that "each time you thought you have made it, you get thrown back ten steps" (Field diary, 2009). What becomes clear here is that the "relational materiality" (Law 1999: 4) of markets is tested particularly along agrarian frontier regions where nature has yet to be transformed into a calculable resource, devices still have to prove their reliability, and farmers are often driven into risky projects.

Against this background, we can conclude with Mitchell (2007: 245) that "[t]he performance of markets involves a mixture of technologies, calculative devices, methods of control, and trials of strength." Materials and nature are imponderable elements in this regard. For OFL, this was a lonely struggle. With little government support (despite its mother company's weighty role in Ghana's agricultural sector), no irrigation, regional cooling and packhouse infrastructure in place, and no high-voltage electricity available, the company managers had to rely on their resourcefulness to solve these problems.

The Terms of "World Market" Enrollment

Mobilizing adherents and translating them into coherent forms, is a precondition for making markets work as "economic" and political schemes. But on which terms does "world market" enrollment occur? Mainstream and agrarian political economists usually have simple answers to this question. Whereas the former would conceive of market encounters between agrobusiness firms and farmers either as encounters of free and self-interested individuals in an equal market space (in the case of neoclassical economics) or as potentially asymmetrical, opportunistic encounters that need to be mediated by contracts (in the case of the *New Institutional Economics*), agrarian political economy accounts are more critical of the formatting of such encounters, even if they are regulated by contracts. Indeed, the literature on contract farming is full of descriptions of unequal encounters or incomplete contracts mediating the relationship between companies and outgrowers (Feder 1976; Glover & Kusterer 1990; Oya 2012). For instance, Watts (1994: 65) argues that contracts in outgrower schemes across the Global South often represent "means of subordination," epitomizing the unequal and pro-capital terms of "world market integration". Such a position needs further qualification from a relational-materialist and performative take on marketization.

First, the translations that enact markets usually comprise a wide range of tactics, such as negotiations, compromises, calculations, intrigues, and even violence (Callon & Latour 1981: 279). Even though the history of "world market integration" in the Global South, and the production of capitalist market orders more generally, has often been shaped by acts of violent enclosure and surplus appropriation (Marx 2008[1867]; Nevins & Peluso 2008a; Bernstein 2010), encounters between "agrocapital" and local farmers/labor are not always a matter of simple power equations. Although contracts as inscriptive devices framing crucial market encounters, roles, and obligations can indeed be crucial redistributive instruments, there exist considerable differences with regard to how such processes work in practice, depending on the configuration of market encounters, of which contracts are but one structuring element.

Second, we should not simply assume that agrobusiness companies or retailers for that matter exercise power over farmers *a priori*, but demonstrate how their power is being composed and what kind of structural artifacts may facilitate its composition (Kleinman 1998). Power is an effect of heterogeneous arrangements, not simply a function of capital or incomplete contracts, as I will show in detail in Chapter 7. The complexity of such heterogeneous arrangements has considerably grown in an increasingly reflexive global agrifood economy (Campbell 2006), with a range of market-makers shaping the terms of "world market" enrollment. This requires us to embrace even more nuanced understandings of the power geometries of global agrifood markets.

The case of OFL arrestingly illustrates this. At first, the setup of the mango project – a corporate player with considerable experience and resources encountering mostly illiterate farmers who had never produced for the "world market" before – immediately raises concerns about power asymmetries. The (potentially unequal) encounter between these two parties was, however, mediated by a number of co-market-makers, most notably DIAROC, AEF, GLOBALG.A.P., and the Organic Movement. Although the critical capacity of these organizations has to be situated within the limitations of market-oriented development agenda (Amanor 2009), they nevertheless transformed, translated, distorted, and modified the contractual arrangement between OFL and the outgrowers.

DIAROC, in particular, acted as an effective intermediary by brokering the first contractual arrangements between OFL and the farmers from 2001/2002 onward.

At that time, the farmers had not yet been organized into AOMO, while DIAROC helped draft the contract on their behalf as a precondition for financial support. While OFL had an interest in mobilizing its own terms of valuation and agendas in an early draft version of the contract at the beginning of the project, DIAROC had a keen interest in ensuring that the farmers would not become part of an exploitative project. DIAROC, which in the past had adopted a more classical development approach based on production-related support to farmers and empowerment, embraced a more value chain-oriented approach around the time it started its engagement with OFL. Yet the "social economists" at DIAROC, having a civic mandate as a faith-based organization, were still skeptical about the distributive power of value chains. They did not believe that value chains simply worked for the poor. They did not just want to accept the discourse that value chains are driven by the single logic of profit maximization and efficiency and saw a need to balance their intervention between "market," "industrial," and "civic goals" (in the register of the *économie des conventions*), aspirations that had, indeed, been at frictional interplay in the organization itself for a while. The DIAROC economists in the "wild" wanted to prevent the unequal allocation of risks and surpluses so inherent in market arrangements by designing the "appropriate mechanisms" in order to "shift power balances" (Interview with program officer, 2009) from a company toward north Ghanaian "peasant farmers."

The mediative and productive role of DIAROC becomes strikingly evident if we move backstage. In 2003, the responsible officer at DIAROC informed the OFL managers and directors that several uncertainties remained about certain sections of the contract drafted by the company and that some paragraphs needed to be clarified, amended, changed, or dropped. DIAROC managed to change many paragraphs of the contract for the sake of clarity, often in favor of the farmers.[19] This touched upon a wide range of issues such as pricing and payment modalities, the marketing of fruits, the removal of "non-performing" outgrowers from the scheme, and conflict resolution.

For instance, DIAROC stipulated that OFL could not take any land or other assets as collateral when farmers defaulted on their contractual obligations or their loan repayment, as the organization wanted to prevent dispossession of farmers. By complying with this stipulation, the debt would effectively become a "dead debt" if a farmer dropped out of the scheme.[20] It dawned on OFL managers from the very beginning that it would not make sense to take a peasant farmer to a local court given the high transaction costs involved and the fact that farmers hardly owned any assets, but DIAROC managed to have this issue dealt with more clearly in the contract.

DIAROC also pushed for the creation of an extra-legal arbitration mechanism in case of conflict between OFL and the farmers, with the result that traditional mechanisms of conflict resolution (*zabili goobu*[21]) were incorporated into the contract. Given the fact that farmers could not provide any collateral or be taken to court, OFL had to seek other means of enforcing its rights and recovering its investment in case a farmer wanted to quit mango farming or was removed from the scheme owing to non-performance. Such a situation represented a dilemma for OFL because farmers were entitled to the land on which credit-financed trees were planted. Neither OFL nor AOMO could simply take over the farm given local customary tenure arrangements. With the support of DIAROC, these arrangements were incorporated into the contract under the so-called "next of kin rule": in case a farmer died, dropped out, or was removed, his next of kin would be approached to take over the farm and the loan, a practice that actually tied in well with customary practices of inheritance (see Abdulai 1986: 85).

Another important issue pushed by DIAROC was the involvement of women in the project. Under Dagbon customary law, it is difficult for women (though not impossible if they have the resources) to acquire direct usufruct rights to land, even though access to land can be granted by their husbands, their husbands' family, or benevolent community members. This fact represented a challenge to DIAROC's plan to turn as many women as possible into mango farmers with secure access to land. Thus, during field trips to Ghana, the organization's officers tried to explore ways to incorporate women. It was found in discussions with farming communities that women had the right to use fruits of trees in general, and thus there would be some scope for incorporating them; DIAROC attached this wish to its loans and grants. Even though in practice female participation in the project was often difficult to push for, DIAROC's intervention prompted OFL to focus more strongly on what had until been then a neglected issue. Furthermore, though less intrusive, AEF also had a close look at the accounting activities of OFL, ensuring that those farmers who had been supported with AEF money were not exploited by the company.

In 2009, the contract was amended to include commitments toward GLOBALG.A.P. and the Organic Movement. Both organizations usually interfere strongly with the farming practices of a client (Ouma 2010) and have made it obligatory that a commitment to their principles is incorporated into contracts in cases where a company provides technical and marketing assistance to farmers.

The fresh-cut encounters were formatted quite differently. Contrary to the case of OFL and its outgrowers where an NGO helped to specify a contract that left little space for ambiguities that would disadvantage the outgrowers, here the underlying contract was in fact "not really hard and fast," as a senior manager of the company admitted herself during an interview in 2008. Even though it also incorporated a range of terms stipulated by standard-setting bodies such as GLOBALG.A.P., it did not specify in any more comprehensive terms contractual obligations for both parties, nor did it give any buying guarantees to farmers or outline what would happen in case of a conflict between the two parties. It was instead a simple "future purchase agreement"[22] (Watts 1994: 26).

The practice of global supply chain management often reframes such loose institutional arrangements as "gentlemen agreements." In the vernacular of JIT, this meant the following: "Yes, we trust them. We don't write, we don't want to go into agreement, writing long term paper. Gentlemen's agreement, this is what we have said, let's trust each other, we shake hands and it works" (Interview with supply chain manager, 2008). In today's global agrifood markets, such enrollment formats are outcomes of encounters between sociotechnically unequally equipped agencies and, therefore provide considerable space for the uneven distribution of risks and surpluses (see Callon

1998a: 46; Çalışkan & Callon 2010: 13). Retail markets in the Global North are full of "gentlemen's agreements," given the unwillingness of many supermarkets to enter into fixed contracts that would undermine their scope for flexible accumulation. Alternatively, the term "gentlemen's agreement" mobilized here can be understood as a "black box" (Callon & Latour 1981) for the "relations of domination" (Çalışkan & Callon 2010: 13–14) that permeate global retail markets and make them highly differentiated "space[s] of possibles" (Bourdieu 2005: 76).

The examples discussed here show that contracts are not necessarily means of subordination, but that they can also be objects of contestation and negotiation depending on the equipment of the agencies involved. The rearrangements of power, inequality, and property that are characteristic of new agrarian frontier regions are not automatically a unidirectional matter. In the mango project, farmers, indeed, had considerable power over the company as they could simply withdraw from the project without having to fear legal repercussions. Furthermore, DIAROC, aspiring to act on behalf of largely illiterate and poorly organized farmers, helped specify the terms of the contract, acting as a crucial intermediary.[23] In turn, AOMO, despite being heavily understaffed, could refer to these fixed terms in a legal situation. Other intermediaries, such as GLOBALG.A.P. and the Organic Movement, mobilized their own frames of valuation. The contract itself was a "compromising device" (Thévenot 2001a) – an outcome of various translations "during which the identity of actors, the possibility of interaction and the margins of maneuver" (Callon 1986: 203) were negotiated and delimited, putting the encounters between OFL and the farmers on a more equal footing.[24]

The involvement of other co-market-makers also points to the growing role of mediators of all kinds in agriculture and development, and, indeed, the global economy more generally. These often create new alliances and new meanings, and forge new potentialities (Lendvai & Stubbs 2009: 678). The involvement of different mediators in the organic mango project is also a striking example of the new power-laden connectivities that shape the contemporary global agrifood economy: the rights and obligations of two transacting parties in northern Ghana are shaped by organizations in spatially distant but institutionally close Europe. It makes the mango frontier a truly relational place.

Good(s) Connect(ions)

The life of commodity is indeed an ongoing series of movements and *stasis* (Appadurai 1986). Unpacking such dynamics is a requirement for understanding how global market connections are being forged in practice. In this regard, it is helpful to again invoke the distinction between a product and a good – between a process and a state. Making "products" and achieving "goods" lie at the heart of market-making. An immersion into the production and qualification of goods in the JIT project strikingly underpins this. Before the suppliers start growing pineapples, they are allocated a temporal slot in a planting schedule that roughly reflects future expected orders by the retailers. Each farmer is given a supply quota according to his individual farming capacities, on which he (there is no "she") bases the number of fruits he is planting. Prior to planting, the farmers have to check on the quality and health of their suckers (infant plants) and must perform risk assessments on the land they selected in order to avoid planting on contaminated land. During the actual production of fruits, farmers have to check for erosion, weeds, and pests, yet only by resorting to fertilizer and pesticides approved by the company. Fruits mature for eight to nine months, after which flower production is induced with the chemical *ethephon*, a practice known as "forcing." On top of that, the farmers have to meet a range of private food safety and quality standards that carry their own catalog of specifications, requiring, for instance, that farmers keep records, ensure hygienic practices, treat their workers well, or implement a sustainability program on their farms.

The whole production process is supervised by the company's agronomists, who occasionally check on the farmers, give technical advice, or conduct internal audits on whether the farmers comply with the private standards, which are later audited by an external certification body. As such, farmers are part of an extended "metrological network" (Callon et al. 2002: 214) that links them to agronomists, external auditors, and standard setters. When the fruits have reached maturity 150 days after the forcing, the agronomists check again on the physical quality of the fruits as part of the so-called "pre-harvesting." Are the sugar levels alright? Do the fruits have appropriate size? Is their texture fine? If the results meet corporate standards, farmers are then scheduled to deliver them to the factory a few days later. It is a time of uncertainty. The farmers never know how many of their fruits will pass the strict quality checks at the factory. Sometimes they are shifted to other days owing to demand volatilities. On the day of delivery, they bring their fruits to the factory in their own or hired vehicles. Only authorized crates must be used to transport the pineapples. At the so-called fruit intake, the quality assurance officers screen the load. It is always a controversial encounter. If the fruits meet the quality specification, the pineapples are moved into the factory for processing where they are further qualified to enter the world of the retailers.

★ ★ ★

The process of pineapple production described here may not be that different from that in the past, but its entanglement with the sociotechnical and spatiotemporal orders of JIT makes a crucial practical difference. In the 1980s and 1990s, the process of bringing pineapples to "the market" was much less formatted. Farmers would usually prepare the land and plant pineapple suckers of the local Smooth Cayenne variety, not worrying about pesticide applications, food safety, or workers' welfare. No talk of "good agricultural practices" or certification schemes. When fruits were mature, an exporter would come to degreen them with *ethephon* to give them a yellowish color that makes it more appealing to Northern consumers. The fruits would be picked up on-farm by the exporter, who usually brought his own workers. Everything was rather makeshift: "Pineapples were packed in the fields, sorted inside trucks due to lack of equipment to lift pallets, sent straight to the port, and pineapples were not cooled until they were in the refrigerated vessel" (Whitfield 2010: 21).

As mentioned in Chapter 3, before 1995, Ghanaian exporters served niche markets in Europe mainly on an air-freight basis, exporting a relatively high quality. From the mid-1990s onward, they converted to sea-freight pineapple after the Sea Freight Pineapples Exporters Association of Ghana (SPEG) was founded in 1995. Given the lack of a proper cooling and logistics infrastructure for sea-freighted pineapples and because many new pineapple exporters with little experience rushed into the business, the quality of exports deteriorated sharply (Voisard & Jaeger 2003). Whitfield (2010: 22–23) argues that "Ghana's quality and yields were more inconsistent than production in Central America and Côte d'Ivoire. Standardized production practices, key to achieving homogenous, good quality fruits, were not achieved among producer-exporters, much less among smallholders, and quality was checked only at individual exporters' packing stations." While the problematizations underlying these words are by no means unproblematic (because they are silent on the question who actually defines what counts as "quality" in global agrifood markets), they nevertheless serve well to convey that the introduction of a tightly coordinated JIT supply chain with complex quality framings at its center represented a new sociotechnical and spatiotemporal order of things. Unpacking how this order came into being and what it meant for participating farmers is crucial for understanding how retail markets are being governed.

While TF could tap into a base of farmers with previously acquired skills in export-oriented pineapple production and had already built up a large network of market relations with retail customers in different countries at the time of research, OFL still had to find markets for its goods and singularize them. The company was still in a process of "search," that is, positioning itself, gradually building up relationships with buyers in Europe, and experimenting with how to get produce to markets in the first place.

Having the "Right" Product

When asked why TF has been able forge global market connections, some of the senior managers would simply reply that "we had the right product." This indeed sounds like a simple formula, but it in fact black-boxes the intricate work that goes into market-making. Neither resources – as shown earlier – nor products/goods simply lay waiting to be discovered by resourceful entrepreneurs; rather, they have to be made. The sociotechnical arrangements had to be created that enabled the qualification, objectification, calculation, legitimate exchange, and circulation of goods in the global marketplace.

Enrolling farmers was only the first step in market-making. In order to tap into the most demanding retail markets in Europe, the Smooth Cayenne pineapple many farmers were used to needed to be reframed into high-quality goods that could relate to the modalities of valuation circulating in those markets. Such reframing required more or less organized and stabilized encounters with farmers that made new qualculations possible (Callon & Muniesa 2005: 1245):

> What comes off the farm is extremely important, and thus our philosophy to be close to where the farms are so that we can have an influence over the quality of the raw material

that we receive and we can have a dialogue with farmers about recent arrivals, future arrivals, next year's arrivals, how we going to plan, do you need some money, shall we change this or modify that. That is the message that we try to convey to the retailers. [...]. So we feel we are in a stronger position to offer the best quality, and the advantage that we must continue to maintain is that of being close to the farmer and therefore offering a discernable quality advantage. (Interview with senior agronomist, 2009)

Accomplishing such a "discernable quality advantage" required the mobilization of a whole range of sociotechnical devices that regulated the ontological reconfigurations of Smooth Cayenne pineapples (and other fruits) into high-value convenience goods sold to quality-conscious retailers and consumers in the Global North. In order to permanently secure this advantage in a market with a high substitutability of products and the constant threat of price-based competition given many retailers' concern with shareholder value (Gibbon & Ponte 2005), TF tried to position its new goods in a way that allowed for the creation of protected niches (White 1981) and stable market relationships (Fligstein 2001). This positioning built on extending existing markets for fresh-cut fruits – the field where the founder of the company had gathered considerable experience – but at the same time required a singularization of goods and their close attachment to retailers and consumers alike (Callon et al. 2002: 201, 205).[25]

Part of this singularization was achieved by nurturing constant product and process innovation. Over the years, TF managed to create a range of ready-to-eat fruit assortments. Sophisticated organizational frames were constructed in order to serve a range of customers with different products, many of them customized to the individual needs of the buyers. In 2008, the Ghanaian subsidiary alone produced dozens of different products. The ability to source raw material "fresh from farm" and to offer a wide range of customized products gave the company its competitive advantage.[26] Additional market niches were carved out in 2003, when the company expanded into other countries in order to exploit geography-bound seasonal differences and resources that were not available in Ghana. This extensive production network complemented the company's product portfolio in important ways, helping it ensure a year-round and consistent supply of fruit assortments in which pineapples and mangoes were strategic ingredients. A consistent and perennial supply of mangoes constituted TF's "unique selling point" (USP) over its larger competitors, but was indeed a hard-earned competitive advantage. Losses frequently accrued during the last quarter of the year, when no mangoes were available in Ghana and had to be imported, in order to sustain "the market." Altogether, continuous product innovations and the construction of unique – but sometimes quite costly – selling points stabilized attachments to customers and nurtured the company's reputation in the marketplace.

Performing the Audit Economy

The other way attachments were created was by invoking more sophisticated quality framings. As indicated earlier, besides meeting technical production standards that regulated the size, shape, texture, juiciness, sugar levels, and fruit color, TF became compliant with many major retailer-owned and sector-specific standards at both the factory and farm level. The adoption of these standards was a Janus-headed issue. Although some managers were critical about the flood of standards that had flooded the markets since the early 2000s and complained about retailers imposing these standards on their suppliers without being subjected to a similar form of "public engagement" (Thévenot 2001b), others considered them as opportunities for leap-frogging and niche creation.

Although concerns have been raised more generally that firms and farms in the Global South may be excluded by private standards from Northern markets owing to their technical complexity and associated compliance costs (Fold 2008; Ouma 2010), the TF management embraced these standards pro-actively. The company had an active role in the qualification of products/goods, unlike the farmers, who had no choice but to comply with the new standards if they wanted to remain part of the JIT market arrangement. In many cases, such a proactive stance toward standards was not only facilitated by resource endowments such as access to capital and technical know-how – resources many other local agribusiness firms often lacked – but also by a privileged access to consultancy and standard-setting circles owing to the company's close foreign connections. Although I will delve into the organizational disarticulations of the audit economy and its "imperialist charge" (Blowfield & Dolan 2008: 11) in the Chapter 6, it is worth highlighting that the ability to continuously comply with new standards eventually ensured the durability of JIT connections in rapidly changing market environments. In a market where various notions of quality have become one of the defining properties of competition, standards represent "investments in forms" (Thévenot 1984, 2009) that ensure temporally, spatially, and materially stable relations among participants. Of course, such stable relations are more beneficial to some actors than to others.

This account of "capitalizing on the audit economy" should, however, not downplay the exclusionary potential of standards and retailer-driven supply chains (Maertens & Swinnen 2009; Amanor 2009; Ouma 2010) that create "certified spaces" (Mutersbaugh 2005). It is also not to downplay the fact that the ability to comply with the rules of the audit economy is unevenly distributed among producers across the Global South. Many small producers find it increasingly difficult to comply with many standards whose Eurocentrism and programmatic form must be subject to critical debate in the very first place.

Relational Properties of Competition

Although the adoption of private standards qualified TF's goods according to a wide range of framings that allowed for their positioning in different markets, they were in principle accessible to anyone who met them. Thus, they did not represent unique properties of competition that could create permanent attachments to buyers and consumers alike. Against this background, the company mobilized other strategies to stabilize its market connections. As already hinted at in the beginning of this chapter, in part this included performing a culture of corporate social responsibility (CSR) at both factory and farm level. Since the 1990s, such strategies of marketizing relations between capital, labor, suppliers, and the environment have been developed by a number of companies in African horticulture and other industries (see Freidberg 2004; Blowfield & Dolan 2008: 2). Apart from establishing a regime of paternalistic care and responsibility for workers at its factory, in 2007 and 2009, TF created community-development foundations with two of its largest customers. Such ostentatious techniques of enacting "ethical capitalism"[27] did have some philanthropic impetus reflecting the values of the founder of the company, but likewise they attached the retailers more firmly to TF as both parties became mutually dependent on each other for exploiting this newly created relational asset in the marketplace. In the register of the manager entrusted with the implementation of these projects, this relational arrangement protected TF from a quick substitution with other first-tier suppliers in increasingly competitive retail markets. At the same time, this arrangement reframed the company's products as serving a "civic" cause, or a "general interest" (Boltanski & Thévenot 2006 [1991]: 190), and enhanced its "reputational capital" (Blowfield & Dolan 2008: 2) by creating associations that had previously not existed.

Another corporate strategy for stabilizing market arrangements was to directly connect operations to consumers, now a more widespread strategy in global agrifood markets. In 2007, the company developed an electronic traceability system in partnership with one of its most important customers. It allowed consumers to directly connect via the Internet with the farmer supplying a product. This sociotechnical device helped enact discourses about alternative visions of trade (trade as a "lattice," as one manager called it) and distributed new "cognitive competencies" (Callon et al. 2002: 194) among consumers. It allowed the differentiating of pineapple chunks made in Ghana, sourced from the hard-working "smallholders" of Densu Valley, from those that were simply imported by giant agribusiness corporations such as *Del Monte* to Europe from large mechanized farms in Latin America. In this way, the device reframed goods by internalizing elements that had previously not been factored into transactions, invoking a transnational economy of affection based on connectivity and personal interaction.[28]

In tandem with other tactics, the strategy outlined here can be regarded as an effort to stabilize market arrangements by creating non-price-based properties of competition (Fligstein 2001: 69). Such strategies of differentiation aim at creating stable hierarchies in markets, where both the status/worth of a good as well as the status/worth of the producer define the relative opportunities open to that producer *vis-à-vis* those available to its competitors (Podolny 1993: 830).

Ongoing Struggles for Retail Worth

In today's JIT retail markets, supply chains compete against supply chains on a daily basis (Gibbon & Ponte 2005; Busch 2007: 441). In these highly competitive markets, the qualification and positioning goods are ongoing struggles as "quality" and the status of suppliers is constantly under threat. Although TF tried to evade the relationally disruptive dynamics of competition, the threat of "displacement" was increasing with sharpened competition and the intensification of "value retailing" (Hughes 2012: 38).

For retailers who cared more about price and physical quality than about the diverse quality framings of TF's goods, larger-scale competitors cutting fruits in Europe became a viable alternative more recently, especially with the onset of the global economic crisis from 2008 onward (see Chapter 8). For instance, the company lost two major product lines and one customer to a competitor in 2008. In order to prevent such detachments from the outset, TF managers also sought more "osmotic" (Ponte & Gibbon 2005: 15) ways of convincing buyers of their superior quality. This included inviting buyers to come to Ghana to see the story behind the product with their own eyes, a strategy that was not always successful. In fact, many retailers fear the personal attachment of their staff to suppliers and therefore rotate their procurement managers on a regular basis to let calculation prevail, not empathy and affection (see Boltanski & Thévenot 2006 [1991]: 263).

What we can conclude from the dynamics of qualification described in this section is that the qualification and requalification of goods are "at the heart of economic competition and the organization of markets" (Callon et al. 2002: 201). In this regard, performing global retail connections was a long series of (re)qualifications and (re) positionings (Callon & Muniesa 2005: 1235), often with significant impact on the making of agencies and encounters within the agribusines outgrower complex. As the *économie des conventions* reminds us, the qualification of goods always "presupposes the qualification of the labor and the organizations involved in their production" (Wilkinson 1997: 331) (see Chapter 8).

The Orderings of JIT

In this last section on the JIT frontier, I would like to discuss how the process of making products and achieving goods was marked by controversies and disruptions. Within the everyday practice of global agrifood connections, processes of qualification (including production) are not as smooth as portrayed here but are grounded in the sticky materiality of economic practice, as well as in the frictional, power-laden encounters of differently equipped agencies. A whole range of factors repeatedly destabilized the JIT market arrangement, often with a serious impact on the farmers. In this regard, two issues deserve a more detailed discussion.

The first point that warrants emphasis is what I would call "the temporal (dis-) orders of JIT." JIT production is *per definitionem* characterized by flexibility and uncertainty, exposing particular dynamics with regard to the distribution of risks and surpluses. As the TF agronomists can tell us, planning JIT is a huge challenge. Many of company's suppliers would confirm this. Trying to maximize their profits by minimizing their overstock,[29] retailers would frequently change their orders at short notice in response to market demands.[30] This resulted in a volatile demand regime for pineapples (and other fruits), and the company staff were frequently faced with the difficult decision of whether to internalize, share, or externalize risks (see Chapter 7).

Whereas demand was a continuously precarious issue, so was supply. Sometimes, raw material would not be available, and in other cases the weather would fail. Sometimes logistics would break down. Not meeting orders was a serious threat to firm survival as some retailers usually fine their suppliers for failed deliveries; the threat of a supplier switch loomed large in the highly competitive retail markets where "out of stock" is generally considered a no-go. In order to maintain a competitive edge, the company often had to pay dearly. When raw material for pineapples was not available from the smaller suppliers, TF had to buy expensive fruits from other export-ers, who often hiked prices through cartel-like networks. With regard to mangoes, outside the Ghanaian season, the company had to import huge volumes of this most strategic ingredient from other countries in order to maintain its USP. Sustaining markets over large distances was both a logistical and financial nightmare.

Furthermore, in retail supply chains, as in other buyer-driven chains (Gereffi 1994), not all "goods" are possible. This is often neglected in the NES-inspired literature on status goods and status orders in markets (see Podolny 1993), even though some notable exceptions exist (e.g., Fligstein 2001). The qualification of goods is always embedded into a more general "space of possibles" (Bourdieu 2005), in which different modalities of valuation circulate and grant goods their legitimacy and worth. Certain agencies, which are equipped to do so, may impose their terms of valuation on others, which makes them dominant, in that one modality of valuation exerts pressure on another one or in that one modality of valuation is no longer open to political debate (Thévenot 2009: 806). Neither the making of products, nor the achievement of goods remains untouched by such "closures." For instance, TF could not place its own branded products on the supermarket shelves in its most important market, because many retailers hinder their suppliers from doing so in order to prevent a shift in negoti-ating power that could accrue from brand image effects. This indeed supports the claim that in contemporary retail markets, "control over the qualification of specific products is a key source of power for 'lead firms'" (Gibbon & Ponte 2005: 18; Dolan & Humphrey 2004). Thus, the relationship between the worth of a good and power must always be put under detailed scrutiny. Lastly, in markets, it is those actors who manage to impose the rules of valuation on others who are powerful (Callon 1998a: 46).

Conclusion

In this chapter, I have shown how global agrifood connections were forged in the two case studies and how the sociotechnical arrangements that enabled the qualification/objectification, calculation, detachment/exchange, and mobilization of goods were constructed and stabilized. I demonstrated how the small initiatives of two entrepre-neurs grew into organizational complexes of significant size. Even though both case studies represent different frontier regions of export-oriented marketization and exhibit different evolutionary trajectories, two points warrant particular emphasis.

First, in frontier regions, we cannot take resources or certain roles for granted. Neither organic mangoes or JIT pineapples nor outgrowers or suppliers were just ready for export, an argument that will be further qualified in Chapter 6. The market-making projects in question did not simply take over the world; they had to mobilize human and nonhuman adherents and frame their encounters in ways that permitted fruits to be objectified and qualified as goods that can enter the world of Northern buyers. Such connections had to be made before goods could eventually be positioned and exchanged in the marketplace. The processes of enrollment and translation were central to such projects. In this regard, significant differences existed between the two case studies. TF could build upon a body of skills that had already wrestled with the problem of producing pineapples for export markets, even though it had to sociotechnically reformat such skills for the JIT project to take-off. In contrast, OFL had to start from scratch. To put it differently, whereas OFL was still struggling to punctualize a range of complex relations so that the mango supply chain could act "as a single block" (Law 1992: 385), TF had managed to transform many network elements into new routines, sociotechnical devices, and organizational forms. Even if precariously, these could be more or less taken for granted in the process of supply chain management and allowed to perform and reproduce JIT connections across space and time.

Second, both projects are indicative of new ways of arranging global agrifood markets. Markets, however, do not impose themselves naturally and compellingly – there is no single form. Instead, what the case studies support is the view that markets "are complex realities that can be configured differently, as each configuration can be designed to respond to particular orientations and requirements" (Callon 2010: 163).

Building on older models of agribusiness organization, both market-making projects were entangled in a variety of economic models, aspirations, agendas, modalities of valuation, and actors. This was not only because projects of economization can never be simply reduced to one logic and to some extent always represent composite arrangements, but also because both projects were situated at specific historical conjunctures and shaped through worldly encounters of heterogeneous actors across distance and difference. The performance of the markets studied was a function in a series of historical events of market-making, as one could express it in more Foucauldian terms. Treating their performance as events means rediscovering the "connections, encounters, supports, blockages, plays of forces, strategies, and so on, that at a given moment establish what subsequently counts as being self-evident, universal, and necessary" (Foucault 1991: 76). The mango project involved a large number of actors (ARAMIS, OFL, single farmers, AOMO, NGOs, local chiefs, state agencies, consultants, buyers, standard-setting bodies, etc.), each of which was to varying degrees involved in the analysis, equipment, and shaping of market STAs, while each of them contributed to their performance. Owing to this collective and distributed reflexive activity, the project was not only geared toward the accumulation of corporate wealth but was also firmly entangled with ideas about "value chain development," "inclusive markets," "poverty reduction," "empowerment," "community development," and "organic production."

The worldly encounters making up the project took place at a time when a more general shift in development policy circles toward "private-sector-led development" occurred. In a region where the state had largely failed to engineer agricultural development, a "developmental market" took shape. It was through such a performance that the mango project was rendered workable in a "peripheral region" that had not been exposed to export-oriented tree cultivation before and acquired the strength necessary to fulfill its long-term objectives. At the same time, when the mango project was launched, markets themselves increasingly became shaped by a plurality of aspirations to

which the project related. These contextual factors, together with "local" particularities, constituted the "field of possibilities" (Foucault 1982: 790) for the mango project,
which was itself transformed as new co-market-makers became enrolled in the project.
In general, the diverse aspirations, agendas, and modalities of valuation driving the
mango project needed to be translated in order for it to work, even though they sometimes were at frictional interplay, as will be further demonstrated in Chapter 8.

The performance of the JIT market was distinctively different, even though it
shared some commonalities with the mango project. The actor landscape was less
heterogeneous, and market-making was primarily the work of the Ghanaian state, TF,
its customers, suppliers, and service providers. In this regard, we must not forget the
farmers and exporters that had made pineapple an export crop in the Densu area
earlier on. In this case study, the local regulatory framework ("the free zone model"),
mode of organizing production ("JIT"), products envisaged ("fresh from farm"),
competitive dynamics in local raw material markets ("capricious markets"), and
market-orientation ("high-end retail markets") came with a particular performance
of markets. Workers and suppliers were redefined as "stakeholders" in a larger project
to ensure their stable enrollment within a vulnerable supply chain that feared disruption. Fused with ideas about local value addition, CSR, sustainability, and supply
chain management, the JIT market arrangement gained its strengths from weaving
alliances and keeping multiple modalities of valuation in play (e.g., "family and
mutual respect," "contributing to local value addition," "fresh from farm," "profit-
orientation," "efficiency," "commitment," "flexibility," etc.).

Emphasizing the composite yet recombinant quality of the JIT market arrangement, however, should not make us blind to the hardening of positions and interests.
In this concrete case, the performance of markets came along with more unequal
positions and encounters than in the mango project owing to the absence of actors
who could have mediated translation processes to the benefit of the farmers. Thus, we
should not forget that the work of enrollment may result in *unity* but not in *equality*.

Taken as a whole, despite differences in terms of "local" contextual factors, actor-
configurations, the scale of ontological reconfiguration, and the quality of market
performance and market orientation, both case studies attune us to the polyvalent
character of capitalist economization. On the one hand, they show that we cannot
reduce capitalist projects to a single economic logic (Gibson-Graham 2006 [1996]),
and on the other hand, it cannot be refuted that we have reached a stage of "ethical
capitalism" (Barry 2004: 196) in which empirical knowledge about farmers themselves is being marketized.

Endnotes

1   In this book, all names of individuals, of the case study companies and related organiza-
     tions, and their geographical associations have been anonymized, are withheld, or have
     been altered to protect sources. Development organizations and programs associated with
     the Ghanaian agricultural sector more generally are referred to by their original names.
2   This is a problem many outgrower schemes have faced across the Global South (see, e.g.,
     Glover & Kusterer 1990: 127; Jaffee 1994).

3   Access to low-interest capital has been a huge problem for Ghanaian agro-exporters and farmers, with interest rates of most banks ranging from 20% to 32% per annum.

4   The dawadawa or locust tree (*parkia biglobosa*) is a highly valued indigenous multipurpose tree. Various parts of it are used for the preparation of meals, and as medicine and building material (Blench 2012). The leaves of the tamarind tree (*tamarindus indica*) are used for food and medicinal purposes.

5   Note here that a contract *per se* was not a new thing. Many farmers I talked to were using the Hausa term *alkawli* to describe the contract they signed with OFL, an established local expression usually used to denote that one person has a material obligation toward another person. "The contract" may have been new in terms of its complexity but not in terms of its meaning as an object signifying an obligation toward someone else.

6   The loan has a maximum duration of 10 years.

7   Note here that this program had a strong commercial component. It was orchestrated by OFL's mother company, which worked together with a major European fertilizer producer in order to upscale grain production in northern Ghana for domestic markets.

8   Whether the company could live up to such aspirations will be discussed in detail in Chapter 7.

9   These costs would have accrued from expenses for labor and monitoring. In the more recent literature on agrarian change in the Global South, smallholder farms are often said to be more efficient because they are "able to absorb the transaction costs of supervising and screening labor and because the marginal opportunity costs of family labor, including the free labor of women and children, are lower than hiring labor" (Amanor 1999: 135; see also Ramamurthy 2011: 1054).

10   See http://www.growinginclusivemarkets.org/ (accessed: 07/07/2012).

11   On the role of local brokers during the encounters between (transnational) agribusiness and local farming communities, see Vellema (2002: 65–67) on the Philippines.

12   "In trust," because land is perceived to belong to the ancestors and future generations of the inhabitants (Abdulai 1986: 76).

13   In parts of Mamprusi, it is much more common that families are the *de facto* distributional mechanisms of land.

14   I am grateful to Iddrisu Azindow for this comment.

15   This is not to say that these perspectives simply misrepresent an independently given reality. In many cases, such as the MCA's land registration component, they help to organize the material world and make new forms of inclusion–exclusion possible (Mitchell 2007: 248).

16   Because women do not have formal access to land in Dagbon, as in many other parts of Africa, participation of women in the project was rather low, even though their participation was encouraged by DIAROC in particular. Out of 1,295 outgrowers (2010), 122 were women. The women participating in the scheme were granted access to land through their husbands, male relatives, or networks they were able to forge in their communities.

17   It should be noted that "nature" as a self-evident domain opposed to "society" is quite problematic a term. Actor-network theorists would reject such modernist ontologies (see, e.g., Whatmore & Thorne 1997; Goodman 2001; Boeckler 2005: 29–30). Moreover, "nature" has "multitudinous manifestations" (Delaney 2001: 499, cited in Castree 2003: 282).

18   In 2009, as part of a diversification project, the company had trials with drying fruits such as bananas and pineapples in a new drying facility. These were ordered from OFL's sister company in Ghana's south or bought from regional markets.

19   The negotiated contract was later used as a template for all farmers in the scheme, not just for DIAROC-funded farmers.

20   The contract was amended in 2009, and OFL and AOMO agreed to change this point as it represented too unilateral a risk for OFL. The new contract, which applied to all farmers, stated that the debt is taken over by AOMO. Yet this externalization of risks stood on sandy ground. Many managers and some farmers I talked to agreed that any debt would virtually remain a "dead debt" owing to AOMO's limited capacity to pay back debts of defaulting farmers.

21   This is a system that tries to solve conflicts between community members amicably, whereby the conflicting parties have to present their case at the chief's palace, who then tries to solve the issue.

22   Following Feder (1976: 422), such agreements can also be understood as one-sided contracts.

23   Of course, the involvement of NGOs in development projects raises more general questions of accountability: whom are they actually speaking for (Mohan 2002)?

24   Such a formal equal footing does, however, not automatically guarantee that both parties stick to the contract "backstage."

25   This is not to suggest that we can simply separate the supply from the demand side. Retailers, consumers, and other co-market-makers are firmly a part of these qualification processes (see Callon et al. 2002: 202–203; Gibbon & Ponte 2005: 20).

26   With the largest customers, this physical quality advantage had to be continuously demonstrated in benchmarking sessions at their head offices, where the quality of TF's products would be compared against that of its competitors.

27   Following Barry (2004: 196), the term does not denote that "capitalism" has become more moral or ethical. Rather than referring to "a system, or a stage in the evolution of system" it refers to a "set of ways of acting on the conduct of business activity."

28   One could, of course, simply dismiss such reframings as a refetishization of commodities (Guthman 2004).

29   In Northern retail sectors, particularly in the US and UK, large inventories are normally interpreted by "financial markets" as "indicators of inefficiency" (Ponte & Gibbon 2005: 17), which represents a bad judgment for corporations that are largely financed through capital markets (Burch & Lawrence 2009). Yet, being "out of stock" is not an option either (Busch 2007: 440), which eventually puts huge pressure on suppliers.

30   This is indeed a more general practice of many Northern retailers (see Raworth & Kidder 2009; Young 2004). Particularly in markets where buyers occupy quasi-oligopsony positions, suppliers have often no choice but to play by the flexible tunes of the buyer. In fresh produce markets, however, JIT production is even more risk-prone because of the perishable nature of food. Fresh fruits cannot be simply held until market demand resurges. For instance, fresh (whole) pineapples could be stocked in a cool place for a maximum of three days if they still were to meet TF's quality criteria. Many of the company's processed products had a maximum shelf life of six to seven days.

Chapter Six
Enacting Global Connections: The Making of World Market Agencies

When I once talked about the mango project to Musa, an educated outgrower who had worked for Ministry of Food and Agriculture (MOFA) in the past, he said that introducing mango cultivation among the local farmers was like "introducing an alien idea, if you don't guide them, you will go nowhere." The local farmers, he reasoned, were not naturally tree but food crop farmers. However, at the same time, Musa was optimistic. He argued that when the farmers saw the first monetary benefits from mangoes, "they will run for it themselves."

What lies behind these words? First and foremost, Musa's framing of mango cultivation as "alien" not only reminds us that mangoes had not been cultivated commercially in Dagbon before the Organic Fruit Limited (OFL)[1] project was launched, but also that they had not been treated as goods of the "world market." Most farmers, if at all, used mangoes for domestic consumption, and only few of them, often those deemed as having "traveled" by their colleagues, now and then sold mangoes in local markets. The assumption that "they will run for it for themselves" sensitizes us to the "problem" of valuation, namely, the process through which mangoes might become framed as a valuable object fit for exchange through operations of calculation and (practical) judgment. It reminds us once again that "things" do not circulate out of nothing or due to some intrinsic property, but because they are framed as valuable, good, and worthy.

The indeterminate worth of mangoes in northern Ghana sharply contrasted with the status of pineapples in the study region in the south, where many farmers had considered pineapple cultivation as "a first class job" (Interview with farmer, 2008)

Assembling Export Markets: The Making and Unmaking of Global Food Connections in West Africa, First Edition. Stefan Ouma.

until the subsector slid into a major crisis from 2006 onward. Against this background, all the suppliers of Ton:go Fruits (TF) had already developed a sense of "export market worth" with regard to pineapples before they became part of just-in-time (JIT) markets. This is not to deny that the market for JIT pineapples came with new uncertainties about their worthiness. Such doubts, however, were quickly allayed by the fact that TF paid reasonable prices to suppliers and paid within two weeks after the harvest in the early years of the project. In a region that had been exposed to patterns of export-oriented marketization for decades, the context for making new market *agencements* was a different thing.

★ ★ ★

Exploring the formatting work geared toward transforming Ghanaian farmers into competent *homines oeconomici* who play by the rules of the global agrifood economy forms the core of this chapter. It will become clear that market-making is not simply about mobilizing adherents, but also about making them *fit* into new sociotechnical arrangements. Unpacking the more microphysical, disciplinary processes that lie at the heart of "world market integration" helps unsettle some of the taken-for-granted assumptions about global market modernity. In a more Foucauldian register, it helps unsettle the "self-evidences on which our knowledges, acquiescenes and practices rest" (Foucault 1991: 76), making visible the singularity of particular configurations "where there is a temptation to invoke a historical constant, an immediate anthropological trait, or an obviousness which imposes itself uniformly on all" (ibid.: 76). In fact, the global agrifood connections I described in Chapter 5 could not have become effective without the making of particular agencies that value simple crops as "goods" that have (a legitimate) exchange value, take ownership over them, perform the roles assigned to them in the market-making process, and become responsible and accountable. Hard work goes into the making of "outgrowers" and "suppliers" across the frontier regions of global agrarian capitalism (see also Nevins & Peluso 2008a: 22).

In order to grasp the making of new market agencies, it is worth turning once again to the work of Callon (2005: 4–5), who argues that (re)configuring "an agency means (re)configuring the sociotechnical *agencements* constituting it, which requires material, textual and other investments" [italics in original]. This must turn our interest to the careful arrangements and tactics being mobilized to cultivate market agencies among Ghanaian farmers (and workers). The making of particular market agencies is, however, never a straightforward process, but one marked by controversies, trials of strength, improvisations, and recalcitrances. It is a process of mobilizing new associational routines grounded in new collective structures of knowing, yet an often skewed and fractured one.

The formatting of market agencies played out differently in the two case studies. In the first section of this chapter, I demonstrate how difficult it was for OFL managers to create an *agricola oeconomicus*, disentangled from his or her local context, reentangled with the things that matter to organic mango markets, performing individual and group tasks alike, taking ownership over his or her trees, valuating them *vis-á-vis* other crops, and relating present investments to future returns in order to pay off debts.

Formatting farmer agencies who qualculate mango trees as envisaged by the OFL economists in the "wild," in fact, represented a struggle in itself. In the next section, I discuss the making of responsible and autonomous agencies in the context of both case studies. Processes of responsibilization and autonomization have a firm place in the variegated histories of "capitalism," but they have been given a new thrust in the "quality assurance world" owing to the global proliferation of self-improvement technologies such as standards, certification schemes, and audits. As I demonstrate in the last section by reflecting on both case studies, the proliferation of such technologies requires us to put the relationship between "value" and "power" in the global economy of qualities under close scrutiny. By doing so, we can give back meaning to the term "value" in global value chain analysis, which seems to have forgotten about it despite its suggestive name (Gibbon et al. 2008). Untangling the geographies of uneven development in the global agrifood economy is not only predicated upon exploring how value is created, enhanced, and captured (see Henderson et al. 2002; Coe et al. 2008), but also upon unpacking what constitutes it in the very first place.

Qualculating the Mango Tree

The pragmatics of valuation perspective introduced in Chapter 2 suggests that "[m]arkets are not possible without generating and then reproducing a stark distinction between the 'things' to be valued and the 'agencies' capable of valuing them" (Çalışkan & Callon 2010: 5). Having said this, the question is how a mango (or a pineapple, for that matter) was transformed into an object to which farmers as "qualculative agents" assign worth? All this is not self-evident. We have become so used to the naturalizations of neoclassical economics – the rendition of goods as being simply there and having an (unambiguous) exchange value (Orléan 2003, cited in Jagd 2007: 83) – that we tend to forget about the associational work that goes into their making. Furthermore, the economic value of a good is usually conflated with its market price (Fourcade 2011: 42). However, "behind the world of prices" (Heilbronner 1983: 267, cited in ibid.) lies much more.

Indeterminate Framings of Worth

The mango project was marked by various struggles of valuation from the very beginning. Initially, vast tracts of land had to be cleared for the mango trees. Rumors spread quickly that OFL would dispossess the farmers of their land, making many farmers in the area reluctant to join the scheme. Such bad publicity intensified when some farmers uprooted shea trees in order to create space for mango cultivation, which drew suspicion from local radio stations, the Ghanaian Environmental Protection Agency, and some local chiefs. The said land clearings were considered particularly problematic given the manifold worth of the shea tree and its products, which not only serves as a source of fat but also provides additional cash income to many women and their families, especially during the hungry season between January and June when the rains finally set in (see Chalfin 2004; Poudyal 2011). This made paving the ground for the market project a techno-political affair in its own right. OFL, in collaboration with the Association of Organic Mango Outgrowers (AOMO), however, quickly managed to dismiss rumors that farmers were dispossessed of their lands and shea trees were uprooted in large numbers. Both OFL and AOMO staff tried to counter any concerns about the loss of income opportunities by highlighting the comparatively higher income the farmers would gain from the mangoes in the future. What was at stake in the very beginning of the project was to underline the specific worth of mango trees and clear the ground for their legitimate production.

However, this was only the first barrier to creating worthy goods. For the farmers, growing organic mangoes for export was a highly indeterminate issue. In the sense of Dewey (1915: 506), the worth of the mango trees was "unfinished or not wholly given" (see also Stark 2009: 14). Organic mango cultivation required the adoption of sometimes unknown and strange farming techniques. It was unclear whether the mangoes would bring any monetary benefits to the farmers. In the early years of the project, in many villages, rumors circulated that "farmers will suffer for nothing." The farmers still had to take care of their food crops, which competed with mango trees for time and labor. In general, the planting of trees had been not a popular practice in much of Dagbon, even though some exceptions existed such as the *Kapok* tree (*ceiba pentandra*), which had been widely used for fiber production.[2] Against this background, it is no wonder that there was no original Dagbani word for "permanent crop." Trees were simply described as *wumpuni* ("god-given") by most farmers. The most difficult aspect of mango cultivation under contract was, however, the long gestation period of four to seven years. For the majority of farmers, many of whom were struggling to the next farming season, it was difficult to adapt to the long-term frame of the project.

How difficult the introduction of a long-term tree crop was, is probably best highlighted by one particular encounter I had during the course of my fieldwork that provides insights into local modalities of valuation: I once followed Mbema, one of the field assistants (FAs) of OFL supervising the outgrowers, through his daily activities, meeting a group of farmers he supervised on their farm in the eastern part of the outgrower scheme. Mbema, fluent in English and living in the village of the outgrowers, was very reflective about this daily work and, thus, a valuable resource person. With the farmers watching curiously on the fringe of their farm, he told me that the group he was supervising had started mango farming in 2004, and that the subsequent years turned out to be "quite difficult" because the farmers only reluctantly took up mango farming. Fortunately, he said, things started changing in 2006 when farmers heard about some of their colleagues cashing in on their first harvests. Again, in 2009–2010, he saw a dramatic change in the attitude of the farmers as information about the monetary benefits of mango growing had diffused in the outgrower scheme. Upon hearing this, the five farmers present nodded acquiescently, murmuring a collective "*tagbu beni*" ("there is change"). When I asked them why it had been so difficult for so many outgrowers to commit themselves to mango farming, they attributed it to its nature as a future crop (*dahin shali bendirigu*; *dahin shali* = "in the near future"; *bendirigu* = "crop" or "food crop"). *Dahin shali bendirigu*, they explained, is in contrast to a short-term crop (*punpongo bendirigu* = "something we eat now"). The farmers argued that if they fully concentrated on the mangoes, their families would be at risk of not having sufficient food for the next seasons, because of the long gestation period of mangoes and the looming uncertainties about future returns (Field diary, 2010).

Given that mango trees constituted an indeterminate worth in the view of many farmers, OFL managers and AOMO staff struggled hard to create "spaces of tradability" (Fourcade 2011: 45) in the course of the project. Framing the mango tree as a worthy good was, in fact, hard work, particularly during the rainy season when trees and farmers' food crops competed for labor. These practical challenges are also well highlighted by a diary entry of my research assistant, David, who worked for AOMO as an extension officer. Back in June 2010, just around the beginning of the rainy season, he noted:

> Farmers' unwillingness to attend to any activity on their mango plantations during the rainy season is very overwhelming. This frustrates most of the field assistants since they have to carry out most of these activities all alone. According to the field assistants, no amount of words could convince farmers during this part of the year to work on their mango farms. The mango farm is only given consideration after the farmer has completely harvested all his annual crops. This was the response of a farmer I asked why he refuses to help the field assistant spray his farm. "We are very busy on our farms (and) you are also talking about mango? I will only go to my mango farm after I have finished all my work in my annual crops farm. That mango is matured enough to overcompete weeds and diseases." This further demonstrates the short-sighted character of farmers.

What David called depreciatingly "short-sighted" in an act of economic othering, indeed resembles a very practical[3] response. His observations, as well as the explanations of the farmers quoted earlier, suggest that in the beginning, among many outgrowers, the mango tree was neither associated with market worth nor was able to satisfy the seasonal needs of the farmers and their families, many of whom struggled to eke out a living. Such doubts were exacerbated by the fact that many farms did not start to produce fruits the fourth year after planting as initially projected by OFL managers, but only in the sixth or seventh year, with some farmers having worked for a good eight years on their trees without any significant yields – a problem I will delve into in detail in Chapter 8.

In many cases, the farmers also were hesitant to take ownership over the trees at the beginning of the project, either because they thought OFL owned them or because of their indeterminate worth. Many farmers used descriptions such as "*anfaani kani*" ("there is no benefit"), "*ti bi nyari ti wahala nyori*" ("we don't see a benefit for our toil"), or "*ti dirila wahala yoli*" ("we suffer for nothing") to describe the situated economics of mango farming, either because they were not sure of the future monetary benefits or could not independently sell the fruits or eat them according to the terms of the contract. The problems of ownership and valuation were firmly entangled and lay at the core of the market-making project, as can be read from the accounts of two farmers in the village of Limaligu. Both were among the first groups to have joined the project, and they had already harvested twice at the time of the interview. One farmer, Hamza, said:

> When the project first came into this community, we were thinking that the white man would own the project and for that matter if we made a mistake and gave our land to the white man to do the project at the end he is going to benefit [and] we won't get anything until later we realized that we have to own the mangoes but [are] only supported with the inputs. (Group Interview/Hamza, 2008, translated)

With a slightly different tone, his colleague, Fuseini, added:

> Since we planted the trees, no one had a doubt of the ownership of the project again, the doubt was only there when it was first coming, but [...] the effort, the hardworking, the commitment to the field was varied because we were still having that kind of doubt whether we would benefit until our people [the group of the farmers], they had their first export and the second export that actually told us that something good will come out of that. (Group Interview/Fuseini, 2008, translated)

Valuing the mango tree, however, and developing a "sense of ownership" was not only about simple cost-benefit calculations, but required new valuations that contained both quantitative and qualitative elements. Indeed, some farmers realized the monetary value of mangoes when they cashed in on their harvests, but the trees also needed to be judged as "good" or "worth" (*anfaani*) more generally in a social setting where tree cultivation was uncommon and where mangoes competed with other useful and socially "considered"[4] crops such as maize, groundnuts, or cowpeas. The Dagbani term *anfaani* has, in fact, a double meaning. On the one hand, it can be used to indicate that something has a "monetary benefit" or "monetary value," and on the other hand it denotes that something is a "blessing" or "good."[5]

Such valuations of the mango tree could only take place *in-process* (Dewey 1915: 517; Stark 2009: 7, 9) as recursively constituted outcomes "of acts of substitution, juxtaposition and transformation" (Thomas 1991: 31) through frictional encounters, which in turn impacted on the farming practices of, and agencies among, many farmers in the scheme. Consider, for instance, the experience of Abdulai, a mango pioneer from the village of Pulugu and one of the most successful members of a group of five farmers:

> After I got some income from the farm, I tripled the number of visits to my field. So initially, I can abstain from the mango farm for about two weeks, but now every two days I have to visit the farm. The mango project has actually given a lot of experience to farmers like me because of the income we started getting from the mango. That made us now stop some of our farming, like the groundnut, and it was taking a whole lot of our time. Now, I realized that the yield I will get from the mango is better from what I get spending my time for the maize. (Interview, 2009, translated)

It was through such experiences and juxtapositions that mangoes by and by became a matter of "consideration" (Dewey 1915: 516). This suggests that "value" is neither

subjective and disembodied nor symbolic and semiotic, as either economists or anthropologists have often argued (Graeber 2001), but a very practical, materially entangled,
and formed in process through a series of mutual adjustments between "things" and
human beings (Appadurai 1986: 15; Callon & Muniesa 2005: 1233; Beckert & Aspers
2011: 14, 26).

From the viewpoint of the economists in the "wild" supervising them, the farmers
had to learn to equate their present investments into the mango farms with future
returns and levels of indebtedness, which was particularly important given that OFL
offered two different prices for grade A (export quality) and grade B crops (local
market). These categories came with "valuation technologies" (Fourcade 2011: 45)
through which the mangoes were finally qualified and quantified at the time of harvest
and to whose working the farmers, most of them illiterate, had to become accustomed
in the first place. Only good farming practices based on prudent qualculation in the
present would yield good mangoes in the future in both qualitative and quantitative
terms, which in turn would result in high monetary returns and a quick repayment of
the debt. This meant that farmers had to get accustomed to "the whole concept of
things costing money," as one OFL senior manager described the process (Interview,
2009), performing their contractually assigned roles as debtors in the market-making
process. In other words, they had to become used to a new money-debt economy
revolving around the mango tree and contractual obligations, which was about "calculating, enumerating, and the reduction of qualitative values to quantitative terms"
(Simmel 1936, cited in Mitchell 2002: 80)[6]. OFL and AOMO staff, all quite reflexive
in their role as economists in the "wild," pushed such qualculations by mobilizing a
range of "methods for associating" (Law 1987: 114). This comprised the mobilization
of awareness-raising campaigns, such as the screening of a movie[7] about "good" farming
practices in the villages of the project area as well as the introduction of so-called
"intermediate-value crops" such as groundnuts and maize on credit. These were
meant to bridge the long gestation period of the mango trees and provide incentives
for other farmers to join the project. Such crops created a "proxy value," reducing the
ambiguities surrounding the market-making project. As we can read from an interview with John, who took over the outgrower department from Charles in 2009, such
strategies were guided by the insight that

> [...] the farmer will only see the value of the mango when he gets money from it. Even if
> you tell him it will do this it will do that in five years time, what he wants is now, what will
> sustain him now, so the mangoes will only attract the farmer's attention when it produces
> good money for the farmer and that was the very reason why I introduced the intermedi-
> ate-value [crops] so that it will bridge that gap, that long gestation period. (Interview, 2009)

Struggling for the Agricola Oeconomicus

Even though the OFL managers registered changing agencies among farmers within
the course of the project, especially among those who received proper returns from
their first harvest, framing the mango tree as a worthy good that needed attention and

care was a strenuous, unfinished accomplishment, marked by many setbacks, overflows, and frictions. The contractually assigned roles and responsibilities (such as those of a "debtor") evolved by no means naturally, but needed to be constituted in an inter-active and performative process that often only produced precarious results. The frictional nature of market-making in northern Ghana was well highlighted in an interview with a senior manager. In a moment of sober reflection on his years in the agribusiness–outgrower complex, he reckoned: "You think you are on top things, then [laughter] your boat rocks over and you start all over again. So it is every day is some-thing new, every day something new […]" (Interview, 2009). Friction, one might add following Tsing (2008: 28), is nothing else than "the everyday crisis of the value form." The frictions of market-making became even more evident during another moment of reflection after the company had lost tens of acres of mango trees to bush fires due to negligence on the side of the farmers in early 2010 (see Figure 6.1). Ignoring the fact that the company actually developed its outgrower scheme in a fire climax ecozone,[8] he offered a problematization we frequently encounter when experts try to explain the "failed commercialization" of peasant agriculture in West Africa and elsewhere: "It will take them [the farmers] another ten years to become like the farmers in Mali or Burkina [Faso], but they will never be commercial farmers. […]. It just seems that they are happy with the little they get, they don't need much" (Field diary, 2010).

Figure 6.1   A mango farm destroyed by bush fires in 2010. (From Author's photo.)

Such was, indeed, a frequent tone adopted by many OFL economists in the "wild." Couched in the words of modern economics, the mystery was that farmers appeared more to be satisficers than maximizing *homines oeconomici*. They had to go a long way to live up to the idea of the *agricola oeconomicus*. Indeed, the outgrowers to be were often entangled in a close web of kinship relations, governed by an "affective regime" (Boltanski & Thévenot 1999: 362), that clashed with the "anthropological monster" (Bourdieu 2005: 83) of the calculating-optimizing farmer. Many farmers could simply not sanction or remove other group members who were tacitly perceived as "lazy" and "not committed" (for instance, those responsible for bush fires) because they feared being castigated as *o ka yurilim* ("he has no love for others") within their communities. Others used water meant for irrigation for domestic purposes. In a region were many villages usually face serious shortages of water, it seemed legitimate to put people before trees. Such farmers, it was said, felt a moral obligation to do so.

Although we should, following Thomas (1991: 8), avoid rendering the mango farmers as non-calculating, risk-averse "economic others" who adopt a safety-first approach to agricultural production – a topos frequently encountered in development economics and anthropology (Feeny 1983) – the hetero- and self-descriptions of farmers remind us that making a market for organic mangoes in northern Ghana was not only a struggle against nature, but also one for accomplishing particular *agencements*. As the term suggests, agencies are not effects of a universal model of agency but are the result of heterogeneous engineering, which, sometimes, may fail to fully achieve its aspirations.

What can we take from this account for intelligibilizing the making of new market agencies in the frontier regions of export-oriented marketization? First and foremost, it shows that having a sense of ownership over a thing and valuating it as having a market worth are two sides of the same coin. The "problem" of invoking agencies that qualculate objects as market goods and assume ownership over them has material, relational, and temporal dimensions that form part and parcel of the ontological reconfiguration on which markets thrive more generally. It is only when worth, grasped in its relational ("an organic mango for export is different from a wild mango tree and can substitute/complement food crops as a source of income"), temporal ("the future value of a good depends in part on present investments"), and material ("the physical quality of the mango tree and the farm directly affects the market value of the crop") dimensions, is ascribed to a discretely defined object ("the mango tree") that the textbook *agricola oeconomicus* emerges.

Despite facing several setbacks and recalcitrances, the project of formatting market agencies in the mango project was all about forging new associations. It was about linking the past, present, and future through qualculative procedures. Couched in the vocabulary of the pragmatics of valuation, the formatting of market agencies in the mango project was marked by a paradoxical sequential interplay of entanglement and disentanglement (Callon & Muniesa 2005: 1233). For the agribusiness–outgrower complex to take off, "the mango tree" needed to be disentangled from established social and material associations, reentangled within the overall organizational arrangement of the market-making project, and framed as a worthy good by situating it in a new spatiotemporal frame of collective qualculation. For the mango market to achieve the form envisaged by the OFL economists in the "wild," self-interested agencies obsessed with calculation-optimization according to their own interest were required (Rose 1996: 136; Holm 2007: 236). Such a program of calculative individualization also required hard work. Rendering such a modality of valuation as "economic" and formatting farmers who were mentally and technically equipped to do so was a project of "subjectification" (Çalışkan & Callon 2009: 389) in its own right, albeit an extraordinarily strenuous one, with varied results across the outgrower scheme.

The notion of subjectification is useful to reflect on for a moment because it reminds us of the cognitive-cum-embodied (market agents need to be equipped with the capacity to develop and exercise particular skills), affective (through particular desires, people become market subjects), and relational dimensions (market subjects always engage in action with others, including "objects") of market-making (Thrift 1997: 127–129; Foucault 1982). At the same time, market agents may be part of many conventional registers – effects of the wrestling and crossing of different lines of sub-jectivity (Deleuze 1992: 159). However, and here we have to move beyond established notions of subjectification, new subjectvities cannot be detached from particular soci-otechnical arrangements with the capacity to produce them, to channel them, and to support them while excluding others. Eventually, the making of global agrifood market connections in northern Ghana was not a subjectification but a performance struggle (Callon 2007: 343) during which the *agricola oeconomicus* could not just be assembled according to plan.

Responsibilizing/Autonomizing Farmers

The making of qualculative agencies is only one facet of the varied performance pro-cesses that characterize the new frontier regions of the global agrifood economy. Another facet is the responsibilization and autonomization of agencies (Hughes 2001; Freidberg 2004; Loconto 2010). Everything that makes it possible to locate sources of action, establish origins, and assign responsibilities plays a strategic part in shaping market agencies (Callon 2005: 4–5). In fact, the variegated history of capitalist mar-ketization, and indeed "capitalism" itself, has been one of creating responsible, auton-omous, and accountable agencies who take their life into their own hands and "produce according to the specific needs of the commodity" (Nevins & Peluso 2008a: 22–23; see also Rose 1996: 139; Escobar 2005: 142).

As already hinted at in Chapter 2, such aspirations have been taken to a new level in various economic fields, including the global agrifood markets, with the rise of standards, audits, and certification schemes over the past two decades as part of neo-liberal governance agendas (see Power 1997; Shore & Wright 2000; Freidberg 2007; Guthman 2007). In agriculture, these technologies aim at directing the behavior of farmers, workers, and managers "at a distance," aspiring to create responsible and autonomous agencies who act in their own interest and in that of the caring retailer and its consumers (Hughes 2004; Higgins & Larner 2010). In this sense, responsibi-lization and autonomization always imply a particular qualification of labor (Boltanski & Thévenot 2006 [1991]: 328).

The making of responsible agencies was no straightforward process in both market-making projects, however. In fact, one should refrain from mobilizing a closed and univocal notion of "subjectivity" in a world endowed with multiple modalities of valuation and potential agencies. Contestation, struggles, heterogeneity, and plastic, reconfigurable material devices are part of the messy actualities of market sociotechnical *agencements* (STAs) (Callon 1998a: 25–26; Higgins & Larner 2010: 5). As highlighted previously, the notion of *agencement* allows for the capture of a wide range of subjectivities (qualculative/non-qualculative, rational/non-rational, reflexive/non-reflexive, individual/collective, and, for that matter "responsible"/"irresponsible") and material arrangements. But how are the *agencements* created that produce "responsible" actions executed by autonomous agents?

Standardizing Market STAs

Figure 6.2 shows a group of pineapple farmers sitting in a circle. Enticed by beverages, they listen to the words of the TF agronomists. Today's training is about integrated pest management (IPM), a requirement under the recently revised GLOBALG.A.P. standard, to which many suppliers of European retailers have to adhere. Over the years, the suppliers had gone through a number of "exotic" (at least from the perspective of the farmers) standard schemes that sought to qualify them according to a wide range of technical, sanitary, phyto-sanitary, social, ethical, and environmental framings of worth.

Figure 6.2   Pineapple farmers attending an IPM meeting. (From Author's photo.)

As elsewhere in the rural South (Neilson & Pritchard 2009; Ouma 2010), these standards had had a profound impact on supply chain relations, production and management practices, and labor relations in the agribusiness–supplier complex. Although many managers had become increasingly critical toward the inflation of standards and the stream of outward-oriented accountability they created over the years, their adoption had been key to remaining competitive in the market. Given the technical complexity and costs of standard compliance, many suppliers, as well as their farm workers, had also become quite skeptical about the benefits of these standards. For instance, to comply with GLOBALG.A.P.'s stipulations regarding the quality and safety of food, producers have to make knowledge- and capital-intensive investments in upgrading the infrastructure of farms (pesticide stores, and toilet and shower facilities to ensure hygiene on farms), implement a quality management system (QMS), and apply new farm management and agricultural practices. Rigid input documentation and plot labeling are crucial metrological technologies for ensuring the traceability of fruits. Farmers are subjected to a strict regime of internal control points that serve as "form-giving instruments" (Thévenot 1984: 8) (see Table 6.1).

Table 6.1   Major control points of GLOBALG.A.P.

Area of performance	Practice
Traceability	Growers must guarantee that the produce can be traced back to the farm level by registering the exact planting and harvesting date of produce on signs attached to individual plots.
Record-keeping and internal self-inspection	Producers are required to keep records of all substances applied to crops, the exact amount, and the date of application. An internal self-inspection must be performed at least once a year.
Varieties and rootstocks	Only certified/authorized seed varieties may be used.
Site history and site management	The history of a farm site has to be checked for environmental issues, for example, if trees were felled for cultivation or whether the land has been contaminated (e.g., through heavy metals).
Risk assessment	Potential risks during the production process have to be systematically identified, assessed, and reduced. Water and soil analyses have to be taken and checked for heavy metals. Maximum residue samples have to be taken at least once a year for a certain number of plots. Health risks must be assessed for workers.
Fertilizer use	Only approved fertilizers may be used; inorganic and organic fertilizers have to be stored separately from crops or seeds.
Irrigation	Contaminated water must not be used for irrigation.
Integrated pest management	Pests must be dealt with in ecologically sensitive ways. Crops must be treated with pesticides punctually if affected. Producers must ensure a minimum time between spraying and harvesting.
Harvesting and produce handling	Hygienic treatment of harvested produce must be ensured.

Source: Ouma, S. (2010). Global Standards, Local Realities: Private Agrifood Governance and the Restructuring of the Kenyan Horticulture Industry. *Economic Geography* 86 (2), 197–222. Reprinted with permission from John Wiley & Sons.

Standards such as GLOBALG.A.P. propagate Eurocentric framings of quality and "personhood" (Dunn 2005: 186; see also Campbell 2005) that often clash with local ways of doing things. Thus, for many of the TF suppliers, the new practices that GLOBALG.A.P. (and some other standards) sought to invoke represented a new sociotechnical order of things they had to get adjusted to in the first place.

The training session shown in Figure 6.2 is part of this new sociotechnical order of things. According to GLOBALG.A.P., IPM is about a

> careful consideration of all available pest control techniques and subsequent integration of appropriate measures that discourage the development of pest populations and keep plant protection products and other interventions to levels that are economically justified and reduce or minimize risks to human health and the environment. IPM emphasizes the growth of a healthy crop with the least possible disruption to agro-ecosystems and encourages natural and/or non-chemical pest control mechanisms (Foodplus 2009: 42)

The TF suppliers have been gathered to get introduced to this "natural" and "non-chemical" way of controlling pests. One agronomist explains in Twi, the local language, what this training is all about:

> The reason for all the trouble is that, when there are foreigners out there and you grow pineapples here and he hasn't seen with his own eyes how your farm is, he doesn't know what chemicals you have used on the farm and he has to go to a shop to buy some of your products and eat, then there must be some standards that will guarantee the consumers that, the product that he or she is going to buy, when he or she eats it, it is safe and has no problems. (Recording, translated, 2008)

And he continues:

> So if we don't add too much chemicals, then it means some of the environmental hazards caused by these chemicals have been reduced. So we will use another new way to eliminate the diseases rather than to use the chemicals. So as you see this is the motive. It's all about chemicals and how much they [the foreigners] are afraid [of]. Because they see that the chemicals are good but how we use them is what causes the problems. (Recording, translated, 2008)

With regard to this scene, one could easily say "business as usual" in global commodity chains. But let us not treat this situation as something given but as something that raises questions. Let us treat it as a "diagnostic event" (Moore 1987) in its multiple relations rather than simply a node in a global commodity chain. Let us treat it as an anthropological situation (Rabinow 2003). From such a vantage point, the situation resembles a formative setting that emerges in relation to the more general processes we usually abstractly call "the market." It brings to the fore the fact that things are not born as commodities but turned into them. Things are not "economic" *per se* but have to be rendered as such.

But the situation is about more than simply objectifying and abstracting "things", producing them for exchange. It is likewise about the production of things judged as "good" for exchange, of pineapples good for "foreigners." What is good needs to be justified by the manager, and utterances such "the reason for all this" and "the motive behind" indicate such justifications. The agonomist justifies the introduction of new production practices by relating to a *particular* modality of valuation (let us call it "sustainability") and not others. As Thévenot et al. (2000: 237) put it, "[j]ustifications can involve positive 'arguments,' claims, or position statements, but might also be critical 'denunciations' of opposing views in the dynamics of public disputes."

In one way or another, such justifications "also provide a second order description of how the social world should be formatted" (Latour 2005: 232). But they are problematizations at the same time, such as when hierarchies of worth are established between "substandard" local pineapples and the goods that retailers want. Problematizations often call for specific solutions (Foucault 1997[1984]; Callon 1986; Rabinow 2003): Not all elements are allowed to enter the "good." "Externalities" such as negative environmental impacts are to be internalized, and ambiguities about the state of the good have to be reduced. All this can be done by complying with the principle of IPM:

> IPM's first principle is prevention. Make sure you do all that you can to prevent the disease. If you become careless, then you will get a problem. I always say that and I always repeat it during our meetings that "failure to plan is planning to fail," and if you fail to plan then you are planning to fail. [...]. There should be a monitoring system. If you really want to buy the idea of IPM, then go by it. (Recording, translated, 2008)

★ ★ ★

Along with a range of other procedures and devices we cannot see here, the standard is eventually made an "obligatory passage point" (Callon 1986: 205) within a complex network of power, knowledge, and methods for normalizing associations (such as metrological devices). All this is part of the objectification and qualification work that makes up pineapples fresh from farm, and this is a "diacritical process" (Boeckler 2005) that results in a specific framing of objects.

Although the training obviously represents only a snapshot of the ongoing work aimed at standardizing and reconfiguring agencies along the JIT frontier – GLOBALG.A.P. was just one of the many standards shaping it – it nevertheless shows that the implementation of standards is not a mere *technical* process but also a *political* one. On the ground, the properties of goods are objectified and rendered visible via the use of metrological devices such as monitoring sheets, annual audits by certification bodies, and the issuing of certificates so that goods can enter the world of Northern retailers and consumers in unambiguous and legitimate ways. Such systems are materializations of voluntaristic and market-based technologies of control and accountability (Power 1997; Shore & Wright 2000; Hughes 2004) – of a sort of technopolitics that should be put under postcolonial scrutiny (Seth 2009). To be accountable in the "quality assurance world", TF agronomists busily kept records throughout the year, documenting their own and the farmers' practices. In fact, they were often so occupied with accounting that they did not have time for anything else, including, for instance, improving production techniques.

When I asked the agronomist responsible after the training and during a more general discussion on standards, whether GLOBALG.A.P. was not sufficient as a generic standard, he just responded: "That is what I ask myself [....] The supermarkets want us to be audited, but not them. They are too powerful" (Field diary, 2008). Thus, standards might not only be understood as investments in forms (Thévenot 1984) that allow for enrolling at a distance in more Foucauldian terms (Larner & LeHeron 2004: 226); they are also power-laden framing and qualculation devices that shape and stabilize market encounters by invoking particular forms of agency while suppressing others. Such inscribed framings decide what is taken into account during an action and what is not, delineating acceptable from non-acceptable practices as well as worthy goods from non-worthy ones. In this way, standards instantiate new forms of material relationality along the supply chain (Barry 2006: 242). By doing so, they seek to normalize particular associational practices to achieve the outcomes retailers, standard bodies, or consumers aspire to.

Although often messy in practice, normalizing for "the market" must be understood as a socio-spatial project of realigning a given practice with a given standard or modality of valuation (Callon 1991: 142; Gibbon et al. 2008: 324). In other words, normalizing for global retail agrifood chains is about creating pacified, docile, and self-regulative agencies that can be compared to each other on a global scale. This eventually enhances the cognitive scopes of centers of calculation such as retailers and standard setters because differences among market participants are reduced to manageable problems (Larner & LeHeron 2004: 223).

All this makes contemporary export-oriented agrarian frontier regions in many parts of the Global South comprehensive technological zones that accelerate and intensify agencies in particular directions and not in others (Barry 2006: 241). Barry (2006: 243) reminds us, in resonance with Foucault's sensitivity to "events" (Foucault 1991: 76), that such technological zones are not inevitabilities. Instead, they must be unpacked with regard to their historical and pluricausal constitution as well as in terms of the specificities of the materials, ways of knowing, and practices they mobilize to shape particular economic configurations (Barry 2006: 250). This makes their study a critical project in its own right.

★ ★ ★

The historical work of making responsible, autonomous agencies as part of creating and stabilizing market *agencements* becomes particularly manifest in the case of OFL. The farmers had to adopt new farming practices that would allow for the attachment of goods to the world of Northern buyers, as we can read from the following account by John, the company's assistant general manager. According to him, the OFL agronomists often had to remind the farmers that

> [...] you are farming not just for chop [food], you are farming for money. And just like you take your goat to the market and somebody will look at how fine your goat is and how fat it is, then he can give the price, then he will now bargain and buy. So it is with the mango! Somebody is going to buy, he wants you to make the mango this way so that

when that mango is that way then he will buy, so that was one important thing. And secondly, [...] it's change that brought human beings into the world and it's change that will take them away so if you're a human being and you don't want to change, that means you are never growing. [...]. You can only be a good farmer if you're able to adapt to new things that can improve your life. (Interview, 2010)

"Farming for money" rests on extensive ontological reconfigurations. "Organic mango farmers" had to become compliant with the rules of GLOBALG.A.P. and the Organic Movement as well as with a range of farming prescriptions developed by OFL. As in the case of TF and its suppliers, the responsibilization of mango outgrowers was worked upon through a mixture of "external subjection and internal subjectification" (Shore & Wright 2000: 61). The outgrowers underwent extensive training in personal hygiene and new husbandry practices, and it was through such training that new associations between hitherto unlinked elements were forged.

This included, for example, learning about the "connection between going to the toilet, and feces making it into your food – the fecal-oral cycle"[9] as part of the training on personal hygiene to ensure a sanitized export production. Hygiene and husbandry practices were closely monitored by OFL's FAs, who lived in the farming communities and thereby transcended the boundary between "firm, farm and society" (Vellema 2002: 20). These FAs had to fill field activity sheets and document whatever pesticides had been applied, whether problems had occurred and note if progress had been made on the farms. The outgrower manager regularly checked on these field activity sheets. They also kept records for the farmers, most of whom were illiterate, and instructed them when to spray the trees with pesticides and micro-nutrients such as boron and cinc. Spray instruction sheets (signed by the outgrowers) and spraying reports (signed by the assistant outgrower managers) were part of an overall QMS, an inscriptive device with productive power. It was the QMS that (partly) rendered a whole range of new practices as market-economic and whose design and performance finally decided whether the farmers would pass an external audit or not. The QMS was being constantly refined in a reflexive and circular process, constituted by external prescriptions (GLOBALG.A.P., Organic Movement) as well as by internal regulations and everyday experiences. Such external prescriptions played a major role in setting up the frames of qualification for both goods and agencies in the outgrower scheme.

With regard to North–South agrifood relations, we often read that such arrangements facilitate "governing at a distance" (Miller & Rose 1990; Larner & LeHeron 2004), perpetuating sanitizing-cum-civilizing missions that rely on colonial modalities of power (Campbell 2005; Freidberg 2004). But what does it actually mean *in practice*? Let us ask the OFL outgrower manager. He will tell us that if a careless non-outgrower farmer sprays a non-selective herbicide such as glyphosate up to the fence of a neighboring outgrower farm, he will have to send an e-mail to the Organic Movement to inform them of such a contamination. If he is lucky, someone will respond by informing him that the responsible committee agreed that the organic land and trees adjacent to the sprayed fence should retain organic status, but likewise warn him that if a similar event occurs in future, the mango trees within 15 m of the affected area will lose their organic status. They may also demand that, in addition, a system should be put in place that eliminates the potential for contamination of organic land. They will probably also make suggestions on how to prevent contamination in future: erect a physical barrier and/or set up a formal agreement with the neighboring farm. Of course, all this will be checked during the next annual inspection. He will then inform his assistant managers that all outgrowers ought to be actively informed of the major risk neighboring crops pose to the organic status of their mango trees. They should engage with the non-mango farmers bordering their farms about selecting crops that do not interfere with organic mango farming. To be on the safe side, he will recommend that all farms should have a safety belt surrounding the farm and that no crops should be cultivated up to the boundary fence. And, of course, he will likely remind his assistants to convey this message to all their farmers, and to be proactive about activities happening outside the mango farms.

This *typical* diagnostic event gives life and sweat to the idea of "governing at a distance." It likewise tells us what it means to engage market universals. In the global economy of qualities, such more distant attempts to create responsible agencies are usually followed by annual visits by auditors, who check on whether farmers and staff of the contracting company comply with a given standard (Ouma 2010). If non-compliances are registered, the auditees have to improve on themselves and their organizational practices, and implement the "corrective actions" the auditors suggested. Altogether, this account of a diagnostic event highlights the critical tension that may emerge when local practices are exposed to more general modalities of valuation and the justifications and controversies that may accompany such a process (see Thévenot 2001a: 72).

Standards and the Stubborn Social

The aspirations and modalities of valuation standards seek to invoke are not always effective, nor are they undisputed. All kinds of politics and practical controversies surround both the definition and implementation of standards. Certainly, standards represent closures where things no longer seem to be up for debate (Thévenot 2009: 806), but in practice not all market participants may accept such closures. Farmers, like any other agency to be framed and pacified, are not just "clean slate[s] awaiting inscription" (Li 2007b: 279). A look backstage confirms such assumptions. Not all TF suppliers were present during the IPM meeting, and some had only sent their farm managers. After the IPM training, the agronomist even complained to me in frustration that "it is some four or five guys who are not committed. So I have to sanction them. We do not compromise anymore. First, I will give them a warning, and then we may suspend them from supplying or even drop them" (Field diary, 2008). On the farm, workers often refused to wear the protective gear GLOBALG.A.P. demanded, arguing that it disturbed them while working in the tropical heat. Ebeneezer, one of the farmers, here tells us how stubborn the social can be:

> In the Ghanaian system, you realize that our minds are not used to certain things, or "I'm farming, so what about toilets in the farm, why should I waste a whole lot of books recording," you see there was no education on the importance of our having toilets on the

farm. So when you introduce such a system in the Ghanaian system, introduce such methods in our system, they will say, "Ah! What is this?" Even in their house they hardly put up toilets [...]. So something like this, if you are not on them, they will not do it. Yes, if you are not on them, they will not do it. (Interview, 2008)

Even the agronomists themselves sometimes struggled to live up to the local aspirations of global standards. This became very clear when I once talked to a senior agronomist when he was busily preparing the pineapple suppliers for an audit under a retailer-driven standard scheme, which the company had just recently adopted. Prior to the audit, the agronomists had been occupied with instructing farmers on what arrangements must be in place in order to survive the audit, rushing from farm to farm. Indeed, many farmers usually received panicky calls from agronomists when audits were coming, and some farmers mocked them for such practices. Some farmers also proved to be quite stubborn as they were skeptical about the benefit of the new standard.

Although one could refer to such practices of neglect and resistance variously as virtual compliance (Blowfield & Dolan 2008), ritualistic compliance (Power 1997), or "backstage activities" (Ybema et al. 2009: 5), I would instead argue that such practices emerge from the coexistence of different modalities of valuation among market participants and that markets are spaces in which these modalities clash and need to be translated (Ouma 2010). Both the TF agronomists and the farmers, in fact, turned out to be quite critical of the proliferation of standards when I got to know them better, disputing both the legitimacy as well as the aspirations of those market devices when judged against the background of their own practical situation. One senior agronomist, for instance, who probably spent 60% of his working time with "reading standards," "reading new versions of standards," and "preparing audits against those standards," remarked quite critically:

You know this is a proliferation of standards in which most of the people who are being audited don't care. They don't really want to have that, and they don't want to learn all about the standards, and in my view the requirements of those standards for people to learn about those standards is merely promoting their [the retailers'/standard-setting bodies'] own self-interest [...]. (Interview, 2008)

* * *

In the case of OFL, the agronomists did not so much struggle with enforcing the rules of global standard setters but with making farmers perform internally defined husbandry practices at individual and group levels. Given the indeterminate worth of the mango tree and the competition of labor between the mango trees and other subsistence crops, many farmers neglected their farms. Farms were often not watered sufficiently or grass was not slashed, leaving them susceptible to the bush fires that frequently plague large parts of northern Ghana during the dry season between December and March. The bush fires had disastrous consequences for the project, destroying or damaging 250 acres of mangoes during the course of the project (see Figure 6.1). Other farmers did not attend to scheduled activities such as the spraying of trees, leaving desperate FAs behind. The most difficult thing, as one field assistant once remarked, was "to get them to do the right thing at the right time" (Field diary, 2011) – to make them perform the roles and responsibilities they had been contractually assigned. The daily struggles of market-making in the outgrower scheme, and the communicative flows between AOMO and OFL, often circled exactly around this issue. Alarming e-mails about so-called "problem farms" were a regular occurrence.

Although the company initially had a more lenient stance toward such farms and tried to "save every farmer," as a senior manager once remarked (Field diary, 2009), this changed during the course of the project when the project budget was repeatedly cut by the shareholders (see Chapter 8). Eventually, the managers would introduce more formalized performance measurement criteria in order to assess the practices of farmers. Those farmers who scored badly or had their trees destroyed by roaming animals or bush fires owing to poor farm management either lost the right to receive OFL inputs and services on credit or were removed from the scheme. When no next of kin could be found who could take over the farm (see Chapter 5), the farmer's debt became virtually a "dead debt." In this way, the market-making project not only introduced the line between those "inside" and those "outside" the market in the first place, but also redrew it repeatedly.

Value/Power

The standardization of sociotechnical relations along market frontiers points to a larger issue. Standards define the terms of engagement in markets, as I already touched upon in Chapter 5. The terms of engagements in markets more generally are effects of power-laden sociotechnical arrangements. For instance, all of the standards companies such as TF and OFL comply with are set and "rendered technical" (Li 2007a: 270) by Northern retailers and standard setters with little or no say from Southern producers. Yet, retailers often do not follow the principles embodied in some of these standards themselves. This was, for instance, the case with ethical and fair trade standards that some retailer customers of TF were so eagerly promoting in their stores. One large retail customer, who claimed to be at the forefront of the fair trade movement, was, in fact, one of the most cutthroat customers.

Such asymmetries make contemporary agricultural markets semi-public spaces, where retailers use their panoptical power to make their suppliers legible and transparent, while their own relationships with suppliers are exempt from public scrutiny and remain black-boxed. In this way, producers, be it farmers, or the companies they are linked to, are dispossessed "from [the] power to decide what matters or, in other terms, what is value" (Elyachar 2005: 8).

When we talk about new enclosures in frontier regions of the global agrifood economy, we should not talk only about material dispossessions (Nevins & Peluso 2008b; Peluso & Lund 2011), but also about symbolic ones: only those producers who have been granted property rights over certain certificates that indicate a conformity with (externally defined) standards are allowed to participate in privately regulated markets (see Mutersbaugh 2005: 399; Guthman 2007). The work of standardization is embedded into highly asymmetrical relations of definition and accountability:

[T]he retailers are very powerful and it is they who like to say to their suppliers, "You must reach this standard, you must reach that standard, you must do this, you must do that," so it's your part to do it [...]. But ask the auditors, ask the retailers themselves to submit to an audit, it is a bit difficult: "Oh no, no, no, we don't actually receive audits, we give audits," but it's not really fair. Why shouldn't supermarkets receive ethical audits along with the farmers and the processors and other suppliers? (Interview senior TF agronomist, 2008)

The criticism mobilized here, though formulated toward ethical standards, points to the broader definitional asymmetries shaping audit encounters between farmers, exporters, and retailers as well as standard-setting and certification bodies in the "quality assurance world". Audits create semi-public spaces – "panoptic 'partnerships,'" as Freidberg (2007: 331) calls these [retailer-driven] "schemes to improve the human condition" (Scott 1998), with the realm of production being engineered to be fully legible while the realm of exchange (between exporters and retailers) remains a black box. The words of the agronomist also underline that "powerful" are those actors who "practically define or redefine what 'holds' everyone together" (Latour 1986: 273).

Furthermore, they bring to the fore the fact that "exchange is always, in the very first instance, a political process, one in which wider relationships are expressed and negotiated in a personal encounter" (Thomas 1991: 7). Although both TF and OFL managers could sometimes influence the implementation of standards during personal encounters with auditors, both companies, like so many other producers, were, nevertheless, part of a highly asymmetrical game in which European retailers and standard-setting bodies managed to co-format markets by putting their own programs into circulation (Callon 2007: 335). This points, in fact, to something larger. Mimicking what Wal-Mart started in the United States in the 1990s, many Northern retailers now go beyond exploiting market inequalities – they reshape the very *possibilities* of trade (Busch 2007: 445; Tsing 2009: 157).

Another problem with the surge of private standards is that they create a largely outward-oriented production model that is more concerned with performing the retail economy of qualities than with improving internal organizational practices such as fruit production or supply base management. This was the case in particular with TF, which complied with a whole range of different standards. A senior agronomist summed up the organizational disarticulations of a continuously morphing economy of qualities as follows:

There should be some harmony now because now, the standards are getting too much for more customers. [...]. It means the whole year you do nothing but prepare farmers to meet standards. Instead of maybe concentrating to improve upon systems and farming practices and methods, you will be thinking more of standards because now standards take up most of our time. (Interview, 2008)

What this excerpt shows is that relations of domination permeating and structuring retail markets are fundamentally inscribed in relations of definition. In the "quality assurance world", instead of "swarms of possibilities, we find lines of forces, obligatory passing points, directions and deductions" (Callon & Latour 1981: 287; see also Daviron & Ponte 2005).

Conclusion

In this chapter, I dealt with the frictional enactment of global market connections. Whereas Chapter 5 outlined how farmers became enrolled into the two market-making projects and how markets were arranged so that goods could be qualified, objectified, mobilized, and exchanged, this chapter demonstrated how things to be valued and agencies capable of qualculating them where actually constituted *in situ*. Having somewhat black-boxed such processes for the frontier in southern Ghana, I unpacked what hard work might go into the making of the *agricola oeconomicus* and what mundane and materially entangled processes of subjectification define the very moment of "world market integration." Often, however, such formatting work might be threatened by overflows, setbacks, as well as competing forms of agency and modalities of valuation, which need to be channeled and directed in the process of market-making. As Tsing (2005: 5) notes so adequately, "[i]n the historical particularity of global connections, domination and discipline come into their own, but not always in the form laid out by their proponents." Accordingly, it is in frontier regions, where certain agencies and modalities of valuation are often still a matter of controversy, where new alignments have to be forged so that markets can eventually work smoothly. The case of OFL and its outgrowers shows how difficult such alignment work can be, disqualifying accounts of markets that see an ahistorical reality and an anthropological constant where there is ontological reconfiguration and formatting.

However, the making of qualculative agencies is only one facet of the variegated performance processes that characterize the new frontier regions of the global agrifood economy. Although advanced capitalist markets cannot exist without responsible and autonomous agencies who produce in the interest of the commodity and/or according to contractual obligations, such processes of responsibilization and autonomization have been given a new thrust with the global spread of various process standards and certification schemes, which aim to govern firms and farms *at a distance*. Their implementation and conduct is never a mere technical process. They "transform the objects and subjects they aspire to govern" (Higgins & Larner 2010: 9), thereby reshaping the identities of and relations between farmers, agronomists, retailers, consumers, and standard-setting and certification bodies.

Farmers no longer produce simply "pineapples" or "mangoes," but goods whose "value depends on their relation with a set of more or less standardized assessments of their quality" (Barry 2006: 242) – goods that can enter the world of Northern retailers and consumers in unambiguous and legitimate ways. In this manner, the global economy of qualities produces new forms of material relationality. In new frontier regions of the global agrifood economy, this results in a complex bricolage of processes of external subjection and internal subjectification that are governed at both proximity and a distance, making them technological zones in their own right. Yet such processes always carry with them disciplinary struggles that are the result of co-existing and competing modalities of valuation. Such processes are firmly shaped by definitional asymmetries inscribed into "relations of worth" (Boltanski & Thévenot 2006 [1991]: 143). This is once more a demonstration that markets are not only sites where the quality of goods is tested and evaluated, but likewise spaces of possibles (Bourdieu 2005). In general, this chapter comes to an important conclusion. Any study of marketization must not only unpack what constitutes value/worth, but also what undermines it and what defines how it *cannot* be realized (Elyachar 2005: 7).

Endnotes

1   In this book, all names of individuals, of the case study companies and related organizations, and their geographical associations have been anonymized, are withheld, or have been altered to protect sources. Development organizations and programs associated with the Ghanaian agricultural sector more generally are referred to by their original names.
2   I am indebted to Iddrisu Azindow for this point.
3   I use the term "practical" instead of "rational." What is at stake here are practical valuations of the mango tree, valuations that can only take place in process.
4   Dewey (1915: 516) once aptly noted that "[a] value, in short, means a consideration."
5   For example, childhood or the shade of a tree may be referred to as *anfaani*.
6   Obviously it is difficult to transplant Simmel to northern Ghana without provoking the anger of postcolonial theorists. His conception of the money economy as being constitutive of the "modern" world needs the significant other of the non-market economy of "traditional" worlds. Although we should be sensitive to such otherings, there is, nevertheless, something we can take from it: That the rise of particular forms of qualculation is connected to particular moments in history, where some exchange framings become more dominant than others; that the money economy is about a series of transformations and measurements; and that no commodity can emerge without those transformations.
7   The film, shot with local comedians in *Dagbani*, showed the various encounters between "serious" and "lazy" farmers, thematizing crucial issues such as husbandry practices, gender roles, success, group work, and information sharing.
8   I am indebted to Kojo Amanor for this point.
9   Quote taken from an e-mail-discussion with the person who conducted the training, 2011.

Chapter Seven
Markets, Materiality, and (Anti-)Political Encounters

Just-in-time (JIT) is not just a principle, it has likewise a materiality. If JIT is all about power (Cox 1999), then so must be the "things" that hold it together. Let us follow its materiality. Let us move backstage. Let us see how a supplier typically brings his fruits to market – or not …

It is delivery day. After harvesting his fruits, a pineapple farmer grades his fruits into three weight categories (I, II, III) at his farm as demanded by Ton:go Fruits (TF)[1] guidelines. Upon arriving at the factory's fruit intake, he lines up his delivery according to each weight category. He offloads all estimated category III fruits and puts them into one line, as with the assumed category II and I fruits. Caution is required. Small fruits (category III) should not make up more than roughly a third of the delivery. A quality assurance officer performs a cross-check, takes twelve fruits from each line as a sample and weighs them. If these fruits are found to be in another category, the whole line will automatically be in this weight category. Fruits heavier than category I will also be weighed as category I fruits, because, apparently, the cutting machines in the factory cannot process any larger fruits.

It is not all about weight. The fruits are evaluated against a whole series of quality criteria. Applying various techniques of metrology and documentation, the history of each consignment is written. Is the farmer delivering an approved supplier? Are benchmarks for external color, condition, bruising, maturity, sugar context (measured in Brix), maturity (measured by translucency), aroma (measured by smell), flavor (measured by acidity), and texture met? Have the pineapples been transported and stored the right way?

Assembling Export Markets: The Making and Unmaking of Global Food Connections in West Africa,
First Edition. Stefan Ouma.
© 2015 John Wiley & Sons, Ltd. Published 2015 by John Wiley & Sons, Ltd.

But the intake is not just a site of evaluation, it is also one of ambiguous qualification and decision-making. It is here that circulation is further guaranteed if pineapples are judged as good, or halted if they are not. Fruits may be rejected, provisionally accepted, or accepted outright – depending on the score a pineapple achieves on a recording form. "Provisionally accepted" means that visually underripe fruit might eventually be rejected and invoiced back to the farmers. Such conclusions will be made in process inside the processing plant. The action is where the farmers are not.

★ ★ ★

When talking about the encounters between large agribusiness companies and smallholder farmers in the Global South, narratives of unequal bargaining power, informational asymmetries, one-sided contracts, and value redistribution inevitably pop up (Feder 1976). In his magisterial piece on contract farming, Watts (1994: 63) notes that

> [...] The history of contracting is replete with company manipulation and abrogation of contracts. [...]. The volatility of world markets, especially in fresh fruit and vegetables, has also contributed to companies reneging on their contractual obligations to purchase the totality of a grower's output.

Such classic insights into agribusiness–farmer encounters are still a valuable starting point for studying the new frontier regions of the global agrifood economy (Oya 2012), but these narratives tend to conceive power as a substance, with "capital" being rendered a force that exploits poor smallholders according to the general law of capitalist accumulation. Even though the global agrifood economy has profoundly changed since Watts published his piece and the global commodity/value chains and production networks literatures have developed more nuanced notions of power with regard to increasingly complex and global trade relations (see Gibbon et al. 2008; Hess 2008; Neilson & Pritchard 2009), power often remains unspecified in its mundane and technical manifestations in this literature. As I have already outlined in Chapter 2, the agrarian political economy and chain literatures have largely not accounted for "*how* hierarchies come to be told, embodied, performed, and resisted" (Law 1994: 134). Such manifestations of power, as well as the "'hidden conditions' for the production of deeply uneven transnational market orders" (Berndt & Boeckler 2011a: 1062), are usually less visible, and we have to move backstage to study them. It is here where we can draw on Latour's practical take on power. What exactly happens when "big" agribusiness meets "small" farmers? How (un-)equal are those encounters? And what (re)distributive effects may come along with them?

This chapter addresses these ostensibly simple questions with regard to both case studies. Answering them will further qualify the previously made argument that market sociotechnical *agencements* (STAs), depending on their configuration, can create differentiated positions and agents in the market (Çalışkan & Callon 2010), which may result in the uneven allocation of risk, loss, and gain. The crucial question that critical ethnographies of marketization ask is when are "economic agents" such as "suppliers" or "outgrowers" in a position to contest the performance of markets

and when not? In other words, what needs to be explored is when the market as a *process* turns political, that is, when its organization and operation are disputed and become a matter of controversy, and when not? To make sense of such dynamics, I conceive of the making and remaking of global agrifood markets as a series of (anti-)political encounters. I demonstrate that whether "critical dynamics" (Eymard-Duvernay et al. 2003: 16) ensue during the process of marketization depends to a large extent on the distribution of the qualculative power and critical capacities of the agencies involved in market transactions, their resource mobilizations, and materially grounded interactions. Material devices and algorithms are crucial mediators in this regard. Often hidden from the general public, they reconfigure global agrifood connections. Eventually, this chapter demonstrates that power is not only articulated in specific relations of definition, as the previous chapter has shown, but also in specific relations of qualculation and accounting. Markets are not as flat as neoliberals usually tell us.

The Hidden Conditions of Global Markets

When Mr. Sneijder, the founder of TF, set up his JIT business in the late 1990s, he was aware that markets can be sites of struggle. Having worked in a factory in Europe for some years in the heyday of unionism, he had learned of "the oppressive nature of unionism, of the 'them-and us-culture,' which unionism caused." Although convinced that "there is no reason why actually one shouldn't sit around a roundtable [...], no reason why we can't discuss and try and find an equitable and fair way what the solution is" (Interview, 2009), he perceived the *ancien* union system as conflict ridden, leading all too often to a confrontation between "capital" and "labor." When setting up his business in Ghana, he therefore wondered how to initiate a different relationship with workers and suppliers alike, one not based on confrontation but on a "corporate culture" of "trust" and "mutual respect."

When looking backstage, however, matters become complex. As I have argued in Chapter 5, buying into the rhetoric of trust deployed in the interview risks neglecting other forces stabilizing market *agencements* such as the very "visible hands of particular market agents" (Zafirovski 2000: 276) and the transformative power of market devices. Ordering an organization is not just a matter of building trust among its members – it is likewise about *productive* power. Although ordering is not *all* about power, it diffuses even in environments shaped by the very best intentions (Foucault 1982)! Because the structural imperative of JIT is to accurately meet the lead times of supermarkets, which nowadays fiercely compete over leaning supply chains, partly mimicking the accumulation strategies of "Toyotaist" manufacturing enterprises (Gibbon & Ponte 2005; Raworth & Kidder 2009), suppliers to big Northern retailers must always be "in the pipeline" – otherwise they may be quickly substituted. This is the organizing principle of "supply chain capitalism" (Tsing 2009; see also Busch 2007). Under such structurating conditions, disruptions from labor or supplier strikes represent a potential threat, and this is actually what the interview cited earlier invites us to think about.

Hence, making the JIT model work *in situ* rested on a whole scheme of carefully controlled systems. It required particular market arrangements based on distinct translations and role definitions. Workers and suppliers needed to be peaceful – not confrontational. Given the rather easy substitutability of (low-skilled) labor in Ghana, having a pacified supply base was key to enacting global JIT connections. No raw material, no market! Thus, the argument to be advanced here, in line with Fligstein (2001: 34), is that the internal organization of the JIT agribusiness–supplier complex was a direct response to the prevailing conventions of competition in retail markets. Machiavellian politics were at work, invoking the *raison d'etre* of SCM. Farmers were divided instead of coming together – for good reasons. Some were paid differently, and some could get more produce to the market than others. Indeed, the allocation of supply quotas can be an effective means of translation because they help manage critique in supply chains. Critique, for instance, with regard to certain pricing or quality assurance practices, hardly became collective because group formation rests as much upon hard work as does group failure:

> Yes that is where we are falling down, we don't have [a] union. If you want to try to organize something some people will disorganize themselves and then later on we have to stop it [...]. There is no pineapple suppliers union or farmers' union until now. So we don't have [a] common front. (Interview with farmer, 2008)

JIT orderings are powerful orderings, and they prompt us to ask a set of questions about the performativity of SCM in retail markets (Busch 2007). Why it is that farmers do not come together? Why do they act individually rather than collectively, even though other possibilities exist? Or, in other words, "how is it [...] that the heterogeneous bits and pieces that make up organization generate an asymmetrical relationship between periphery and center? [....] How is it that a manager manages?" (Law 1992: 390). The questions are firmly about power. The ordering of the JIT arrangement reminds us, however, that power is not simply held as a stock by those rendered "powerful", but composed of the wills of other people (Latour 1986: 269). The translation of farmers into individual suppliers, in association with the systems of metrology in place at the factory level (see the next section) and the rather low educational level of many farmers resulted in the uneven distribution of risks, losses, and gains along the supply chain. It provided space for a market order that was in many respects hardly effectively challenged by most pineapple suppliers of TF. Even though some farmers used the exit option over the course of time, many arranged themselves within the temporalities and materialities of JIT.

This is not a critique of the corporate interviewees who so willingly gave me access to their field of practice – it would be far too easy to deem what I describe here as an agrobusiness-engineered manufacture of consent among peasants so that "surplus appropriation is not obscured at the point of production" (Watts 1994: 62; see also Feder 1976). This is a critique that problematizes what is often neglected when theorizing South–North trade relations: the power-laden nature of market devices and the structural inscriptions they bear in relation to the market social. It is a reminder that power is part and parcel of even those spaces that often well-intended practitioners imagine as egalitarian, including some of my interviewees. All market STAs are powerful and translative. I shall substantiate this claim in the following section by arguing that the JIT market ordering was based on the black-boxing of a range of sociotechnical devices (including the systems of metrology described in the beginning) and overflows that farmers failed to challenge collectively. In this regard, what follows takes up the argument about the relation between black boxing and enrollment made in Chapter 5.

Powerful Valorimeters

The materialities of JIT are organized around flexibility and selective permeability. Large retailers often cancel their orders, a practice many suppliers around the world have learned to fear (Young 2004). Ask the TF managers! The practices of flexible accumulation employed by some of its customers resulted in a volatile demand regime and the staff responsible were frequently faced with the difficult decision of whether to internalize or externalize these risks to suppliers. A complete internalization of risks would have threatened the company's survival, whereas a complete externalization would have created broad-based unrest among suppliers. Under these structurating conditions, the costs of canceled orders were sometimes internalized. Sometimes, however, a low-demand regime led to an increased rejection (or "rejects," as they were called by the farmers) of fruits by the staff responsible for fruit intakes, which were often not justified on grounds of under-demand or canceled orders, but by advancing technical arguments. The intake personnel, for instance, would argue that the fruits supplied did not meet the company's quality criteria (e.g., translucency levels, sugar content/Brix levels, texture, etc.). For the farmers, having worked for a good 14 to 15 months on their pineapples, such rejects came with financial losses and personal frustrations. "The rejects are killing us" was a frequent refrain among many pineapple suppliers (see Chapter 8).

Although earlier work on contract farming highlights similar practices of risk and cost redistribution (e.g., Glover & Kusterer 1990: 129; Watts 1994: 63; Singh 2002: 168; Vellema 2002: 75), it should be noted that the material infrastructures that enable such practices do not just deserve a side note but must take center stage when talking about the production and maintenance of relational asymmetries in the global agrifood economy.

Let me further qualify this argument. A crucial and materially entangled choreography during the intake encounter was the assessment of the sugar content of pineapples, which the intake personnel measured by using a so-called refractometer (see Figure 7.1). During the use of this device, a specimen of pineapple juice would be applied to it to ascertain the sugar content of the solution. Ideally, the Brix levels had to score values from 1x to 1y on a scale from 1 to 35, even though sometimes values lower or higher than this would be accepted. The quality assurance officers at the fruit intake would use their own refractometer, and the farmers usually had little opportunity to contest their assessments. The majority of the farmers did not even own refractometers themselves; they were literally "badly equipped agencies" (Callon 2007: 349) and thus could often not challenge the consignment history that the quality assurance officer wrote.

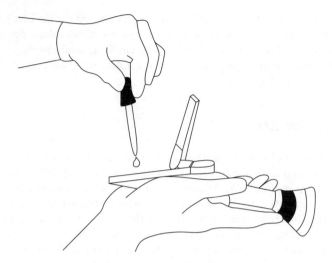

Figure 7.1   A refractometer. (From Design by Elke Alban. Reprinted with permission.)

Rejecting fruits on the grounds of a technical assessment at times represented "a numerical way of displacing and resolving political disputes" (Pinch & Swedberg 2008: 11) about actually existing supply chain orders. Materially and politically disabled farmers often found it hard to challenge such displacements. Under the flexible JIT demand regime, quality became a flexible category itself. For instance, the Brix would be handled quite differently in terms of high and low market demand. Of course, the farmers could have pushed for less ambiguity if they had become a collective, but as one intake manager put it very well: "Everybody wants a favor, so if I get a favor [...] why should I fight for you? [...]. When you see the forest, you see it as a group, but when you enter you see the single tree" (Field diary, 2009).

What this account shows is that the JIT market ordering was based on the design and effects of a range of black-boxed (because unchallenged) "valorimeters." Valorimeters are "the various tools, procedures, machines, instruments or, more generally, devices effecting this controversial translation of values into figures and, more precisely, into monetary amounts" (Çalışkan & Callon 2010: 17). Calculative agencies who are able to achieve the imposition of their valorimeters and calculations on others are in a position "to transform their own valuation into an obligatory passage point and can spread the definitions of value that are more closely aligned with their interests" (ibid.: 17).

To be fair, the tactics presented here did not emerge from some overall corporate strategy – as argued earlier, organizations are neither monoliths (Thrift & Olds 1996) nor can they be separated from their "market environment" (Schatzki 2005). Instead, they were often the result of distributed coping strategies and framings of worth among company staff, who judged farmers and the fruits supplied according to specific situations. Sometimes these situations[2] were framed by mere technical arguments, sometimes by market imperatives when produce was scarce (and quality criteria suddenly mattered less), sometimes by subtle personal connections between gatekeepers at the factory and individual farmers who managed to negotiate the quantity of produce to be accepted at the intake. At times, the agronomists would intervene in the encounters between quality assurance personnel and the farmers and as such played a crucial role as mediators. On the one hand, they had to perform their role as custodians of the farmers because they had assessed the Brix content of the fruits on-farm and told farmers to harvest in the first place, and on the other hand they had to act in the interests of their organization. Given these organizational ambiguities, no wonder that one farmer described the performance of the intake as a "game" (Field diary, 2009).[3]

All this made the JIT market arrangement, like many other market arrangements, a relational *bricolage* of trust, mutual dependency, affection, consent, and domination. It is no contradiction that the ongoing exchange relationship between two parties may be characterized by various forms of sociality (Thomas 1991: 31), for it all depends on the situational arrangements, their materially entangled interaction, the resources the parties manage to mobilize, and their qualculative and critical capacities. My account is, indeed, a reminder that translations are comprised of a wide range of practices – negotiations, intrigues, calculations, acts of persuasion, and force can be all part of the *same* game (Callon & Latour 1981: 279).

Yet, not all pineapple farmers accepted the imposition of JIT valorimeters and translative tactics. A few better-educated ones at least brought their own refractometers and challenged the rule of experts at the factory. Moreover, some of the biggest suppliers, who were exporters themselves, gradually pushed to have their own weighing bridges on their farms to calculate the accurate weight of their fruits. These suppliers had different cognitive and technical capacities and had the option to export their fruits themselves, something which enhanced their negotiating power *vis-à-vis* the company's management.

Pricing, Returns, and Visible hands

Not only are the definitions and evaluations of product properties such as quality or weight effects of specific, power-laden sociotechnical arrangements, but so are prices – the final outcome of every market. As argued in Chapter 2, prices are not just results of supply and demand based on marginal utilities, as neoclassical economists usually posit (Arrow 1998), or of power constellations and "social influences," as economic sociologists, old and new, have argued (Weber 1922 [1978]; cited in Swedberg & Granovetter 1992: 8; see also Zafirovski 2000: 286; Beckert 2011). This argument gains more weight if we reflect upon the general development of prices in the market for JIT pineapples. In the beginning, the TF management used prices as prostheses to enroll farmers into its market-making project. Prices paid for pineapples were set above the industry average and even increased in times of high market demand in order to prevent farmers from side-selling to other exporters. At the same time, tactics were gradually developed to deal with the threat of farmers controlling input prices, a common problem of market-making (Fligstein 2001: 17), which would have jeopardized the stability of the JIT market order.

As argued earlier, from the very beginning the company used prices as "productive devices" in "a political process of deliberation" (Çalışkan 2007b: 257), basically creating a "structured" supply base, whereby the most important suppliers would be paid in foreign currency, while others would be paid in local currency. From 2006 onward, TF stopped making temporal price adjustments despite the fact that suppliers faced rising costs for labor and inputs. As will be shown in more detail in Chapter 8, this was partly due to the fact that price competition increased in output markets from 2006 onward, narrowing pricing scopes (see Excursus 7.1). In 2008, however, the company agreed to pay all suppliers in foreign currency after it had transpired that some farmers had been treated more equally than others, which gave farmers a small price increase when the exchange rate was favorable. Nevertheless, from the farmers' perspective, this was not enough, and they sought an adjustment of prices, as one farmer remarked in 2009:

> So I think what Ton:go Fruits should do is, when there is going to be [a] review on prices, there should be [a] review, there should be [a] review if there has been increase in cost of production and the review should not [be] based on only Ton:go Fruits, they should sit down and discuss prices with the farmers. They have to sit down with the farmers, and we put our cost of production across and the price we intend to collect. Maybe there should be a form of discussion so that we come out with a fair price which will benefit Ton:go Fruits, which will benefit the farmers, too. (Interview with farmer, 2009)

Why did the farmers not revolt against such pricing practices, or drop out of the JIT business altogether?

Part of the answer has already been given. Although some of the TF suppliers indeed left TF or dropped out of pineapple farming completely over time because

---

Excursus 7.1   Prices are treacherous "things"

Contrary to what mainstream economic price theory argues, firms do not usually set prices "at the point where marginal revenue equals marginal costs" (Beckert 2011: 22). Prices often do not represent the actual costs a producing firm is incurring. TF, for instance, had to pay for promotions of new products at retail stores (see Gibbon & Ponte 2005: 20–21). It is also a common but controversial practice among some Northern retailers to make their customers pay a specific sum of money to provide them with free capital to fund their expansion or to compensate for efficiency losses naturally occurring when relations move away from a market regime and become more stable and "personal." Such "special payments" (Gibbon & Ponte 2005: 21) contribute significantly to the overall profits of some Northern retailers. At times, retail suppliers such as TF may also make losses to sustain the market, as I showed in Chapter 5. It is also common that large retailers employ reverse auctioning tactics, where the bidder with the lowest price will get a specific product line (Busch 2007: 448). The hope for suppliers making such bids is that in time they may be able to increase their prices. In the case of TF, large competitors with a certain market power adopted such strategies and thus represented a considerable threat. Altogether the existence of a whole range of redistributive backstage practices makes the study of prices in retail markets (and elsewhere) an elusive quest.

they thought it was no longer profitable, the majority never did engage in any mean-ingful collective action because they were not able to develop structures of common interest.[4] The voice option had been organized away, and the exit option remained equally elusive for most farmers as market demand for the local Smooth Cayenne pineapple variety dropped rapidly from 2005 onward owing to rising global demand for MD2. The latter pushed many Smooth Cayenne farmers and exporters out of the pineapple business. This change in variety posed a real problem to several farmers as they had taken up bank loans backed up by TF as part of an ambitious expansion program launched in 2006.

Furthermore, effective demand dropped in the wake of the global economic crisis from 2008 onward (see more in Chapter 8). Owing to the cumulative effects of pref-erence change and global economic crisis, the smaller TF suppliers had no real choice but to engage with these orders as TF remained the only major exporter of the Smooth Cayenne variety between 2006 and 2009. Back in the summer of 2008, Kojo, a supplier, described the situation the farmers where caught in as follows:

> Actually, Ton:go Fruits is trying their best to keep the relationship or to keep the busi-ness, but the problem is they are also not taking; according to them, they are facing a lot of problems, market strategies and challenges over there, so increasing the price will make them go out of the business. So we can't force them much because they are the only buyer, so we are looking up to them. (Interview, 2008)

In late 2008, the farmers even agreed to a price reduction for two consecutive months in order to help TF, which landed in financial trouble owing to the global economic crisis and its costly internationalization program (see Chapter 5).

Many farmers subscribed to such supply chain orders not only because they did not have access to alternative markets, but also because they were not able to calculate their real returns from pineapples sales because they lacked the management skills or the material equipment to do so. Thus, many of them became enmeshed in an opaque thicket of loans, rising production costs, and "rejects", making it difficult to find out "where one really stood." When some of the farmers in 2008 forwarded their own calculations to prove that the business had become gradually less profitable, the TF agronomists subsequently devised their own calculations that eventually served as a yardstick for all other calculations in the system, silencing the concerns of the farmers.

What this account shows is that relations of domination in markets are firmly anchored in relations of calculation, or better, qualculation. In this regard, Çalışkan and Callon (2010: 16) are right when they assert that "[f]ixing a price is always the outcome of a struggle between agencies trying to impose their modes for measuring a good's value and qualities." This mandates we must turn our attention to the "visible hands" of market agents during the process of price formation and supply chain management more generally, rather than attributing prices to the invisible hand of the market (Zafirovski 2000: 276; Busch 2007: 456).

Not all attempts to redistribute risk and value succeeded. One of the few practices the TF suppliers challenged collectively because they were all affected by it was the exter-nalization of labor costs to the farmers in the wake of the global economic crisis. TF started to shift these costs to farmers when competition in output markets increased, and profit margins dwindled. The company had already externalized the first round of grading fruits to farmers in 2008, a decision that remained unchallenged. When the Swiss headquarters of the TF holding company, however, decided to externalize the decrowning of fruits to farmers in the same year, the farmers became more proactive. Externalizing the decrowning to farmers not only reduced the *payable* weight for fruits, it also transferred additional labor costs to them. For example, one farmer reported that instead of using five people for harvesting he had to use eight, sometimes even ten, workers to harvest and decrown the fruits. Decrowning the fruits on-farm also made them vulnerable during transport and virtually unsalable in local markets (where they would have to be taken if they had been rejected by TF). It was for this reason that not all local managers of TF supported this practice, even warning the managers in the headquarters that it could adversely affect the quality of the fruits or lead to unrest. Leaving some quite frustrated agronomists behind, the headquarter management, nevertheless, pushed for externalizing the decrowning cost to the farmers.

Although the management could pass the order without much open resistance, the suppliers eventually became more critical of this practice and joined forces because it affected all of them without exception. Farmers were thus in the same boat without some of them being "more equal than others." The practice soon became a thing of the past.

Power Relations as Relations of Accounting

Markets are, above all, sites where the quality of goods is tested, evaluated, and translated into prices. Their organization hinges on activities of "abstraction" (Muniesa et al. 2007: 4) that prepare those tests and format them: activities of classification, measurement, codification, certification, and pricing (Eymard-Duvernay et al. 2003: 12). As was shown in the previous sections, all these activities are open to "performation struggles" (Callon 2007). They can be materially tinkered with, affecting the organization of markets, which in turn may shape the distribution of risk, loss, and gain. Such a perspective can accommodate some findings of earlier works on contract farming (Watts 1994; Vellema 2002) and markets more generally (Fligstein 2001: 15; Beckert 2011), which suggest that the organization of market encounters usually bears enormous potential for conflict, as it may directly affect the returns to market participants. Against this backdrop, it is in instances when the organization of markets is no longer contested that one should become suspicious.

Unequal market encounters, of course, may be contested, but the pineapple case study suggests that the quality of the calculative, reflexive, critical, and associational capacities of affected market agents (be they individual or collective) – political capacities in their own right (Eymard-Duvernay et al. 2003: 16) – are crucial in this regard. To a great extent, however, critical dynamics in markets not only depend on the political capacities of particular agents that could challenge the modalities and materialities of qualification and exchange but also on the relations of accountability shaping market encounters. A crucial question in this regard is how "the market" is organized as a sequence of encounters of accounting? When do such encounters become "critical moments" (Boltanski &Thévenot 1999: 359) and "matters of concern" (Latour 2005: 87)?When do overflows turn political and "misfire" (Butler 2010: 151)? When do performance struggles occur and when not? Framed somewhat differently, these have been crucial questions in other studies on outgrower schemes (seeVaughan 1991: 181;Vellema 2002: 68) involving more complex flows of inputs, credit, products, payments, and loan deductions as is the case with Organic Fruits Limited (OFL) and its 1,295 outgrowers.

A valuable starting point for developing a critical analysis of accounting within global agrifood connections is the insight that organizing an accounting system in contract farming schemes, and within and between organizations more generally, is about inventing a "particular way of understanding and administering events and processes" (Vellema 2002: 68). Accounting, usually a crucial practice in the performation of concrete capitalist markets, gives meaning and form to economic practices, constituting those realms commonly rendered as "economic" (Miller 1994: 4; Muniesa et al. 2007: 3). In loan-financed contract farming schemes, accounting transforms the flows of money, debts, inputs, services, products, and returns into numeric data.

Like other activities of abstraction (classification, measurement, etc.), accounting may decide the redistribution of risk, loss, and gain during market encounters. It is by no means a *neutral* practice "that merely documents and reports 'the facts' of economic activity" (Miller 1994: 1). It is transformative, opening up new possibilities for action, while closing down others. It has "economic consequences," as Miller (1994: 7) notes accurately. But broadly speaking, accounting is not just about transforming different physical flows and practices into numeric form: it is also about giving narrative accounts (Stark 2009: 26), making things visible and intelligible. In this vein, market encounters can be "understood as sites in which actors engage in practices of justifying worth" (ibid.: 24). In organizations or markets, it is often during physical encounters between people that rather abstract accounting structures working *backstage* are translated into narrative accounts *frontstage*, or that these structures are fed with new data produced during such encounters.

The problem of accounting is worth investigating with regard to OFL and its outgrowers, who, in contrast toTF and its suppliers, were linked through other organizational arrangements and served seasonal markets with different redistributive outcomes. Initially, there seemed to be huge asymmetries between OFL and the mango farmers in northern Ghana, for the latter had no experience with loan-financed export agriculture and, compared to their southern counterparts, exhibited high levels of illiteracy. Not without cause, some public servants familiar with the project were worried about the setup of the mango project from the very beginning. For instance, a close industry observer and former employee of the Ministry of Food and Agriculture then heading the Export Marketing and Quality Assurance Programme (EMQAP) aired his concerns about the obvious power asymmetries between OFL and the outgrowers. According to him, the fact that the company was working with "peasant farmers that have never grown cash crops before" gave it a "huge advantage," and he saw "a chance that this could be abused" (Interview, 2008). He was concerned that OFL could use its virtual monopsony power to "exploit the farmers" (ibid.), basically echoing what authors such as Watts (1994: 63–64) and Amanor (1999: 28, 78) describe as an almost generic feature of outgrower schemes. For the official, public policy had to ensure "that farmers are not exploited" (Interview, 2008), or, to put it differently, that there is "accountability."

Given such concerns, the crucial question is how encounters of accounting were framed and formatted in the case of OFL and its outgrowers? When addressing this question, we should first be aware of the diverse configurations market encounters may take and, second, avoid giving in to an *a priori* binary opposition between the powerful corporation and its powerless outgrowers. Such an opposition would, in fact, be blind to the ordinary weapons of the weak (Scott 1986), as well as to the fact that power is actually made up of the wills of others (Latour 1986: 269). Despite the ostensible asymmetries existing between OFL and the outgrowers, the market encounters in the mango project stood on a very different footing than those along the JIT frontier.

First, owing to the involvement of DIAROC as a mediator, a detailed contract regulated crucial encounters between OFL and the outgrowers. The contract left little space for ambiguities and, in fact, was even framed in favor of the farmers as they could virtually not be taken to court in cases of default (see Chapter 5).

Second, although a more comprehensive contract itself does not automatically ensure equal encounters as contracts as framing devices are often incomplete *in practice* (Feder 1976; Glover & Kusterer 1990; Vellema 2002: 56), the OFL directors and managers wanted to be transparent in their dealings with farmers. As argued in Chapter 5, every contract has its non-contractual elements. In a frontier region where trust in a hitherto unknown market still needed to be established and where onto-logical reconfigurations of significant scale and scope had to take place for "the market" to thrive, the OFL directors and managers knew that it was crucial to foster a good relationship with the farmers and their communities. The OFL directors and senior managers were aware that a poor relationship could discourage farmers from investing in the mango farms, create a space for the side-selling of produce in times of production, or even turn political. This would have jeopardized the long-term invest-ment of the company, including the loan recovery. "Everything starts with the farmer" (Interview managing director, 2009); such was the corporate credo. If he made money, the company would make money, too. That credo had worked particularly successfully in another agricultural venture of OFL's parent company, which had managed to enroll around 16,000 farmers into its corporate network.

Third, the market for organic mangoes was seasonal. On top of that, OFL never dealt directly with retailers but with large distributors of fresh fruits in Europe. These markets bore little resemblance to the highly risky, demanding, and squeezing retail chains that TF delivered to just in time.

Fourth, the loan advancement, the provision of inputs, the harvesting and market-ing, the loan recovery, and the sheer number of outgrowers involved required a very comprehensive system of accounting.

Fifth, albeit notoriously understaffed and run only by two permanent employees (administrator, accountant) and a board of farmers (chairman, vice-chairman, secre-tary, and treasurer), the Association of Organic Mango Outgrowers (AOMO) and its executives acted as a voice speaking on behalf of the farmers and checking on the technical practices of the company. Moreover, DIAROC and the African Enterprise Foundation (AEF) as funding parties also checked occasionally on the quality of the relationship between OFL and the farmers.

Unpacking how worth was actually accounted for in the agribusiness–outgrower complex within the structurating context outlined requires a two-step approach. First, I discuss how accounting (price setting, grading, harvest payments, loan repayments) worked frontstage. Then I show what controversies surrounding accounting practices were at play backstage. Such a comparison will provide us with a better understanding of the multifarious nature of accounting as a relational, materially entangled practice.

Accounting: Frontstage

The market encounters between producing outgrowers and OFL as "world market" mediator was based upon a contractual agreement that stipulated a wide range of issues. According to the contract, farmers would receive inputs such as mango tree seedlings, farming equipment, organic manure, pesticides, chemicals,[5] and water tanks, and be supported with technical services. Inputs would be allocated at the prevailing market rates, attracting no interest. Each year, farmers would be given a detailed loan statement for their plot. Such a *samli gbang* ("debit paper"), as it was called by the farmers, gave a detailed cost account of all items and services provided to the farmers.

When the first batch of farmers started to produce mangoes in 2006, the OFL management entered into agreements and price negotiations with importers in Europe, a ritual that repeated itself for the following years even though the buyers changed. They would agree on a price through an open book system, whereby both parties would disclose their costs in order to reach a price agreement. Once the seasons' price for export quality fruit was determined and communicated to AOMO, the net price for export fruits would be calculated by deducting the transport, packaging, and handling costs (reviewed every year and submitted to AOMO in advance of the harvesting season) from the gross price. The harvesting of fruits would start in April or May. Fruits would be harvested with the help of OFL staff, classified into high-quality (grade A) and low-quality grades (grade B)[6], weighed, and transported to the packhouse, where the fruits would be reclassified into export (grade 1) and local sales (grade 2) at the company's packhouse after the fruits had been washed and a more nuanced assessment of their quality was made. The payment for the mangoes would be organized as stipulated in the contract. About a third of the net sales value would be used for loan repayment to OFL.

Living up to the aspirations of the contract required creating a "space of calculability" (Callon 1998a: 24) that would allow for taking into account the flows of entities, transactions, and the sequence of algorithms that constituted crucial market encounters in the agribusiness–outgrower complex. Creating such a space of abstraction required a range of social, material, and procedural investments that were part of the ontological reconfigurations on which market-making rests. In 2002, just after the first outgrowers had joined the project, OFL set up its accounting system. First, the company's accountants used a special software package to administer the farmers' loan accounts and on which the provided inputs and services were recorded. The program, however, only allowed a manual entry of data, which entailed a huge work-load and left considerable scope for error.

In 2006, just when the first farmers were about to harvest, OFL implemented a new integrated accounting system with the help of Indian IT specialists, who would come to Ghana's north from time to time. According to the OFL chief accountant, the system was not only implemented for internal purposes but also because the vision of the company's directors was "not to exploit, but to share" (Interview, 2009). Through the new integrated accounting system, all the departments of the company were linked to its finance department. The departments were separated into modules, and the day-to-day activities of those departments automatically fed into the central accounting system. There was, for instance, a packhouse, an input and equipment store, and an outgrower module, which were linked to the accounting module. In this way, the OFL accountants could immediately charge a farmer when he or she received inputs from the store, or could deduct a certain percentage of his or her net harvests for loan repayment after he delivered to the packhouse when fruits were ready. The accounting system, and the devices it mobilized (e.g., computerized farmer data, indi-vidualized debit notes), aimed at reciprocal control and transparency of costs, debts, and profits. Accounting would be done in USD as it was still the most widely used currency and more stable than the GHS. Inputs and local sales, however, would be priced in GHS, whereas exports would be remunerated in €. Thus, the debts of the farmers as well as their remuneration from exports had to be revalued in USD at the given exchange rate at the end of each year. Accordingly, the debit note listed debts in GHS, the USD equivalent, and the exchange rate used to calculate the equivalent.

Accounting: Backstage

What may be missed from my rather smooth account of encounters of accounting in the mango project, largely derived from the propositional content of interviews held with OFL accountants and managers, is the fact that "algorithms cannot be described and defined in an abstract way, independently of the material conditions of their enactment" (Callon & Muniesa 2005: 1241).

"Accounting for the market" was thus not as smooth as depicted. This is, in fact, a reminder of how important it is to study the backstage activities of global connec-tions. The farmers generally described their relationship with OFL as "good, very faithful and transparent," "heartful," and "trustful," and attested to OFL having a "good reputation" in the area whereby no one had come "out to accuse the work they are doing" during focus group discussions in 2009. However, encounters of accounting were often marked by controversies and misunderstandings unfolding during the course of the project. Such hidden controversies mainly revolved around five issues, of which the first two were closely related: the price setting for export and local markets;

the worth of prices for export and local markets; payments; the grading of fruits; and the adding of unforeseen costs to the farmers' loan account. Because the latter point will be taken up again in Chapter 8, in what follows I will only address the first four issues:

Price setting: As Watts (1994: 61) already noted with respect to older generations of outgrower schemes across the Global South, price relations can be a definite source for the redistribution of risks and value between buyers and producers. In contract farming schemes, there principally exist two different ways of determining prices: (1) through a fixed price contract, which fixes a price in advance, as in the case of TF, or (2) through a formula price contract, which calculates a price later "as a residual after subtracting processors' costs from revenues obtained" (ibid.: 61), as in the case of OFL. The former generally increases the risk for the processor-buyer, guaranteeing a price floor (even though there may be other complementary means in place to redistribute risks and value), whereas in the latter case, the firm neither can make losses, nor can it make large profits (ibid.: 61).

In aggregate terms, however, price manipulations can make a big difference to returns in large loan-financed outgrower schemes, *a fortiori* because price negotiations between the exporter-processor and buyers abroad are either often complicated, or hidden from the outgrowers. Thus, price-fixing procedures may raise multiple issues of conflicting accountability (Stark 2009: 25). This was precisely the case in the mango project, but AOMO as well as the farmers pushed for one of their representatives to be present during the price negotiations between OFL's management and buyers in Europe. Such a push came after the company had harvested the first batch of mangoes in 2006 at rather short notice, neither informing the farmers about price negotiations nor about the marketing of the mangoes. Even though such an overnight harvesting was necessary owing to weather conditions, it created an atmosphere of mistrust among many pioneer farmers, as can be read in the minutes of an AOMO meeting held after the harvest in 2006:

> The emergency harvesting of mangoes by OFL management this year 2006 has created great suspicion. The outgrowers complained that the time they were informed to harvest their mangoes was very short. The price, they said, was solely determined by the OFL management which should not have been the issue. They also complained that they were deceived that their mangoes were to be sent abroad only to be told later that they were sold at the local market and above all, the AOMO executives who are their mouthpiece were not involved. The executives, in responding told their members that they took this matter up and had discussions with the management, and measures have been put in place to ensure that such a thing never happened again. The executives mentioned that some of the measure included AOMO executives would be around during harvesting time and marketing periods. This is to ensure transparency [...]. (minutes AOMO meeting, June 17, 2006)

Following this complaint, an AOMO representative was present during price negotiations between OFL and buyers in Europe in 2007, a practice that was meant to be continued in subsequent years, but OFL, struggling with financial problems due to the low yields, argued that there were no additional funds available to fly out AOMO representatives. This state remained unchanged until 2010, when AOMO, now headed by a new, formally educated, and proactive chairman, pushed for more transparency. He had already bemoaned the state of affairs in 2009 after he had taken up office and told me straightforwardly during an interview that

> before I joined them, I was told a representative from AOMO was part of the delegation that went for the negotiation of price. But this year it didn't happen and what I was told was finance was the reason. And sometimes certain things happen; my problem is that they don't put us in their negotiations [...]. At least they should always put us, when they want to engage in a policy change [...]. Something that is going to affect us, at least we must have a representative. (Interview, 2009)

Owing to the insistence of AOMO and its chairman, in 2010, the OFL management gave an assurance that it would become more transparent on price negotiations, promising to forward the e-mail communications between the company and the buyers in Europe to AOMO and its executives.

The worth of prices: Setting prices at a reasonable level was central for enrolling the farmers into the project. The company managers were aware that low prices could discourage farmers from mango growing or lead to side-selling. Although most of the farmers were satisfied with the prices paid for export and local sales in 2007 and 2008, discontent developed from 2009 onward because yields turned out repeatedly to be far below expectations, farmers had been excluded from price negotiations, and some of them perceived the prices for local fruits to be too low. Consider, for instance, the field note that David, my field assistant and a technical staff member of AOMO, took in 2010 after he had visited some farmers just before the harvests began:

> Farmers in Song-Issakae and Lapalsi complained of OFL local prices for mango this year being very low and economic wise it doesn't make any sense to sell their mango at that price. This perception of the farmers has a tendency to result in some of them secretly harvesting their fruits and selling at the local market. (Field diary, 2010)

Although the farmers later saw that OFL's local prices were eventually better than the prices offered in local markets and not a single act of side-selling could be documented, such an observation hints at an important issue, namely, the fact that prices may disrupt stable market relationships. As already highlighted in Chapter 5, the OFL managers were aware of the prosthetic function of prices and thus tried whatever they could to avoid controversies with regard to prices for both export and local sales.

When it came to export sales, the company would pay the farmers the guaranteed prices in 2009 and 2010, even though the fruits fetched far less than the price agreed with the outgrowers and buyers prior to the harvests owing to quality problems.[7] OFL was vigilant to ensure that prices for non-export mangoes were higher than those in the local market in order to reduce the likelihood of farmers side-selling fruits to traders.

What this case shows is that, in tightly coordinated and power-laden global agrifood chains (and markets more generally), prices are often "purposefully tinkered

[with]"; they "are done but they can do things too" (Muniesa 2007: 378), such as sending out signals and signs:

> We just have to tell the farmer what goes on in the market [...]. And I told AOMO also this year that "if you do have a client that is willing to pay more than OFL link him with OFL and we will give you a higher price but don't go and bypass OFL to sell the mangoes." Because [...], for instance, the farmers in the south get GHS 45 per kilogram, that is what they pay them [...]. We pay our farmers between GHS xx and GHS xy. Very good price. So for anybody to come in here and to start buying my farmers' mangoes, the only that will happen [is] cash! That is the only thing. They say "here's GHS 10,000 give me all your mangoes," but that will happen even if you give the farmer double the price. So, I think that the farmers, I feel some understand what is happening. (Interview senior manager, 2009)

Grading: As I have already shown in the case of TF and its suppliers, and as, indeed, the history of contract farming tells us more generally, the grading of harvests may be a controversial procedure, full of backstage practices, adjustments, and redistributive struggles. But compared to the JIT frontier, there was more at stake in the mango project. Grading as a market practice had to be rolled out in the very first place. It was not just part of the encounters of accounting shaping agribusiness–outgrower relations but central to the broader ontological reconfigurations at work when a simple mango became a good for the organic fruit market and "peasants" became loan-financed "outgrowers." It was during the grading of fruits that the final link between the properties of a mango and its worth would be made, and such links were by no means uncontested. After many farmers had become more experienced, they started questioning the grading of their fruits in 2010. The farmers were confused by the grading algorithm, which stipulated a series of classifications and reclassifications by which the best-quality fruits would be selected for exports. They were puzzled by the fact that "somebody could harvest plenty of mangoes but that the quality was so bad, that, when they come to the packhouse, they screen it and if you have less grade A, then you don't get much money" (Interview farmer, 2010, translated). Such controversies stemming from divergent framings of worth are well reflected in a field note by David, my research assistant, who was present during the April 2010 harvest:

> Pulugu farmers complained of [a] very rigorous sorting procedure by [the] OFL harvesting team. This results in increasing quantities of grade B thereby reducing their total net income. Personally I was deeply involved in the whole process of harvesting, sorting, and weighing, and I had no reservation with the sorting procedure since the company had to ensure that grade A fruits meet the required quality standards for export. (Field diary, 2010)

Like the Pulugu farmers, many others were confused by the grading practices, and OFL staff together with AOMO had to organize several public encounters with farmers in different areas of the outgrower scheme, where they justified the grading procedure, rendering it an "objective process," as Amin, the chief accountant, once tried to explain to me (Interview, 2011). During such public encounters of accounting, the rather abstract accounting mechanisms largely working behind the back of the outgrowers were translated into narrative accounts of how situations had been evaluated. This underlines the close entanglement of bookkeeping and narration in the process of *account*-ing (Stark 2009: 25; see also Vellema 2002).

Furthermore, the OFL management agreed to have a representative of AOMO supervise the grading from 2011 onward in order to avoid disputes associated with accounting practices. In the words of Boltanski and Thévenot (2006 [1991]: 35), such decisions were part of the struggle to create "natural situations" during market encounters – situations "in which agreement over associations is perfectly established." Such natural situations, in which linkages between specific human and nonhuman elements have been normalized, are exactly the opposite of "critical moments," in which two agents interpret a situation according to different modalities of valuation, and controversies may develop (Boltanski & Thévenot 1999).

Payments: The way payments were conducted was an equally controversial issue. When some farmers had become more experienced by 2009, they started to challenge OFL's practice of not issuing statements with a detailed breakdown of the harvest payments. Instead of the bulk figure OFL had provided, the suspicious farmers wanted to know exactly how much OFL had deducted from their gross revenue for its technical services and for loan deduction in relation to the previously agreed price and the volumes sold in the domestic and export markets.

Tempers were heated all the more as many farmers experienced very low yields in 2009, unlike in 2006, 2007, and 2008, when expectations had been more modest. This became evident in 2010 during a focus group discussion with the chairman of a group that had scored the highest yields from 2006 to 2008, but was disappointed in 2009 and 2010. During an encounter in 2010, the chairman told me the following:

> I only got 100 GHS for my 2 acres. It was so low that I didn't get much. We initially said OFL cheated us because there was no breakdown of costs, but the OFL accountant went round to explain prices to us. So next year we want to see the exact items priced listed on the breakdown. That was it, the argument we had with them. Once the accountant came around and explained to us how the breakdown was calculated, we understood. Another complaint was that the loan repayment rate was considered as too high, given the fact that the yields were so low. (Group interview, 2010, translated)

On top of that, in the same year a technical problem in 2010 with the accounting system, managed at a distance by the IT specialists in India, delayed the payment of farmers, creating discontent among them. Resolving this required many public encounters during which the OFL accountant explained together with AOMO staff how deductions had been made in order to cool down tempers among the farmers. Learning from such instances, the OFL management started to provide a detailed breakdown of the harvest payments from 2011 onward.

Another part of the translation problem was the factoring in of the exchange rate. According to the contract, OFL should have converted the USD/€ to GHS at the interbank exchange rate of the date the company had credited the customer's payment to its account. This would have shifted the potential scope of action to the side of OFL. What OFL did, however, was to use the exchange rate prevailing at the time of price negotiations with AOMO in January or February in order to reduce the scope for misunderstandings. According to the chief accountant and a senior manager, the whole concept of exchange rate was difficult to translate into the local systems of reference, and one way to fully disclose to farmers what they would get after the harvest had been sold in Europe was to use a pre-fixed exchange rate. Depending on the development of the exchange rate between the time of fixation and the sale of mangoes in Europe, such an arrangement could be beneficial to either party. Until 2011, the exchange rate had been favorable for the farmers, resulting in a better deal than expected for those who sold their fruits in export markets. Nevertheless, the OFL management repeatedly had to make its pricing practices public, explaining to AOMO and the farmers how exchange rate volatilities affect returns in intricate ways.

What we can take from my reconstruction of the multifarious encounters of accounting in the agribusiness–outgrower complex is that the algorithmic configurations of such market encounters "are not structures that already exist in which calculative agencies simply circulate and develop. Agencies may, and often are, engaged to varying degrees in the design and negotiation of architectures that organize market encounters" (Callon & Muniesa 2005: 1243). In order to investigate the (re)distributive effects of global agrifood market connections, it is thus crucial to unpack when such reflexive, critical, and truly political dynamics ensue and when they do not.

Conclusion

In this chapter, I have shown that market STAs, depending on their configuration, can create differentiated positions and agents, which often bring with them the redistribution of risk and value. I have demonstrated for the pineapple case study that enacting agrifood connections "JIT" may rest, among others, on the development of tactics, relations, and material layouts that structure the possible spaces for action among suppliers (Foucault 1982: 794). In this case, the staff of the organization scrutinized often succeeded in imposing their scripts of qualculation on them in order to make things "work." Their power was composed of the differential access the suppliers had to possibilities within a series "practice-arrangement bundles" (Schatzki 2005: 479). This brings to the fore the "specific relation between politics, technology, and the economy" (Barry 2005: 87).

In order to highlight the techno-political character of market-making, it is important to open the black boxes of global market connections "through a critical unveiling of entangled links that [...] [their] closure[s] mask" (Thévenot 2009: 806). To do so, however, one has to move beyond the politically rather unspecified notions of translation/black-boxing deployed in the actor-network-theory and social studies of economization and marketization literatures, or the notion of compromise used in the *économie des conventions*, respectively. I would rather put forward the notion of everyday anti-politics to capture the hidden struggles for closure and the subsumption of critique that often lie at the heart of forging and maintaining global agrifood market connections. This notion speaks directly to a critical research program that asks questions about the organization and operation of markets, and when and under what conditions these become a political matter and when they do not (see Barry 2005: 87; Butler 2010). Although principally applicable to a wide range of social encounters, the everyday anti-politics of markets refers to all the mundane processes that smooth over conflicts about supply chain management and market-making and narrow the spaces for the political – for disagreement (Barry 2005: 86). When the performance of markets and the everyday "investments in form" (Thévenot 1984) supporting it have anti-political effects, we can talk of anti-politics. During social encounters, including economic ones, everyday anti-politics restricts critical dynamics, invisibilizes over-flows (Callon 2010: 164), or closes "down debate about how and what to govern and the distributive effects of particular arrangements" (Li 2007a: 265), often through reference to technical arguments and authoritative forms of expert knowledge (Mitchell 2002). For a long time, supply chain anti-politics shaped market encounters along the JIT frontier even though new critical dynamics were induced from 2009 onward (see Chapter 8).

Contrary to the pineapple frontier, the design of the market encounters in the mango project turned more political in several instances owing to the agency of AOMO and the sensitive cultural setting, but also due to the fact that the power structure of the contractual arrangements was balanced more toward the farmers. Not only was the contract very specific owing to the intervention of DIAROC, but the power of OFL in general was composed of risky elements given that farmers could practically default on their obligations without having to fear legal consequences. Thus, the OFL sharehold-ers had a keen interest in ensuring accountability on both sides in order to save their long-term investments in a legally precarious and politically sensitive environment. This is not to deny that many encounters between agribusiness firms and farmers across the Global South still stand on a far less equal footing (Singh 2002) and that many agrobusiness companies are moving toward more calculative agendas (e.g., vertical integration, contracting of more commercially oriented farmers, etc.) to secure a competitive advantage in the global agrifood economy (Dolan & Humphrey 2004; Maertens & Swinnen 2009; Amanor 2009; Oya 2012).

In sum, research on global (agrifood) market connections should be particularly sensitive to those moments when political turn into anti-political economies. The anti-political, the stable, and the normalized should attract our suspicion because these states are all effects of a power that is as much productive as it is constraining. The crucial question is when and within which concrete sociotechnical arrangements does this happen? An anthropology of markets and equipments can help us address such a truly political question.

Endnotes

1   In this book, all names of individuals, of the case study companies and related organizations, and their geographical associations have been anonymized, are withheld, or have been altered to protect sources. Development organizations and programs associated with the Ghanaian agricultural sector more generally are referred to by their original names.

2 It is appropriate to characterize the intake as an "ambiguous situation," in the register of Boltanski and Thévenot (1999: 374).

3 In this regard, one must also differentiate between the interest of the firm and the self-interest of particular employees (see Glover & Kusterer 1990: 128).

4 That the heterogeneous composition of contract growers may impede their organization is, of course, not a new finding (see, e.g., Glover & Kusterer 1990: 143).

5 Under the Organic Movement standard, the use of a limited number of chemicals is still allowed.

6 Grade A was reserved for all fruits with a potential export quality, whereas grade B was not suitable for export and was sent to the drying facility of OFL. At the pack-house, a grade A fruit could still be reclassified to a grade B fruit during a more detailed assessment.

7 Since OFL agreed with its largest buyer in Europe on an open book costing arrangement based on a flexible price, the final prices paid for mangoes could either be under (in the case of dropping market demand, or poor quality) or above the agreed price. Because OFL exported only small volumes and was still not yet in full production at the time of research, the flexible price was the better deal. This meant that OFL at least got back some money on substandard fruits instead of having them rejected, as would be the case with fixed prices.

Chapter Eight
Market Crises: When Things Fall Apart, or Won't Come Together

We had [...] a terrible year, we got to admit, but we survived it, and we got to look forward to the next decade, thinking about the sort of things, which we learned during the previous decade, if you like, and in particular over the last year. We all know the expression between a rock and a hard place – I think we were between two rocks and a hard place [...]! (Senior manager, company xy, Ghana, sometime between 2009 and 2011 during a staff meeting).

cri•sis noun \\'krī-səs\ : a difficult or dangerous situation that needs serious attention; the decisive moment (as in a literary plot); a situation that has reached a critical phase[1]

If markets are made, they can also be unmade, not only through critical ethnographies but also by market agents themselves. Crises and change are part of the capitalist market game. This seems obvious, and most practitioners would confirm this. A Ton:go Fruits (TF)[2] supply chain manager once told me that "[e]very day, every day brings forth challenges," and a senior manager of Organic Fruit Limited (OFL) once sarcastically remarked that "you think you are on top of things, then [laughter] your boat rocks over and you start all over again. So it is every day is something new, every day something new" (Interview, 2009).

When we look into the social studies of economization and marketization (SSEM), the *économie des conventions* (EC) or the sociological and geographical literature on interfirm relationships, global commodity/value chains (GCC/GVC), and global production networks (GPN), crises and change are often absent processes. These literatures are obsessed with order, institutionalization, and the reproduction of roles,

Assembling Export Markets: The Making and Unmaking of Global Food Connections in West Africa, First Edition. Stefan Ouma.

structures, and relations, not with crisis, destruction, and change. There are, however, a few notable exeeptions in economic sociology (see, e.g., Schumpeter 1947; Baker et al. 1998; Beckert 2009) and the chain literatures (Bair & Werner 2011b), not to speak of the larger field of critical political economy, where "crisis" is foundational vocabulary (Marx 2008 [1867]; Harvey 2011).

Fligstein (2001) offers a promising entry point for discussing market crises. According to him, there are three phases of market evolution – *emergence* (when roles/identities of market agents still have to be defined and interorganizational relations still have to be stabilized), *stability* (when stable relations have developed and a status hierarchy of goods and firms has been established), and *crisis* (a state where a firm can no longer reproduce itself) (ibid.: 75). Following this model, one could indeed assume that we should conceive of crises (the breakup of internal or external firm relations) as extraordinary moments of economic life. Fligstein, however, underlines the point that the survival of a firm is being *constantly* threatened:

> First, suppliers can control inputs, raise prices, and make firms who require their inputs unprofitable. Second, competitors can engage in price competition, take over market share, and eventually drive the firm out of business. Third, gaining cooperation from managers and workers in the firm presents problems of interpersonal conflict, and politics can jeopardize the ability to produce goods and services. Finally, products may become obsolete. (ibid.: 17)

The two major sources of instability in markets are the tendency of firms to engage in price competition and the problem of keeping the firm together as a political coalition (ibid.: 70). As already touched upon in Chapter 2, Fligstein and other market sociologists argue that market agents are trying to develop stable social structures to control these sources of instability in an often uncertain environment (ibid.: 29), whereby the key challenges are, first, to create a system of power (or a "social organization") in the so-called "market field" and, second, once it is in place, to maintain it. Such a take on markets allows us to distinguish between *crises* and *Crises*. The former refers to the everyday struggles of managing the survival of a firm (or other organizational arrangements such as supply chains or outgrower schemes), whereas the latter refers to grand destructive moments – when things fall apart, relations break up, new technologies take over, or a firm (or another organizational structure) collapses.

Although Fligstein's take on markets represents a valuable starting point to think about the stabilization and destabilization of market arrangements, it obviously suffers from two shortcomings. First, despite its potential to bridge the micro–macro divide, it operates at a fairly abstract level and has little to say about how market agents may maneuver through crises *in situ* – how they may reconfigure market sociotechnical *agencements* (STAs) through embodied practices of realignment. Second, because it, like so many other economic sociology accounts, focuses on the social rather than the socio*material* organization of markets (Pinch & Swedberg 2008), it is blind to the heterogeneous elements that make up market architectures – goods, relations, diverse agencies, multiple ways of knowing, laws, modalities of valuation, procedures, technical devices, "nature" itself, etc. – and which no longer hold together in times of *Crises*. Practitioners would tell us that each of these elements can be a source of disruptive dynamics – that each of them can destabilize the ostensibly coherent economic formation we often simply call "the market."

A perspective that takes seriously the sociomaterial and heterogeneous nature of market STAs offers a significantly different take on market crises/Crises. Although the heterogeneous engineering of markets faces challenges and controversies on a daily basis (the everyday crisis of the value form, to use Tsing's expression again), Crises can be understood as moments when the drawing together of heterogeneous elements has become increasingly difficult or is no longer possible, leading to the breakdown and disintegration of particular market STAs. Framings of goods may overflow, agencies may cease to be pacified and disenroll from existing arrangements, authoritative forms of knowledge stabilizing market STAs may be challenged, the organization of encounters may be contested, the material devices supporting market STAs may fail, and even nature may "refuse" to be turned into resources. Ostensibly solid points in market STAs may be crucial sources of relationally disruptive and even destructive dynamics.

Employing a very "social" sociology, the sociology of markets and the chain literatures have no place for such kinds of messy dynamics. However, a performative take on marketization that is sympathetic to the symmetry principle of actor-network-theory (ANT) (Callon 1986; Law 1994: 101–102; Busch & Juska 1997: 691) can accommodate such sources of crises and its effects. Doing so, however, requires moving beyond the empirical foci of much of the SSEM literature. Even though some of its proponents highlight that markets must be conceived as a "process" (Callon 1998a: 32), as "continuously emerging and reemerging" (Callon 1998b: 247) – a perspective that principally allows the accommodation of crises/Crises and change – much of the literature seems to be more preoccupied with market design, maintenance, and stability (Overdevest 2011). This applies in particular to studies mobilizing the performativity argument (Butler 2010), for instance, when they find that an economic model shapes its world (but see MacKenzie 2007 for an exception). Such a focus is, indeed, puzzling given the literature's pragmatist ANT roots. It is ANT after all that invites us to think of disorder, not order, as the normal state of affairs (Latour 1986: 275; Law 1994: 1–2). Thus, making sense of crises/Crises and change in markets requires sensitivity to these roots (Overdevest 2011).

Keeping such sensitivity in mind, this chapter shows how market arrangements in the two frontier regions were destabilized into different directions over the course of time. In the case of TF and its suppliers, I illustrate how its market model slid into Crisis owing to the cumulative effects of changing preferences in the global pineapple market ("goods could no longer be legitimately exchanged"), the global economic crisis ("goods were no longer sought after"), and the erosion of its supply base amid new dynamics of competition in local raw material markets ("suppliers disenrolled from the market arrangement"). The Crisis of this model was firmly entangled with the more general Crisis of the Ghanaian pineapple subsector.

The entry point into the mango case study is a different one altogether. Here, I highlight how "nature" itself was the source of Crisis, impacting in significant ways the organization and trajectory of the outgrower scheme. The narrative I am going to construct underscores earlier warnings: we cannot simply take "nature" for granted as a resource of "the market" (see Chapter 5). As pragmatism reminds us, crisis cannot be separated from change (Overdevest 2011). Thus, in each of the case studies, I am also just interested in how market STAs are being *reconfigured* as sociotechnical accomplishments. Such an endeavor, however, warrants a brief reminder about the pragmatist roots of both ANT and the SSEM. For pragmatists such as Dewey, crises are always situations when established practices within a certain context can no longer solve problems successfully, or when the environment of practices has changed in such ways that a reconfiguration of practices is necessary to yield desired outcomes. But they are also situations that create an opportunity for new reflection – moments for "intelligence" and "reconstruction" (Overdevest 2011: 536) – and change may take place through a process of inquiry, practical judgment, and search (Dewey 1915; Stark 2009). This at least applies when Crisis does not lead to collapse.

In the following sections, I capture moments of reconstruction, and the reconfiguration processes they may induce, through the notion of *reassembling* (Latour 2005: 7). It is not just social theorists who can reassemble the social; so can economists in the "wild," where reassembling is a moniker for heterogeneous *re*engineering. I show that such a process often implies controversial adjustments, as frames for evaluating objects, processes, and people are in motion. Following Boltanski and Thévenot (2006 [1991]: 25), moments of Crisis can likewise be understood as moments of "disequilibrium, critique, dispute, and contestation" with regard to the framings of worth and ways of knowing at play within a certain setting.

What follows is *my* account of crisis and reengineering in the two frontier regions, although it is obviously also a smoothed and partly rationalized account that does not fully do justice to the messiness, personal frustrations, controversies, misery, and problem-related coping practices that mark everyday market-making and remaking.

A Model in Crisis

TF and its farmers lived through many crises. As has already been said, every day was a challenge. Sometimes these crises turned dangerous, for instance, when TF became part of the so-called air-freight war. The "war" started in 2007 and intensified in 2008 after the major organic certification body (the Organic Movement) in one of the company's main markets started to consider a ban on air-freighted organic produce. Ostensibly responding to the rising awareness about climate change among Northern consumers, the standard-setting body became concerned about the ecological footprint of air-freighted produce imported to Europe, arguing that it was incompatible with the idea of organic and sustainable consumption. A boycott of produce in the name of climate change would have seriously affected TF in direct and indirect ways.

At that time, between 5% and 10% of TF's fruit output was organically certified, representing an important niche market for the company. These fruits were sourced from pineapple, coconut, and papaya farmers in regions outside of Densu Valley, and a ban would have resulted in the exclusion of these farmers from the market. Even worse, such a ban could have eventually spilled over to the conventional product lines, which would have had disastrous consequences for the company and its conventional suppliers, undermining the possibilities for trade altogether. In October 2008, the standard's board eventually succumbed to public pressure from a coalition of African exporters (of which TF was part), development organizations, scientists, supermarkets, and the air-freight lobby, and abandoned its plans for a ban, and the market crises was solved.

What this brief account should remind us of is that Crises could alternatively be understood as "hot situations" (Callon 1998b) – historical moments when established frames of exchange overflow and products become "delegitimated" (Fligstein 2001: 32; see also Boltanski & Thévenot 2006 [1991]: 80).

Although TF and its farmers managed to win the air-freight war, another crisis ensuing in the same year brought major disruption. It was a layered, proliferating crisis – a crisis articulating a variety of internal and external processes and forces. Although, at least from the viewpoint of TF, its market model had been stable and successful for almost one decade, ensuring the expansion and growth of the company, the situation started to change from 2007 onward. TF and its farmers were consecutively hit by changing preferences in the world pineapple market, the global credit crunch, the Icelandic ash cloud shock, the intensification of price-based competition in retail markets, and an increasing shortage of raw material in Ghana. The cumulative effects of these resulted in the partial disintegration of its supply base. In the following, I shall map out these processes. For the sake of analytical clarity, I separate them by sections, but in practice, these processes were articulated in intricate and messy ways.

MD2 Takes Over the Market, or How Goods Become Delegitimated

In 1996, something changed in global pineapple markets. Qualifying those changes requires a little detour into the world of transnational agribusiness. In that year, Fresh Del Monte Produce,[3] a US-headquartered, transnationally organized producer, distributor, and marketer of fresh fruits, vegetables, and other products, brought to market what some call "arguably the most valuable new fruit product in the world"[4]: its Gold Extra Sweet Pineapple, often cryptically called MD2. It was an industrial crop that came out of Del Monte's laboratories in Hawaii, produced for the plains of Costa Rica, meant to change the market to the advantage of the agribusiness giant (Vagneron, Faure, & Loeillet 2009). Until the mid-1990s, the world pineapple market had been clearly partitioned. South East Asian countries such as Thailand, the Philippines and subsequently Indonesia had become centers for canned and juiced pineapples. Central American exporters, particularly Costa Rica, had been mainly serving the US market with the Champaka variety, which was not as popular with European supermarkets and consumers owing to its less sweet taste and greenish color (Whitfield 2010: 22). Thus, Central American supplies to Europe had been rather negligible, and the European fresh pineapple market had been largely served by Côte d'Ivoire and Ghana with the Smooth Cayenne variety (Fold & Gough 2008; Vagneron, Faure, & Loeillet 2009).

MD2 was meant to redraw the geography of the global pineapple market by virtue of its attested superior quality. MD2 was promoted for its golden color and sweeter taste, which differentiated it from the then popular Smooth Cayenne variety. It was designed to be more rounded in shape, yielding consumer-friendly slices of approximately identical size (Fold & Gough 2008: 1688). MD2 was also promoted as offering a longer shelf life, an important purchasing criteria for Northern retailers obsessed with enhancing their efficiency and returns on capital. Given its quality framing and storability, Del Monte's designer pineapple could be easily transported from Latin America to Europe by sea, thereby threatening the comparative advantage of countries such as Côte d'Ivoire and Ghana, which, until then, had competed by virtue of their proximity to Europe. Like many other transnational agribusiness companies, Del Monte had considerable supply chain power, controlling the whole fruit chain comprising research, production, logistics (refrigerated containers, specialized vessels, own trucking companies), distribution, ripening centers, and category management (Fresh Del Monte Produce Inc. 2011). Backed up by a sophisticated marketing machine and an opaque intellectual property rights strategy, MD2 gradually conquered the European pineapple market from 1999 onward (see Figure 8.1) (Fold & Gough 2008: 1688; Whitfield 2010).

When other transnational agribusiness companies turned to MD2 in 2003, it eventually became an "obligatory passage point" (Callon 1986: 205) for most players in the pineapple market. Production in Côte d'Ivoire started to fall after the turn of the century owing to insufficient investments in MD2 production and political turmoil, but, as Fold and Gough (2008: 1688) observe, West African supplies to the European Union (EU) remained relatively constant since Ghana managed to increase its exports

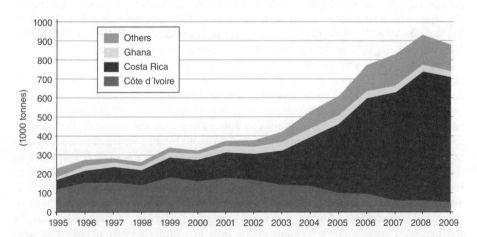

Figure 8.1 EU imports of pineapple from Ghana, Côte d'Ivoire, and Costa Rica, 1995–2009. [Adapted from Whitfield, L. (2010). Developing Technological Capabilities in Agro-Industry: Ghana's Experience with Fresh Pineapple Exports in Comparative Perspective. DIIS Working Paper 28. Copenhagen. Reprinted with permission.] *Imports refer to all extra-EU imports. EU is the EU-15 group for the period 1995–1998, EU-27 group from 1999 onward. The category "Others" refers to the total imports from all countries other than Côte d'Ivoire, Costa Rica, and Ghana.*

until 2004 (see Figure 8.1). Since early 2004, however, the growing demand in the EU was covered by pineapples from Costa Rica. Whereas Costa Rica had an EU-15 market share of about 44% in 2003, it had increased to 69% in 2007. Alongside this, imported volumes increased from 184,175 mt to 573,832 mt during the same period. Between 2003 and 2007, European pineapple imports from Côte d'Ivoire and Ghana fell by 55% (Whitfield 2010: 28). Ghana's share of the EU-15 pineapple market came down from 7%–9% in the late 1990s to 3% in 2010[5] (Loeillet & Paqui 2010). Ghana, already having commanded a low share of the market, lost even the little it had. Despite Smooth Cayenne's good taste and popularity among consumers, Ghana's industry, with its low investments in quality assurance and supply chain infrastructure, had little means to counter the quality framing of the designer pineapple, just at a time when food safety and quality became a huge topic in European retail markets. Consequently, the variety slipped to the bottom of the price spectrum of the fresh pineapple market (Whitfield 2010: 22).

The sudden switch to MD2 was a huge blow to the Ghanaian pineapple subsector. Many exporters could no longer sell the fruits they had sourced from smallholders, and they ended up owing them huge amounts of money. Obviously, the industry was badly equipped for the MD2 shift. Even though farmers and exporters had heard of the new variety from 2000 onward, neither the Ghanaian state nor individual industry players were responding proactively to the challenge. It was only in 2004 when the World Bank, as part of Horticultural Export Industries Initiative (HEII), in alliance with the Ministry of Food and Agriculture (MOFA) and the Trade and Investment Programme for a Competitive Export Economy (TIPCEE) (see Chapter 3), tried to reconnect smallholders and exporters to markets. These players supported farmer groups with plantlets cultivated in a tissue culture laboratory of a major pineapple exporter, which had been set up with the help of TF, in order to cultivate low-cost MD2 suckers.[6] 87% of the plantlet costs were to be covered by HEII, and 13% by the farmers; 30% to 40% of the revenues were to go back to the World Bank.

The project was able to supply 100 farmer groups (1,000 farmers in total) with about 5 million plantlets by the end of 2007. However, it faced serious problems delivering them in time. Each party, farmers and exporters, deeply mistrusted each other given that the former had frequently side-sold produce in the past, and the latter had run away with the farmers' money in 2006. Therefore, the multiplication project failed to reconnect farmers to exporters. As I was told by the former manager of HEII at a rather cathartical moment during an interview in 2008, the project managers of TIPCEE and HEII thought that covering 70% to 80% of the plantation costs would be enough to reconnect farmers to markets, but they underestimated the practical and monetary challenges MD2 would pose to smallholder farmers. After all, it was an industrial crop designed for the plains and harvesting machines of Costa Rica, not for the hands of smallholders farming in the hills of southern Ghana, raising critical questions of why smallholders should be pushed into such markets in the first place. Farmers also did not have the operational capital or the know-how to cultivate such a designer pineapple. MD2 required different land preparation techniques, investments in mulching foliage, and additional fertilizer,[7] as well as careful post-harvest handling, including a functioning cold chain (see Figure 8.2). Many pineapple farmers were

Figure 8.2   A field planted with MD2. (From Author's photo.)

particularly cash strapped, as the exporters had not paid them after the sudden demand drop in 2006. The result was a gradual exodus of many exporters and farmers, as shown in Figure 8.3.

The operations of TF were affected in two ways by the MD2 shock. First, its major customer shifted from the popular Smooth Cayenne to the MD2 pineapple variety, which seriously affected all smaller and medium-sized suppliers. To make matters worse, many of the farmers went for bank loans in 2006 after they had been encouraged by TF to expand their production. Second, alternative marketing channels went dry as other exporters either collapsed or shifted to the MD2 market. Previously, TF suppliers would sell excess produce to other exporters, a recourse that was then no longer possible, as was well described by a TF agronomist back in 2009:

> The major problem that I can talk about is the shift from Smooth Cayenne to MD2. It was not well thought of, and it really has affected us. Because for about the past five, six years, we had about almost 38 exporters, who bought excesses from our farmers for their exports. So they had other markets for their surpluses. But then with the shift from Smooth Cayenne to MD2, there wasn't any exporter for Smooth Cayenne except for Somarts, who was doing bits. It was all MD2. And we only had a few key players in the MD2 industry. And as I talk to you, I think we have about only eight major exporters in the country. It reduced from thirty something to eight because everybody was out. (Interview, 2009)

To cope with the MD2 shift, the company consequently had to source MD2 pineapples from larger exporters, who would often engage in price hiking through

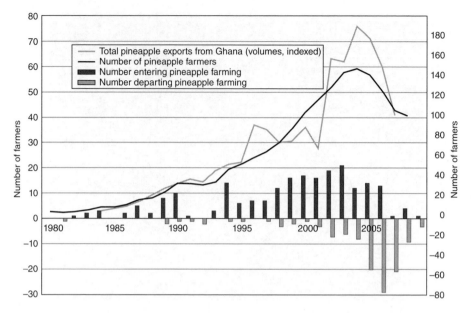

Figure 8.3   Pineapple market participation in southern Ghana, 1980–2009. [Modified after Barrett, C. B. et al. (2012). Smallholder Participation in Contract Farming: Comparative Evidence from Five Countries. *World Development* 40 (4), 715–730. Reprinted with permission of Elsevier.]

cartel-like structures, squeezing the company's profit margins. The non-exporter suppliers of TF, like many other farmers in Densu Valley, incurred considerable financial losses and consequently struggled to convert parts of their production to MD2 when plantlets became cheaper and the knowledge about MD2 production had spread.

As argued in Chapter 3, the general impact of the MD2 shock was a strongly contracted industry. While in the late 1990s there were between 50 and 70 companies exporting pineapples at any one time and about 40% of exports came from smallholder production (Dixie & Sergeant 1998), these figures had come down drastically by 2009. The market was now dominated by only seven serious exporters, with two of them accounting for over half of the exports, and many smallholders had been pushed out of business.[8] This included farmers of the cooperative Farmapine, a World Bank–funded farmer-owned company of 370 farmers, which until 2004 was the largest single exporter of pineapples in Ghana and which failed to switch to MD2 (see also Danielou & Ravry 2005: 20–21).[9] The surviving exporters, some of them with access to foreign capital, carved out a new MD2 frontier west of Accra, where they acquired vast tracts of land for an increasingly mechanized form of agriculture, resulting in many migrant (nonindigenous) smallholders with weak land rights in their host communities losing their access to land (Amanor 2012; Fold & Gough 2008). The MD2 shock was the source of TF's crisis as it had considerable repercussions for its supply base as well as many other farmers in Densu Valley.

Trading Down in Times of Crisis

In addition to the MD2 shock, TF was price-squeezed by one of its major customers in 2008 as the per unit price for its largest pineapple-based product line with the retailer was reduced considerably. Competition in output markets increased from 2009 onward. As consumers started saving on pricy convenience food in the wake of the global economic crisis, many European supermarkets increasingly engaged in "value retailing" (Hughes 2012: 38). This eventually favored some of TF's larger competitors, who were aggressively fighting for market share. The situation became financially more dramatic in October 2008, reaching a full-blown Crisis of survival in January 2009. As a reaction, many permanent workers were laid off in March 2009, and a foreign subsidiary of TF had to temporarily close down.

It was a painful and conflict-ridden adjustment. The greatest challenge was to get approval for the corporate restructuring from staff, consumers, and the general public alike. New cutting and peeling machinery was brought to Ghana and other branches to save on labor costs. The situation began improving from April 2009 onward as savings on labor and the newly launched sale of bottled fruit juice for the Ghanaian market materialized, but they worsened again when the largest buyers put renewed pressure on TF. During the global economic crisis, even more benevolent retailers were pushing for price adjustments. In times of Crises, "even friends started to get tough," as the marketing manager put it during a staff meeting I attended (Field diary, 2009). His words were a marker for the great uncertainty that loomed over the just-in-time (JIT) model. The price pressures described here were the result of the increasingly fierce competition among retailers, with competitors[10] trying to take over market share by pushing down prices or openly offering lump sum payments.

Responding to the new pressures in its markets, TF laid off workers again. This resulted in considerable unrest among workers, who threatened to go on strike over redundancy compensation issues, leading to a tedious negotiation between the management and the workers.[11] The strike was eventually averted through a collective bargaining agreement at the factory level, but, more generally, the rules of the game in output markets had changed considerably, and the TF managers struggled to meet the expectations of workers, suppliers, buyers, and the wider public alike. In times of "economic downturn" (Hughes 2012), TF's goods were increasingly being evaluated merely in terms of "price" and not in terms of "freshness," "long-term relationships," or "developmental impact." Such revaluations became an object of critique during several corporate meetings I attended.

Currency and Capital Volatilities

It is common development economics knowledge that the cost-return structure of air-freight exports is heavily affected by currency and oil price fluctuations. Between June 1 and November 1, 2008, the operational currency of TF depreciated against the US dollar, making air-freight fuel paid in USD more expensive. The margins of the company were further squeezed because of the exchange rate and the monetary policy of the Ghanaian government. This had already been an issue in early 2008 when I started my research. In fact, it was one of the first issues my counterpart, a senior manager of TF, singled out during an interview as being one of the biggest challenges export-oriented companies in Ghana were facing. From his perspective, the Ghanaian cedi had been overvalued *vis-à-vis* the US dollar and the corporate currency for several years. Inflation was high, reaching an annual rate of 16.52% in 2008 and 19.25% in 2009[12] owing to increased government spending prior to the general elections in January 2009.[13] An overvalued, inflated Ghana cedi again eroded the company's margins. For instance, in late 2008, the costs of labor and inputs alone suddenly increased by 30% owing to currency fluctuation. Even though things started to turn around in June 2009 under the auspices of the new NDC government (which decided to let the cedi float at its "natural" level and aimed at achieving a one-digit inflation rate), the currency volatilities had resulted in serious financial losses for TF by August 2009.

The losses due to the retailers' price squeezes and currency volatilities were exacerbated by serious cash-flow problems. This was, first, due to the corporate expansion that took place in 2007 (see Chapter 5) and, second, due to the global credit crunch that resulted in a contracted market for capital to ensure day-to-day liquidity. Bringing equity investors on board was not an option as the shareholders did not want to lose control of the company. Eventually, in 2010, the company turned to the private sector financing arm of a development organization, which provides low-interest loans to companies operating in developing countries. This was a move the senior management wanted to avoid at all costs because this organization wants a strong say in corporate governance issues in exchange for its loans.

When the Supply Base Disenrolls …

In addition to an already difficult corporate situation, competition for raw material increased from 2009 onward when new competitors entered the pineapple game. This was a problem because the shift to MD2 had pushed many exporters and smallholder farmers out of the Smooth Cayenne business from 2006 onwards, leading to a contracted Smooth Cayenne market. Whereas many farmers and exporters left the pineapple business altogether, some gradually converted part or all of their production to MD2 following the encouragement of the government, HEII, TIPCEE, and the MCA. This ran counter to the view of the TF senior management, which had repeatedly warned the government and donors not to embrace a unidirectional adjustment strategy for the industry, suggesting that MD2 should not make up more than 50% of the supply base. Consequently, the Smooth Cayenne variety gradually lost ground in the industry. TF, however, still depended heavily on this variety for certain product lines.

Even its own small and medium suppliers either gradually converted to MD2 or dropped out of the business altogether. How could this happen without the knowledge of the upper management? Backstage, the stark demand volatilities between 2007 and 2009 had seriously impacted the relationship between TF and its suppliers, who were increasingly left stranded with their produce. The company failed to rework its relationship with its farmers as it had developed some sort of organizational complacency, in part as a result of the virtual monopsony it had on Smooth Cayenne pineapples after demand for this variety had evaporated in many export markets from 2006 onward. Only in 2009 did the senior managers realize that the stability of the relationship with suppliers was under a serious threat when some suppliers dropped out of pineapple production or increasingly supplied fruits as brokers sourcing from other farms,[14] basically exploiting the labor power and weak market position of even less fortunate farmers in Densu Valley. Farmers had become frustrated with increasingly adverse terms of trade, high rejects, and prices that were "killing" them. Take, for instance, Kweku, a long-time TF supplier to whom I talked in mid-2009:

> Yes [...] it's not easy. You see you grow the thing [the pineapple]. You can force yourself to grow the thing. Like I was saying 2006, I acquired land in 2006. Over 30 acres, I bought all the suckers [...]. So I was buying suckers, fueling my truck to transfer the suckers to my field, planters, chemicals, workers for over one year. When I harvest, when it's time for harvesting, the market was not there. I put about 250 million [25,000 New Ghana cedis] in that business by then. I couldn't even get 50 million [5,000 New Ghana cedis]. So you can see. You can see. And then the cost in the business is killing us, so the price they [TF] are buying the fruit is not enough. Yes, it's not enough. (Interview, 2009)

Other farmers became aware of the new opportunities provided by increased demand from new competitors. "There is no pineapple in the system" was a frequent saying among agronomists around that time, who were "chasing pineapples" from dusk till dawn. Among the new players in the market field were several juice processors that tried to tap into the underexploited domestic market, local market women who responded to increased domestic demand, and a foreign-owned exporter-importer who had a niche market for Smooth Cayenne pineapples in France, Switzerland, and Italy, and several petty exporters who entered the game from 2010 onward when the Ghanaian government introduced a corporate tax rebate for any firm or person engaged in agricultural production. All this led to increased demand, and the spot prices paid by new market entrants at times exceeded those paid by TF.

This competitive moment prompted some farmers to challenge the prevailing order of the JIT market arrangement, no longer accepting how their fruits were valuated. For instance, Kofi, the educated son of a major pioneer supplier, started selling his pineapples to a customer of TF – the aforementioned foreign-owned exporter-importer – at a better price and service (pickup at farm level). He had become frustrated with the prices and rejects associated with the JIT model. Moreover, his father, once a so-called "big time farmer" and the biggest non-exporter supplier of TF who had gone for an ambitious expansion in 2007 with the encouragement of the company, had suffered dearly from the MD2 shock. Kofi had a simple explanation for his disenrolling from the JIT market arrangement:

> So once you don't take very good care of me and somebody is ready to assist me, why wouldn't you leave and go? Your girlfriend keeps telling you "I need money to do my hair, I need money to buy my dress" and you don't mind her, she finds somebody and she runs

away to that person. She doesn't care whether you have bought a car for her or you have bought a house for her, she will still leave you and go [...]. We are all fighting for market isn't it? (Interview, 2009)

Kofi's disenrollment from the JIT arrangement threatened the stability of the TF's supply base. It "denatured" (Thévenot 2002: 191) the prevailing market social because he no longer agreed "on the nature of the reality test for the evaluation" (ibid.: 191) of pineapples. Kofi, well known to the other farmers, thus induced new critical/political dynamics (Eymard-Duvernay et al. 2003: 12; Overdevest 2011: 535) into the scheme. What the JIT model needed least were more Kofis, as this would have threatened the order of the arrangements described in detail in the Chapter 7. Kofi also acted as a broker for other farmers who did not have market access, thereby maintaining a grip on fruits TF could have made use of. As if he had just read Latour's warning that power is "made of the wills of all others" (Latour 1986: 269), in August 2009, a senior manager of the company complained to an agronomist that they had done so much for the family of the farmer, and it had been simply unfair and unprofessional that the son went on a rampage in their very own turf (Field diary, 2009).

The flawed shift to MD2 and its repercussions, as well as the breakdown of TF's supply base, were eloquently described to me by an obviously concerned Mr. Sneijder in mid-2009, when he reflected on the multiple origins of the Crisis of the pineapple subsector:

> Smooth Cayenne was an important variety of pineapple, which would support the farmers and for some years, 2002 to 2004, 2005 maybe even, very little happened, MD2 didn't really take off, and the Smooth Cayenne remained and we continued to grow. And then, about two and a half years ago, we had the government and NGOs making noise about the benefits of MD2. We'd already got the country into it by setting up tissue cultures and the like, we got it going but it just began to become a *cause célèbre* for the authorities and we started shouting the loudest, "Don't go too far, don't go too far, please." And we warned against it, because the Smooth Cayenne is smooth, is cheaper to produce, it's easier to produce it in these mountains here, MD2 suits the great plains in Costa Rica and northern Brazil, where the Americans have, you know, basically flattened thousands of kilometers of land, in order to produce economically, very low cost, using machinery and no people, vast numbers of fruit. Of course, seeing this, the Africans [sic!] thought, "well, this is a market that's growing very fast," but it grew very fast because of the strengths of the marketing powers of the Americans, and again we continued to warn people. At the same time, about a year ago – this is something we didn't know was happening and I'm crossed with my own intelligence for not really getting the message through – but a year ago or so, just over a year ago, our own farmers started to get out of Smooth Cayenne and into MD2. We expected them to do half of it, but they didn't; they got out of Smooth Cayenne altogether or just abandoned their fields, and concentrated and put all the inputs into MD2. The results of that was evident in January [2009], when suddenly the first forcings started to come through and we saw, "my goodness me, what's happening, something awful," and we weren't getting Smooth Cayenne and for six months now we've been struggling to get Smooth Cayenne. (Interview, 2009)

Reassembling the Market Social?

The years 2008 and 2009 were bad. Although many farmers were nostalgic about the "good old days," by 2009 many of them had lost hope. At times, farmers would use strong words to describe their situation. Take John, a seasoned pineapple farmer:

> Formerly, we were enjoying the business, everything was going on smoothly but recently things are working against us yeah, very, very, very, we are in a difficult era, particularly since, that's since last, I think last we had a difficult time from, that was 2008.(Interview 2009)

Mawuli, another supplier reports with a similar thrust:

> OK, you know, way back in 1996, where the market is good, you realize that most of the guys there, like if as we walk through the bush, if it were to be in 1996, like you will not see any land left uncovered with pineapple. Like all those areas you see pineapple there. So now as the market flopped like that, most people cannot farm. [....] And the second issue that I see, they were using the money that they get from the pineapple to put up structures, buildings. So most of the buildings were put up through these pineapple exports. During that time, I can say the level of education was very high, was very high, because people are getting enough money, they cater for their people [...] but as the market flopped, we realized that most of the people cannot pay the school fees they used to pay. [...] And also, apart from that, during that time the standard of living was high. Because there was money in the system, cash flow was good. (Interview 2008)

It was not just TF farmers who suffered from the MD2 shock and global economic turmoil, Densu Valley more generally was full of unfinished houses; farmers were nostalgic for better days; youths who in the past had migrated back from towns to their villages to work on pineapple farms were "idling around" because of lack of work or had left to urban areas altogether. By 2009, some surviving Densu Valley farmers had become suppliers to other TF farmers. Rent-seeking through brokerage appeared more lucrative than production. Other TF farmers simply dropped out of the trade. Between 2007 and 2009, at least six of the company's Smooth Cayenne farmers had stopped planting. It was an alarming situation, and the TF managers eventually realized that something had to be done about it. Nothing was certain anymore. Because the flow of raw material was threatened by the partial disintegration of the supply base, the heterogeneous engineers of TF had to reassemble the market social.

Consequently, company managers worked hard throughout 2009 to realign their supply base, trying to reestablish legitimacy for the JIT model. In August 2009, the upper management called for a "farmer emergency meeting," in which I was fortunately allowed to participate. The meeting was rich in justifications and accounts. It started with a reconstruction of what went wrong and ended with an emotional plea to the farmers to work jointly with the company to solve the crisis. A senior foreign manager put particular emphasis on the supply shortage, blaming the government and donors for a unidirectional push toward MD2, complaining that some customers were threatening to switch to competitors if the supply did not improve. Somewhat shoving aside the problems that had amassed over the years within an ostensibly "sustainable relationship," he added that he did not want to blame anyone, and that both the company and the farmers should "work together and get things done better." He continued his account, suggesting that the company would like to renew its commitment to stable orders. But the manager also emphasized that what the company had in mind was not only commitments "through orders," but also "financial commitments," in this case, loans. Blurring the boundary between firm, farm, and community, he invoked notions of close personal relations, trust, and place-based attachments to protect his business from the market forces "out there." Emphasizing that TF had been around for 12 years, protecting the interests of its "farming community" and its "staff," he underlined that there was a need to renew this relationship through an "agreement in both ways," because the farmers failed to supply what had been actually agreed upon six months ago (Field diary, 2009).

The meeting was an exercise in realignment and "managing failures" (Li 2007a: 265), whereby the crisis was portrayed as "an outcome of rectifiable deficiencies" (ibid.). The senior manager promised a new approach to supply chain management and additional credit to farmers in order to secure raw material amid new competitive pressures in input markets. By assuring new commitment, the manager tried to re-forge connections with the farmers, while at the same time black-boxing the systemic flaws of JIT retail agrifood chains: their inherent volatility and the frequent shifting of costs and risks further upstream. By invoking notions of family, community, trust, and commitment, the manager tried to re-enroll the suppliers into a collective project. Loans and commitment were mobilized as "interessement devices" (Callon 1986: 209). New ways to evaluate routines in the supply chain were promised at the meeting, although the practice of keeping different evaluative principles in play (see Stark 2009) – for instance, when it came to the assessment of product weight and quality – had contributed successfully to the reproduction of the JIT model for a long time.

The re-enrollment of all suppliers, however, was an uncertain issue, as some became aware of their new negotiating power or saw the need to diversify their markets. "Gone are the days when farmers were fools. Competition is booming, markets are everywhere. They [the buyers] are even begging us for fruits," as Kofi boldly described to me the new window of opportunity that had suddenly opened for many farmers (Field diary, 2010). Other suppliers started to secretly disenroll from the network, side-selling produce to other exporters and local market women, either because they were offered higher prices or because this was a chance to circumvent the repayment of the loan granted by TF in 2009, which was to be retrieved from the farmers' supplies to the factory. Eventually, some farmers failed to pay back their loans and "ran away with the money," as one agronomist put it (Field diary, 2010). One of the threats to a company's survival identified by Fligstein (2001: 17) became harsh reality. The Densu Valley suppliers ceased to be pacified, becoming aware of their power to control inputs and push for higher prices in a changing market environment. Because of price squeezes by retailers in Europe, TF found it difficult to increase its prices for pineapples, fearing that price increases could lead to an upward price spiral. Between a rock and a hard place ...

Given a contracted raw material market and the fact that at least two of the ten farmers who had been given loans failed to honor the loan commitment ("loans for fruits"), the undersupply problem had still not been solved by August 2010. For the first time, TF was forced to import pineapples from neighboring countries such as Togo, Côte d' Ivoire, and Benin. Raw material costs skyrocketed.

Matters were worsened by the nominal and real appreciation of the Ghana cedi against the US dollar and the corporate currency in the first three quarters of 2010, which resulted in loss of price competitiveness of made-in-Ghana goods and services in international trade more generally. On top of that, TF suffered severe losses from the strike of a major European airline in March and the eruption of Eyjafjallajökull in April 2010, whose ash cloud grounded exports for four consecutive days. The JIT model had come under pressure from virtually all sides. Among the upper management, questions about its future were raised. The whole organization of the company's supply chain became a matter of discussion. In September 2010, many permanent workers had to be laid off again. Furthermore, plans were discussed to relocate some production lines to other African countries that offered enough raw material supply at lower costs (such as Benin and Nigeria) or special government subsidies (such as Gabon). Other ideas included developing sea-freightable products and new distribution channels to lower the costs of the company's products.

As a response to the raw material shortage in Ghana and the ash cloud shock, the company opened a back-up factory for its MD2 line in Europe in mid-2011. Fruits were now imported for the first time from the industrialized plains of Latin America and processed in Europe. This represented a drastic change in business strategy and was a reaction to the critical moments through which the company had passed. It was a realignment of supply chains, though not one in the interest of Ghana's pineapple farmers. It remained unclear what would happen to the Smooth Cayenne line as several of the company's smaller suppliers had stopped production. Consequently, the company joined up with some leftover farmers of Farmapine and planned to venture into a new frontier in the Brong-Ahafo Region, which still offered a potential for "less demanding" farmers, as one agronomist put it (Field diary, 2011).[15]

All in all, in the wake of increased competition and the global economic crisis, the location of Ghana itself had become a critical node in the multinational production network of TF. Although its market model fared well in the early years and farmers had good returns, the terms of trade deteriorated when competition became more price based, input costs rose, and contextual factors changed. The durability of the JIT arrangement depended heavily on the willingness of retailers to pay comparatively more for fruits fresh from farm, a pacified supply base, a favorable exchange rate regime, and, not to forget, free zone rents.

Recalcitrant "Nature" and the Crisis of the Developmental Market

The notion of "creating history," the term Claire used to describe what it meant to introduce export-oriented organic mango farming in northern Ghana (see Chapter 5), was a marker for the wide range of ontological reconfigurations that had to occur for the market-making project to "take off." Roles and responsibilities had to be defined; new forms of qualculative agency needed to be bred; mundane trees had to be turned into export goods; new encounters had to be organized. All this required hard work, marked by "irritations, disjunctures, and paradoxes which surface when heterogeneous actors practically enact" particular production/market models (Berndt & Boeckler 2011a: 1058). Even though I have repeatedly underlined that all of this work was materially entangled, one may quickly forget that agrifood markets cannot thrive if the biogeophysical dimensions of production are not effectively controlled.[16] Scholars of global agrifood connections and the historical expansion of capitalist modernity more generally all too often tend to forget that nature is not a passive, external object that can be easily tamed in a Promethean fashion (Mitchell 2002: 29), but is unpredictably active and often the cause of troubles or even crises. I have black-boxed such problems for the pineapple case study. Yet, as economic geographer Ray Hudson notes so perceptively:

> Every economic activity – production, exchange, consumption – [...] necessarily involves material transformations, chemical and physical transformations of matter from one state to another but material transformations that chronically exceed their intended effects, as unruly matter escapes the frame defined by a given transformative process. Consequently, at every stage in the economy the transformation of materials has both intended and unintended – the latter often invisible or otherwise undetected as well as unwanted – effects. (2008: 188)

Of course, Hudson is not the first one to emphasize the materiality of economic processes. According to Mitchell (2002: 30) and Pinch and Swedberg (2008: 7), it was Marx who was foremost in acknowledging that material things and processes form hybrids with the consciousness of humans. Building on Marx's sensitivity to the material base of "economic" processes, from the 1980s onward agrifood scholars have emphasized that agriculture represents an "anomaly within capitalism, arising from the singularities of its natural production process" (Goodman 2001: 185). In this literature, consequently, nature is largely considered a rather passive obstacle to the process of capital accumulation, affecting the organization of production as well as the structure of industries and markets (Mann & Dickinson 1978).

More recent work in political ecology has broken with such positions and treats nature "as a set of obstacles, opportunities, and surprises that firms confront in their attempts to subordinate biophysical properties and processes to industrial production" (Boyd et al. 2001: 556). How to make biogeophysical systems act as a force of production and "the market" more generally is then a salient question when it comes to the marketization of nature.[17] This question also preoccupied the OFL managers, and they would be quick to tell us how difficult it was to transform nature into a resource that could be counted on *in practice*. Their project of market-making was not only a struggle over the engineering goods, agencies, and market encounters, but also about the "production of nature" (Smith 1984) itself.

Yet, to understand this production of nature, we have to move beyond the modernist ontology described in many political ecology and economy texts, which often still advance a binary opposition between the "human" and the "nonhuman" (Goodman 2001: 185, 190; Mitchell 2002: 52). In the case of OFL's market-making project, as is the case with all "nature"-based market-making projects, "nature" was the medium, constraint, and effect of an ongoing process of heterogeneous engineering; *medium* because it had to be turned into a form of (production) capital and commodity (Prudham 2003: 637), *constraint* because it shaped and constrained the practices of heterogeneous engineering in specific historical and geographical circumstances, and *effect* because the mango trees as engineered nature were themselves relational effects of a whole range of discursive-cum-material practices at work in the outgrower scheme that recursively defined the sort of market arrangements that were possible. It was during Crises moments, when "nature" did not act in the name of the market, that the precarious "relational materiality" (Law 1994: 102; see also Goodman 2001: 192) of marketization became most evident. Unpredictably active and full of surprises, "nature" often escaped the frames defined by the heterogeneous engineers of OFL and its consultants.

All this had significant consequences for the returns on capital, practices of economization, frames of qualification, and organizational relations within the agribusiness–outgrower complex.

(Mis-)calculating "Nature" and other Surprises: Mango Trees as Precarious Commodities

The mango project started with ideal calculations advanced by consultants hired by the OFL director and his associates. Drawing on their own expertise in conventional mango farming and on international standards for conventional mango production, these experts provided the foundational knowledge for the project. By mobilizing such generalized, abstract knowledge about mango cultivation, they necessarily operated with simplifying assumptions about factor costs, climatic dynamics, labor intensity, yields, growth cycles, and prices, and necessarily bracketed a whole range of other factors lying outside their narrow frame of abstraction (Scott 1998: 292). With little regard for local climatic, edaphic, hydrological, vegetative, and micro-social particularities, the OFL director and his associates based their calculations about investments and returns on a "normalized acre" (ibid.: 289) of mango trees that had been constructed in the bounded realm of scientific expertise. They projected that the mango trees would start to yield in the fifth year after planting, starting with 300 kg per acre, which would steadily increase until the tenth year, when the yields would total 6,300 kg per acre. Irrigation, according to the consultants, would only be required for the first three years of production. For the outgrowers, it was assumed that this would result in considerable net returns from year eight onward. It was thought that the outgrowers could pay back their debts after the fifth year and from the eighth year onward they would not have to rely on credit anymore but could finance OFL services from their mango-related savings. Within 12 to 15 years after planting, the credit would have been paid back.

It was a promising calculation. Thus, 2,000 outgrowers were quickly targeted. It was assumed that by 2015, these 2,000 outgrowers, combined with the nucleus farm, could produce 20,000 mt of fruits per annum, which would have made OFL one of the biggest players in the global mango market – organic, on top of that. Consequently, OFL staff was busy registering farmers, expanding the outgrower scheme to reach the goal of 2,000 outgrowers by 2008. "We have to reach our project goal" was frequently heard during that time.

These calculations became a linchpin for the mango project. Everything was based on them: the enrollment of shareholders, farmers, and NGOs; the content of the contract; the organizational and material layout of the outgrower scheme; and the staffing of OFL. To reach the goal of 2,000 outgrowers by 2008, a lot was done faster and on a larger scale than it should have been. Seduced by target-based bonuses, OFL staff would often hastily register farmers without doing proper background checks. Farmers scattered uneconomically over a wide geographical area would be registered often with a disregard for the microclimatic and edaphic variations between different locations.

The expansion drive came with huge investments in equipment, farm infrastructure, seedlings, and staff, even though tree cultivation is a delicate issue that demands a step-by-step approach. Trees are tricky commodities. In fact, they can become the spatiotemporal nightmare of every capitalist, as OFL shareholders and managers would soon find out. Unlike seasonal crops such as pineapples, they can never be "fully produced" and "the time required for biogeophysical (re)production processes to occur, and the fact that natural resources are extensive in space, found in particular locations, and vary in quality, all affect the capital accumulation process in unique and important ways" (Boyd et al. 2001: 556). Tree cultivation has "'built-in' delays in the turnover of capital" (Mann 1990; cited in Prudham 2003: 641). You never know what you may get, and, as the saying goes, only time will tell. There remains a constant uncertainty regarding the correspondence between investments, "observed traits in young trees and the realization of gains at commercial maturity" (ibid.). Malpractices of the past can hardly be corrected. Fields cannot be abandoned if the water level or soil quality in a given location is poor. Often, there are also serious constraints with regard to technical manipulation, all the more with organically grown trees, where the range of chemical or even genetic manipulation is limited or forbidden altogether. All this makes trees a kind of spatially fixed capital and precarious commodities at the same time.

Soon it became clear that the practicalities of mango cultivation in northern Ghana were at odds with the normalizing assumptions and abstract knowledge of the foreign consultants. It also became evident that many of the calculations and management decisions based on this expertise would have a negative impact on the future course of the project. "Nature," and not least the outgrowers themselves, had many ways of escaping the visions of the experts.[18] When the nucleus farm and the first bunch of farmers had harvestable fruits in 2006, the yields were already below expectations. This suboptimal development continued in the subsequent years.

The year 2007 saw a slight increase in yields, with some farmers harvesting considerable volumes of mangoes – yet, on average, yields remained below expectations. The same was true for 2008, and 2009 was a disastrous year, with yields even regressing in many farms. The agribusiness–outgrower complex slid into a state of crisis and uncertainty. The shareholders cut the budget by half for 2010, putting huge pressure on OFL staff to improve yields. Everything was downsized. 2010 was again a disappointing year. Only in 2011 did yields increase again, and there was renewed hope for the project.

Crisis Accounts

What I described earlier with the agnosticism of a "distant observer" was in fact an embodied and difficult process of adjustment. It was full of trials of strength, clashing bodies of farming knowledge, disappointments, and conflict, and resulted in several sociomaterial rearrangements of the market-making project. But how could it happen that the project – which from the very beginning was so sensitive to local cultural particularities – could slowly slide into Crisis?

During my time in the outgrower scheme, managers and farmers would produce many accounts. What became generally evident, however, was that the crisis was an articulation of different factors emanating from the very setup of the market-making project and the ways the relational materiality of "nature" was taken into account when the project was set up[19]: the imported mango seedlings from Burkina Faso, which were planted on 75 acres of the scheme (see Chapter 5), turning out to be of poor quality; the farmers, who had obviously been registered in locations with poor soil quality, planting their trees virtually on top of the laterite crusts that are so common in parts of the tropics; the mango trees suddenly needing more water during their first three years than expected; the tree flowers proving to be more vulnerable to the semi-arid climate of northern Ghana (with its heat waves and the dry and dusty *Harmattan*) than the consultants had predicted; and the alignment of farmers and trees with the overall program of market-making being harder work than had been envisaged. Claire's words are indicative in this regard:

> So we started out with projections that were given to us at international standards, you know. So we have put international standards on trees growing in Dagbon raised by Dagombas and Mamprusi people, and they didn't have irrigation at that time and they are organic and there's so many issues that weren't put into those projections [...]. (Interview, 2008)

> Yeah you know, I think [...] it obviously wasn't realized in the beginning how huge effects of the, the climate would be on mango production [...]. So I think the, the possible negative effects of, of high temperature here probably was sort of overlooked or, or not realized [...]. (Interview, 2009)

In an effort to counter some of the effects of past management decisions, OFL repeatedly made costly adjustments in order to realign "nature" with its project of market-making. In 2002, after it was clear that the seedlings imported from Burkina Faso were of poor quality and diseased, the company invested in a nursery to produce high-quality seedlings that could be used for planting new mango orchards or for regrafting old ones. In the same year, an irrigation system was set up at the nucleus farm because the mango trees, planted on poor soils, needed more water than expected during their early growth years. The system was extended to the outgrower farms in 2006 to substitute for the labor-intensive bucket irrigation system the outgrowers had been using until then.

The harvests in 2006 and 2007 were both below expectations, and projections were reworked. Although some managers already had doubts about the trajectory of the project, there was still widespread hope that the reworked projections and investments would materialize in the future. For 2008, the company projected eight containers of exportable fruits (160 mt) but eventually exported only less than half of it from its nucleus farm and even less from the 500 or so outgrowers in production. This was partly because of the heavy rains in August and September 2007[20] that flooded large parts of northern Ghana and which impacted the flowering behavior of the trees. Following this disappointment, the directors put the expansion of the project on hold, and the target of reaching 2,000 outgrowers faded away.

From 2008 onward, the shareholders of OFL were becoming increasingly nervous. After the huge and often unforeseen investments they had made up to 2008, they expected something major for 2009. Bonuses and salary increments were cut. The OFL staff got the directive to yield 500 mt of mangoes from the nucleus and outgrower farms, of which 350 mt should be exportable. The directive came close to a Damoclean sword, putting huge pressure on the outgrower department in particular. This pressure could be felt during many encounters I had with the OFL managers.

It became particularly evident during a weekly outgrower manager meeting I attended back in September 2008. Pressured by the expectations of the ARAMIS shareholders, production problems, and an incoming audit by the Organic Movement, the outgrower manager Charles had a serious word with his four assistants, each of whom supervised another 14 field assistants (FAs) working with the outgrowers on a daily basis. He informed the managers that "bacterial black spot,"[21] a leaf and fruit disease caused by a bacterium (*xanthomonas campestris pv. mangiferaeindicae*), was a serious problem in some farms, while others exhibited low levels of weed uprooting and mulching.[22] Charles was obviously not happy with the progress his staff had made since the last harvest in April, all the more because they expected an external audit by the end of the month. He made an emotional appeal to all his assistants, urging them to work more committedly toward improving on the internal control system that the Organic Movement required, as well as toward getting better at production management more generally:

> Please gentlemen, [...] we want to fully be able to participate in international trade. It is clear that there should have been some things happening which have not been addressed at an according pace [...]. I am responsible as the outgrower manager for the scheme, so all things not being done are shifting back to me. We are here to meet targets, to meet objectives. And let us do our very best, so that we all can benefit. It is part of the reason why we never got out yields in the past season. There are no wishy-washy things anymore. So attention to detail, please. So all issues not related to mangoes, push them aside! It's gonna drag you down, it's gonna drag us down! (Field diary, 2008)

The harvest in April and May 2009 came as a shock. While the yields on the nucleus farm had increased by 10%, the harvests from the outgrowers' farms were even less than in the previous year. The agribusiness–outgrower complex had to undergo a complete restructuring as the shareholders cut the budget by half. OFL also decided to withdraw its truck-based water delivery services given to those farmers not connected to the pipe irrigation system.

The mood was depressed when I arrived after the harvest for my field research. The managers were working under high pressure from both the farmers' and the shareholders' side. The outgrower department was downsized, and the chief agronomist, Charles, was made redundant owing to budget cuts. Uncertainty loomed large, and during many encounters, several managers would repeatedly express doubts about the future of the project. In some outgrower fields, the yields were as low as 10% of the initial projections. Even groups who had experienced relatively successful harvests in the past had low yields in 2009. Many farmers were discouraged by these developments, as the chairman of the Association of Organic Mango Outgrowers (AOMO) succinctly summarized in 2009:

> They are actually not so encouraged considering the number of years the trees have actually attained and not fruiting [...]. And considering the initial projections we made, they are getting discouraged. And actually, that is what is pulling some of them back. (Interview, 2009)

On top of that, the low yields were increasing the relative indebtedness among the outgrowers as costly technical services and inputs continued to be given to them, but at the same time there was no income to service the loans. This raised concerns among AOMO executives and some of the outgrowers.

In early 2010, it dawned on the OFL managers that history would repeat itself as flower production set in too early, exposing the flowers to heat during the hot dry season from January to March, which negatively affected fruit production. A consultant visiting in March also found out that in many locations, trees had only developed poor root systems. During the drive to reach 2,000 outgrowers as quickly as possible, many trees had obviously not only been planted on poor soils, but also in planting holes that were too small. To make things worse, 2,400 trees were burned by bush fires because the respective farmers had not maintained their fire-belts. Although some farmers were enjoying satisfactory yields, other farmers became increasingly discouraged, and the mood in the outgrower scheme was at an all-time low. In January 2010, some of OFL's shareholders and senior managers even had to tour different areas of the outgrower scheme to appease the farmers and assure them that they still had faith in the project. The management was still optimistic that the project could be turned around because it had hired new mango experts from the Netherlands, Senegal, Australia, and Brazil in order to solve the production problem.

Despite the renewed optimism, already the 2010 pre-harvest time came as a big blow to OFL staff and many farmers alike. Many trees lost their fruits, and even previously successful farmers had less yields than in the past. David, my research assistant, made some striking observations prior to the harvest. As expected, the yields turned out to be very disappointing, as David later remarked in his diary for two specific sites, even though other farms faced similar problems:

> Total harvest in Zulungu zone indicates that this year yields have fallen by 60%. This was the same for Pulugo zone, where successful farmers like Pulugo chairman got a total harvest of less than 100 kg. Generally, most of the farmers were not happy with their total yields at the time of harvest *but who is to be blamed?* (Field diary, 2010, italics in original)

Despite the yield problems, the shareholders were willing to continue investing in the project. The newly hired consultants brought in fresh knowledge from different production areas around the world, and the yields increased significantly again in 2011. Things *seemed* to turn for the better.

Regrouping

What the previous section shows is that "nature" must not be "understood primarily as a feature of the firm's external environment" but rather "as part and parcel of the basic problem of organizing and implementing production" (Boyd et al. 2001: 561). It is thus part and parcel of the assumingly social "thing" we call "the market." Along the mango frontier, the problem of transforming "nature" into resources that could be counted on came along with painful adjustments, controversies, and disappointment. Established frames for qualifying farming practices, goods, and agencies, as well as the organization of market encounters, came into question as unintended side effects of past management decisions and nature's recalcitrance produced considerable overflows. The failure to enroll "nature" as a reliable resource led to the reordering of the market arrangement as new calculations of "nature," investments, and profits became "matters of concern" (Latour 2005: 114):

> Well, I think OFL had a plan of by 2007, [by] year 2008 that we are going to push as fast as we can to reach 2,000 growers […] so, we were actually overspending to be able to reach our goals. But with the yield dropping down, the shareholders said "no." Investment on irrigation was huge, and also the irrigation did not make a difference in the yield. [....] So immediately, we had to make a total turn-around and regroup again. And secondly, we had to find out now, what are the problems? Why aren't we getting flowering in certain areas? [....] So yeah, then the shareholders came to me and said to me, "Right, you have to make a decision. Your budget's been cut by 50%, so you have to make decisions, how you adapt to that budget." So the shareholders were saying "that is what we can afford and from the next phases now, OFL has to start generating its own income." (Interview senior manager, 2009)

As can be seen from the quote, regrouping had three dimensions. First, the OFL management altered its calculatory calculus, and the agribusiness–outgrower complex had to undergo a considerable restructuring, including a downsizing of the outgrower department. Second, the management sought new recombinations of knowledge in order to solve the yield problems. Third, OFL had to look for other sources of income generation. For the sake of space, I will only address the first two dimensions in the following sections.[23]

The Corporate Calculus of the Crisis

With the yields repeatedly being below expectations, OFL became increasingly calculative in its relations with the outgrowers. Whereas in the past the policy had been not to lose any outgrowers and many "poorly performing" farmers even had trees replaced after they had been burned by bush fires, destroyed by animals, or died from water stress, from 2008 onward the company's management became much stricter and laid a greater emphasis on efficiency. This was evident during the general meeting of AOMO in July 2008 when one OFL senior manager burst into the room and announced that the company would no longer be willing to carry on with "non-performing farmers." After the meeting, I made the following field diary entry:

> The executive meeting started with an announcement of one obviously concerned senior manager. Farmers are not performing well, and AOMO is urged to step in on this issue. For instance, farms in Larba are abandoned. He made it clear that the company can no longer afford to give out seedlings and loans just like that, saying: "I want things fixed, and how things are done, I don't care, I can no longer bear farmers, who are not performing, those days are gone [...]." Referring to some problem plots, e.g., along Larba-Manbagla Road, he said he would give out a list with non-performing farmers and that he then expects consequences from AOMO members. He either expected a change of ownership or a delisting, asking AOMO officials who would then pay for it?[24] He closed his speech by warning that "the days that OFL was giving out money just like that are gone. We are not an NGO, we are not World Vision, we are not Oxfam, our pockets are closed." (Field diary, 2008).

In 2008, the company introduced a measurement system to requalify the farmers' performances, and in June 2009, the company decided to delist 90 farmers (90 acres) who were not performing according to those measurements.[25] Farmers were graded into three categories, whereby the first group of farmers (category A farmer) would receive all inputs, the second group would receive an amount of inputs according to their rating and had to pay for any additional inputs they required (category B farmers), and the third group of farmers (category C farmers) would be delisted:

> We are also going to start deleting bad farmers. Farmers that pull the project down, we are going to remove them. We will write off the debt, we won't take him to court or anything. The shareholders are willing just to write it off. Because some of the farmers you just continue giving and giving and it never stops. [...] [I]t sounds a bit harsh but the company loses too much money. (Interview senior manager, 2009)

The group of "performers" was also allowed to join a program set up by OFL's mother company (ARAMIS) that gave out high-yielding grain varieties to farmers in various parts of Ghana on a loan basis, with the loan being retrieved from the sale of harvests (organized by ARAMIS). This was meant to keep up the morale of the farmers. What this account shows is how, in the wake of crisis, processes and people were reevaluated according to new framings of worth that were informed much more by the imperative for efficiency. This contrasted with the past aspiration to save every farmer, and to nurture personal relations and attachments.

In addition, as already hinted at earlier, the management also cancelled truck-based irrigation services to the 700 farmers (700 acres) not connected to the irrigation system and considerably reduced the number of FAs in the outgrower department in order to cut down on technical service costs. *De facto*, such practices of economization went against the content of the contract, which stated that OFL would provide all inputs and services necessary to grow organic mangoes on a credit basis.

Although the OFL management claimed that in cases of *force majeure* such adjustments were justified, AOMO staff and even some OFL managers feared that the sudden changes could backfire on the company–outgrower relationship and create a major controversy. When meeting him on one of his last days on duty, even the fading outgrower manager noted with concern, "I am not so much bothered about myself, but more about the farmers. We made so many promises, and now farmers see us withdrawing all these things, selling trucks and tanks" (Field diary, 2009). The AOMO administrator, who joined our conversation, was equally concerned about the effects of the "OFL regrouping." In several locations, rumors were spreading that the company would abandon the farmers. It was obvious that the policy changes of OFL had not been communicated well. Only in the course of many public encounters between the AOMO secretary, its executives, the OFL management, and the farmers could trust in the company be reestablished. Such public encounters helped to restore some confidence in the project to some extent, and the relationship between OFL and the outgrowers started to improve when farmers in some locations obtained increasing yields in 2011.

Fixing Yields: Contested Pathways of Qualification

From the beginning, the OFL managers relied on the expertise of foreign consultants with regard to mango cultivation. After repeated yields that were below expectations, the company intensified its search to solve the yield problems from 2009 onward. The foundational knowledge on which the project and much of the management decisions were based increasingly became a matter of controversy. Such an opening was necessary because for many years the company had relied only on one pair of consultants from abroad, who, to make matters worse, were not specialists in organic tree farming. As new consultants were incorporated and some farmers had themselves become increasingly knowledgeable about mango farming, two lines of controversy emerged.

The first one was the frictional relationship between different bodies of expert knowledge mobilized to solve the yield problem. The second one was the relationship between expert knowledge and the practical knowledge of the farmers. Although such frictional relationships could be approached from a conventions school perspective as a clash of different evaluative principles (Boltanski & Thévenot 2006 [1991]: 269–270;

Truninger 2008), Scott's notions of *episteme* and *mētis* (1998: 311) are particularly useful to help grasp the dynamic yet often frictional interaction between different ways of knowing in the course of market-making projects (and social ordering schemes more generally). Writing on state-driven schemes to improve the human condition, such as the mobilization of scientific agriculture in colonial and post-colonial societies in the Global South, *mētis* describes the forms of knowledge embedded in local experience, whereas *episteme/techne* describes the abstract knowledge deployed by the state and its technical agencies as part of agricultural modernization projects. Despite Scott's state centrism, I feel comfortable with using such categories in the context of "private sector-driven modernization projects," too.

After the disappointing 2009 harvest, the company's management brought in a new organic consultant through the help of a buyer in Europe. The consultant visited the project for one week and afterward produced a sharp-edged report that basically outlined all the major mistakes that had been made in the past with regard to organic tree cultivation, from the selection of sites and seedlings, to composting and watering. He argued that the previous consultants' advice was essentially based on a chemical approach to organic farming and that this had contributed to the problems the agribusiness–outgrower complex faced at that moment. Convinced that knowledge of formal organic principles existed within OFL, but that this knowledge had never been translated into *know-how*, he came to the conclusion that composting, a cornerstone of organic agriculture, had never been practiced seriously. He dismissed the other consultants' advice as reductionist and full of chemical mastery. For him, organic farming was not something one could implement from acquired knowledge alone but was based on an understanding of biological processes and nature itself (Field diary, 2009). The reductionist *techne* the conventional experts deployed simply could not do justice to the complex mechanics of "nature" and their variegation in time and space.

Apart from the fact that the company had not tapped into alternative forms of epistemic knowledge that embrace a different way of transforming "nature" – transforming by understanding, not transforming by chemically controlling – it also became clear that the company's agronomists had not recognized the considerable *mētis* some outgrowers had acquired over the years with regard to tree cultivation and the microclimate in their specific location. Instead, to cite Scott (1998: 273), "[i]mported faith and abstraction [had] prevailed [...] over close attention to the local context." Yet scholars critical of scientific agriculture remind us that "the rule of experts" (Mitchell 2002), and their disregard for contextuality and practical knowledge, has led to the failure of many agriculture modernization projects around the world[26]:

> The power of practical knowledge depends on an exceptionally close and astute observation of the environment [...]. Nor should we forget that the peasant cultivator [...] lives year in and year out in the field of observation. He or she will likely know things that neither an absentee cultivator nor a research scientist would ever notice. (Scott 1998: 324)

Indeed, in 2009 – just after the first dramatic yield failure – many farmers raised the concern that their voices had not been heard enough when it came to managing the mango trees. For instance, Abukari, the chairman of one of the pioneer groups, reckoned:

> OFL, especially last year had a problem with that, they didn't want to share ideas with us, they always try to say what they know is final. And we, I have an experience with that because last year, they used to install the irrigation system on our mango fields, so when the rains stopped we told them [OFL] never to start irrigating around that time because around that time the trees needed no water and when we said it they refused, they went ahead and irrigated the trees. I think that it was arrogant because they should listen to us even though we are not technical people but we know the condition and the weather here. (Interview 2009, translated)

The problem described by the chairman was brought up during several encounters with other farmers. Around that time, the OFL upper management became aware of this problem and tried to be more attentive to the practical knowledge of the farmers in the future.

The management's becoming more sensitive to the local geographical context of particular farms and to the opinion of farmers opened up new pathways for solving the yield problem. More consultants from Brazil, Senegal, and Australia – all countries with large populations of mango trees – were hired to fix the yield problem. Together with the organic consultant they would visit the project, exchanging ideas on how to solve the problem. The team slowly put together the pieces of the yield puzzle. Apart from poor soil quality and water stress, it turned out that the main problem was the time of flowering. Instead of flowering in December, some of the fruits did so only in January, exposing the buds and consequently the fruits to temperatures of up to 43 °C. Some of the newly hired consultants remarked that a potential solution would be to chemically trigger flower induction with *Paclobutrazol*, a plant growth retardant, and treatment with potassium nitrate (KNO_3), but this would have resulted in the scheme losing its organic status. The shareholders and the organic consultant were against such an approach, the former for commercial reasons, the latter for reasons of principle.

The OFL management was caught up in an indeterminate situation (Dewey 1915) given the different, at times even opposing, accounts produced by the consultants. "I don't know where to go," one obviously frustrated senior manager admitted when I met him in March 2010. He thought that the solution would probably lie in a mixture of organic principles when it comes to composting, and chemically induced flowering to save the project, and the company indeed started some non-organic farming trials on its nucleus farm, but at the same time he was pessimistic about quick-fix solutions. There were "so many factors," the senior manager said, ranging from management, to production, to chemical application, to weather to soil types. "If you change one thing, the other things may also change," he described the complex mechanics of organic mango farming in northern Ghana. He said that the company was gradually building up capacity to deal with edaphic and climatic intricacies in the region. However, he frankly admitted that there was a problem that had not been solved, and this was water. The groundwater tables in the region were just too thin, unlike neighboring Burkina Faso or Mali, where mango trees could develop extended root systems.

Furthermore, many of the trees in these countries were reasonably mature, with some of them even having been planted during colonial times. This was another flaw in the initial projections, as another senior manager eventually concluded: "[t]oo many things were taken for granted" (Field diary, 2010). The OFL managers and shareholders could only hope that the trees would adapt to the water and heat stress, while mitigating some production problems with sound irrigation and organic crop management.

In nature, changes take time. Against this backdrop, it was not surprising that 2010 was a bad year again. Only in 2011 did yields improve. There was light at the end of the tunnel, even though the shareholders had long abandoned the idea that the mango project would yield quick returns, and its breakeven point had been corrected from year 15 to year 20. Despite yield improvements, converting the scheme to conventional agriculture was not off the table. All in all, there still hovered a cloud of uncertainty over the project. Despite the director's assurance that ARAMIS would not abandon it, farmers and company staff alike steered into an uncertain future. Frontiers have always been spaces of uncertainty and risk alike.

Conclusion

In this chapter, I have shown how market arrangements in both case studies were destabilized over the course of time. Market crises can have many sources. Crisis is when networks fail (Law 1992: 389) – when the bits and pieces that make up the market social cannot be pacified anymore, become recalcitrant, are challenged by new bits and pieces, become obsolete, or do not come together in the first place. In the first case study, crop varieties, capital, prices, workers, suppliers, exchange rates, retailers, and competitors became problematic elements in the market arrangement, calling for the realignments of supply chains. Crisis was a matter of "things falling apart." It was the result of a supply chain model being pressured by both internal and external dynamics.

The Crisis of the mango project was a different matter altogether. It was a manifestation of the failure of "drawing things effectively together." At the same time, some materials had not yet the right shape to effectively punctualize the market social. Materials are themselves relational effects (Law 1994: 101). The mango trees could only produce yields with the right inputs, climate, soil, water supply, and husbandry practices. All became critical elements in the organic market STA, hampering the yield production and qualification of the mango trees. Mango tree production in northern Ghana rested on the unpredictable interaction of a whole range of human and nonhuman elements that could not be placed in a neat frame of calculation, which in turn affected the practices of economization in the agrobusiness–outgrower complex. The Crisis was both a material and a relational one. What we can finally take from this account is a warning to those strands of social theory that disregard nonhuman actors and have an unbroken faith in the human mastery of the "external environment." As Mitchell (2002: 30) notes, nonhuman actors such as "nature" do not just interact with the activities of human agents. They make possible a world that somehow seems the outcome of human rationality and programming. They shape a variety of social processes, sometimes according to human plans, but just as often not, or at least not quite. How is it, we need to ask, that forms of rationality, planning, expertise, and profit arise from this effect?

My accounts of critical moments in the history of both market-making projects point to something larger that warrants attention in the study of global market connections. Capitalist marketization is often a collection of hybrid, dynamically and reflexively interrelated agents that are engaged in the performance of markets. The concept of performance, or better co-performance, allows us to consider the observable reality "as the temporary outcome of confrontations between different competing programs, including scientific ones" (Callon 2007: 335). It emphasizes the historical dimension of market-making processes, as well as the fact "that the economy and markets are the temporary and fluctuating result of conflicts and the constantly changeable expression of power struggles" (ibid.). Crisis is then a moment when the performance of markets shifts in such ways that the enactment of established programs of surplus production for one or more actor(s) is no longer possible or when the "practical realities" in a specific site are no longer compatible with the prevailing performance of markets.

Endnotes

1   Source: http://www.merriam-webster.com/dictionary/crisis, accessed: 05/12/2013.
2   In this book, all names of individuals, of the case study companies and related organizations, and their geographical associations have been anonymized, are withheld, or have been altered to protect sources. Development organizations and programs associated with the Ghanaian agricultural sector more generally are mentioned by their original names.
3   Fresh Del Monte Produce has operations in South and Central America, the US, Africa, the Middle East, South East Asia, and Europe. It had a turnover of USD 3.55 billion in 2010 (Fresh Del Monte Produce Inc. 2011: 3).
4   See http://www.bsfllp.com/news/firm_reports/000011/002.5, checked on 30/10/2011.
5   It should be noted, however, that "Ghana's total exports did not fall so drastically, because in 2003 Compagnie Fruitière (a multinational corporation) established a subsidiary in Ghana called Golden Exotics in a decision to move its production from the Côte d'Ivoire, and started exporting MD2 pineapple in 2004" (Whitfield 2010: 28).
6   In 2006, plantlets of MD2 would cost USD 0.36 per piece, an enormous difference compared to the USD 0.01 farmers paid for Smooth Cayenne suckers (Banson 2007: 42).
7   In 2005, one acre of MD2 pineapples (25,000 plants) required USD 9,000 for planting material, USD 77 for land preparation, USD 1,495 for agrochemicals and fertilizers, and USD 741 for labor. For Smooth Cayenne, the values were USD 250, USD 77, USD 498, and USD 258 (Banson 2007: 42). By 2009, the costs for planting material had come down to 10% of the initial value. According to calculations of TF agronomists, one acre of MD2 (18,000 plants) had come down to USD 2,103 while planting 1 acre of Smooth Cayenne (20,000 plants) required USD 2,085.
8   Even though no exact figures are available, other studies confirm that the number of smallholder farmers in export value chains has dropped drastically (Fold & Gough 2008; Whitfield 2010; see also figure 8.3).

9   I met many of these former Farmapine farmers in the villages I conducted research in, where they struggled to make a living or tried to get reconnected to the market with the help of NGOs or the Millennium Challenge Account (MCA) program.

10 Some of these companies had a strong competitive edge when it came to prices because they were buying sea-freighted fruits with the crowns removed in the countries of production. This enhanced packaging efficiency. They also used mechanical peelers and often cheap migrant labor at their factories in Western Europe.

11 Note here that the valuation of workers according to an industrial (efficiency-oriented) framing of worth in the wake of the economic crisis clashed with the rendition of the company as a "family" based on long-term relationships and trust that was part of factory life (see Chapter 5; see Boltanski & Thévenot 2006 [1991]: 244; Thévenot 2001a: 413).

12 Inflation rates are given in consumer prices. Source: http://www.indexmundi.com/facts/ghana/inflation#FP.CPI.TOTL.ZG; accessed: 30/10/2011.

13 The National Democratic Congress (NDC) won and took over power from the then ruling National Patriotic Party (NPP).

14 Many of these were former Farmapine members, who had been assisted by donor organizations such as the German Technical Cooperation (GTZ, now GIZ) to acquire GLOBALG.A.P certificates.

15 On the agribusiness strategy of "shifting to uninformed growers in new regions," see Glover and Kusterer (1990: 131).

16 The "taming of nature" has indeed been key to the extension of capitalism's frontiers, as Mitchell's account of colonial Egypt (Mitchell 2002) or Scott's account of "high modernist agriculture" (Scott 1998) clearly show.

17 Nature-based industries are those industries that confront nature directly, but these should always be analyzed in their own terms and specific historical and regional contexts (Boyd, Prudham, & Schurman 2001: 556). Thus, we should distinguish between nonbiologically based industries based on extraction, where the physical properties of materials cannot be manipulated (e.g., mining), and biologically based industries based on cultivation, where the biophysical properties of organic material can be manipulated to achieve a desired outcome (e.g., tree cultivation, aquacultures). Such a conception of "nature" may still risk perpetuating a nature/society divide, but can likewise be part of a relational materialism as favored by ANT scholars and myself in the remainder of this chapter.

18 See Mitchell's work on the building of the Aswan Dam in early 20th century Egypt for a particularly insightful example of how nature may evade the calculatory frames of experts (Mitchell 2002: 37–38).

19 Another factor that contributed to the crisis of the project was the fact that there had hardly been any government support. OFL had to use a diesel generator for 10 years to run its operations due to the government's inability to connect its office and pack-house to the national grid. Roads to the outgrower farms had been in a particularly poor state, resulting in high maintenance costs of vehicles used by the company. Furthermore, no mango-related research and development was locally available, forcing the company to hire expensive foreign consultants. As part of the MCA project, the operations were at least connected to the national grid in 2011, and some feeder roads in the region were repaired. States are firmly part of market-making (Fligstein 2001: 23), even if this might only be through their absence.

20 See, e.g., http://www.irinnews.org/report.aspx?reportid=74278, checked on 18/11/2011.

21 The bacterial black spot disease, an infection that negatively affects fruit production and produces black spots on leaves and fruits, was just one of the imponderables of nature the managers and farmers encountered. Other threats included fruit fly attacks and Athracnose,

a fungal disease caused by *colletotrichum gloeosporioides*. The disease devastates young leaves and often causes severe blossom blight, which can destroy flower panicles and prevent fruiting from setting in.

22   Indeed, many farmers' lack of attention to farm hygiene and tree husbandry – particularly the watering of trees – had been a persistent problem in the scheme and contributed to the low yields, but from 2008 onward the OFL senior management became stricter on issues such as farm hygiene, watering, and fertilizer application, which the assistant outgrower managers and their field assistants were pushed to enforce.

23   From 2009 onward, OFL started to generate additional income from the sales of seedlings and from the drying of large quantities of fruits (purchased from outside) in its drying facilities. The dried fruits were sold both locally and for export.

24   The issue of financial liability with regard to canceled farms was a black box in the contract mediated by DIAROC (see Chapter 5). The contract was amended in 2009 in this respect, stipulating that in such a case, all debt would be borne by AOMO and that the relationship between OFL and the outgrower would be ended. Even though OFL managers were aware that any debt would be virtually a "dead debt" owing to the limited financial resources of the organization, the amendment was meant to transfer responsibility from OFL to AOMO at least symbolically.

25   Furthermore, 70 farmers (70 acres) who were registered but had not yet planted were dropped from the scheme.

26   Note that Mitchell, despite being equally concerned with the role of experts during a project of techno-political engineering, eventually takes a different track than Scott. Rather than setting up modern science, misused by states, in opposition to practical knowledge, Mitchell investigates what social and political practice "produce simultaneously the powers of science and the powers of modern states" (Mitchell 2002: 312).

Chapter Nine
Conclusion

In a now classic article, Latour (1983) poses the question of what we can learn about society from the study of laboratory practice, the study of a single place? Similarly, but coming from a very different corner, Burawoy (1998) asks us to "extend out" from a particular site we have researched and situate it into the broader historical dynamics of global capitalism. Obviously, any study on export-oriented marketization should take such positions seriously and attempt to qualify the links that have been forged and the broader dynamics that bring certain frontier regions into being. But what lies at the end of these suggested paths? How exactly do we qualify the connections that come along with marketization, what notion of "society" and "capitalism" do we deploy? How do we account for the disconnections and processes of marginalization that simultaneously shape the geographies of export-oriented marketization (Berndt & Boeckler 2011a: 566)? These are intricate questions yet to be fully answered.

Two points, however, should be clear at this stage: the complex relational materiality of marketization processes in the global agrifood economy cannot be grasped by a single disciplinary perspective still trapped in a modernist division of labor (Mitchell 2002: 28), which mobilizes a sovereign narrative of universals ("capitalism," "globalization," "development," "value," "modernity," etc.) largely detached from actual practices and situations, and, which has already decided on "who counts as an agent" and who does not (ibid.: 29). Although we must come to terms with how what happens in particular frontier regions of agrarian marketization relates to global structures of competition and accumulation, science and technology, regulation, consumerism, developmentalism, and models of investment, we must also explore *how* such structures

Assembling Export Markets: The Making and Unmaking of Global Food Connections in West Africa,
First Edition. Stefan Ouma.
© 2015 John Wiley & Sons, Ltd. Published 2015 by John Wiley & Sons, Ltd.

are assembled in the messy materiality of economic practice rather than assuming their power and pervasisveness *a priori*. What this book has shown is that the novel framing of goods, agencies, and encounters that constitute the process of export-oriented marketization are often historical assemblages that expose a great deal of contingency owing to their enactment across cultural, spatial, and material differences (Tsing 2008: 40). Emphasizing the contingency of global agrifood connections does not mean to "discount the linking process, with its requirements for economic intelligibility" (Tsing 2008: 41). Too often, however,

> we let the requirements for intelligibility take over our analysis instead of considering how every link is merely "intelligible enough," that is, formed with friction. We imagine the linking process as guided by a uniform economic logic that lines up places and people like products in an assembly line (ibid.).

This book has shown how global agrifood market connections are carved out from a heterogeneous world, how they are rendered intelligible and technical, and what opportunities, costs, risks, and disciplinary forces accompany them.

How then to make sense of the "limited intelligibility" and "heterogeneity" of economic relations? These questions lie at the core of the *économie des conventions* (EC) project, and so does the desire to qualify the links sustaining market connections by invoking a range of orders of worth, which facilitate coordination across different and often ambiguous situations. Such a focus on ordering principles seems to be welcome. However, rendering the making of global agrifood market connections intelligible through a close reading of the pragmatist strand of the EC still risks invoking an "external principle" (Boltanski & Thévenot 2006 [1991]: 216) to which actors revert during "economic" interactions, despite the intention of authors such as Boltanksi and Thévenot to position themselves against all social theories that operate with a notion of inscription, such as "habitus," "society," "system," or "discourse" (Thévenot 2001a: 406).

Why not develop a more grounded analytical position? Why not follow the engaged *agencements* of "the quality assurance world" and the manifold form-giving activities that sustain them instead of resorting to a formalist description of economic practices? There are three ways to think about per-*form*-ing global agrifood market connections (even though these are not the only ways!):

First, there are "investments in forms" (Thévenot 1984) such as designer crop varieties, standards, or devices of metrology, which help to shape marketization at a distance. The MD2 pineapple, the Brix scale, and the GLOBALG.A.P standard are perfect examples in this regard.

Second, there are "quasi-standards" (Latour 2005: 229). As I have shown throughout the empirical chapters, the procedures, and framings of economics at large ("producing things for the market," price and cost calculations, the concepts of debtor and creditor, accounting procedures, contracts, performance-measurement technologies, supply chain management principles, open-book costing, etc.) are such quasi-standards. These help to qualculate, to take into account. Profit, value, redistribution, and exploitation "depend entirely upon such niceties" (ibid.), though such form-giving activities can be quite messy in practice. Often, they do not correspond to the strong notion of performativity that Callon (1998a) initially came up with. Take, for instance, one senior manager of Organic Fruits Limited (OFL) who described the making of markets in northern Ghana as a process of "trial and error." There was no way that he could "go to a book and say this is what I have to do" (Chapter 5). Or take the case of TF, where Jan, a university-trained manager, claimed that their "business is built upon various different beliefs or values, let's say, and the company's strategy as well tends to take those values into account" (Interview, 2010) and that "you don't get a sense that there is a kind of school of thought that is directing the company down a particular model that has been talked about in textbooks" (ibid.).

At the same time, many ideas of modern economics have indeed have become circulating artifacts that are no longer contested and can be counted on as reliable resources during the process of market-making. These are often unconsciously used to render some practices "economic," while calling others into question, or singling them out as objects deficiency and improvement. This is exemplified by Claire's observation about the "satisficing" behavior of the mango outgrowers, which clashed with her ideas about calculation and maximization:

> It's very difficult to tell a farmer that GHS 500 is small money […]. He's standing there with this in his hands saying, "I've never in my life, had this much money and you're trying to tell him it should have been GHS 2,000." And meanwhile, his whole year is taken care of. He doesn't have to think of GHS 2,000 because a GHS 500 is working, you know. And that I think is a very huge underlying fact that we're battling with is. You know the farmers know the minimum that they need do to get that GHS 500, not about the maximum they could do to get the GHS 2,000, and so it's something like that. And I've heard that this is a, this is a fact in Côte d'Ivoire and other places. (Interview, 2008)

Claire has her own view on what behavior counts as "economic," and obviously the practices of the outgrowers do not correspond to that.

Third, there are circulating and collecting statements that are not continuously materialized but whose movements can have the same effects, "on condition that we don't see them as simply 'representing' or 'distorting' existing social forces" (Latour 2005: 231). Collecting statements can comprise a wide range of points of reference on which actors rely during the processes of marketization. There are numerous examples: the aspiration of the OFL shareholders to "see development in the north" (Interview with Claire, 2008); or the notion of "a private company with an NGO think" (Interview with senior manager); or the narrative of the firm as a family (Chapter 5); or the discourses on inclusive markets, empowerment, and socializing the value chain (Chapter 5); or Ton:go Fruit's (TF)[1] ambition to tell the story of a product (Chapter 5); or the concept of "gentlemen's agreements" that was offered as a "substitute" for formal contractual relations in the just-in-time (JIT) supply chain (Chapter 5); or the statement that the mango farmers "will never be commercial farmers" (Chapter 5); or John, the OFL outgrower manager, cautioning the outgrowers that they were "farming not just for chop (food)," but for money (Chapter 6); or the warnings of the TF agronomist to his farmers that "failure to plan is planning to fail" (Chapter 6); or the finding of the OFL organic consultant that "[o]rganic is based on an understanding of biological processes and its inspirational source must be nature itself."

Others have strikingly shown how collecting statements such as "development," "modernity," "capitalism" (Mitchell 2002), "entrepreneurship" (Elyachar 2005), or "the tragedy of the commons" (Holm 2007) have aided the reengineering of the economy. Like justifications, collecting statements "not only trace new connections but also offer new highly elaborated theories of what it is to connect" (Latour 2005: 232). Collecting statements may become inscribed into quasi-standards (e.g., the notion of "profit" inscribed into accounting procedures) or into policy papers such as Ghana's second Food and Agricultural Development Policy (FASDEP II), and they are often part of grand visions to recollect society. Most often, however, owing to their circulation and situational enactment, they expose a great deal of mutability. Consider, for instance, the notion of "inclusive markets" to which the case of OFL can be linked. It cannot be couched in neat categories. It is a new collecting statement, fused with several ideas, drawing inspiration from many other sources than neoclassical economics! Thus, collecting statements are not external principles but proliferations of how to (re)assemble and perform "the social."

Collecting statements, in alliance with other elements, give market arrangements some order and their normalcy. However, as I have shown throughout this book, normalized market arrangements frequently overflow. The networks of the market social, especially if they span large distances, are constantly reconfigured, and mediated by both human practices and material objects, as well as by mobile and mutable collecting statements. They cannot simply be couched into Weberian ideal-type orders that, furthermore, are rooted in European moral and political philosophy. Does one really want to mobilize such very particular categories to historicize and scale down networks that, for instance, link Dagomba and Mamprusi farmers, local chiefs, staff from different corners of Ghana, managers from different countries, a Belgian director and his associates, NGOs from New York and Brussels, customers in Belgium, certification bodies in different European countries, and consultants from South Africa, the Netherlands, Australia, Brazil, and Senegal?[2]

Opting for a more grounded approach to qualify global market connections does not mean that we end up with flat ontologies. On the contrary! Hierarchies matter, but we must show how they "come to be told, embodied, performed and resisted" (Law 1994: 134): how is it that a firm becomes a "lead firm" in a supply chain? How is it that standards standardize? How is it that value, costs, and risks are produced and (re)distributed? How is it that actors become individual rather than collective? What I have excavated in large parts of this book are the new arrangements of knowledge, power, and materially entangled practices that accompany export-oriented marketization in frontier regions. A notion of power meandering between Foucault, ANT, the SSEM, and Thévenot's more recent engagement with economic *dispositifs* (Thévenot 2009) has been fruitful in this regard. I demonstrated that what counts as worthy in today's global agrifood markets is shaped in bundles of practice arrangements with differentiated possibilities for action (Schatzki 2005). It warrants special emphasis that some worlds of justification (or collecting statements) are not accessible to everyone (e.g., the world of agrifood standards backed up by technical expertise of Northern provenance) because actors such as farmers in the Global South lack the *legitimate* knowledge, resources, and equipment to do so, or because there are multiple tactics that facilitate translations that result in something other than compromises. The configuration of the sociotechnical *agencements* shapes whether agencies emerge that acquire power (reflexive, calculative, judgmental, individual, collective) to challenge certain arrangements that shape the distribution of "goods" and "bads" along agri-food chains. In this regard, we always have to focus on the intricate relationship between the political and anti-politics, between openness and closure, between dissi-dence and translation. As much as it is a fact that retailers actually do not *receive* audits but *give* audits, it is a fact that auditees may just prepare for these audits a few days in advance. As much as it seems that a company with considerable resources and educated staff is in an advantageous position over largely illiterate outgrowers with no experience in export-oriented tree farming, it is also a fact that its power is made of the wills of these outgrowers. In any case, it should be clear that domination and injustices arising from flawed trials of strength are not tolerated forever. The dynamics of disenrollment and Crises in the JIT case study described in Chapter 8 remind us of this.

Beyond Inclusion

When we "zoom" out to reflect on how a particular market social comes into being in the global agrifood economy, we risk sliding into the terrain of abstraction (Jazeel & McFarlane 2010). Such a disembedding of knowledge may neither do justice to those who have participated in a research project nor to those who want to know what we can learn from the study of two cases about the state of a country's agrarian political economy more generally. These are legitimate concerns, especially when considering that the promotion of (global) agricultural value chains has become part of what Hart (2001) called the "big D" millennial Development project, aiming at connecting Southern farmers to the "quality assurance world" (Neilson 2014). Ghana has expe-rienced a range of interventions in this regard since 2004. The common denominator of these projects has been that "the starting point is the market" (Fynn 2011: 4), and that agriculture has to be conducted "in a more business-oriented fashion" (MOFA 2010: 36). Linking up with such aspirations, a plethora of consultancy reports and strategy papers have made recommendations on how to place Ghanaian farmers in global agrifood chains. The orientation of the Medium Term Agriculture Sector Investment Plan (2011–2015), the implementation framework for Ghana's second Food and Agriculture Sectoral Development Plan, is telling in this regard:

> The integration of smallholders into international markets will have to be through lead firms that have access to markets. Government will need to facilitate that linkage and provide the enabling environment for the industry, plus linkages to firms that have the technical capacity for production and exports. The industry is private sector led and government will provide infrastructure of public goods nature and facilitate export trade

through promotion, information generation and dissemination, support for meeting quality standards, appropriate legal framework and enforcement of regulations (MOFA 2010: 34).

Such recipes often tend to ignore the fact that agricultural development is not just a matter of creating an "enabling environment" for individual firms leading farmers into the "world market," but must be organized as a national strategic project (Neilson 2014). For instance, the drama unfolding in the Ghanaian pineapple subsector after the rise of the MD2 variety was not only caused by the reshaping of buyer markets by transnational agrobusiness interests, but also by a lack of strategic public–private sector coordination (Whitfield 2010). Furthermore, such recipes tend to ignore broader structural questions of how inequality is produced and reproduced in the global agrifood economy (Bair 2005; Neilson 2014). Indeed, the practice of actually existing value chain development (with a small d; see Hart 2001) across the agrarian South has often been inherently risky and marked by new patterns of divergence, differentiation, and disconnection (3Ds). Although there are different models to organize agrobusiness value chains (and the two case studies presented here, despite the serious crisis moments they lived through, are at the better end of the spectrum for a variety of reasons such as a non-financialized ownership structure, directors with a developmental orientation and rather good relationship with farmers and local communities), we nevertheless can take them as starting points to reflect upon a range of critical issues related to the 3Ds of actually existing value chain development. This book invites us to think of them along three axes.

Exclusion. My case studies highlight the ambivalent interplay between inclusion and exclusion that is characteristic of the new frontier regions of the global agrifood economy. Although the development of Ghana's pineapple subsector with TF as a focal actor seems to support the point of Amanor (2012: 737), who argues that the "expansion of global markets integrates smallholders into market oligopolies, subjects them to increasing competition, and ensures the exit of those unable to compete, and the appropriation of their land by sectors better integrated into the technology treadmill of global capitalist agrifood chains," the case of OFL shows that agrobusiness still may rely on less "commercial" smallholders in certain regions for a variety of economic, political, and moral reasons. This, however, is not to downplay the fact that, more recently, in response to the financial and food price crisis of 2007/08, transnational agrobusiness companies and genuine financial investors have been flocking into African agriculture on a large scale ("the great land grab") (Cotula 2013). These have joined hands with both state agencies and donors, advancing a capital-intensive and finance-oriented form of value chain agriculture that may integrate outgrowers as a supply chain backup (McMichael 2013). However, as my case studies have shown, the expansion of agrarian capital does not happen smoothly in a law-like fashion, but requires tactics of enrollment and local engagement, or it may fail altogether.

Disarticulation. The second way we could think of the 3Ds of actually existing value chain development is through the concept of disarticulation. Drawing on older work in agrarian political economy, as well as on poststructuralist takes on positionality in the global economy, Bair and Werner (2011a: 989) recently introduced it to bring to the fore "production volatility, precipitous booms and busts, and historical patterns of dis/investment" as well as processes of devaluation and dispossession in order to counter the "inclusionary bias" (ibid.) of the global commodity/value chains and production networks literatures. Such a perspective advances a "processual understanding of the production of goods, places, and subjects and their iterative incorporation and expulsion from primary circuits of capital accumulation" (ibid.). Although global connections need particular "conditions of existence" (Hall 1985) and are usually an articulation of many elements and relations, they often display a "dark side," which may nevertheless be deeply entangled with their ongoing reproduction. At this stage, I can only qualify some of the disarticulations of marketization in the two frontier regions. Take, for instance, the Densu Valley farmers excluded from markets owing to the MD2 shock who were later turned into "shadow outgrowers," and were thus productively reincorporated into JIT supply chains that had become increasingly risky for some original suppliers; or the expansion of a new frontier region west of Densu Valley, where large-scale exporters, some owned by transnationals such as Dole, have claimed new land to the detriment of migrant farmers with weak land rights in their host communities (Chapter 8); or the introduction of tree cultures that affect established patterns of land tenure and entitlement as they lead to a quasi-privatization of land (Chapter 5); or the fact that producers in the Global South are dispossessed of the power to define what good is worthy and what not owing to the proliferation of various retailer-driven standards and certification schemes (Chapter 6).

In sum, we can only speculate on the full range of contemporary and future disarticulations in the cases under scrutiny, as I have not delved into a range of issues that are characteristic of agrarian frontier regions. These include processes of social stratification and intra-community conflicts (Amanor 2010a), livelihood struggles (Neilson & Pritchard 2009), changing land tenure arrangements (Murray et al. 2011; Boamah 2014), or the transformation of household and gender relations (Carney 1988).

Displacement. Another way to think about the disconnections that accompany export-oriented marketization processes is through the notion of "displacement" (Callon 1986: 223). As nature, people, and things are incorporated into new market arrangements, agencies not compatible with the rules of the game are dispelled, objects framed as unworthy are denied market access (e.g., the Smooth Cayenne pineapple variety), and local modalities of valuation have to give way to the standards, quasi-standards, and collecting statements circulating in global agrifood markets.

As I have shown in several instances, and as anthropologists of global market connections have put it so perceptively, "commodification [...] brings people and places together in new ways, blending identities, creating new ones, and marginalizing others" (Nevins & Peluso 2008a: 23). Farmers need to be "performers" and become "compliant" with global food safety and quality standards. They need to change their farming routines and be "committed" if they want to be part of "the quality assurance world." They have to change their "mindsets" if they want to be part of "modern supply chains," and those who cannot adjust have no place. Rural spaces in the Global South are being increasingly characterized by fragmenting development (Bernstein 2010).

Global horticultural markets position, subjectify, and size, and such effects challenge established notions of agrarian class formation and rural stratification. The words of Mensah, a TF supplier, underline this strikingly:

> Some people, some farmers are not serious, they have to put more effort in the farm work, monitor [...], they have to see everything in order, every day they have to be on the farm, farm every day, even if you have managers, you have to be there on the farm. (Interview, 2010)

Or consider the words of Dauda, the chairman of the Association of Organic Mango Outgrowers, who during one of our frequent conversations in the organization's office told me that he was keen on "changing the mentality of our people" from a "conception that things are for free and that you just open your hand to a more business-oriented thinking" (Field diary, 2009).

In a more Foucauldian register, one could argue that in the course of marketization projects along the new frontier regions of the global agrifood economy, the laboring farmer "comes into view as an object of knowledge and a target of intervention, as an individual to be assessed, evaluated and differentiated from others, to be governed in terms of individual differences" (Miller & Rose 1990: 201). This is also the tenor of the current market-oriented development agenda: only those subjects and objects that fit into the new register of global individual differences can be part of "the market."

"Market Modernity," Alternatives, Critique

Lastly, my account also prompts us to ask specific questions about the new forms of associations wrought by and enacted through particular forms of marketization, and what this may mean for society and economic relations in general. This ambition is in line with the kind of critique advanced in this book, which aims at defamiliarization (Roy 2012), not at immediately proposing alternative ways to organize the economy. While I think that "lifting the veil" already equips us well to think about alternatives in a more normative way, I am aware that the question of "[w]hat sort of a world do we want to see performed" (MacKenzie 2006: 275) is a legitimate and important one. The undeniable fact is that "African agriculture" needs more investment, needs to capture more value by developing agro-processing industries (Ouma & Whitfield 2010), and develop economic models that better the lives of poor rural and urban households alike. My two case studies aimed to achieve this, contributing to employment and income generation in the local economy, albeit with different degrees of success. However, I also showed that global agrifood connections can be inherently risky, shaped by profound power asymmetries. From this, it follows that the social and technical organization of outgrower schemes need careful consideration in order to protect the interest of farmers. Local and regional markets, which require a less demanding and costly *agencementization*, should be considered as viable alternatives when reflecting upon corporate strategy and industrial policy in the context of African agrifood industries. The thrust of this book has been, however, to move beyond an instrumentalist critique of actually existing value chain development. The perspective embraced here opens the door to an analysis of how markets as calculative collective devices "transform daily life" (Fourcade 2007: 1026). It builds a bridge to those strands of social theory that adopt a more *longue durée* perspective on the variegated trajectories of economization, including the often colonial modalities of power engrained in them (see also Freidberg 2004; Campbell 2006; Werner 2012). Global agrifood connections have transformed the daily lives of farmers in Ghana and elsewhere, and they seek to invoke specific projects of modernity that come into being through new ways of performing the social. But what is the "nature" of this "modernity"? Is it simply about the enactment of the "modern producing subject" (Escobar 2005: 142), or the "dynamics of capitalist social relations of production and reproduction" (Bernstein 2010: 10), or about the increasing reflexivity of global agrifood markets (Campbell 2006), or about the proliferation of new apparatuses (Agamben 2009) that start to furnish the lives of people in frontier regions?

The "truth" lies probably in between these very different takes on the historization of the market social. What is clear, however, is that the answers to such questions cannot be couched in a purified, totalizing, and synchronic take on modernity that leaves it operational as a grand historical narrative (Mitchell 2000). After all, what does it mean when northern Ghanaian farmers produce organic- and GLOBALG.A.P-certified mangoes for European consumers on communal land that has been quasi-privatized under a loan-based contract arrangement shaped by both local and translocal actors? What does it mean when the working patterns on pineapple farms and the returns on the farmers' investments in southern Ghana are determined by the supply chain management practices of Northern retailers that are in turn profoundly shaped by the competitive dynamics of a financialized sector?

Beyond Agrifood: Profanizing Marketization

Although this book is about the construction of agro-export markets in Ghana, it relates to wider debates on the expansion of markets and new processes of commodification in various social domains and places. Markets seem to have become ubiquitous and all-pervasive, the prime movers of a diverse range of goods and services at a national and global scale, the mantra of our time, apparently permeating every sphere of society: the marketization of education, CO_2, water, land, genes and genomes, arts and culture, body parts and blood, or even the weather are all examples of how the frontier regions of marketization have been extended. Such new frontier regions are often associated with the ongoing neoliberalization of economy, society, and "nature," but the very mechanisms of market expansion and commodification are the product of centuries of "cultural workouts" (Amin & Thrift 2000: 5).

Thus, at a time when development, society, and nature seem to be all about markets – when markets have become the "new religion" (Chakrabortty 2010) – and when the developmental prospects of large parts of the Global South are rethought through the prism of "market-oriented development," it seems to be important to take markets, their making, and their governmental effects seriously. Against this backdrop, this book pleads not only for a denaturing of markets but also for their "profanation" (Agamben 2009; Berndt & Boeckler 2011a: 561). Profanizing markets means relocating them in the realm of politics and sociotechnical practice at a time these have gained a sheer metaphysical quality. If we know what profane sociotechnical arrangements make up markets, then there is nothing natural or universal about them anymore. Much will be won if the means, arrangements, and translations that facilitate marketization processes are unveiled and made available for debate.

Endnotes

1   In this book, all names of individuals, of the case study companies and related organizations, and their geographical associations have been anonymized, are withheld, or have been altered to protect sources. Development organizations and programs associated with the Ghanaian agricultural sector are generally referred to by their original names.
2   A question I have not engaged with sufficiently in this book is what happens if we provincialize actor-network-theory (ANT) and its derivatives. If one should put economics and political economy under postcolonial scrutiny (see, e.g., Chakrabarty 2011), then why not ANT, the social studies of economization and marketization (SSEM), and the EC?

References

Abdulai, M. (1986). Land Tenure among the Dagomba of Northern Ghana. *Cambridge Anthropology* 11 (3), 72–101.

Abdulai, R. T. & Ndekugr, I. E. (2008). Indigenous Land Holding Institutions as an Impediment to Economic Use of Land: Case Studies from Tamale. In Simons, R. (ed.), *Indigeneous People and Real Estate Valuation.* Springer, Dordrecht, pp. 19–37.

Abolafia, M. (1998). Markets as Cultures: An Ethnographic Approach. In Callon, M. (ed.), *The Laws of the Markets.* Blackwell, Oxford, pp. 69–85.

Addo, E. & Marshall, R. (2000). Ghana's Non-Traditional Export Sector: Expectations, Achievements and Policy Issues. *Geoforum* 31 (3), 355–370.

Afari-Sefa, V. (2006). Export Diversification, Food Security and Living Conditions of Farmers in Southern Ghana, Göttingen.

Agamben, G. (2009). *"What is an Apparatus?" and Other Essays.* Stanford University Press, Stanford, Calif.

Agergard, J., Fold, N., & Gough, K. V. (2010). Introduction. In Agergard, J., Fold, N., & Gough, K. W. (eds.), *Livelihoods, Mobility and Markets in African and Asian Frontiers.* Routledge, London, pp. 1–9.

Akerlof, G. (1970). The Market for "Lemons": Quality Uncertainty and the Market Mechanism. *Quarterly Journal of Economics* 84 (3), 488–500.

Al-Hassan, R. & Diao, X. (2007). *Regional Disparities in Ghana: Policy Options and Public Investment Implications.* Washington, DC.

Amanor, K. (1999). *Global Restructuring and Land Rights in Ghana: Forest Food Chains, Timber and Rural Livelihoods.* Nordiska Afrikainstitutet, Uppsala.

Amanor, K. S. (1994). *The New Frontier.* Farmers' Response to Land Degradation. A West African Study. Zed Books, London, New Jersey.

Assembling Export Markets: The Making and Unmaking of Global Food Connections in West Africa, First Edition. Stefan Ouma.
© 2015 John Wiley & Sons, Ltd. Published 2015 by John Wiley & Sons, Ltd.

Amanor, K. S. (2009). Global Food Chains, African Smallholders and World Bank Governance. *Journal of Agrarian Change* 47 (2), 247–262.

Amanor, K. S. (2010a). Family Values, Land Sales and Agricultural Commodification in South-Eastern Ghana. *Africa* 80 (1), 104–125.

Amanor, K. S. (2010b). Participation, Commercialisation and Actor Networks: The Political Economy of Cereal Seed Production Systems in Ghana. www.futures-agricultures.org. Accessed 10/10/2013.

Amanor, K. S. (2012). Global Resource Grabs, Agribusiness Concentration and the Smallholder: Two West African Case Studies. *Journal of Peasant Studies* 39 (3–4), 731–749.

Amin, A. & Thrift, N. (2000). What Kind of Economic Theory for What Kind of Economic Geography? *Antipode* 32 (1), 4–9.

Amin, A. (2002). Spatialities of Globalization. *Environment and Planning A* 34 (3), 385–399.

Anderson, B., Kearnes, M., McFarlane, C., & Swanton, D. (2012). On Assemblages and Geography. *Dialogues in Human Geography* 2 (2), 171–189.

Annan, K. (1998). Unite Power of Markets with Authority of Universal Values, Opening Address World Economic Forum. Davos. http://www.un.org/News/Press/docs/1998/19980130. SGSM6448.html. Accessed 6/18/2013.

Appadurai, A. (1986). Introduction: Commodities and the Politics of Value. In Appadurai, A. (ed.), *The Social Life of Things: Commodities in Cultural Perspective*. Cambridge University Press, Cambridge, pp. 3–63.

Arrow, K. (1998). What Has Economics to Say about Racial Discrimination? *The Journal of Economic Perspectives* 12 (2), 91–100.

Arthur, P. (2006). The State, Private Sector Development, and Ghana's "Golden Age of Business." *African Studies Review* 49 (1), 31–49.

Aspers, P. & Beckert, J. (2008). Märkte. In Maurer, A. (ed.), *Handbuch der Wirtschaftssoziologie*. Springer VS, Wiesbaden, pp. 226–246.

Aspers, P. (2009). How Are Markets Made? http://www.mpifg.de/pu/workpap/wp09-2.pdf. Accessed 6/18/2013.

Bachmann, V. (2011). Participating and Observing: Positionality and Fieldwork Relations During Kenya's Post-Election Crisis. *Area* 43 (3), 362–368.

Bair, J. & Werner, M. (2011a). Commodity Chains and the Uneven Geographies of Global Capitalism: A Disarticulations Perspective. *Environment and Planning A* 43 (5), 988–997.

Bair, J. & Werner, M. (2011b). The Place of Disarticulations: Global Commodity Production in La Laguna, Mexico. *Environment and Planning A* 43 (5), 998–1015.

Bair, J. (2005). Global Capitalism and Commodity Chains: Looking Back, Going Forward. *Competition & Change* 9 (2), 153–180.

Baker, W. E., Faulkner, R. F., & Fisher, G. A. (1998). Hazards of the Market: The Continuity and Dissolution of Interorganizational Market Relationships. *American Sociological Review* 63 (2), 147–177.

Banson, K. E. (2007). Effects of Innovations on the Production and Marketing of Fresh Pineapples for Export in Ghana: Master Thesis, Hannover.

Barber, B. (1995). All Economies Are Embedded: The Career of a Concept, and Beyond. *Social Research* 62, 387–401.

Barber, B. (1977). Absolutization of the Market: Some Notes on How We got from There to Here. In Dworkin, G., Bermant, G., & Brown, P. G. (eds.), *Markets and Morals*. Halsted Press, Washington, New York, pp. 15–31.

Barnes, T. (2001). Retheorizing Economic Geography: From the Quantitative Revolution to the "Cultural Turn." *Annals, Association of American Geographers* 91 (3), 546–565.

Barnes, T. (2005). Culture: Economy. In Cloke, P. & Johnston, R. (eds.), *Spaces of Geographical Thought. Deconstructing Human Geography's Binaries*. Sage, London, pp. 61–80.

Barnes, T. J. & Sheppard, E. (2010). "Nothing Includes Everything": Towards Engaged Pluralism in Anglophone Economic Geography. *Progress in Human Geography* 34 (2), 193–214.

Barnes, T. J. (2007). Methods Matter: Transformations in Economic Geography. In Tickell, A., Sheppard, E., Peck, J., & Barnes, T. (eds.), *Politics and Practice in Economic Geography*. Sage, London, pp. 1–24.

Barrett, C. B., Bachke, M. E., Bellemare, M. F., Michelson, H. C., Narayanan, S., & Walker, T. F. (2012). Smallholder Participation in Contract Farming: Comparative Evidence from Five Countries. *World Development* 40 (4), 715–730.

Barrientos, S., Gereffi, G., & Rossi, A. (2011). Economic and Social Upgrading in Global Production Networks: A New Paradigm for a Changing World. *International Labour Review* 150 (3–4), 319–340.

Barry, A. & Slater, D. (2005). Technology, Politics, and the Market. An Interview with Michel Callon. In Barry, A. & Slater, D. (eds.), *The Technological Economy*. Routledge, New York, pp. 101–121.

Barry, A. (2004). Ethical Capitalism. In Larner, W. & Walters, W. (eds.), *Global Governmentality: Governing International Spaces*. Routledge, London, pp. 195–211.

Barry, A. (2005). The Anti-Political Economy. In Barry, A. & Slater, D. (eds.), *The Technological Economy*. Routledge, New York, pp. 84–100.

Barry, A. (2006). Technological Zones. *European Journal of Social Theory* 9 (2), 239–253.

Beckert, J. & Aspers, P. (2011). Value in Markets. In Beckert, J. & Aspers, P. (eds.), *The Worth of Goods: Valuation and Pricing in the Economy*. Oxford University Press, Oxford, pp. 1–40.

Beckert, J. (2005). Trust and the Performative Construction of Markets. *MPIfG Discussion Paper* 05 (8).

Beckert, J. (2009). The Social Order of Markets. *Theory and Society* 38 (3), 245–269.

Beckert, J. (2011). Where Do Prices Come from? Sociological Approaches to Price Formation. *Socio-Economic Review* 9 (4), 757–786.

Berndt, C. & Boeckler, M. (2007). Kulturelle Geographien der Ökonomie: Zur Performativität von Märkten. In Berndt, C. & Pütz, R. (eds.), *Kulturelle Geographien*. Transcript, Bielefeld, pp. 213–258.

Berndt, C. & Boeckler, M. (2009). Geographies of Circulation and Exchange: Constructions of Markets. *Progress in Human Geography* 33 (4), 535–551.

Berndt, C. & Boeckler, M. (2011a). Geographies of Markets: Materials, Morals and Monsters in Motion. *Progress in Human Geography* 35 (4), 559–567.

Berndt, C. & Boeckler, M. (2011b). Performative Regional (Dis)integration: Transnational Markets, Mobile Commodities, and Bordered North – South Differences. *Environment and Planning A* 43 (5), 1057–1078.

Bernstein, H. (2010). *Class Dynamics of Agrarian Change*. Fernwood Publishing; Kumarian Press, Halifax, NS., Sterling, Va.

Blench, R. (2012). Dagbani Plant Names, Cambridge, UK. http://www.rogerblench.info/Ethnoscience/Plants/General/Dagbani%20plant%20names.pdf. Accessed 6/18/2013.

Blench, R. (1996). *Agriculture and Environment in Northeastern Ghana: A Comparison of High and Medium Population Density Areas*. Overseas Development Institute, London. http://www.rogerblench.info/Development/Ghana/ODI/Northern%20Ghana%20-agriculture.pdf. Accessed 6/18/2013.

Blowfield, M. & Dolan, C. (2008). Stewards of Virtue? The Ethical Dilemma of CSR in African Agriculture. *Development and Change* 39 (1), 1–23.

Boamah, F. (2014). How and why Chiefs Formalise Land Use in Recent Times: the Politics of Land Dispossession through Biofuels Investments in Ghana. *Review of African Political Economy*, 1–18. Online first, DOI: 10.1080/03056244.2014.901947

Boeckler, M. (2005). *Geographien kultureller Praxis. Syrische Unternehmer und die globale Moderne.* Transcript, Bielefeld.

Boeckler, M. & Berndt, C. (2012). Geographies of Marketization. In Barnes, T., Peck, J., & Sheppard, E. (eds.), *The Wiley-Blackwell Companion to Economic Geography.* Wiley-Blackwell, Oxford, pp. 199–212.

Boeckler, M. & Berndt, C. (2013). Geographies of Circulation and Exchange III: The Great Crisis and Marketization "After Markets." *Progress in Human Geography* 37 (3), 424–432.

Boltanski, L. & Thévenot, L. (1999). The Sociology of Critical Capacity. *European Journal of Social Theory* 2 (3), 359–377.

Boltanski, L. & Thévenot, L. (2006 [1991]). *On Justification: Economies of Worth.* Princeton University Press, Princeton.

Bourdieu, P. (1977). *Entwurf einer Theorie der Praxis: Auf der ethnologischen Grundlage der kabylischen Gesellschaft,* 2nd edn. Suhrkamp, Frankfurt am Main.

Bourdieu, P. (2005). Principles of an Economic Anthropology. In Smelser, N. & Swedberg, R. (eds.), *The Handbook of Economic Sociology,* 2nd ed. Princeton University Press, Princeton, pp. 75–89.

Bowen (2006). Grounded Theory and Sensitizing Concepts. *International Journal of Qualitative Methods* 5 (3), 1–9.

Boyd, W., Prudham, S., & Schurman, R. (2001). Industrial Dynamics and the Problem of Nature. *Society and Natural Resources* 14 (7), 555–570.

Bräutigam, D. (2005). Strategic Engagement: Markets, Transnational Networks, and Globalization in Mauritius. *Yale Journal of International Affairs* (Summer/Spring), 63–78.

Brüntrup, M. & Peltzer, R. (eds.) (2006). Outgrowers: A Key to the Development of Rural Areas in Sub-Saharan Africa and to Poverty Reduction, Bonn.

Burawoy, M. (1998). The Extended Case Method. *Sociological Theory* 16 (1), 4–33.

Burawoy, M. (2000a). Introduction: Reaching for the Global. In Burawoy, M., Blum, J., & George, S. et al. (eds.), *Global Ethnography: Forces, Connections, and Imaginations in a Postmodern World.* California University Press, Berkeley, pp. 1–40.

Burawoy, M. (2000b). Grounding Globalization. In: Burawoy, M., Blum, J. & George, S. et al. (eds.), *Global Ethnography. Forces, Connections, and Imaginations in a Postmodern World.* California University Press, Berkeley, pp. 337–350.

Busch, L. & Juska, A. (1997). Beyond Political Economy: Actor Networks and the Globalization of Agriculture. *Review of International Political Economy* 4 (4), 688–708.

Busch, L. (2007). Performing the Economy, Performing Science: From Neoclassical to Supply Chain Models in the Agrifood Sector. *Economy and Society* 36 (3), 437–466.

Burch, D. & Lawrence, G. (2009). Towards a Third Food Regime: Behind the Transformation. *Agriculture and Human Values* 26 (4), 267–279.

Butler, J. (2010). Performative Agency. *Journal of Cultural Economy* 3 (2), 147–161.

Çalışkan, K. (2010). *Market Threads: How Cotton Farmers and Traders Create a Global Commodity.* Princeton University Press, Princeton.

Çalışkan, K. & Callon, M. (2009). Economization, Part 1: Shifting Attention from the Economy Towards Processes of Economization. *Economy and Society* 38 (3), 369–398.

Çalışkan, K. & Callon, M. (2010). Economization, Part 2: A Research Programme for the Study of Markets. *Economy and Society* 39 (1), 1–32.

Çalışkan, K. (2007a). Markets and Fields: The Ethnography of Cotton Exchange and Production in a Turkish Village. *New Perspectives on Turkey* (27), 115–146.

Çalışkan, K. (2007b). Price as a Market Device: Cotton Trading in Izmir Mercantile Exchange. In Callon, M., Millo, Y., & Muniesa, F. (eds.), *Market Devices.* Blackwell, Malden, pp. 241–260.

Callon, M. & Latour, B. (1981). Unscrewing the Big Leviathan: How Actors Macro-Structure Reality and How Sociologists Help Them to Do So. In Knorr-Cetina, K. & Cicourel, A. (eds.),

Advances in SocialTheory and Methodology:Toward an Integration of Micro- and Macro-Sociologies, Boston, Mass., pp. 277–303.

Callon, M. & Law, J. (1995). Agency and the Hybrid Collectif. *South Atlantic Quarterly* 41 (2), 481–507.

Callon, M. & Law, J. (2005). On Qualculation, Agency, and Otherness. *Environment and Planning D: Society and Space* 23 (5), 717–733.

Callon, M. & Muniesa, F. (2005). PeripheralVision: Economic Markets as Calculative Collective Devices. *Organization Studies* 26 (8), 1229–1250.

Callon, M. (1986). Some Elements of a Sociology ofTranslation: Domestication of the Scallops and the Fishermen of St. Brieuc Bay. In Law, J. (ed.), *Power,Action, and Belief:A New Sociology of Knowledge*. Routledge; Keagan Paul, London, pp. 196–229.

Callon, M. (1991).Techno-Economic Networks and Irreversibility. In Law, J. (ed.), *A Sociology of Monsters: Essays on Power, Technology and Domination*. Routledge, London, New York, pp. 132–161.

Callon, M. (1998a). Introduction:The Embeddedness of Economic Markets in Economics. In Callon, M. (ed.), *The Laws of the Markets*. Blackwell, Oxford, pp. 1–57.

Callon, M. (1998b).An Essay on Framing and Overflowing: Economic Externalities Revised by Sociology. In Callon, M. (ed.), *The Laws of the Markets*. Blackwell, Oxford, pp. 244–269.

Callon, M. (2005). Why Virtualism Paves a Way to Political Impotence. A Reply to Daniel Miller's Critique of the Laws of the Markets. *Economic Sociology European Electronic Newsletter* 6 (2), 3–20.

Callon, M. (2007).What Does it Mean to Say Economics is Performative? In MacKenzie, D., Muniesa, F., & Siu, L. (eds.), *Do Economists Make Markets? On the Performativity of Economics*. Princeton University Press, Princeton, pp. 311–358.

Callon, M. (2009). Elaborating on the Notion of Performativity. *Le Libellio d'AEGIS* 5 (1), 18–29.

Callon, M. (2010). Performativity, Misfires and Politics. *Journal of Cultural Economy* 3 (2), 163–169.

Callon, M., Méadel, C., & Rabeharisoa,V. (2002). Economy of Qualities. *Economy and Society* 31 (2), 194–217.

Carmody, P. R. (2011). *The New Scramble for Africa*. Cambridge, UK; Polity Press, Malden, Mass.

Campbell, H. (2005).The Rise and Rise of EUREPGAP: European (Re)Invention of Colonial Food Relations? *International Journal of Sociology of Food and Agriculture* 13 (2), 1–19.

Campbell, H. (2006). Consultation, Commerce and Contemporary Agri-Food Systems: Ethical Engagement of New Systems of Governance under Reflexive Modernity. *The Integrated Assessment Journal* 6 (2), 117–136.

Carney, J. (1988). Struggles over Crop Rights and Labour within Contract Farming Households in a Gambian Irrigated Rice Project. *Journal of Peasant Studies* 15 (3), 334–349.

Carrier, J. (1997). Introduction. In Carrier, J. (ed.), *The Meanings of the Market:The Free Market in Western Society*. Berg Publishers, Oxford, pp. 1–68.

Castree, N. (2003). CommodifyingWhat Nature? *Progress in Human Geography* 27 (3), 273–297.

Chakrabarty, D. (2011). Can Political Economy be Postcolonial? In Pollard, J., McEwan, C., & Hughes, A. (eds.), *Postcolonial Economies*. Zed Books, London, NewYork, pp. 23–35.

Chakrabortty, A. (2010). Are the Markets Our New Religion? *The Guardian*, May 18.

Chalfin, B. (2004). *Shea Butter Republic: State Power, Global Markets, and the Making of an Indigenous Commodity*. Routledge, New York.

Chamberlin, J. (2007). It's a SmallWorld After All: Defining Smallholder Agriculture in Ghana. International Food Policy Research Institute. Washington, DC (IFPRI Discussion Paper, 00823).

Clifford, J. (1986). Introduction: Partial Truths. In Clifford, J. & Marcus, G. (eds.), *Writing Culture: The Poetics and Politics of Ethnography*. University of California Press, Berkeley, pp. 1–26.

Coase, R. H. (1988). The Firm, the Market and the Law [5. print]. University of Chicago Press, Chicago.

Coe, N. M., Dicken, P., & Hess, M. (2008). Global Production Networks: Realizing the Potential. *Journal of Economic Geography* 8 (3), 271–295.

Collier, P. & Dercon, S. (2014). African Agriculture in 50 Years: Smallholders in a Rapidly Changing World? World Development 63, 92–101.

Cook, L. (2000). Free Zones and Export Growth in Ghana. CAER II Discussion Paper No. 76. Harvard Institute for International Development.

Cotula, L. (2013). The Great African Land Grab?: Agricultural Investments and the Global Food System. Zed Books, London.

Cowen, D. (2012). The Deadly Life of Logistics. http://technosalon.wordpress.com/2008-9-salon/2010-11-open-concept/concepts-and-conceptacles/logistics-deb-cowen/. Accessed 6/18/2013.

Cox, A. (1999). Power, Value and Supply Chain Management. *Supply Chain Management: An International Journal* 4 (4), 167–175.

Crang, M. & Cook, I. (2007). *Doing Ethnographies*. Sage, Los Angeles, Calif.

Crang, P. (1997). Cultural Turns and the (Re)Constitution of Economic Geography. In Lee, R. & Wills, J. (eds.), *Geographies of Economies*. Arnold, London, pp. 3–15.

Czarniawska, B. (2008). *A Theory of Organizing*. Edward Elgar, Cheltenham.

Danielou, M. & Ravry, C. (2005). The Rise of Ghana's Pineapple Industry. From Successful Take-Off to Sustainable Expansion. Africa Region Working Paper Series No. 93, World Bank. Washington, DC.

Davies, C. A. (2008). *Reflexive Ethnography: A Guide to Researching Selves and Others*, 2nd ed. Routledge, London.

Daviron, B. & Ponte, S. (2005). *The Coffee Paradox: Global Markets, Commodity Trade and the Elusive Promise of Development*. Zed Books, London, New York.

Deleuze, G. (1992). What is a Dispositif? In: Armstrong, T. J. (ed.) Michel Foucault, Philosopher: Essays Translated from the French and German. Routledge, New York, pp. 159–168.

DeSoto, H. (2001). *The Mystery of Capital: Why Capitalism Triumphs in the West and Fails Everywhere Else*. Black Swan, London.

Dewey, J. (1915). The Logic of Judgments of Practise. *The Journal of Philosophy, Psychology and Scientific Methods* 12 (19), 505–523.

DFID (=Department for International Development) & SDC (=Swiss Agency for Development and Cooperation) (2008). A Synthesis of The Making Markets Work for the Poor (M4P) Approach. http://www.enterprise-development.org/page/m4p. Accessed 6/18/2013.

Diaz-Bohne, R. (2008). Économie des conventions – ein transdisziplinäres Fundament für die neue empirische Wirtschaftssoziologie. Paper presented at the Jahrestagung der Sektion Wirtschaftssoziologie der DGS, Berlin, 18–19th of February.

Dicken, P. (2011). Global Shift: Mapping the Changing Contours of the World Economy, 6th ed. Sage, London.

Dicken, P., Kelly, P., Olds, C., & Yeung, H. W.-C. (2001). Chains and Networks, Territories and Scales: Towards a Relational Framework of the Global Economy. *Global Networks* 1 (2), 89–112.

Dixie, G. & Sergeant, A. (1998). *The Future of the Ghanaian Export Horticulture Industry*. Dorset.

Dolan, C. & Humphrey, J. (2004). Changing Governance Patterns in the Trade in Fresh Vegetables between Africa and the United Kingdom. *Environment and Planning A* 36 (3), 491–509.

Dunn, E. (2005). Standards and Person-Making in East Central Europe. In Ong, A. & Collier, S. (eds.), *Global Assemblages: Technology, Politics and Ethics as Anthropological Problems*. Blackwell, Malden, pp. 174–193.

Durkheim, É. (1977 [1893]). *Über die Teilung der sozialen Arbeit*, 1. Aufl... Suhrkamp, Frankfurt am Main.

Eaton, C. & Shepherd, A. W. (2001). *Contract Farming Partnerships for Growth: A Guide*. FAO, Rome.

Elden, S. (2010). Land, Terrain, Territory. *Progress in Human Geography* 34 (6), 799–817.

Elyachar, J. (2005). *Markets of Dispossession: NGOS, Economic Development, and the State in Cairo*. Duke University Press, Durham, London.

Emerson, R. M., Fretz, R. I., & Shaw, L. L. (1995). *Writing Ethnographic Fieldnotes*. University of Chicago Press, Chicago.

England, K. & Ward, K. (2007). Introduction: Reading Neoliberalization. In England, K. & Ward, K. (eds.), *Neoliberalization: States, Networks, Peoples*. Blackwell, Malden, Mass., pp. 1–22.

Escobar, A. (2005). Economics and the Space of Modernity: Tales of Market, Production and Labour. *Cultural Studies* 19 (2), 139–175.

Eymard-Duvernay, F., Faverau, O., Orléan, A., Salais, R., & Thévenot, L. (2003). Values, Coordination and Rationality: The Economy of Conventions or the Time of Reunification in the Economic, Social and Political Sciences. Paper presented at the Conference "Conventions et institutions: Approfondissements théoriques et contributions au débat politique," Paris, 11–12th of December. http://www.parisschoolofeconomics.com/orlean-andre/depot/publi/ART2004tVALU.pdf. Accessed 10/18/2013.

Feder, E. (1976). How Agribusiness Operates in Underdeveloped Agricultures: Harvard Business School Myths and Reality. *Development and Change* 7 (4), 413–443.

Feeny, D. (1983). The Moral or the Rational Peasant? Competing Hypotheses of Collective Action. *The Journal of Asian Studies* 42 (4), 769–789.

Ferguson, J. (2006). *Global Shadows: Africa in the Neoliberal World Order*. Duke University Press, Durham.

Fine, B. & Milonakis, D. (2009). *From Economics Imperialism to Freakonomics: The Shifting Boundaries between Economics and other Social Sciences*. Routledge, London.

Fine, B. (2003). Callonistics – A Disentanglement. *Economy and Society* 32 (3), 478–484.

Fligstein, N. & Dauter, L. (2007). The Sociology of Markets. *Annual Review of Sociology* 33 (1), 105–128.

Fligstein, N. (2001). *The Architecture of Markets: An Economic Sociology for the 21st Century*. Princeton University Press, Princeton.

Fold, N. & Gough, K. V. (2008). From Smallholders to Transnationals: The Impact of Changing Consumer Preferences in the EU on Ghana's Pineapple Sector. *Geoforum* 39 (5), 1687–1697.

Fold, N. (2004). Spilling the Beans on a Tough Nut. Liberalization and Local Supply System Changes in Ghana's Cocoa and Shea Chains. In Hughes, A. & Reimer, S. (eds.), *Geographies of Commodity Chains*. Routledge, London, New York, pp. 63–80.

Fold, N. (2008). Transnational Sourcing Practices in Ghana's Perennial Crop Sectors. *Journal of Agrarian Change* 8 (1), 94–122.

Foodplus (2009). Globalgap General Regulations Integrated Farm Assurance Version 3.1, Cologne. http://www.globalgap.org/cms/upload/The_Standard/IFA/English/GRs/GG_EG_IFA_GR_Part_I-V_ENG_V3_1_Nov09_update.pdf. Accessed 13/07/2011.

Fortman, L. (1985). The Tree Tenure Factor in Agroforestry with Particular Reference to Africa. *Agroforestry Systems* 2 (4), 229–251.

Foucault, M. (1980). *Power/Knowledge. Selected Interviews and Other Writings, 1972–1977*. The Harvester Press, Brighton.

Foucault, M. (1982). The Subject and Power. *Critical Inquiry* 8 (2), 777–795.

Foucault, M. (1997 [1984]). Polemics, Politics and Problematizations. In Rabinow, P. (ed.), *Essential Works of Foucault 1954–1984*. New Press, New York, pp. 111–119.

Foucault, M. (1991). Questions of Method. In Burchell, G., Gordon, C., & Miller, P. (eds.), *The Foucault Effect: Studies in Governmentality; With Two Lectures and an Interview with Michel Foucault*. University of Chicago Press, Chicago, pp. 73–86.

Fourcade, M. (2007). Theories of Markets and Theories of Society. *American Behavioral Scientist* 50 (8), 1015–1034.

Fourcade, M. (2011). Price and Prejudice: On Economics and the Entchantment (and Disenchantment) of Nature. In Beckert, J. & Aspers, P. (eds.), *The Worth of Goods: Valuation and Pricing in the Economy*. Oxford University Press, Oxford, pp. 42–62.

Frances, J., Levacic, R., Mitchell, J., & Thompson, G. (1991). Introduction. In Thompson, G., Frances, J., Levacic, R., & Mitchell, J. (eds.), *Markets, Hierarchies and Networks: The Coordination of Social Life*, reprinted. Sage, London, pp. 1–20.

Freidberg, S. (2004). *French Beans and Food Scares: Culture and Commerce in An Anxious Age*. Oxford University Press, New York.

Freidberg, S. (2007). Supermarkets and Imperial Knowledge. *Cultural Geographies* 14 (3), 321–342.

Friedmann, H. (1993). The Political Economy of Food: A Global Crisis. *New Left Review* (197), 29–57.

Fresh Del Monte Produce Inc. (2011). Annual Report 2010. Coral Gables.

Fynn, M. (2011). Ghana: Joint Sector Review of Agriculture, 2011. Analytical Summary Report on Value Chain Development in the Agriculture Sector in Ghana. GIZ-MOAP. Accra. (unpublished report).

Garfinkel, H. (1967). *Studies in Ethnomethodology*. Prentice Hall, NJ.

Geertz, C. (1973). *The Interpretation of Cultures: Selected Essays*. Basic Books, New York.

Geertz, C. (1978). The Bazaar Economy: Information and Search in Peasant Marketing. *American Economic Review* 68 (2), 28–32.

Gereffi, G. (1994). The Organization of Buyer-Driven Global Commodity Chains: How U.S. Retailers Shape Overseas Production Networks. In Gereffi, G. & Korzienewicz, M. (eds.), *Commodity Chains and Global Capitalism*. Westport, pp. 205–221.

Gereffi, G., Humphrey, J., & Sturgeon, T. (2005). The Governance of Global Value Chains. *Review of International Political Economy* 12 (1), 1–27.

Gereffi, G., Humphrey, J., Sturgeon, T., & Kaplinsky, R. (2001). Introduction: Globalisation, Value Chains and Development. *IDS Bulletin* 32 (3), 1–12.

GEPC (Ghana Export Promotion Council) (2008a). *Export Market Opportunities for Fruits and Vegetables in the European Union*. Accra. (unpublished document).

GEPC (Ghana Export Promotion Council) (2008b). *Ghana: Snapshot of the Performance of the Non-traditional Export Sector in 2007*. Accra. (unpublished document).

Gibbon, P. & Ponte, S. (2005). *Trading Down: Africa, Value Chains and the Global Economy*. Temple University Press, Philadelphia.

Gibbon, P. & Ponte, S. (2008). Global Value Chains: From Governance to Governmentality? *Economy and Society* 37 (3), 365–392.

Gibbon, P., Bair, J., & Ponte, S. (2008). Governing Global Value Chains: An Introduction. *Economy and Society* 37 (3), 315–338.

Gibson-Graham, J. K. (2006 [1996]). *The End of Capitalism as We Knew It*, 2nd ed. University of Minnesota Press, Minneapolis.

Giddens, A. (1979). *Central Problems in Social Theory: Action, Structure and Contradiction in Social Analysis*. MacMillan, London.

Giddens, A. (1983). *Profiles and Critiques in Social Theory*. University of California Press, Berkeley.

Gidwani, V. K. (2004). The Limits to Capital: Questions of Provenance and Politics. *Antipode* 36 (3), 527–542.

Gille, Z. & Riain, S. Ó. (2002). Global Ethnography. *Annual Review of Sociology* 28 (1), 271–295.

Glover, D. & Kusterer, K. (1990). *Small Farmers, Big Business: Contract Farming and Rural Development*. MacMillan, London.

Goffman, E. (1974). *Frame Analysis: An Essay on the Organization of Experience*. Harvard University Press, Cambridge.

Goldstein, M. & Udry, C. (2008). The Profits of Power: Land Rights and Agricultural Investment in Ghana. *Journal of Political Economy* 116 (6), 981–1022.

Goodman, D. & Watts, M. (1997). Agrarian Questions: Global Appetite, Local Metabolism: Nature, Culture, and Industry in Fin-de-Siecle Agro-food Systems. In Goodman, D. & Watts, M. (eds.), *Globalizing Food*. Routledge, New York, pp. 1–32.

Goodman, D. (2001). Ontology Matters: The Relational Materiality of Nature and Agro-Food Studies. *Sociologia Ruralis* 41 (2), 182–200.

Goody, J. (1980). Rice-Burning and the Green Revolution in Northern Ghana. *Journal of Development Studies* 16 (2), 136–155.

Gould, M. (1991). Parsons' Economic Sociology: A Failure of Will. *Sociological Inquiry* 61, 89–101.

Gouveia, L. & Juska, A. (2002). Taming Nature, Taming Workers: Constructing the Separation Between Meat Consumption and Meat Production in the U.S. *Sociologia Ruralis* 42 (4), 370–390.

Grabher, G. (2006). Trading Routes, Bypasses, and Risky Intersections: Mapping the Travels of "Networks" between Economic Sociology and Economic Geography. *Progress in Human Geography* 30 (2), 163–189.

Graeber, D. (2001). *Toward an Anthropological Theory of Value: The False Coin of Our Own Dreams*. Palgrave, New York.

GRAIN (2010). Turning African Farmland over to Big Business. http://www.grain.org/article/entries/4062-turning-african-farmland-over-to-big-business. Accessed 4/18/2013.

Granovetter, M. & McGuire, P. (1998). The Making of an Industry. Electricity in the United States. In Callon, M. (ed.), *The Laws of the Markets*. Blackwell, Oxford, pp. 147–173.

Granovetter, M. (1985). Economic Action and Social Structure: The Problem of Embeddedness. *The American Journal of Sociology* 91 (3), 481–510.

Grosh, B. (1997). Contract Farming in Africa: An Application of the New Institutional Economics. *Journal of African Economies* 3 (2), 231–261.

Gupta, A. & Ferguson, J. (1997). Discipline and Practice: "The Field" as Site, Method, and Location in Anthropology. In Gupta, A. & Ferguson, J. (eds.), *Anthropological Locations: Boundaries and Grounds of a Field Science*. University of California Press, Berkeley, pp. 1–46.

Guthman, J. (2004). The "Organic Commodity" and other Anomalies in the Politics of Consumption. In Hughes, A. & Reimer, S. (eds.), *Geographies of Commodity Chains*. Routledge, London, New York, pp. 233–249.

Guthman, J. (2007). The Polanyian Way? Voluntary Food Labels as Neoliberal Governance. *Antipode* 39 (3), 456–478.

Hall, S. (1985). Signification, Representation, Ideology: Althusser and the Post-Structuralist Debate. *Critical Studies in Mass Communication* 2 (2), 91–114.

Hann, C. M. & Hart, K. (2011). *Economic Anthropology: History, Ethnography, Critique*. Polity Press, Cambridge.

Hart, G. (2004). Geography and Development: Critical Ethnographies. *Progress in Human Geography* 28 (1), 91–100.

Hart, G. (2001). Development Critiques in the 1990s: Culs de Sac and Promising Paths. *Progress in Human Geography* 25 (4), 649–658.

Harvey, D. (2011). *The Enigma of Capital: And the Crises of Capitalism*. Profile, London.

Henderson, J., Dicken, P., Hess, M., Coe, N., & Yeung, H. W.-C. (2002). Global Production Networks and the Analysis of Economic Development. *Review of International Political Economy* 9 (3), 436–464.

Herod, A. (2001). Implications of Just-in-Time Production for Union Strategy: Lessons from the 1998 General Motors United Auto Workers Dispute. *Annals of the Association of American Geographers* 90 (3), 521–547.

Hess, M. (2004). "Spatial" Relationships? Towards a Reconceptualization of Embeddedness. *Progress in Human Geography* 18 (2), 165–186.

Hess, M. (2008). Governance, Value Chains and Networks: An Afterword. *Economy and Society* 37, 452–459.

Higgins, V. & Larner, W. (2010). Standards and Standardization as a Social Scientific Problem. In Higgins, V. & Larner, W. (eds.), *Calculating the Social: Standards and the Reconfiguration of Governing*. Palgrave MacMillan, Houndmills, pp. 1–18.

Hill, P. (1963). *The Migrant Cocoa-farmers of Southern Ghana: A Study in Rural Capitalism*. Cambridge University Press, Cambridge.

Holm, P. (2007). Which Way is up on Callon? In MacKenzie, D., Muniesa, F., & Siu, L. (eds.), *Do Economists Make Markets? On the Performativity of Economics*. Princeton University Press, Princeton, pp. 225–243.

Hudson, R. (2008). Cultural Political Economy Meets Global Production Networks: A Productive Meeting? *Journal of Economic Geography* 8 (3), 421–440.

Hughes, A. & Reimer, S. (2005). Guest Editorial: Publishing Commodity Chains. *Geoforum* 36 (3), 273–275.

Hughes, A. (2001). Global Commodity Networks, Ethical Trade and Governmentality: Organizing Business Responsibility in the Kenyan Cut Flower Industry. *Transactions of the Institute of British Geographers, New Series* 26 (4), 390–406.

Hughes, A. (2004). Accounting for Ethical Trade: Global Commodity Networks, Virtualism and the Audit Economy. In: Hughes, A. & Reimer, S. (eds.), *Geographies of Commodity Chains*. Routledge, London, New York, pp. 215–229.

Hughes, A. (2012). Corporate Ethical Trading in an Economic Downturn: Recessionary Pressures and Refracted Responsibilities. In *Journal of Economic Geography* 12 (1), 33–54.

Humphrey, J. & Schmitz, H. (2002). Developing Country Firms in the World Economy: Governance and Upgrading in Global Value Chains. INEF Report 21.

Hutchins, E. (2001). Distributed Cognition. In Smelser, N. J. & Baltes, P. B. (eds.), *International Encyclopedia of the Social & Behavioral Sciences*, 1st ed. Elsevier, Amsterdam, New York, pp. 2068–2072.

ILRF (International Labour Rights Forum) (2008). *The Sour Taste of Pineapple: How an Expanding Export Industry Undermines Workers and Their Communities*. Washington, DC.

Jaffee, D. (2007). *Brewing Justice: Fairtrade Coffee, Sustainability, and Survival*. University of kfornia Press, Berkeley.

Jaffee, S. (1994). Contract Farming and Shadow Competitive Markets: The Experience of Kenyan Horticulture. In Little, P. & Watts, M. (eds.), *Living under Contract*. University Press of Wisconsin, Madison, pp. 97–139.

Jagd, S. (2004). Laurent Thévenot and the French Convention School: A Short Introduction by Søren Jagd. *Economic Sociology European Electronic Newsletter* 5 (3), 10–16.

Jagd, S. (2007). Economics of Convention and New Economic Sociology: Mutual Inspiration and Dialogue. *Current Sociology* 55 (1), 75–91.

Jazeel, T. & McFarlane, C. (2010). The Limits of Responsibility: A Postcolonial Politics of Academic Knowledge Production. *Transactions of the Institute of British Geographers* 35 (1), 109–124.

Jones, A. & Murphy, J. T. (2011). Theorizing Practice in Economic Geography: Foundations, Challenges, and Possibilities. *Progress in Human Geography* 35 (3), 366–392.

Karikari, I. (2006). Ghana's Millennium Challenge Account and the Land Component: A Holistic Approach? Paper presented at the XXIII International Federation of Surveyors Congress, Munich. http://www.fig.net/pub/fig2006/papers/ts45/ts45_04_karikari_0916.pdf. Accessed 5/18/2013

Kasanga, K. & Kotey, N. A. (2001). *Land Management in Ghana: Building on Tradition and Modernity*. International Institute for Environment and Development, London.

Kasanga, K. (1995). Land Tenure and Regional Investment Prospects: The Case of the Tenurial Systems of Northern Ghana. *Property Management* 13 (2), 21–31.

Khor, M. (2006). *The Impact of Trade Liberalisation on Agriculture in Developing Countries: The Experience of Ghana*. Third World Network, Penang.

Kleinman, D. L. (1998). Untangling Context: Understanding a University Laboratory in the Commercial World. *Science, Technology, & Human Values* 23 (3), 285–314.

Knorr-Cetina, K. & Bruegger, U. (2002). Global Microstructures: The Virtual Societies of Financial Markets. *American Journal of Sociology* 107 (4), 905–950.

Knorr-Cetina, K. (1989). Spielarten des Konstruktivismus. *Soziale Welt* 1 (2), 86–96.

Krarup, T. M. & Blok, A. (2011). Unfolding the Social: Quasi-Actants, Virtual Theory, and the New Empiricism of Bruno Latour. *The Sociological Review* 59 (1), 42–63.

Krippner, G. R. (2001). The Elusive Market: Embeddedness and the Paradigm of Economic Sociology. *Theory and Society* 30 (6), 775–810.

Konings, P. (1984). Capitalist Rice Farming and Land Allocation in Northern Ghana. *Journal of Legal Pluralism* 22, 89–119.

Larner, W. & LeHeron, R. (2004). Global Benchmarking: Participating "at a Distance" in the Globalising Economy. In Larner, W. & Walters, W. (eds.), *Global Governmentality: Governing International Spaces*. Routledge, London, pp. 212–232.

Latour, B. & Woolgar, S. (1979). *Laboratory Life: The Construction of Scientific Facts*. Princeton University Press, Princeton, NJ.

Latour, B. (1983). Give Me a Laboratory and I Will Raise the World. In Knorr-Cetina, K. & Mulkay, M. (Eds.), *Science Observed: Perspectives on the Social Study of Science*. Sage, London, pp. 142–170.

Latour, B. (1986). The Powers of Association. In Law, J. (ed.), *Power, Action and Belief: A New Sociology of Knowledge?* Routledge & Paul, London, pp. 264–280.

Latour, B. (1999). On Recalling ANT. In Law, J. & Hassard, J. (eds.), *Actor Network Theory and After*. Blackwell, Malden, pp. 15–25.

Latour, B. (2005). *Reassembling the Social: An Introduction to Actor-Network-Theory*. Oxford University Press, New York.

Law, J. (1986). On the Methods of Long Distance Control: Vessels, Navigation, and the Portuguese Route to India. In Law, J. (ed.), *Power, Action, and Belief: A New Sociology of Knowledge*. Routledge; Keagan Paul, London, pp. 234–263.

Law, J. (1987). Technology and Heterogeneous Engineering: The Case of Portuguese Expansion. In Bijker, W. E., Hughes, T. P., & Pinch, T. J. (eds.), *The Social Construction of Technological Systems: New Directions in the Sociology and History of Technology*. MIT Press, Cambridge, Mass., pp. 111–134.

Law, J. (1992). Notes on the Theory of the Actor-Network: Ordering, Strategy, and Heterogeneity. *Systems Practice* 5 (4), 379–393.

Law, J. (1994). *Organizing Modernity*. Blackwell, Oxford.

Law, J. (1999). After ANT: Complexity, Naming and Topology. In Law, J. & Hassard, J. (eds.), *Actor Network Theory and After*. Blackwell, Malden, pp. 1–14.

Legg, S. (2011). Assemblage/Apparatus: Using Deleuze and Foucault. *Area* 43 (2), 128–133.

Lendvai, N. & Stubbs, P. (2009). Assemblages, Translation, and Intermediaries in South East Europe: Rethinking Transnationalism and Social Policy. *European Societies* 11 (5), 673–695.

Li, T. M. (2007a). Practices of Assemblage and Community Forest Management. *Economy and Society* 36 (2), 263–293.

Li, T. M. (2007b). Governmentality. *Anthropologica* 49 (2), 275–281.

Lie, J. (1997). Sociology of Markets. *American Sociological Review* 23, 341–360.

Lindner, P. (2008). *Der Kolchoz-Archipel im Privatisierungsprozess: Wege und Umwege der russischen Landwirtschaft in die globale Marktgesellschaft*. Transcript, Bielefeld.

Little, P. & Watts, M. (1994). Introduction. In Little, P. & Watts, M. (eds.), *Living under Contract*. University Press of Wisconsin, Madison, pp. 3–18.

Little, P. D. & Dolan, C. S. (2000). What It Means to be Restructured: Nontraditional Commodities and Structural Adjustment in Africa. In Haugerud, A., Stone, M. P., & Little, P. D. (eds.), *Commodities and Globalization: Anthropological Perspectives*. Rowman & Littlefield, Lanham, Md., pp. 59–78.

Loconto, A. (2010). Sustainability Performed: Reconciling Global Value Chain Governance and Performativity. *Journal of Rural Studies* 25 (3), 193–225.

Loeillet, D. & Paqui, T. (2010). L'Ananas. *Fruitrop* (176), 23-50.

MacKenzie, D. A. (2006). *An Engine, Not a Camera: How Financial Models Shape Markets*. MIT Press, Cambridge.

MacKenzie, D. (2007). Is Economics Performative? Option Theory and the Construction of Derivatives Markets. In MacKenzie, D., Muniesa, F., & Siu, L. (eds.), *Do Economists Make Markets? On the Performativity of Economics*. Princeton University Press, Princeton, pp. 56–86.

MacKenzie, D. (2009a). *Material Markets. How Economic Agents are Constructed*. Oxford University Press, Oxford, New York.

MacKenzie, D. (2009b). Making Things the Same: Gases, Emission Rights and the Politics of Carbon Markets. *Accounting, Organizations and Society* 34 (3–4), 440–455.

MacKenzie, D., Muniesa, F., & Liu, L. (2007). Introduction. In MacKenzie, D., Muniesa, F., & Siu, L. (eds.), *Do Economists Make Markets? On the Performativity of Economics*. Princeton University Press, Princeton, pp. 1–19.

Mann, S. & Dickinson, J. (1978). Obstacles to the Development of a Capitalist Agriculture. *Journal of Peasant Studies* 5 (4), 466–481.

Maertens, M. & Swinnen, J. F. M. (2009). Trade, Standards, and Poverty: Evidence from Senegal. *World Development* 37 (1), 161–178.

Marcus, G. (1995). Ethnography in/of the World System. The Emergence of Multi-Sited Ethnography. *Annual Review of Anthropology* 24, 95–117.

Marston, S. A., Jones, J. P., & Woodward, K. (2005). Human Geography without Scale. *Transactions of the Institute of British Geographers* 30 (4), 416–432.

Marx, K. (2008 [1867]). *Das Kapital: Kritik der politischen Ökonomie*, 34. Aufl., unveränd. Nachdr. d. 11. Aufl. 1962. Dietz-Verl, Berlin.

Mbembe, A. (2001). *On the Postcolony*. University of California Press, Berkeley.

McMichael, P. & H. Friedmann, H. (2007). Situating the Retailing Revolution. In Burch, D. & Lawrence, G. (eds.), *Supermarkets and Agri-Food Supply Chains*. Cheltenham: Edward Elgar, pp. 100–128.

McMichael, P. (1998). Development and Structural Adjustment. In Carrier, J. G. & Miller, D. (eds.), *Virtualism: A New Political Economy*. Berg Publishers, Oxford, pp. 95–116.

McMichael, P. (2013). Value-chain Agriculture and Debt Relations: Contradictory Outcomes. *Third World Quarterly* 34 (4), 671–690.

Miller, D. (1998). Conclusion: A Theory of Virtualism. In Carrier, J. G. & Miller, D. (eds.), *Virtualism: A New Political Economy*. Berg Publishers, Oxford, pp. 187–216.

Miller, D. (2002). Turning Callon the Right Way up. *Economy and Society* 31 (2), 218–233.

Miller, P. & Rose, N. (1990). Governing Economic Life. *Economy and Society* 19 (1), 1–31.

Miller, P. (1994). Accounting as Social and Institutional Practice: An Introduction. In Hopwood, A. G. & Miller, P. (eds.), *Accounting as Social and Institutional Practice*. Cambridge University Press, Cambridge, pp. 1–39.

Mitchell, T. (2000). The Stage of Modernity. In Mitchell, T. (ed.), *Questions of Modernity*. University of Minnesota Press, Minneapolis, pp. 1–34.

Mitchell, T. (2002). *Rule of Experts: Egypt, Techno-Politics, Modernity*. University of California Press, Berkeley.

Mitchell, T. (2007). The Properties of the Markets. In MacKenzie, D., Muniesa F., & Siu, L. (eds.), *Do Economists Make Markets? On the Performativity of Economics*. Princeton University Press, Princeton, pp. 245–279.

Mitchell, T. (2008). Rethinking Economy. *Geoforum* 39 (3), 1116–1121.

MOFA (Ministry of Food and Agriculture) (2010). *Medium Term Agriculture Sector Investment Plan (METASIP)*. Accra.

MOFA (Ministry of Food and Agriculture) (2007). *Food and Agricultural Development Policy II: Draft Version*. Accra.

Mohan, G. (2002). The Disappointments of Civil Society: The Politics of NGO Intervention in Northern Ghana. *Political Geography* 21 (1), 125–154.

Moore, S. F. (1987). Explaining the Present: Theoretical Dilemmas in Processual Ethnography. *American Ethnologist* 14 (4), 727–736.

Muellerleile, C. (2013). Turning Financial Markets Inside Out: Polanyi, Performativity and Disembeddedness. *Environment and Planning A* 45 (7), 1625–1642.

Muniesa, F. (2007). Market Technologies and the Pragmatics of Prices. *Economy and Society* 36 (3), 377–395.

Muniesa, F., Millo, Y., & Callon, M. (2007). An Introduction to Market Devices. In Callon, M., Millo, Y., & Muniesa, F. (eds.), *Market Devices*. Blackwell, Malden, pp. 1–12.

Murdoch, J., Marsden, T., & Banks, J. (2000). Quality, Nature, and Embeddedness: Some Theoretical Considerations in the Context of the Food Sector. *Economic Geography* 76 (2), 107–125.

Murphy, J. T. (2008). Economic Geographies of the Global South: Missed Opportunities and Promising Intersections with Development Studies. *Geography Compass* 2 (3), S. 851–873.

Murphy, J. T. (2012). Global Production Networks, Relational Proximity, and the Sociospatial Dynamics of Market Internationalization in Bolivia's Wood Products Sector. *Annals of the Association of American Geographers* 102 (1), 208–233.

Murray, W. E., Chandler, T., & Overton, J. (2011). Global Value Chains and Disappearing Rural Livelihoods: The Degeneration of Land Reform in a Chilean Village, 1995–2005. *The Open Area Studies Journal* 4 (1), 86–95.

Mutersbaugh, T. (2005). Just-In-Space: Certified Rural Products, Labor of Quality, and Regulatory Spaces. *Journal of Rural Studies* 21 (4), 389–402.

Nash, J. (1981). Ethnographic Aspects of the World Capitalist System. *Annual Review of Anthropology* 10 (1), 393–423.

Neilson, J. & Pritchard, B. (2009). *Value Chain Struggles: Institutions and Governance in the Plantation Districts of South India*. Wiley, Chichester.

Neilson, J. (2014). Value Chains, Neoliberalism and Development Practice: The Indonesian Experience. *Review of International Political Economy*, 21 (1), 38–69.

Nevins, J. & Peluso, N. L. (2008a). Commoditization in South East Asia. In Nevins, J. & Peluso, N. L. (eds.), *Taking Southeast Asia to Market: Commodities, Nature, and People in the Neoliberal Age*. Cornell University Press, Ithaca, pp. 1–26.

Nevins, J. & Peluso, N. L. (eds.) (2008b). *Taking Southeast Asia to Market: Commodities, Nature, and People in the Neoliberal Age*. Cornell University Press, Ithaca.

Neyland, D. (2008). Organizational Ethnography. Sage, Los Angeles.

Nicolini, D., Gherardi, S., & Yanow, D. (2003). Introduction: Toward a Practice-Based View of Knowing and Learning in Organizations. In Nicolini, D., Gherardi, S., & Yanow, D. (eds.), *Knowing in Organizations: A Practice-Based Approach*. M.E. Sharp, New York pp. 3–31.

NRI (Natural Resource Institute) (2010). Ghana Export Horticulture Cluster Strategic Profile Study: Part II – Recommended Actions and Part III Background Papers, Greenwich.

Ouma, S. & Whitfield, L. (2012). The Making and Remaking of Agroindustries in Africa. *Journal of Development Studies* 48 (3), 301–307.

Ouma, S. (2010). Global Standards, Local Realities: Private Agrifood Governance and the Restructuring of the Kenyan Horticulture Industry. *Economic Geography* 86 (2), 197–222.

Overdevest, C. (2011). Towards a More Pragmatic Sociology of Markets. *Theory and Society* 40 (5), 533–552.

Oya, C. (2012). Contract Farming in Sub-Saharan Africa: A Survey of Approaches, Debates and Issues. *Journal of Agrarian Change* 12 (1), 1–33.

Peck, J. & Tickell, A. (2002). Neoliberalizing Space. *Antipode* 34 (3), 380–404.

Peck, J. (2005). Economic Sociologies in Space. *Economic Geography* 81 (2), 129–175.

Peck, J. (2012). Economic Geography: Island Life. *Dialogues in Human Geography* 2 (2), 113–133.

Peluso, N. L. & Lund, C. (2011). New Frontiers of Land Control: Introduction. *Journal of Peasant Studies* 38 (4), 667–681.

Phillips, J. (2006). Agencement/Assemblage. *Theory, Culture & Society* 23 (2–3), 108–109.

Pinch, T. J. & Swedberg, R. (2008). General Concerns: Economy, Materiality, Power. In Pinch, T. J. & Swedberg, R. (eds.), *Living in a Material World: Economic Sociology Meets Science and Technology Studies*. MIT Press, Cambridge, Mass., pp. 1–29.

Podolny, J. M. (1993). A Status-Based Model of Market Competition. *American Journal of Sociology* 98 (4), 829–872.

Polanyi, K. (1992[1957]). The Economy as Instituted Process (1957). In Granovetter, M. S. & Swedberg, R. (eds.), *The Sociology of Economic Life*. Westview Press, Boulder, Colo., pp. 29–52.

Polanyi, K. (2001 [1944]). *The Great Transformation: The Political and Economic Origins of our Time*, 2nd ed. Beacon Press, Boston.

Pollner, M. & Emerson, R. (2008). Ethnomethodology and Ethnography. In Atkinson, P., Coffey, A., Delamont, S., Lofland, J., & Lofland, L. (eds.), *Handbook of Ethnography*, Paperback ed., reprinted. Sage, Los Angeles, pp. 118–136.

Ponte, S. & Gibbon, P. (2005). Quality Standards, Conventions and the Governance of Global Value Chains. *Economy and Society* 34 (1), 1–31.

Poudyal, M. (2011) Chiefs and Trees: Tenures and Incentives in the Management and Use of Two Multipurpose Tree Species in Agroforestry Parklands in Northern Ghana. *Society & Natural Resources* 24 (10), 1063–1077.

Poulton, C. (1998). Cotton Production and Marketing in Northern Ghana: The Dynamics of Competition in a System of Interlocking Transactions. In Dorward, A., Kydd, J., & Poulton, C. (eds.), *Smallholder Cash Crop Production under Market Liberalisation*. CAB International, Oxon, New York, pp. 56–107.

Power, M. (1997). From Risk to Audit Society. *Soziale Systeme* 3 (1), 3–21.

Prudham, S. (2003). Taming Trees: Capital, Science, and Nature in Pacific Slope Tree Improvement. *Annals of the Association of American Geographers* 93 (3), 636–656.

Rabinow, P. (2003). *Anthropos Today: Reflections on Modern Equipment*. Princeton University Press, Princeton.

Raj-Reichert, G. (2013). Safeguarding Labour in Distant Factories: Health and Safety Governance in an Electronics Global Production Network. *Geoforum* 44, 23–31.

Ramamurthy, P. (2011). Rearticulating Caste: The Global Cottonseed Commodity Chain and the Paradox of Smallholder Capitalism in South India. *Environment and Planning A* 43 (5), 1035–1056.

Rankin, K. N. (2004). *The Cultural Politics of Markets: Economic Liberalization and Social Change in Nepal*. University of Toronto Press, Toronto.

Raworth, K. & Kidder, T. (2009). Mimicking 'Lean' in Global Value Chains: It's the Workers Who Get Leaned On. In Bair, J. (ed.), *Frontiers of Commodity Chain Research*. Stanford University Press, Stanford, pp. 165–189.

Rorty, R. (1979). *Philosophy and the Mirror of Nature*. Princeton: Princeton University Press.

Rose, G. (1997). Situating Knowledges: Positionality, Reflexivities and Other Tactics. *Progress in Human Geography* 21 (3), 305–320.

Rose, N. (1996). Identity, Genealogy, History. In Hall, S. & Du Gay, P. (eds.), *Questions of Cultural Identity*. Sage, London, pp. 128–150.

Roy, A. (2012). Ethnographic Circulations: Space-Time Relations in the Worlds of Poverty Management. *Environment and Planning A* 44 (1), 31–41.

Schatzki, T. (2001). Introduction: Practice Theory. In Schatzki, T., Knorr Cetina, K., & Savigny, E. von (eds.), *The Practice Turn in Contemporary Theory*. Routledge, New York, London, pp. 1–14.

Schatzki, T. R. (2005). Peripheral Vision: The Sites of Organizations. *Organization Studies* 26 (3), 465–484.

Schatzki, T., Knorr Cetina, K., & Savigny, E. von (eds.) (2001). *The Practice Turn in Contemporary Theory*. Routledge, New York, London.

Schumpeter, J. A. (1947). The Creative Response in Economic History. *The Journal of Economic History* 7 (02), 149–159.

Schwartz-Shea, P. & Yanow, D. (2009). Reading and Writing as Method: In Search of Trustworthy Texts. In Ybema, S., Yanow, D., Wels, H., & Kamsteeg, F. (eds.), *Organizational Ethnography: Studying the Complexities of Everyday Life*. Sage, Los Angeles, pp. 56–82.

Scott, J. C. (1986). Everyday Forms of Peasant Resistance. *Journal of Peasant Studies* 13 (2), 5–35.

Scott, J. C. (1998). *Seeing Like a State: How Certain Schemes to Improve the Human Condition Have Failed*. Yale University Press, New Haven.

Seth, S. (2009). Putting Knowledge in its Place: Science, Colonialism, and the Postcolonial. *Postcolonial Studies* 12 (4), 373–388.

Selwyn, B. (2012). Beyond Firm-Centrism: Re-integrating Labour and Capitalism into Global Commodity Chain Analysis. Journal of Economic Geography 12 (1), 205–226.

Shane, S. (2000). Prior Knowledge and the Discovery of Entrepreneurial Opportunities. *Organization Science* 11 (4), 448–469.

Shepherd, A. (2007). Approaches to Linking Producers to Markets: A Review of Experiences to Date. FAO. ftp://ftp.fao.org/docrep/fao/010/a1123e/a1123e00.pdf. Accessed: 1/04/2012.

Shore, C. & Wright, S. (2000). Coercive Accountability: The Rise of Audit Culture in Higher Education. In Strathern, M. (ed.), *Audit Cultures: Anthropological Studies in Accountability, Ethics and the Academy*. Routledge, London, pp. 59–87.

Singh, S. (2002). Multi-National Corporations and Agricultural Development: A Study of Contract Farming in the Indian Punjab. *Journal of International Development* 14 (2), 181–194.

Silverman, S. (1979). The Peasant Concept in Anthropology. *Journal of Peasant Studies* 7 (1), 49–69.

Slater, D. & Tonkiss, F. (2001). *Market Society*, 2nd ed. Polity, Cambridge.

Smith, N. (1984). *Uneven Development: Nature, Capital, and the Production of Space*. Blackwell, New York.

Swedberg, R. (2005). Markets in Society. In Smelser, N. & Swedberg, R. (eds.), The Handbook of Economic Sociology, 2nd ed. Princeton University Press, Princeton, pp. 233–253.

Songsore, J. (2011). *Regional Development in Ghana: The Theory and the Reality*, 2nd ed. Woeli Publishing Services, Accra.

Stark, D. & Bruszt, L. (2001). One Way or Multiple Paths: For a Comparative Sociology of East European Capitalism. *American Journal of Sociology* 106 (4), 1129–1137.

Stark, D. (2009). *The Sense of Dissonance: Accounts of Worth in Economic Life*. Princeton University Press, Princeton.

Strauss, A. L. & Corbin, J. M. (2003). *Basics of Qualitative Research: Techniques and Procedures for Developing Grounded Theory*, 2nd ed., reprinted. Sage, Thousand Oaks.

Sunley, P. (2008). Relational Economic Geography: A Partial Understanding or a New Paradigm? *Economic Geography* 84 (1), 1–26.

Swedberg, R. & Granovetter, M. (1992). Introduction. In Granovetter, M. S. & Swedberg, R. (eds.), *The Sociology of Economic Life*. Westview Press. Boulder, Colo., pp. 1–28.

Thévenot, L. (1984). Rules and Implements: Investment in Forms. *Social Science Information* 23 (1), 1–45.

Thévenot, L. (2001a). Pragmatic Regimes Governing the Engagement with the World. In Schatzki, T., Knorr Cetina, K., & Savigny, E. von (eds.), *The Practice Turn in Contemporary Theory*. Routledge, New York, London, pp. 56–73.

Thévenot, L. (2001b). Organized Complexity: Conventions of Coordination and the Composition of Economic Arrangements. *European Journal of Social Theory* 4 (4), 405–425.

Thévenot, L. (2002). Conventions of Coordination and the Framing of Uncertainty. In Fullbrook, E. (ed.), *Intersubjectivity in Economics: Agents and Structures*. Routledge, London, New York, pp. 181–197.

Thévenot, L. (2009). Postscript to the Special Issue: Governing Life by Standards: A View from Engagements. *Social Studies of Science* 39 (5), 793–813.

Thévenot, L., Moody, M., & Lafayette, C. (2000). Forms of Valuing Nature: Arguments and Modes of Justification in French and American Environmental Disputes. In Lamont, M. & Thévenot, L. (eds.), *Rethinking Comparative Cultural Sociology: Repertoires of evaluation in France and the United States*. Cambridge University Press, Cambridge, pp. 229–272.

Thomas, N. (1991). *Entangled Objects: Exchange, Material Culture, and Colonialism in the Pacific*. Harvard University Press, Cambridge, Mass.

Thrift, N. & Olds, K. (1996). Refiguring the Economic in Economic Geography. *Progress in Human Geography* 20 (3), 311–337.

Thrift, N. (1997). The Still Point. Resistance, Expressive Embodiment and Dance. In Pile, S. & Keith, M. (eds.), *Geographies of Resistance*. Routledge, London, pp. 124–151.

Thrift, N. (2000). Pandora's Box? Cultural Geographies of Economies. In Clark, G., Gertler, M., &. Feldmann, M. (eds.), *The Oxford Handbook of Economic Geography*. Oxford: Oxford University Press, Oxford, pp. 689–701.

Truninger, M. (2008). The Organic Food Market in Portugal: Contested Meanings, Competing Conventions. *International Journal for Agricultural Resources, Governance and Ecology* 7 (1/2), 110–125.

Tsing, A. (2005). *Friction: An Ethnography of Global Connection*. Princeton University Press, Princeton.

Tsing, A. (2008). Contingent Commodities: Mobilizing Labor in and Beyond South East Asian Forests. In Nevins, J. & Peluso, N. L. (eds.), *Taking Southeast Asia to Market: Commodities, Nature, and People in the Neoliberal Age*. Cornell University Press, Ithaca, pp. 27–42.

Tsing, A. (2009). Supply Chains and the Human Condition. *Rethinking Marxism* 21 (2), 148–176.

Turner, F. J. (1921). *The Frontier in American History*. Henry Holt and Company, New York.

Vagneron, I., Faure, G., & Loeillet, D. (2009). Is There a Pilot in the Chain? Identifying the Key Drivers of Change in the Fresh Pineapple Sector. *Food Policy* 34 (5), 437–446.

Vaughan, A. (1991). Cane, Class and Credit: Small Growers in the Glendale Mill Area. *Antipode* 23 (1), 172–184.

Vellema, S. (2002). Making Contract Farming Work? Society and Technology in Philippine Transnational Agribusiness. Dissertation. Wageningen University, Wageningen. Technology and Agrarian Development Group.

Voisard, J.-M. & Jaeger, P. (2003). *Ghana Horticulture Sector Development Study*. Accra. (unpublished report).

Watts, M. (1994). Life under Contract: Farming, Agrarian Restructuring, and Flexible Accumulation. In Little, P. & Watts, M. (eds.), *Living under Contract*. University Press of Wisconsin, Madison, pp. 21–77.

Werner, M. (2012). Contesting Power/Knowledge in Economic Geography: Learning from Latin America and the Caribbean. In Barnes, T. J., Peck, J., & Sheppard, E. S. (eds.), *The Wiley-Blackwell Companion to Economic Geography*. Wiley-Blackwell, Chichester, West Sussex, pp. 132–146.

Whatmore, S. & Thorne, L. (1997). Nourishing Networks: Alternative Geographies of Food. In Goodman, D. & Watts, M. (eds.), *Globalizing Food*. Routledge, New York, pp. 287–304.

White, H. C. (1981). Where Do Markets Come From? *The American Journal of Sociology* 87 (3), 517–547.

Whitfield, L. (2010). Developing Technological Capabilities in Agro-Industry: Ghana's Experience with Fresh Pineapple Exports in Comparative Perspective. DIIS Working Paper 28. Copenhagen.

Wilkinson, J. (1997). A New Paradigm for Economic Analysis? Recent Convergences in French Social science and an Exploration of the Convention Theory Approach with a Consideration of its Application to the Analysis of the Agrofood System. *Economy and Society* 26 (3), 335–339.

Williamson, O. E. (1979). Transaction-Cost Economics: The Governance of Contractual Relations. *Journal of Law and Economics* 33, 233–261.

Wolfinger, N. (2002). On Writing Fieldnotes: Collection Strategies and Background Expectancies. *Qualitative Research* 2 (1), 85–95.

World Bank (1993). *Ghana 2000 and Beyond Setting the Stage for Accelerated Growth and Poverty Reduction*. Washington, DC.

World Bank (2007). *World Development Report (2008): Agriculture for Development*. Washington, DC.

World Bank (2011). *Tackling Poverty in Northern Ghana*. Washington, DC. http://www.deza.admin.ch/ressources/resource_en_172765.pdf. Accessed: 06/14/2011.

Yaro, J. A. (2010). Customary Tenure Systems under Siege: Contemporary Access to Land in Northern Ghana. *GeoJournal* 75 (2), 199–214.

Ybema, S., Yanow, D., Wels, H., & Kamsteeg, F. (2009). Studying Everyday Organizational Life. In Ybema, S., Yanow, D., Wels, H., & Kamsteeg, F. (eds.), *Organizational Ethnography: Studying the Complexities of Everyday Life*. Sage, Los Angeles, pp. 1–20.

Yeung, H. W.-C. (2003). Practicing New Economic Geographies: A Methodological Examination. *Annals of the Association of American Geographers* 93 (3), 442–462.

Young, W. (2004). *Sold Out: The True Cost of Supermarket Shopping*. Fusion Press, London.

Zafirovski, M. (2000). An Alternative Sociological Perspective on Economic Value: Price Formation as a Social Process. *International Journal of Politics, Culture and Society* 14 (2), 265–295.

Index

Assembling Export Markets: The Making and Unmaking of Global Food Connections in West Africa,
First Edition. Stefan Ouma.
© 2015 John Wiley & Sons, Ltd. Published 2015 by John Wiley & Sons, Ltd.